DEDICATION

DEDICATED TO Adolph Ausubel. The lessons in life that he taught me: devotion to family, to the Jewish people and to Justice will reverberate in my ears as long as I live. "If you do anything in life, do it as well as you possibly can, and then a little better than that."

CONTENTS

PREFACE

I HAVE ASKED myself the question, "Why me? Why should I be the one to tell the story of the Jewish people?"

This is my reply: To remain silent when there is injustice anywhere in the world is to become an accomplice to the wrongful acts that are being committed. And so I have an obligation to speak out forcefully against injustice, particularly the injustice done to my people, the Jews. But why should I be the one to tell this story? After all, I have a career in medicine. To keep up with scientific advances requires a full-time commitment. To care for the sick at any and all hours of the day and night for more than half a century requires total dedication.

I am compelled to tell this story because I am, in a sense, the link between the Old World and a new life in America. I had three missions in writing this book. A tree must have its roots sunk deep into the earth or it will not long survive in the turbulent world in which we live. The Jewish child who is unaware of the history of his people, and to whom a Bar Mitzvah is just a big party, has the potential for becoming a lost sheep. And so the first mission of my book series is to give every Jewish youth an identity, to inform him of the unbelievable courage of the Jewish people, and the indomitable human spirit that enabled his ancestors not only to survive, but to achieve despite almost unending oppression. The second goal of my series is to educate the non-Jewish world to the spectrum of the Jewish experience. Finally, reflecting on Santayana's prophetic words: "Those who do not remember the past, are condemned to repeat it." I seek to point out the wrongs done to the Jewish people in the past, with the goal of persuading mankind not to repeat those tragic errors, whether done to Jews in Germany, Muslims in Bosnia, or Tutsis in Rwanda.

I was the recipient of an oral history handed down over the generations. At the same time, I was a student of written history. Furthermore, I was a member of a family that had accomplished much in the literary world: they were the weavers of stories about a world now gone. Finally, I had come to recognize the power of stories to influence human conduct. For example, the fact that six million Jews were killed in the Holocaust is horrible. But six million is only a number, as horrific as it is. By contrast, reading *The Diary of Anne Frank* enables the reader to identify with the victims of the Holocaust. The reader is compelled to ask, "Why would anyone do such terrible things to a sweet, innocent child and her family?" By identifying with the victims of oppression, the reader is better able to recognize the wrong and, hopefully, make efforts not to repeat those tragic mistakes in the future.

A second question might be asked of me, namely, "When did I start and for what reason did I continue to pursue the work to its completion?"

In our religious congregation, it is customary for the child, as part of the preparation for a Bar or Bat Mitzvah, to do something of religious significance. One child might build a model of the Temple of Solomon. Another might spend many hours assisting the elderly in a senior citizens' residence.

At my and my wife's recommendation, our son's project was to write a history of his ancestors. With the help of parents and grandparents and many others, Ian wrote a fifty-page report. The completed text was presented to the synagogue library and copies were given to all those who attended the celebration.

Subsequently, I decided that the project should be continued. The objective would be more than simply to tell the history of a family; it had to use that history to achieve a higher goal.

Each member of the family was assigned tasks. My son was a member of the Long Island Youth Orchestra. In addition to performing in their concert series in Long Island, the orchestra traveled overseas each summer, performing concerts in distant lands. One such trip was to Australia. I asked that Ian visit relatives in Melbourne and get more details on how they came to emigrate from Galicia to Australia.

On another such summer concert tour, the orchestra was to perform in Portugal. Ian's assignment would be a big one for such a young man. His mission was to wrest from the Portuguese government the transcript of the trial of Portugal's greatest playwright, Antonio José da Silva, a member of our ancestral family, who was the last Jew burnt at the stake during the Portuguese Inquisition. Ian treated each of these requests as a command from a higher authority.

Ian went to the University of Lisbon to see if he could find someone, namely a student who spoke English, who would be willing to help him find the documents if, in fact, there were any still in existence. After great effort, he found a student who was eager to help him.

It turned out that if there were records of the trials in the Inquisition, they would be located in a special building that housed national archives.

When Ian and his newly found friend went to the building, it was locked. A man finally opened the door. Ian explained that he needed to see the transcript of the trial of Antonio José da Silva, which took place during the Inquisition. The man informed him that such records were not open to the public. For Ian to see the records, he would have to obtain permission from either the Archbishop of Lisbon or the President of Portugal. Needless to say, he had neither.

At this point, the student accompanying him pointed out that neither the Archbishop of Lisbon nor the President of Portugal were in the city at this time. Ian, in a most forceful voice, then said to the man in charge, "Do you know President Reagan?"

"You mean the President of the United States?"

"Yes, the President of the United States! He'd be very upset if you didn't allow me access to those records!"

The man appeared quite concerned. "I'm familiar with the trial; it was a famous one. But the record is quite lengthy. Can you read Portuguese?"

"No. But if you microfilm the record, I can then have it translated."

The man then let them in. He went to a back room where the records of trials were hidden in the back of dusty shelves hidden by curtains. When the transcript was finally found, the man took it out and counted up the pages requesting $99.00, including shipment. Ian then handed the man most of the spending money he had saved for the trip, and left.

We subsequently had the several hundred pages translated into English, as just part of the background material for writing one chapter.

My wife, Stephanie, and I spent thousands of hours over a period of thirty years, traveling to the ends of the earth, scouring through documents and conducting interviews. Then I spent many more hours writing the stories.

The voices of my ancestors spoke to me in the Yiddish idiom spoken by my grandparents as they related the stories passed down to them by their forebears. Stephanie, in the idiom of the English language, then rewrote the tales of the past. And so the work is a collaboration of the two of us, just as the book series tells the stories of both our roots, enabling us to record the spectrum of the Jewish experience.

BAR MITZVAH DAY

It is not even dawn, but I cannot sleep. The sheer lace curtains covering my bedroom window are faintly illuminated in the pale light of a street lamp below. I should turn over and get more rest, but the excitement of the day to come won't allow it.

Ian, our firstborn son, will ascend the platform in the synagogue and conduct a service. He will read from the Torah (the Five Books of Moses), assuring the continuation of a 3,000-year-old tradition.

My wife, Stephanie, and I will look on with pride from front-row seats. Our daughter, Lara, will be there beside us. Lara, too, has been preparing for the day when she will assume her role as an adult member of the community – the Followers of Moses. The grandmothers will be there. So will uncles and aunts, cousins, neighbors and friends by the score.

But others shall be there too, not in person, but in spirit: millennia of ancestors and other family members who have persevered to keep the faith even at the cost of their lives, those who have remained loyal to the Covenant first made by the Almighty with Abraham, our father, some 3,500 years ago, relatives too far away or too ill to make the journey, and men and women suffering in prison cells for their beliefs; we feel their presence. I, living in a land of freedom, can discern their figures, their faces.

As my son reads from the Torah and from the Prophets, I remember those whose voices have been silenced by oppression. My mind calls them forth, not only out of reverence for their suffering, but because we have no Bar Mitzvahs, no *simchas*, no Jewish life, without them.

The Jewish child, who is unaware of the history of his people, may someday be lost to his people. For those of other faiths, or of no faith at all, it is important to know our history, to learn the tragedy of prejudice and hate, to recall the indelible response to Cain's question, "Am I my brother's keeper?"

I therefore feel compelled to tell the story of *The Other Guests* who are there in spirit. There are six families: three from my line, and three from my

1

wife's. It is our family tree, but it is also the story of all Jews, a microcosm of the Hebrew people. Indeed, it is the story of all humanity, all children of the Father of the Universe, our triumphs and our tragedies and our struggle to build a better world.

THOSE WHO DO NOT REMEMBER THE PAST...

"THOSE WHO DO not remember the past are condemned to repeat it."

Philosopher George Santayana's caution became the driving force of my work as a Jewish historian.

In light of the horrendous persecution which my people – the Jewish people – have suffered during the past 2,000 years, Santayana's prophecy has served as a beacon guiding my study of history since early youth.

In my childhood, my peers considered me a nerd. I would read the *World Almanac* from cover to cover and commit to memory the height of each mountain, the population of each city and country. Name the country or the continent and I could draw a map of it and show you the locations of its cities and of the battles that had taken place over the centuries. I could name its tribal and religious groups and explain how well they co-existed.

I wore horn-rimmed glasses and was the smallest boy in my class (even smaller than any of the girls), a brown-haired, brown-eyed spare little fellow who could run like an antelope and play basketball, but who retired to his home to read when others were still out having fun. When other children were reading comic books, I was poring through history books, picturing the events and the places so that the past came alive in my mind's eye. I would mold people and places out of clay, and I could describe how Joshua fought the battle of Jericho, moving the pieces of clay around like pieces on a chessboard.

We lived in a four-room apartment in a working-class neighborhood in Brooklyn, New York, with as many as four sleeping in the bedroom that I shared with my grandfather and older brother and an uncle until he married. It was crowded, but my mind was never confined. As I read of past civilizations, my mind flew out the window and I was there in ancient Israel or in Athens or Rome. My bedroom window opened onto a fire escape, and in the heat of summer, a faint breeze through that window was the only means of cooling.

My family had strong ties to the Old World. My father was a spare man, with intense eyes above sagging bag-like lower lids that carried the weight of the tragedies of his people and his struggle to put food on the table and keep a roof over our heads during the Great Depression. The pictures of him clothed in formal dress in Vienna as a young writer of poetry and plays, and executive in the largest shoe factory in Austria, showed a handsome man. He had come to the United States to escape persecution. The first post-World War I anti-Semitic riots in the Austrian capital had been to him as the message written on the wall had been to Daniel. The European continent was a dead place for a Jew.

My mother's older siblings were born in Russian-ruled Poland. She was the first of her family born in this country, a dark-haired, dark-eyed woman of medium height, who spent little of her time making herself "beautiful." Her children were everything. She would wash floors in the halls of the six-family apartment house which we owned and where we resided along with five tenant families. (My father had purchased the building with the savings from his work in the shoe industry.)

Before the sun rose, my mother would stoke coal in the building's furnace in the light of a single ceiling bulb. The coal was heavy, and she would rub her back when the shoveling was done. Then she began tending to all the household chores, never complaining. From time to time, she suffered horrific, colicky pain that, when I became a physician, I learned came from gallstones. My mother would moan until the pain passed and then go on with her work.

My paternal grandfather was one of my roommates from childhood until I became a physician. He was a small, bald, gray-bearded storyteller who never had an unkind word to say about anyone. My mother's parents – a tall, lean, gray-bearded husband and a thin, much shorter wife, whose small head was always covered with a *sheitl* (wig) of piety – lived just a block away from us. Each of these grandparents would tell me stories about the Old World – an oral history that had been transmitted over the generations. As I listened to their tales in the bedroom or at the kitchen table, I would attempt to identify the period in which the events took place.

My youth coincided with the most tragic period in modern Jewish history. The dark shadow of Nazi Germany was spreading across the European continent. Eight million Jews, the major portion of world Jewry, were in mortal danger. I became an avid reader of newspapers and listened to the radio as I lived history. Yet, as a Jew born in the United States, what could I do in the midst of these tragic events? I would inform the older people in the neighborhood of what was going on and how dangerous were the times. "Hitler is determined to rid all Europe of Jews. He must be stopped!"

I would cry out. I would carry maps I had obtained in school down to the street below our apartment and use them to outline the battlefield to adults who were decades older than I was. Soon I became their Walter Winchell and their H. B. Kaltenborn (newspaper and radio commentators).

But I had to get on with my life. Unlike so many of my forebears in Europe who were blocked by prejudice from achieving that which their intellect and hard work would have allowed, America was a land of opportunity. Education would be my means for achieving success in the United States. And so I worked harder than all those around me and did well in high school and college. And that became my ticket to Harvard Medical School. I was always aware that I was alive because I was living in this greatest of nations.

I had thought first of becoming an historian. Then the study of the Constitution and the liberties that had made this country the haven for the poor and downtrodden who yearned to be free, prompted me to move on to the law. But I was told that the goal in the legal profession was to win. How could I justify winning for a client I believed to be in the wrong? Finally I settled on medicine, a field in which I was not required to make a judgment as to the worthiness of the individuals for whom I was caring.

My older brother enlisted and served in the armed services during World War II, and I had the same obligation to defend this country. So when I turned seventeen, I signed up in the naval reserves.

After completing my medical school education at Harvard Medical School, I returned to New York City. I entered an internship and followed that with a residency in a series of Cornell-affiliated hospitals. That period was interrupted by two years of service as a physician in the armed services, during which time I served with the 3rd Marine Division in the Far East.

It would turn out that my dual careers as physician and historian were to intersect at a hospital, a fateful irony I would later understand.

In July 1959, I began my final year of residency training at Mt. Sinai Hospital in Manhattan. On weekends off, I would leave my room in the staff quarters at the hospital and stay at my parents' home in Brooklyn.

One Monday morning upon returning to the hospital, my legs weakened when an intern who had served on my ward informed me that my father had been admitted to the hospital. I was perplexed since I had just seen my father two hours before and he was fine. The intern, who was paged to do the H&P (History and Physical Examination), explained to me that my father was scheduled to have an elective urologic procedure.

"Elective urologic procedure? Are you sure you're talking about my father? I'm not aware of any complaints that would prompt urologic care. And I can't imagine him not telling me that he was scheduled to enter the hospital."

"Ma...maybe it's not your father," he stammered. "I just thought...I had never heard the name Ausubel before I met you. I assumed he was your father."

"What's the patient's name?"

"Nathan Ausubel."

"He's my father's cousin," I replied, now a bit more relaxed. "My dad's first name is Adolph. Whew! In any case, I'll go up and see Nathan. Thanks for the info. But in the future, please don't assume that people with the same last name are father and son."

A few minutes later I was at Nathan's bedside. I was aware of his existence because several of his books were in my father's library. He had much of the Ausubel appearance: slim man, medium height, with thinning brown hair flecked with gray above an elongated face. His forehead was lined with decades of concentration. He had those Ausubel eyes, brown, with lower lids weighted down, bag-like, holding centuries of mankind's tragedies. Those piercing eyes focused on me, as through a microscopic lens, and committed the image to memory in the gray cells of his brain.

"So you're Adolph's son," Nathan observed. "Tell me about yourself: Where did you receive your education? That white coat and the stethoscope tell me you're a physician. What brought you to a career in medicine?"

I gave him a brief description of my 29 years, my early love of history, particularly the history of the Jewish people, my initial idea of becoming an historian, the quiz shows I had been on, and finally my decision to become a doctor.

Nathan laughed when I told him that as a 6-year old I had supplied my mother with answers to the general questions given the audience in a program called "The Mrs. Goes A Shopping." The woman in the audience whose written answer was closest to the correct number would receive a modest prize such as a 20-piece set of dishes or a bathmat and matching toilet-seat cover. The show's host, Harry Vonzel, was surprised when my mother's answers were exactly correct, down to the nearest penny in the cost of the first B-14 bomber and to the exact height of the highest mountain in New York State. When my mother won again and again with a perfect answer, Mr. Vonzel was convinced that someone in his show was giving the answers to this housewife with just a high school education. When my mother insisted that it was her little son who had given her the answer and pointed to me (looking more like a 4-year-old), Mr. Vonzel became very annoyed and told her not to come back again.

"So what brings you to Mt. Sinai?" I inquired after the recitation.

"For surgery, so I don't have to go to the bathroom every hour on the hour. The doctor tells me I'll probably be here for a week after the procedure.

Now, come to visit me when you have the time. I'll tell you all about our family history."

"I've heard stories about us from my grandfather, Judah. He was my roommate until he passed away."

"Then we'll compare notes," Nathan smiled.

❖ ❖ ❖

During the following week, Nathan reviewed his life's experience, from his birth in Lacejsk in Galicia, to his family's coming to the United States when he was a boy, to his service in the Jewish Legion in World War I. He related his travels through several continents in search of Jewish communities in order to learn of the Jewish experience, and about his choice of a career as an author. His first work was a biography of Frederick the Great of Prussia. Demand was limited to libraries in teaching institutions.

Finally, he found his niche – the history and folklore of the Jewish people.

On my days off, I would sit there, sometimes for hours at a time, telling him tales I had heard from my grandparents and others. I related stories to him about events that had taken place hundreds of years ago, and how I had tracked them down to exactly when they occurred because of my knowledge of history. I told him about the grave anxiety I had felt in my childhood about the survival of the Jewish people as the German armies seized lands in which the bulk of world Jewry lived, and of the joy I felt at the reestablishment of the State of Israel after two thousand years of exile, and how I feared for the survival of the Jewish state which was surrounded by tens of millions of Arabs eager to destroy Israel, and of my concern for the Jews in the Diaspora in the era of assimilation.

"Jews in the Diaspora need to learn more about the travails our people went through during the past 2,000 years, to develop a stronger sense of identity if we are to survive as a people," I said. Now I was eager to connect the dots: I wanted to know more about our family in that period between Biblical times and the eighteenth century.

"Very well, so now to my knowledge of our family history," he began in return. "Our family name was *Azuvel* – the Hyssop of the Almighty. We were charged with the responsibility to deliver that spice to the Temple of Solomon some three thousand years ago, and so I concluded that our ancestors must have been spice merchants.

"Twenty-five hundred years ago our ancestors were among the Jews forced into Babylonian exile. But we did not return when Ezra led many of the Hebrew people in Babylon back to Israel. Our ancestors remained in Babylon, which had become part of Persia, only to be sent to Anatolia, known today as Turkey, a generation or two later.

"Our ancestors then lived in Sardis, which was capital of the Lydian Empire (a satellite of the Persian Empire). When earthquakes and foreign invasions destroyed Sardis, the later generation of Azuvels moved to Ephesus, where they remained until that great city vanished into history. From there they moved to Smyrna, another Greek Anatolian city on the Aegean coast. Smyrna was renamed Izmir after the Turkish conquest. During this period, our ancestors developed an interest in herbal medicines. They became apothecaries.

"From apothecaries, some of them became physicians. Dr. David Azuvel even served the greatest Turkish sultan in history, Suleiman the Magnificent. When Suleiman died during his conquest in central Europe, our physician ancestor probably concluded that it would be wise not to return to Istanbul, that he might be accused of having some responsibility for the death of the Sultan. So our family took up residence in Turkish-occupied Budapest.

"The Azuvels remained there until the Christian armies captured the city a century later. Upon seizing the city, they slaughtered most of the surviving Jews as punishment for their having been loyal subjects of the Turks.

"From there our family moved to the Kingdom of Poland which, in that era, included most of the Ukraine, as well as modern-day Poland. Our direct ancestors lived in Dzikow and then Rozwadow, in the province of Galicia. Galicia was later taken over by Austria, as Poland's neighbors – Russia, Prussia and Austria – dismembered that country. My father moved to Lacejsk, twenty or so miles from Rozwadow, and finally to the United States.

"So what do you think of that?"

"I'm amazed," I replied. "I learned a lot about the period from Dzikow, from the eighteenth century on. I knew about the origin of the name Ausubel and something about the title Azuvel: It was on the tombstones of ancestors in Rozwadow. But I knew almost nothing about the details of the earlier history. How did you gather all this information? Where is it written down?"

"I haven't written any book about our family. My work has involved the history of the Jewish people as a whole, and their folklore. But in the course of my travels, I uncovered much about our family. Dr. Abraham Galante, who wrote a multi-volume history of the Jewish people in Anatolia, told me about his findings in the various cities I mentioned before.

"You know that on a tombstone of a Jew, you read the person's first name, son or daughter of the father's first name. Before the European rulers required family names (so they could identify people for tax purposes, etc.), there was no last name on the tombstone of a Jew. That was the case unless you were a *Cohen* – a priest, or a *Levi* – a member of the tribe responsible for the care of religious institutions. But we had a family name – Azuvel. The Jewish community would never have permitted the name Azuvel to be carved on the tombstones unless it had religious significance.

"Abraham Galante was able to trace our family history in Turkey by means of tombstone markings, plus the fact that there still were Azuvels in Izmir when he spent time in that city.

"In my travels through Hungary before World War II, I identified the Azuvel tombstones in the Jewish cemetery in Budapest. They dated to the sixteenth and seventeenth centuries, including the oldest tombstone of our family – that of Dr. David Azuvel who served Suleiman the Magnificent. His service to Sultan Suleiman was recorded on the tombstone.

"In my travels through Poland and Russia, I identified the tombstones of descendants in those countries. The dates were all subsequent to those in Budapest. And so now we're down to the present."

"Can those tombstones be identified today?"

"I don't know. The Nazis destroyed many of the Jewish cemeteries and used the tombstones for pavement and the like. Much of the evidence may have been destroyed."

"Do you plan to write up our history?"

"I'm no youngster. I'll tell you as much as I know about our family. Your father is a writer. You should have his blood in your veins. If you ever get the time – and I believe it would take years to do all the necessary research to collect the additional material – you should write it up."

Then came a surprise, one of the greatest rewards of Nathan's lifetime of labor.

"I've got several other projects I'm working on that will take me 'til I'm a hundred, if the good Lord preserves me. One of the most fascinating is about a town in Latin America in which my wife and I spent a year. I do not wish to mention the name of the country. But while it was one of the most fascinating experiences of my life, and while I have all the material in my mind, I will never put it down on paper. And yet, somehow I would like to convey the story without breaking a trust."

"Why not? And to what sort of trust do you refer?"

"Well, let me tell you the story. Then you'll understand.

"I concluded that all the inhabitants of the town are unquestionably of Jewish descent (except the town priest), but they had lost awareness of their heritage and considered themselves to be Catholics. They cannot remember their past... And yet, they remember more of their past than do most of us in twentieth-century America."

"What drew you to the conclusion that they were all of Jewish descent? I don't recall any description of such a people in your *Pictorial History of the Jewish People.*"

"That's true. They are not mentioned in my book. That is because I made a pledge not to do so. I had heard of a town in a Latin American country that had been settled centuries ago – not long after the Spanish conquered the area – in which all the inhabitants appeared to be European.

"It was not simply by chance that I happened to spend a year in that town. The town was located inland, deep in what people might refer to as the jungle. I had considered that before going there. Why would Europeans choose to settle in such a place, and why would the population still appear European? From what I was told, there were no gold mines or other valuable resources in that area. All their European ancestors could gain from taking up residence in such a remote area were malaria and other tropical diseases. Moreover, everywhere else the Spaniards settled to establish agricultural estates, they employed Indian labor. With the passage of time, the populations mixed to produce the typical inhabitant of that country, with a combination of Spanish and Indian features. To still look European after four centuries or so, these Europeans would have had to consciously isolate themselves and not employ Indian labor.

"I had heard of other situations where secret Jews had left Spain for remote parts of the Empire in the hope of escaping the watchful eyes of the Inquisitors. In fact, hundreds of people of Spanish descent living in the American Southwest have discovered their Jewish roots in the twentieth century."

"How so?" I interrupted.

"For example, a locket handed down from mother to daughter through the generations. When a twentieth-century woman managed to open the seemingly sealed locket, it turned out to contain a *Shema.* (Hebrew prayer "Hear O Israel, the Lord is our God, the Lord is One. Blessed be His glorious Name forever and ever.") One thing led to another, and the holder of the locket concluded that her ancestors had been forced to hide their identity for so long, that the very knowledge of their Jewish identity was lost. That woman was angered by the thought that the church had so persecuted her ancestors that they would be forced to conceal their identity from even their own children. She has now returned to the Jewish faith.

"Another example was a woman who had been given a menorah that had been handed down through the generations. Arousing her curiosity, a search through old family documents led her to the same conclusion and a return to the faith of her ancestors.

"I could go on with example after example, but let me get back to the Latin town in question. Could these Europeans be Spanish Jews who had settled in such a remote area to escape the watchful eye of the Inquisitors? Could their appearance still be that of Europeans because they wanted to maintain their identity, and so did not subjugate the surrounding Indians and eventually mix their blood, so to speak? I had to go there and see for myself whether what I had heard was the case. And if the facts were as I was told, could I find evidence of a Jewish past?

"My wife, Marynn, has always taken part in my studies. She was eager to join my 'expedition.'

"When we arrived, it was as if we had gone back to sixteenth-century Spain. A wall surrounded the town, which was located on a plateau. Three sides of the town were separated from the surrounding area by steep bluffs. The fourth sloped sharply through terraced vineyards to the valley below. An undulating road through the vineyards led to the only gate to the town.

"The surrounding valley consisted of a series of fields. There were no telephone poles or any lines bringing electricity to homes or shops. The buildings, with the exception of the towering stone church in the center of the town, were attached to one another. Whitewashed walls, capped by sloping red-tiled roofs, fronted them. The streets were narrow and there was no automobile or truck to be seen on them; only people on foot or on carts drawn by oxen or horses. There were one- and two-story homes along the side streets, and shops of craftsmen lined the slightly wider main thoroughfare.

"The inhabitants viewed us suspiciously. This was not a tourist resort. There were no hotels in the town. And so, after some negotiation, we took up residence with a family who had been selected by the town elders to host us. We were to be guests: There would be no charge for our food or lodging. Our hosts were David and Esther Mendes. David was a farmer. Both farmers and craftsmen resided within the limits of the town. The fields belonging to each farmer were spread throughout the countryside, beyond the walls of the town.

"The townsfolk were curious as to what had prompted two *Americanos* to come to this remote area, let alone stay on. We told them it was an interest in the history of the peoples of Latin America after the ancestors of the townsfolk had emigrated from Spain many centuries ago. Those ancestors had come to the New World from a single hamlet. Unlike the conquistadors who sought gold and went on to subjugate the Indians, the motivation for their voyage was different. They had no desire to enslave the native population or establish great *haciendas* in which Spanish overlords thrived on the sweat of native labor. Rather, their intent was to establish a sort of idyllic society modeled on the way they had lived in Spain. Spain had become a great power, and all of Spain was being molded to conform to this new concept.

They wanted to continue the old ways that existed before Ferdinand and Isabella ruled the land. In order to achieve this goal, they built their new town deep in the jungle, far from the major cities, and far from the peering eyes of government officials. And they directed their descendants to follow their traditions and remain separate from the native population.

"We later learned that boys born in the town were to marry only girls born in the town. This rule, they insisted, had never been violated by anyone living in the town. Descendants were free to leave for up to a week (although such action was discouraged) and to marry outsiders, but once any individual stayed away for longer than a week or married an outsider, he (or she) was permanently expelled from the community, never to return.

"As seeming proof of what I had been told, there was no trace of Indian ancestry in the appearance of the townsfolk. The only resident not born in the town was the priest, sent to administer services in their church that was located in the center of the town.

"But still there was no obvious physical evidence that they were descended from secret Jews — no sealed lockets, menorahs, etc. Everyone we met viewed himself or herself as an observant Roman Catholic. The church was filled to capacity on Sundays, and the priest considered his flock as loyal to the church as any in the country. And yet there were some hints of a Jewish ancestry. One day I observed our host harvesting his field of grain. All harvesting was done with a scythe; there were no modern machines to be seen anywhere. I noted that he never picked up any of the crop that had fallen to the ground. I further noted that he left the crop in the corners of his field, uncut. I asked him why.

"'That *belongs* to the widows and orphans,' he stated.

"'Is that something you alone do, or is that a general rule in the town?' I pursued.

"'It is part of our tradition, going back to our ancestors in Spain.'

"I did not attempt to point out that this custom was precisely what was decreed in Judaic scripture.

"I noted that the townsfolk worked until dusk each day during the week, but they quit work early on Fridays and did not work on either Saturday or Sunday. They streamed to the town hall on Friday evenings, and then returned to their homes later in the evening. What were they all doing in the town hall? Might they be conducting a Sabbath service?

"I spent one day talking to the town priest. His chest inflated as he noted how loyal his parishioners were to their church. 'They never miss a Sunday mass,' he declared with pride.

"But unknowingly, he gave me an additional hint of possible Jewish ancestry when he mentioned that the community met every Friday night in the basement of the town hall, and that he had never been invited to the proceedings. 'It's some sort of town ritual – limited to people born in the town. I'm from the capital, and so I was never a participant. I've learned that some towns in Spain had gatherings of the inhabitants to which outsiders were excluded. They brought that tradition to the New World. And if that's what they like to do, it's all right with me. I don't disapprove of tradition, so long as it does not affect their piety,' he concluded.

"I chose not to question the priest further. The fact that the gathering took place on Friday nights certainly suggested a Sabbath observance, and the fact that the priest was never invited to the proceedings added further flame to my interest in that event. But how would I be able to observe the Friday night gathering? Perhaps, if I pointed out that my wife and I were Jews, we would gain entry.

"'Why do you stop work earlier on Friday than on the other days during the week?' I asked my host.

"'To prepare for the town gathering.'

"I then told him that my wife and I were Jewish and that it was customary among observant Jews to stop work early on Fridays and prepare for the Sabbath observance. David said that he had not heard of a people called 'Jews.' But then again, he had never been outside the town.

"'Do any of the inhabitants of your town ever go to other towns or cities?'

"'Yes, a few of the town elders go, as a group, to the coast once a month. They travel there on a Monday and return before Friday evening. They go by wagon and carry produce, as well as some craft objects produced by our townsfolk. These they exchange for fish and other foods and goods that we do not make in our town.'

"'What sort of fish? Do they bring back lobsters or crabs?'

"'I'm not familiar with those fish. But then, I'm not one of the town elders and so I've never been to the coast. We only consume fish that have scales.'

"'Why are you limited to eating fish which have scales?'

"'That is our tradition,' was the repeated response to every such question, including the absence of pigs among the domesticated animals they kept, and in their never eating the flesh of carnivores. (Jewish law forbids the eating of carnivores or pig. It also forbids the consumption of sea creatures that do not have scales.)

"After several weeks, I concluded that the key to my obtaining proof of Jewish ancestry would be in attending that Friday night gathering of the inhabitants. But how? My expressed interest in attending the proceedings was always rebuffed with a polite, 'It is only for those born in our town. That is our tradition.' As our stay in the town extended into months, I saw no sign

13

of the townsfolk changing their minds. Towards the end of a year, I became ill. Marynn insisted that we return to New York for medical treatment. Reluctantly, I agreed.

"I informed our hosts of my illness and that I would be leaving for the United States the following week. To my surprise, the town mayor came to see us the following day.

"'We held a meeting of the town elders,' he said. 'They think well of you and your wife. It was decided that you can come to our town gathering this Friday evening. But on one condition: We understand that you are a writer in the outside world. We do not want you to do anything that would attract others to come here. That might upset the tranquility we have enjoyed here over the centuries.'

"I thanked him and promised to abide by their request. I would not publish anything about their community.

"On Friday evening, David and Esther Mendes led Marynn and me to the basement of the town hall where all the town's inhabitants were gathered. What I saw and heard left me dumbstruck.

"David Castro, one of the town elders, covered his head with what was plainly a *tallit* (prayer shawl). He stood in front of the assemblage. He uttered a series of sentences that, while somewhat distorted, were plainly Hebrew prayers ending with a *Shema*. At the end, he withdrew a bottle of wine from the cabinet near the front of the room. He poured some of it into a silver cup – with an inscription written in Hebrew. His hand concealed much of the inscription. Then he recited a series of words, somewhat garbled, but plainly a *Kiddush*. ('Sanctification' derived from *kaddesh*, 'to sanctify.' It is a prayer recited over a cup of wine in the home and the synagogue to consecrate the Sabbath or festival in fulfillment of the Biblical commandment to 'Remember the Sabbath day and keep it holy.' *Exodus* 20:8.)

"After the gathering, which was to me, plainly an abbreviated Sabbath service, I spoke to David Castro. He had learned the words by rote from his father, and his father and his father's father before him had learned the words in the same fashion. He did not know their meaning. It was a 'tradition' that had been handed down through the generations. He, too, had never heard of a people called Jews. He insisted that he and all the other townsfolk were Christians, faithful to the Catholic Church.

"When I suggested that the service proved to me that he and his fellow townsfolk were of Jewish ancestry, he smiled thoughtfully. 'Perhaps it is as you say. Perhaps we are of your ancestry. But we are Christians, faithful to the Catholic Church.'

"I went into the Spanish Inquisition in some detail. I told him that his ancestors' fear of being discovered by their oppressors, and ending up being burnt at the stake for their beliefs, had caused them to emigrate, as a group, to the New World. This plainly explained their efforts to ensure total isolation.

"'Not only did the Church deprive you of the right to worship your God in peace, but the fear that the children might accidentally reveal their secret observance, which would inevitably lead to the slaughter of the community at the direction of the Inquisitors, deprived parents of the right to tell their children of their heritage.'

"The elder nodded his head sadly. 'I understand what you tell me and I have no doubt that it is true. But we are as we are: a tranquil town with a people content to live our lives according to our traditions.' He paused for a moment and asked, 'Do your people, the Jews, follow all these observances?'

"I admitted that his townsfolk appeared to have followed the Biblical commandments more faithfully than many Jews in my country. 'We're in the twentieth century, in an age of great change. Jews, like so many others, are caught up in achieving higher status, larger homes and greater comforts.'

"'Then, perhaps, it is best that we remain apart from that world,' he concluded. 'I don't think that the Catholic Church would persecute us now, but I also don't think we could retain our ways if we enter that modern world which you describe. Let my townsfolk remain content with our simple ways. Maybe in some future, better world we can identify ourselves by the faith of our ancestors.'

"The elder raised his hands above his head, directed them towards me and declared in Biblical Hebrew, '*Ye-vaw-rec-cha-cha Ha-Shem vi-yish-me-re-cha.* (May the Lord bless you and keep you safe)'

"'*Kane ya-he ra-zton* (May this be God's will)', I replied reflexively, head bent forward.

"'*Ya-er Ha-Shem pa-nav a-le-cha ve-chu-ne-cha.* (May the Lord shine the light of His countenance upon you and be gracious unto you.)'

"'*Kane ya-he ra-zton,*' I repeated.

"'*Ye-sa Ha-Shem pa-nav a-le-cha v-ya-sam l-cha sha-lom,* (May the Lord turn His countenance upon you and grant you peace.),' he concluded.

"Again, I responded, '*Kane ya-he ra-tzon.*'

"With that, he embraced me and wished me well on my journey back to the United States.

"His words – words spoken by Jews for thousands of years – still echo in my ears. And so you see why I said earlier, that they remember more of their past than do most of us in twentieth-century America."

15

The following day, Nathan was released from the hospital. Years later, I visited Nathan and his brother, Moses, in their homes atop a hill in the Catskills. I told Nathan of my progress in researching our family history.

"Herbert, you're a lover of history, and from what I have learned, listening to you to when I was a patient in Mt. Sinai, you are one deeply concerned not only with the survival of the Jewish people, but with the advancement of civilization. Today, I have listened to you talk for hours, almost non-stop. You have a natural gift as a storyteller, a gift that seems to be quite prevalent in our family, myself included. You are the link: one who has learned much about and can picture the past, and yet is living in the present. That past should not disappear from the consciousness of this and future generations. You must complete the project even if it takes you the rest of your life. You could even include the story of the town with the secret Jews so long as the name and location of the town are not revealed, so their privacy will have been protected and my pledge will not have been broken.

"You should be a voice that reminds others that they cannot and should not forget the past. Perhaps when a vast chorus of voices reminds us of man's tragic mistakes in the past, mankind will learn to respect all human life. Perhaps then we will arrive at the world prophesized by Isaiah, in which 'they shall beat their swords into plowshares and their spears into pruning hooks. Nations shall not take up sword against nation: they shall never again know war.'"

AZUVEL

In late 1957 it was suggested that I date a recent graduate of Barnard College. Her name was Stephanie Gusikoff, a member of a family of world-class musicians. When I completed my day's work at Memorial Hospital, I headed to her family's apartment in the Bronx. I knocked on the door.

"Who's there?" came from a female voice on the other side of the door.

"It's me, Herb Ausubel. We have a date."

I was early, so she asked me to return a bit later. Half an hour later she was ready. We went out for some food and then to a movie. Then we sat in my car, talking for what seemed hours. I was smitten the first time I set eyes on her. She looked like a Nordic princess, but did not exude airs, and she had an inner beauty about her. She was highly intelligent, with accomplishments in fields quite different from those in which I concentrated. I knew I had found my mate.

I saw her every night that I was not on call, and those were precious few. Within a few weeks I was exhausted: running from the hospital to her family's apartment in the Bronx, and then to my family's residence in Brooklyn, only to have to rush back to Memorial Hospital in Manhattan for morning rounds.

"Let's get married," I pleaded after three months of courtship.

She laughed.

Several months later I proposed again.

"I'm still going to Juilliard for my Masters," she smiled in reply.

Another few months went by and I pleaded for a positive response. "I can't keep this up," I insisted. "I need more than three hours of sleep if I'm to take proper care of my patients."

"You'll have completed your final year at Mt. Sinai next June. We might as well wait 'til then."

I was planning to go into private practice in Long Island with Milt Levine, a classmate from Harvard Medical School. "We could buy a house and get to know people in the area beforehand." I would not let up and so eventually Stephanie conceded.

We were married at the St. Moritz Hotel in Manhattan in January, 1960, blending my Old World family with her musical heritage: rabbis and luminaries of the musical world breaking bread together.

We moved into a house in Elmont, Long Island. Two cots were our only furniture at the start. But we had determination, and that was worth more than any money that we did not possess. Besides, I had pride. As long as the good Lord gave me strength, I would be able to care for my wife and the children whom we hoped would enrich our lives.

In June, 1960, I completed my training at Mt. Sinai Hospital and entered practice along with Milt Levine. We worked seven days a week, through the day and into the night. If called to see a patient thirty miles away at 2 a.m., I would rush to the individual's bedside. Often, the person had no money, but I was a doctor, and the care would be given regardless of whether I was or was not paid for my services. There were even a few occasions when my life was in danger from some deranged individual. I concluded that I would have to be a little more cautious if I hoped to survive.

We lived as frugally as possible, never seeing the inside of a fashionable restaurant. Stephanie would travel into the city, and her earnings from giving music lessons were added to the money I was able to put aside after paying expenses.

We had promised ourselves that we would take a "grand tour" of the continent as soon as we had saved enough to do so. After not having taken a single day's vacation for two years, the time had arrived. Our "grand tour" was a trip from England to Israel. We stayed in 4th class hotels and bed and breakfast homes, and mostly took a bus or ferry between cities.

The Holy Land was to be the highlight of the trip. One day we were taken into a cave in the Galilee. "It must have been a cave like this one," I said as I looked around.

"What are you talking about?" Stephanie inquired.

"The one in the story my grandfather told me in one form and my father's cousin, Nathan Ausubel, in another."

"What story?"

The story started 2,800 years ago. Avraham and his son, Moshe, made their way, astride donkeys, over a narrow winding road in the Galilee. They were dressed alike, both wearing woolen robes, girded at the waist with simple sashes. White cotton hats in the shape of truncated cones rested on their heads. The headpieces were turning gray at the edges from soaking perspiration. They wore brown leather sandals.

Avraham's bronzed face was half hidden by his long, cocoa-colored hair and the sidelocks that flowed over his strong, brown beard. The sidelocks flopped up and down with each forward movement of the animal beneath him. Avraham's deep, dark eyes, alert to danger, continuously scanned the landscape. He urged his four-legged transport up the sharp incline with the tap of a stick, as well as with firm pressure by his legs against the animal's belly. He wet his parched lips with a slow circular movement of his tongue and turned to speak to his son.

Moshe, the more relaxed of the two, hummed a tune to himself as his saucer eyes took in the barren, mustard-colored hills, more in search of rabbits than of danger. Having fallen behind, a sharp "Keep up with me" from his father brought him back to the present.

"Giddy-yap," shouted the boy excitedly, as he kicked his donkey several times, as if putting the blame on the poor beast. A third donkey, urged forward by the pull of a rope held firmly in Avraham's hand, brought up the rear. It bore a small load wrapped in a gray blanket tied securely to its back.

The hills were steep and pox-marked with caves – dark, forbidding openings in the high cliffs that towered above the ribbon-like path they followed.

"Keep a sharp eye on each hole," said Avraham, concerned. "You never know what danger may be hidden within."

Their movements slowed as they ascended a particularly treacherous rise. The animals brayed their discontent with every forced step.

"Let's descend and walk alongside the donkeys," directed the father. "The animals are tired and we have a long way to go. Let them feed on the grass wherever you find any. Forage is scarce in these hills in the dry season.

"Why not ride on the other donkey?" suggested Moshe. "It hasn't much of a load."

"No. Its burden is not heavy, but the load is very important. Besides, if one of us sat on the beast, the jar might be broken."

"Is that what's hidden beneath the blanket? What's in the jar?"

"Something valuable. You'll see in Jerusalem."

"Gold?" inquired the lad, his eyes brightening with interest.

"'No, not gold...but something of worth, nevertheless."

"Is that why we watch the caves – to protect the valuables?"

"And our lives, too. A thief looking down from above can't tell whether our cargo is worth a fortune or sells for half a *shekel* until after he attacks. By then it's too late, so we must be on the alert."

They reached the top of the incline and paused in the heat of the noonday sun to dry their brows and rest their donkeys.

"There's nothing for them to eat here," said Avraham, "but in the next valley down at the bottom there's some dried vegetation. They can feed there."

The father studied the horizon as he turned his neck slowly.

"There's the Sea of Galilee," he added, pointing to the east.

Moshe raised a hand to shade his eyes from the glare of the sun. He peered eastward. The land sloped irregularly downward to a vague stretch of blue far in the distance.

"And beyond there are the cliffs of Golan," continued the father.

"How far is that?"

"A long, long way. But that's not the direction in which we travel. We're headed south to the Holy City."

Avraham loosened his sash, and then tugged at his clothing, trying to entice some cooling breeze beneath his skirts. After a while he said, "Come, let's get on. "We must reach the city before the festival."

Darkness came several hours later, followed quickly by a chilly evening wind. Avraham led his son and the donkeys up to the rocks to a cave that was to serve as shelter for the night. The father studied the darkened cavern carefully. Poking his staff into blackened corners, his sharp eyes studied every roughened edge in the den. Satisfied, he unburdened the animals and patted them gently.

"You've had some grass along the way. I've nothing for you now," he said apologetically to the beasts. "When we reach Jerusalem, you'll have a fine meal."

After the heat of the day, night grew cold in the hills, numbing the body rapidly. Avraham lit a fire by rubbing two stones together over a few dead twigs and dried grass gathered along the way. As the evening meal was heating in the flames, father and son sat cross-legged before the fire, each rubbing his hands together to warm them.

Suddenly a change came over Avraham's face. His eyes grew intense as his hand dropped to his side and fingered the stout staff that lay there. He had noted a dark shadow crossing the mouth of the cave, momentarily blocking out the light of the flickering stars.

"Peace be unto you, stranger," he said in seeming tranquility. "Come closer and sit down. We haven't much to eat, but you're welcome to share it with us."

Moshe dropped an empty bowl with a crash. Surprised and a bit frightened, his head spun around.

A form emerged into the light of the fire; a man, yellow and black, the illuminated surface and the dark shadows of the folds. His hair was jet black and oily with a reflecting sheen. His face was unbearded, but not recently shaven. Avraham perceived something sinister behind the overly large smile on the stranger's face. Was it a seemingly forced smile, or was it the hook of his nose pinched together like a sheathed dagger waiting to be drawn? Perhaps it was the sharp chin that resembled an ax impatient to strike, or the curve of the mouth and the moving indentation on a tongue behind it, like that of a cat as it eyes a mouse, anticipating a fine meal as the animal prepares to pounce. It was not one thing, but the sum of all those observations.

But the stranger's hands made no sudden movements. Instead, the man replied, "And peace be unto you both. I thank you for the offer to share... everything."

The delayed last word sent a chill through Avraham's spine, but he made an effort to conceal his inner feelings.

"Get a bowl for our guest, Moshe... Two bowls, come to think of it, since yours is broken. And clean up the pieces."

The boy, filled with curiosity, obeyed.

They all ate. The stranger started immediately with rapid slurping movements, but Avraham and his son waited until a blessing had been uttered.

The stranger finished first. He belched loudly as if to compliment the cook, and then wiped his face broadly with the sleeve of his grimy robe.

"So," began the stranger, "you're Hebrews. I caught that mumbo jumbo of yours. That's not Aramaic." (An ancient Semitic language spoken by many peoples in the Middle East, including the Hebrews, in Biblical times.)

"Yes," Avraham replied, "we're Hebrews. And you?"

The jet-haired mysterious intruder belched even more loudly than before. "A fine meal...for a *fine* gentleman and his son." His voice rose with that last word. "I don't think you spend many days sleeping in caves."

"A humble man and his son," replied Avraham blandly. "And you?"

"What do you have so neatly tucked in the corner?" inquired the stranger in his determined way.

"It's for the Temple," blurted out Moshe to his father's momentarily-unmasked annoyance.

"Hmm," remarked the intruder. "A gift from a gentleman."

"I asked you a question," said Avraham, firmly. "You have not given us the benefit of a reply. You have shared our meal and now it's over. You are in a hurry, no doubt, so peace be unto you on your journey... And be careful as you leave. It's a sharp drop."

"What's the hurry?" the stranger smiled. "It's cold out there and you have a warm fire. Share and share alike. Isn't that what your God teaches you? I have no place to go on a night like this."

"Then share our fire," Avraham answered with a watchful eye. "Just stay where you are now. I'll let you have one of our blankets."

The father, never turning his back to the guest, took a few steps toward the corner where their packages lay. He carefully extracted three blankets from the pile, one for each of them. The fire was growing low and Moshe tossed a few more dried branches onto it.

"Aren't you a Hebrew?" asked Moshe with a flicker of his eye.

"Ha, no. I'm a Canaanite."

"Do you Canaanites go to the Temple?" questioned the boy.

"Temple? No. I've got Baal back home. Made of fine metal, too."

"What's Baal?" the lad asked.

"Baal? Baal's a god."

"But the Almighty has no name," Moshe retorted.

"Well, my god has a name...and he's well made... You ought to get one for your home. Good protection." He laughed a loud, ominous laugh. "You can ask him for favors. And if you give him something valuable in return, he may grant your request."

"I can't," said Moshe.

"Why not?" puzzled the stranger.

"Graven images are forbidden," retorted Avraham. "It's in the Commandments." He studied the stranger's face and then added, "But if you have a home, why are you out here?"

"Why are *you* out here?" pursued the stranger.

"You heard my son. We're on our way to the Temple to pray."

"Bearing fine gifts." The dark-haired intruder's tongue showed itself as it moved in a circular fashion over his lips.

"A humble offering. Nothing of monetary value," said Avraham.

"Nothing of value given; nothing of value received. No. I'm sure you're not traveling all this distance for nothing," shot back the stranger.

"Have it as you wish. We must rest now. An early departure is necessary. Sleep you well." Avraham pulled his blanket up to his chin and became silent.

The fire died down, leaving but a few glowing embers. Avraham was resting not far from his load. The boy was fast asleep, rolled into a ball and completely hidden beneath his blanket for warmth. All was still, save for the occasional crackling of a small, charred branch breaking and falling into the heat.

A faint grating sound came to Avraham's ears, barely audible against the crackling of the fire. It was the sound of leather rubbing against stone, followed by a vibration suggestive of cloth being ruffled.

In a flash, Avraham was on top of the stranger, right next to the Hebrew's load. He had the man pinned to the ground with one hand twisting his wrist until the Canaanite's dagger fell on to a rock, producing a spark.

The Hebrew's other hand firmly gripped a staff, which was now positioned menacingly close to the stranger's windpipe.

"Don't move a finger if you value your life," Avraham warned him.

"Y-you said share and share alike. You must have gold or something else of value in there. I'm a poor man with many mouths to feed. I meant you no harm. Give me a few coins and I'll be off." The oily stranger's eyes were wide with terror.

"I said, 'Share our meal.' Nothing else. I invited you to share our fire. Nothing else. I do not wish blood on my hands when I arrive at the Temple of the Lord, so be off! And be quick about it."

The frightened man disappeared through the mouth of the cave, into the darkness.

"What happened?" asked Moshe excitedly.

"Learn to keep your senses on the alert," replied his father. "We were within inches of a blade. Bear in mind, I will not always be at your side."

A few days later, father and son stood in the Judean hills. Ahead of them was the city of Jerusalem etched against a cloudless blue sky. The yellow faces of the buildings and walls, hewn from the stone of the surrounding hills, glowed softly in the afternoon sun. The city and the hills were as one: a perfect blend of nature and man's work. There was nothing foreign here, only serenity and peace. It was as if the tribulations of the world ended at the city's gates.

A cooling breeze brushed against the bronzed faces of Avraham and his son as they studied the scene in silence. Their donkeys, tired from the long trip south, bent their heads against the rocky ground, searching for hidden food. The precarious journey from the cedars of Lebanon to the city of David in order to bring a cargo to the Temple for the Shavuot festival was nearly over. (The Festival of the Weeks: one of the three ancient harvest and pilgrimage festivals of the Hebrew calendar. It celebrates the first harvest and also commemorates the giving of the Ten Commandments on Mount Sinai.)

"Moshe, this is the holy city, the city of David, and there on the mount is the Temple of Solomon, a Temple to the Lord."

The soft, brown eyes on the boy's unmarked face, saucers filled with eager innocence, took in the sight. He was powerless to speak. Truly, he had never seen anything like it.

"Come," beckoned the father, impatiently. "It's getting late. We must find a place to stay, wash, change our dress, and then complete our task before evening."

They secured quarters just inside the city walls – a room, in the home of others that had served as Avraham's resting place during some of his many visits to Jerusalem. The donkeys were left outside, feasting on a meal of hay, while Avraham and Moshe washed and then changed into garments of pure white.

Appropriately attired, they hastened off on foot before sunset. With them they carried an earthen jar that had been brought with considerable care from the far north. They made their way through the narrow, hilly streets of the city. The lengthening shadows of the late afternoon spread across the streets as Avraham and Moshe moved on below the arches of buildings that crossed the pathway. Finally, they reached a pair of gates at the southern side of the amber-colored stone wall that surrounded the Temple Mount.

They paused before the huge, dark metal gates. Avraham rested his jar on the ground. Then father and son bathed their hands and faces in a nearby stone basin while Avraham kept a protective eye on his jar.

"Why are we washing again?" inquired the boy. "We're clean."

"So it is ordained, just like our white garments, as a token of our modesty as we approach the Temple of the Lord."

The gates were opened from within by a man who, like themselves, was dressed in linen the color of snow. Avraham deposited two silver coins into the man's pale, smooth hand. Then, with his son tagging along at his side, Avraham carried his jealously guarded reddish-brown container into the outer court of the Temple. There were blue, pink and white marble columns rising upward to a colossal height. These great columns, veined like the churning waters of an angry sea, stood on either side of them as they crossed the great mosaic of dark and light stone that floored the outer court.

Moshe seemed unable to move. He could do nothing but gaze, as if star-struck, at the magnificence of the structure. His father had to nudge him to move forward. They ascended concentric circles of polished sandstone, and approached the grand, roofed Temple.

"Father," asked Moshe as they walked, "who are all those men sitting between the roofed columns near the wall? Look at the birds in cages and barrels filled with who knows what. And what's that strange-looking fellow doing with a balance?"

"All with a purpose – business related to the Temple: the sale of doves and oil and wine to those who have come from far and would like to bring gifts to the Temple; money-changers ready to supply the half-*shekel* payment necessary for admission in exchange for whatever currency the pilgrim carries. But hush, a priest approaches."

A balding priest, thin and sallow-faced, clothed in a pure white linen robe and skullcap, was there to receive the jar. The vessel was promptly and unceremoniously taken past a white mesh curtain into the inner court of the sanctuary. Aside from a quick nod from the priest, there was nothing in his conduct to suggest any reward or even recognition for all that effort.

The boy thought: *We have traveled for days, risking our lives amid the many twists and turns of mountain paths where brigands could be lurking. In fact, we have narrowly missed death at the hands of a cutthroat. And all this to carry the jar and its precious contents to the Temple. Having survived those dangers, we had not paused to rest. Instead, we have hurried, almost breathlessly, through the city to the Temple. Was a nod all we were to receive in recognition of such effort?*

Moshe opened his mouth to speak, but an index finger held by Avraham across his lips stilled the boy before he could begin. However, the demand for silence could not still the boy's curiosity.

Others now entered the courtyard, bearing offerings. Some carried wood, others oil. Men brought wheat, flour, the first fruits of the season and young calves. The priests who carried the offerings past the long white veil into the inner court, too, received these gifts.

From their vantage point at the head of the stairs, Avraham and Moshe peered intently through the mesh of the curtain into the inner court. There, a host of priests in the snow-white robes seemingly floated about. Several activities were taking place at the same time, and it was difficult for Moshe to decide which one to follow. In one corner, some priests were mixing a series of dark ground leaves and other materials. The aroma wafted through the air and arrived at the nostrils of Moshe and his father. A pinch of this and a measure of that.

But what is this all about? wondered Moshe. The substances were being extracted from pitchers without labels. *What's in the burnt-orange bottle? And what does that dark vessel contain?*

Aloud, Moshe inquired softly, "What are they doing?"

"They're mixing spices to make incense," whispered Avraham.

"How do they know how much of each to use?" Moshe pursued.

"It's a formula known only to the priests, handed down from generation to generation."

Their attention was now seized by a most dramatic event. A tall, broad-shouldered priest, with muscular arms bulging beneath his snow-white linen robe, lifted a pure red heifer by its legs. It was a display of strength that amazed Moshe.

The boy nearly fell through the curtain as he tried to get closer to the action. Avraham thrust an arm in front of his son, half to keep the lad from falling, and half to prevent him from violating the sanctity of the inner court.

"Careful. Don't touch the curtain," the father whispered with firmness in his voice. "The thin mesh of that curtain, just like the walls of the Temple, stands as a line of demarcation which we are forbidden to cross without first receiving permission."

"'I'm sorry," replied Moshe.

"The father patted the boy on the back comfortingly. "And try to remain silent. Remember we are in the Temple of the Lord," Avraham whispered.

"Look!" cried Moshe before his father could keep him from shouting out. Moshe held his breath while staring straight ahead at a most astonishing sight. His father, although a veteran of countless trips to the Holy City, gaped in awe.

The tall, broad-shouldered priest, employing every ounce of energy in his pulsating arms, had tossed the animal high in the air. The moment the heifer was released from his hands, the priest reached nimbly for a sword resting nearby. Without a wasted motion, he pierced the falling animal like a matador of a later millennium, seeming to know the precise spot that would dispatch the animal. The beast went limp, crashing to the ground, a huge carcass that had surrendered its life force.

The lifeless creature was then placed atop a fiery chamber. Flesh, skin and bowels turned black in the heat of the flames. The air became heavy with pungent smoke. A wizened man in white placed pieces of cedar wood atop the burning carcass. The old priest followed this by pouring the scarlet contents of a nearby container onto the smoking conflagration.

A priest approached the altar – the balding man in white who had received Avraham's earthen jar – and sprinkled some of the jar's menthaceous contents on top of the fiery mixture.

In the end, there was nothing but ashes. It was all that remained of the heifer, cedar wood, scarlet and spice. The balding man in white, using one hand, shoveled the powdery gray residue into a wide-mouthed vessel which he held delicately balanced in the other hand. A splash was followed by a static, hissing sound as the ashes dropped into the huge bowl. It was flame falling into and being extinguished by water.

The balding priest put down his vessel. He prostrated himself before the altar, then withdrew, carrying his precious vessel across the courtyard. He took great pains not to spill any of its contents. When the balding priest reached the other side of the inner court, he paused. He gave a beckoning nod to a young, fair-haired priest standing nearby. The young priest responded by quickly retrieving the jar that Avraham had brought to the Temple with such care.

The two priests then carried their respective vessels past the sheer curtain that separated the inner from the outer court. They passed Moshe and his father along their way.

"Who are they?" Moshe began as the men in white went by.

Again, that signal for silence appeared on his father's face. It was Avraham's firm insistence that Moshe observe the goings-on with his mouth shut.

The priests descended the fifteen steps and continued across the mosaic of dark- and light-colored stones to the very gates of the Temple. There they rested their containers on top of a small wooden table.

Moshe looked perplexed and chagrined as he watched the older priest return to the inner court, again passing the boy and his father without displaying any further recognition.

Suddenly the veil was drawn back. The inner court was now revealed in its full glory. Trumpets were sounded. The gates of the Temple were thrown open. The appointed hour had arrived. Moshe looked back to see hundreds and then thousands of people streaming into the outer court. Some stopped at the gate. The young priest, responding as if by request, sprinkled some of the flaky contents of Avraham's offering upon those who loitered impatiently at the gates. Each recipient dipped his hands in the wide-mouthed vessel resting atop the small table, then joined the others filing into the outer court.

Avraham and Moshe, along with all the others, now moved into the roofed Temple. Again, Avraham stretched out his firm arm to indicate that this was as far as they were permitted to go. Moshe turned his head. The entire court was filled. The crowd extended back far beyond the Temple gates.

Returning his gaze to the sanctuary, Moshe tried to identify each of the components that made up the House of the Almighty. His father's detailed description of the great hall of the Temple had jelled into a mental picture. Now he had the opportunity to compare the engraving, stored in the recesses of his brain, with the real thing.

He stared at the impressive stone structure that dominated the center of the great cuboid chamber. Stairs ascended to a pair of carved oak doors. Moshe studied the writing above the doors. *It's the Holy Ark*, he thought, *containing the Five Books of Moses. It's just as Father described.*

To the left of the Holy Ark, and situated between the Ark and the Israelites who crowded the rear of the great Temple, was a high altar, solemn, silent and unoccupied.

To the right there was a long, narrow platform on which stood a considerable number of men all dressed in the snow-white linen robes and caps required of the servants of the Temple. Most stood erect with hands at their sides, but some held instruments – cymbals, flutes, harps and lyres.

"The Levites," began Moshe. (They were members of the tribe of Levi, singled out during the wanderings in the wilderness after the Exodus from Egypt for the service of the tabernacle and the attending of the duties of the sanctuary.)

A finger of silence held across the lips and an agreeing nod were Avraham's reply.

The sacrificial ritual was repeated in the presence of the multitude, with a calf serving as the offering. All eyes followed the priest, whose muscular arms exhibited unbelievable power coupled with dexterity.

An almost imperceptible murmur was heard as an imposing figure, tall and stately, entered by way of a side door near the front of the great hall. His silvery hair, flowing over slim shoulders like a graceful wintry waterfall, gave him the look of some ancient oracle. He was clothed in the same white linen outer garments and head covering as the other priests, but with added accoutrements. Golden bells, hung from the skirts of his robe, sounded as he walked. A rich girdle of many beautiful colors surrounded his waist. Twelve stones, each soldered with gold, covered his breast. The names of the heads of the twelve tribes of Israel were imprinted in the gold. Crowning his head was a tiara with a miter at its top. The sacred letters of the Almighty were engraved in a gold plate suspended above his eyes. Moshe knew this could be but one man, the High Priest of the Temple.

The other priests gathered around him and assisted the supreme religious authority of Israel in removing all the ornaments and the girdle of many colors that he was wearing. The gold and the glitter that rested atop his head was also shed, so that his attire was now identical to that of the other priests. Barefoot, he led his fellow priests into the inner court.

Thousands of Israelites assembled in the rear of the Temple in the spacious outer court and even beyond the Temple gates. They now joined the High Priest in the chanting of the *Shema*. The priest who had been occupied earlier in the mixing of spices now placed frankincense on the altar. Following this, a burnt offering was presented. The High Priest ascended the stone steps of the altar and then lifted a cup of wine dramatically above his head. With a sudden twist of his hands, he poured the dark fluid out in front of the altar. Trumpets were sounded and all assembled fell with their faces to the earth before the Almighty. The people cried out for the Lord's mercy and prayed. When the last voice stilled, they rose.

The High Priest descended from the altar, and then raised his long, bony hands up high. All the Israelites prostrated themselves for a second time as the High Priest called for the blessing of the Almighty on them all. With the clash of cymbals and the sound of the other instruments, the Levites broke into singing and the service was ended. The priests filed out of the great hall. Then the multitude, packed in the rear of the sanctuary and throughout the entire outer court, slowly made their way out past the Temple gates.

Avraham looked to his son once they were beyond the gates.

"Well," he began, "you've got questions. Now's the time to ask."

The lad let out a low whistling exhalation, as if he had suddenly been released from a command to hold his breath.

"I think I recognized most of the ceremony and most of the people from your earlier description, but there were *two* sacrifices – the red heifer and a small calf. Why?"

"Do you remember which came first?" responded the father to the boy's frustration.

"The red heifer."

"Correct. And when did it occur?"

"Earlier," replied the boy with growing impatience.

"Yes, that's true, but how much earlier?"

"Quite a few minutes. Why is that important?" the lad scowled.

"The red heifer was sacrificed after the Temple gates were opened, but before the trumpet sounded and the multitude entered the outer court. That is important."

"But why?"

"Because the ashes had to be used in a preparation that was needed before some could enter the Temple."

"I remember," the boy smiled. "The priest – the bald-headed one who took your jar – shoveled the ashes into a bowl of water or something and then took it to the gate of the Temple. But first he got the younger priest to take along our jar...with the stuff you brought from the Galilee... What was in the jar?"

"The 'stuff', as you refer to it, is *azuv*. We carried it all the way from the Lebanon. It has a fragile scent, and so fresh *azuv* must be obtained often if it is to be used continuously." (*Azuv* is an aromatic menthaceous herb derived from the blue-flowered hyssop plant.)

"But what has *azuv* to do with the ashes?" asked the boy, perplexed.

"So it is written in the Scriptures: as we are commanded to do so by the Almighty. No better answer can be given. It is written that those who have been in the presence of the dead, for whatever reason, are unclean to enter the Temple of the Lord until they have been sprinkled with *azuv* and have then dipped their hands into a bowl of water containing the ashes of a pure red heifer."

"But why *azuv* and why a red heifer?" pursued Moshe.

"Why, why, why?" said the father with apparent exasperation in his voice. He thought for a long moment and then added, "Now this is just an idea. *Azuv* has long symbolized humility, just as the willow has been used as a symbol of pride. And humility is in order when we appear before the Lord of Hosts. As for the *pure* red heifer, it must be without blemish to represent our purity of purpose when we enter the Temple of the Lord. But as I said, this is only an interpretation. So it is written. That's all that counts."

The boy listened thoughtfully to his father's words. He thought for a while and then posed one more question. "Father, we live far from here, and yet you travel to Jerusalem often. The road is a dangerous one as I can see from our recent experience. You receive no pay for so hazardous a journey, or even compensation for the cost of the *azuv*. Why do you come back again and again?"

"Because, my son, it is our obligation to the Lord. It was my father's, it is mine, and when I'm gone, it will be yours. We were chosen for this honor – yes, I say honor – generations ago, when the Temple was built in the days of King Solomon. But honor requires responsibility and, yes, even grave hazard sometimes. Moshe, service to the Lord is not something you do when you feel like it; it is a sacred duty that must be carried out. That is the meaning of our name."

"Our name?"

"Yes. You are Moshe ben Avraham *Azuvel*. (*El* means "God" and so *Azuvel* is the "Hyssop of God.") Thousands have traveled long distances on a pilgrimage to the Holy City. But some cannot enter the Temple until they have been sprinkled with *azuv* and then have dipped their hands in the water containing the ashes of the heifer. They should not be kept waiting. And so the deliverer of the *azuv* to the Temple of the Lord must not be tardy."

TERROR IN THE NORTH

OUR FIRST BORN, Ian, was an unusual child. Although he was very aware of his surroundings and exhibited great dexterity, he was rather quiet. The pediatrician assured us that there was nothing wrong with the child. Nevertheless, Stephanie expressed concern.

"I'm sure the pediatrician is right," I insisted. "Ian is just trying to figure it all out before he explains it."

"Explains what?" Stephanie said with some annoyance.

"Well, it is said that Albert Einstein didn't speak until he was four. The story was that he was trying to solve the problem of relativity. When he finally came up with the formula $E = mc^2$, he spoke."

"Very funny," Stephanie retorted. "Albert Einstein did not come up with the Theory of Relativity at the age of four. Besides, I've never heard that being slow to start talking was a proof of genius."

At this point I told her a story about myself:

When I was a young child, my mother had similar concerns about me. It was the time of the Great Depression and we were poor. My parents could not afford expensive counseling, so my mother took me to a Jewish Social Agency where we could obtain free assistance. It was there that I spent an hour with a counselor by the name of Nettie Selling. When I entered her office, she was trying to do something with a dictaphone. I asked what the problem was. She said the machine was not working.

"Can I try it?"

"Do you know anything about dictaphones?"

"No. But let me try to figure it out."

She stepped aside and I went to work. I had never seen a dictaphone before. Nevertheless, I solved the problem in less than five minutes.

She spent the rest of our visit questioning me on a number of subjects. At the end of the session, she reassured my mother that I was fine and that there was no need for me to return to the Agency.

"But I have a bit of advice," Ms. Selling went on. "Have him start up a conversation on any subject, with anyone he meets. Within minutes, they will stand there in awe, wondering how one small head can carry all he knows."

Stephanie smiled when I completed my story about Nettie Selling. "So you became a *wunderkind*, winning quiz contests. Did you ever see Ms. Selling again?"

"No. But she will always be in my thoughts."

Despite my attempt to assuage Stephanie's fears, I could see real worry in her eyes. We took Ian to another pediatrician for a second opinion.

He gave us the same assurance as our pediatrician.

"But what if they are all wrong? What if there is something amiss that should be corrected? What if they are going on the assumption that since his parents are smart, Ian will achieve to their level?" Stephanie's voice trailed off.

True to my predictions, Ian was later viewed as some sort of *wunderkind*. At one time, he came up with a formula as to how one could determine this or that in mathematics. He then wrote a paper containing its proof. Although I was very good in mathematics, I was not sure of his formula's significance. I showed Ian's paper to a patient of mine who was the Chairman of the Department of Mathematics at a major university.

"It's worthy of an 'A' as a Ph.D. thesis," was his conclusion after reading the paper.

One day, Ian posed a question to me. "You've told me that our ancestors were spice merchants who delivered hyssop to the Temple of Solomon. That's how we were given the name *Azuvel*. You also told me that our family lived in the northern part of Israel. But the Assyrians conquered Israel 2,700 years ago, and the inhabitants were sent off into exile. So who supplied hyssop for the Temple after that? And how did our name survive?"

As was my custom, I replied with a story:

A hundred years had passed since Avraham and Moshe Azuvel stood together admiring the Holy City in the Judean hills. The bright-eyed little boy who accompanied his father on the long trip south had long since been laid to rest. A fourth generation of his descendants now inhabited the Kingdom of Israel.

Dawvid ben Chaim Azuvel, a slender, tight-framed merchant, paused on a hilltop in the Galilee. His body was half-bent over a long, rough-hewn staff. His face was partially concealed beneath a faded and dust-covered brown cloth that covered his head and neck to below the level of his shoulders. His ashen cheeks were a striking contrast to the dark, crinkly beard below them. His homeland had been invaded by the Terror of the North led by a ruthless king, Tiglath-Pileser III. The Assyrians had been laying waste to much of Israel's farms, villages and great cities. And so Dawvid's great, sad eyes were turned to the north, watching and waiting...for the unknown.

The word "Assyrian" came into focus in the retina of his subconscious, searing his tongue as if fiery-hot coals had been forced into his mouth. His body went numb, sinking, in his imagination, beneath the icy waters of a rising pool as wind-swept, chilling dust enveloped him. He could feel a viper's sting burning its way into his chest and he stood transfixed, his arms and legs paralyzed with fear.

Strange sounds recalled him to reality. The cracking of twigs and the crushing of dried leaves echoed up from a nearby gully, commanding his attention. This was followed by a heavy thud.

In an instant he was in action, descending into the dark gorge. He used his staff to keep from tumbling down the steep decline. At the base, a trail of crushed weeds, broken bushes and snapped branches led deeper and deeper into a ravine. Bits of torn cloth dangled from some of the splintered wood. Some globs of freshly-dried blood, already specked with dust, were splattered over the yellowing plants, dark-brown leaves and gray rocks, as if some gravely-wounded animal had passed that way, spilling out the last bits of his life force with every struggling step. Here and there, pieces of flesh clung to thorny bushes. At last he saw the source of the trail, the blood and the flesh.

"Master of the Universe!" Dawvid cried out as he looked at a horribly mutilated man lying on the ground. "What happened to you?"

What was left of a man of medium height lay there, face up. His glazed eyes stared at a comfortless gray sky. His mouth was wide open, sucking in air with each labored, heaving movement of his chest. The nose and both earlobes were missing, filled in with dark clots mixed with dirt. His arms rested folded on his abdomen, but there were no hands! Here too, large earth-stained clots covered the wrists at the point of amputation. The gasping remnant of what had been a human being lifted his head. Beneath the blood, the face had a ghost-like quality. Hearing Dawvid's inquiry voiced with shock and yet deep compassion, the supplicating eyes of the wounded man turned towards the newly arrived figure.

"Please help me, please. Water. *Please*."

For a moment, Dawvid was unable to move a muscle. At last, he overcame the stupefying dread and knelt beside the dismembered man. He lifted the poor fellow's battered head with one hand while he held a sheepskin pouch to the stranger's lips with the other. The wounded man drank so quickly that he began to choke. After a few coughs and pats on the back from Dawvid, the fellow stopped. He had his fill of water.

"Who did this to you?" asked Dawvid with unrestrained horror as he helped the man sit up.

"The Assyrians." There was hopeless resignation in his voice.

"How did it happen?" Dawvid persisted. "Did you lose your hands and nose and ears in battle?"

"No," was the reply. "I'm not a soldier. I happened to be in a city which they had just captured after a fierce battle."

"But why did they do *this* to you?" Dawvid asked, trying to comprehend. "Was the battle still in progress?"

The wounded man gagged again and Dawvid had to nudge him forward to release secretions. Finally, the stranger was able to speak again.

"The battle was over," he gasped. "They did this as a warning to all the others, the inhabitants of the cities of Israel, not to resist. What they did to me was not the worst."

Dawvid was stunned.

What sort of people are these, he thought, *that cut off hands and noses and ears just as a warning? Worse? What more could they have done?*

The hideous ghost squirmed as he covered his head with the horrid glob of dirt-covered blood and formless matter that was his forearm, as if to shield himself from the terror his answer recalled.

Slowly and breathlessly he continued: "They herded us...all the inhabitants of the city...into the central square. Our leaders...captains and priests... they were flayed and burnt alive! Their skins...hung on the walls of the city! Some of the warriors...they were impaled on stakes! They seized people indiscriminately...and mutilated them. They cut off fingers...hands...or even entire arms! If they were so inclined...legs were hacked off...at the foot...or calf...or thigh! There was no rhyme or reason...to these acts. Ears and noses...were sliced off...as an afterthought! Often with a mocking, ear-piercing laugh! It was as if to emphasize...the glee with which they went about...their gruesome task.

"Some of the Assyrians...seemingly more vile than the rest...if that were possible...tore out men's eyes...as the victims screamed in pain! These...they fed to the dogs like grape dessert...after a meal... But the role of the dogs... was not over. These monsters...the Assyrians...would pat the animals affectionately...and encourage the brutes to lap up the human blood. And if all this were not enough...imagine the hideousness...of their lighting a barn-fire...and then tossing...young men and women...and even children...into the flames...as kindling wood!

"How anyone survived...all that barbarity...is beyond me. Most died... on the spot. A few wretches...like myself...managed to crawl away...under the cover of darkness. Strange, grotesque creatures...with bleeding, torn flesh...we pawed at the earth and rocks...with elbows and knees...struggling to escape."

Dawvid was too shocked to speak. Only his sobs and the gasps of the wounded man broke the silence. After several minutes of weeping misery, Dawvid wiped his reddened eyes and then asked one final question:

"Did anyone escape unharmed?"

"I don't think so," was the sad reply. "If the city had not resisted...they would have taken us back to Nineveh...or one of the other cities of Assyria... as slaves. But as we resisted...they were determined to butcher us...as an example of their terror. We were to serve as an example...of what was in store... for all who would resist their might."

A hush came over them. What more was there to say? The wounded man's breathing became more and more shallow. His hollow eyes looked up to the heavens with hopeless resignation. His mouth opened wide and his head fell back on Dawvid's lap. His breathing ceased.

Flies, buzzing overhead, sensed that their moment of triumph had arrived. They descended onto the blood and the flesh and hummed their sickening tune, as tiny feelers probed for signs of a life that had vanished.

Dawvid, in anger, swatted at the air. It didn't matter. The flies had not killed him; men had. The guilty parties were the barbarians who, despite their cities of gold, had exhibited less humanity than the lowliest of the Lord's creatures. Dawvid looked hard at the motionless body and then closed the dead man's terror-filled eyes. He lifted the head from his lap and placed it gently on the ground. For a moment he thought about what to do. There was no spade nearby with which to dig a grave.

Suddenly, he was yanked out of his thoughts by a sensation of the hill vibrating. Pulling at branches and pushing himself upward with his staff pressed against the rocks, he climbed out of the gully as quickly as he could. By now he could hear a distant rumbling. Puffing and soaked in sweat, he reached the top of the hill and looked north in the direction of the now thundering noise.

An army of men came into view and it was not an Israelite army. There were hundreds and hundreds of men on horseback, and thousands of foot soldiers clad in armor. They were so numerous that the cloud of dust they made blotted out the late afternoon sun and turned the sky an ominous gray.

In a flash, Dawvid realized that he had to get back to Rivkah and the children. He ran down the side of the hill away from the enemy army. Having traversed three smaller hills, he came to the edge of his hometown. He stopped, panting with exhaustion. The memory of the sight of the dying man in the gully flashed before his eyes. A new burst of adrenaline urged him forward. Not stopping for breath, he flew past men, women and children busily engaged in the routines of a weekday.

The sound of sprinting feet and whistling gasps of the runner attracted attention. People looked up and saw the strange sight of the town's spice merchant suddenly transformed into a galloping, wild-eyed ghost driven by some strange, impelling demonic force. His robe puffed like a sail in the wind, and his head covering streamed behind him.

What possesses him? wondered the muscular, soot-covered blacksmith as he checked his swing halfway through the arc of his powerful thrust. *I've never seen such a transformation: from reserved tranquility and meditation to this!*

"Poor fellow," he muttered beneath his breath as he returned to hammering a glowing-hot horseshoe into shape.

"Run for your lives!" shouted Dawvid without interrupting his stride. "The Assyrians are coming...down the Jerusalem road!"

Faces turned gray; eyes widened with mortal dread; all activity ceased for an instant, except for the racing feet of Dawvid. This was followed by panic. People dropped everything and began scrambling. Some began to scream to alarm loved ones. Others, forgetting everything but themselves, fled every which way, with no seeming sense of direction. The town was like one large auditorium packed with people and someone had just shouted, "Fire!"

Dawvid finally reached his home. The door resisted the twist of his wrist, but his momentum was so great that it flew open as he crashed into it. There was a resounding bang as the door came to a smashing halt against the wall and then bounced back. The entire house seemed to shake. Dishes fell from the kitchen table, breaking into a hundred pieces on the floor.

Rivkah was a plumpish woman in her thirties. Dark-brown hair framed her olive-skinned face. She had been busy preparing the evening meal. Frightened by the terrible noise and the vibrations of the aftershock, she turned to see what had caused it.

Channah, a round-faced, dark-eyed girl, their oldest child, jumped up. She pushed back a lock of raven hair from her forehead. She seemed about to speak, but her tongue clung to the roof of her mouth as she stared at the cadaverous pallor of her father's face. Unable to speak, she knelt down to pick up the pieces of the shattered dishes.

Yosef, a thin, undersized lad of ten with dark, curly hair, dropped the scoop with which he was transferring spice from a large sack to a smaller container. The yellowish-green flakes flew about, scattering over much of the kitchen floor. His reflex response was to clean up the mess, except that he couldn't take his eyes off the heaving chest and terror-filled face of his father.

Naphtali, a happy, rosy-cheeked little boy of six, had been playing a game by himself. Despite the noise and the vibrations of the walls, he had not panicked. But he did put aside his simple, homemade *dreidel* (spinning top). Not fully comprehending the meaning of Dawvid's look, he ran, arms outstretched, to greet his father.

Only Dawvid had no time for hugs.

"Not now," he said grimly. "We've got to get out of here."

"What's happened?" asked his wife, excitedly. "Why do we have to go?"

"There's no time for questions. Rivkah, put some dried food in sacks – three will do. Channah, stop picking up the broken pieces. There's no reason to clean a house we're abandoning. Help your mother instead. Yosef, forget about the spice on the floor. Get some blankets – two for each of us. All of you, put on something warm; we must leave immediately."

Rivkah and the children obeyed in silence, despite the intense bewilderment and anxiety they each felt. A few minutes later they were trailing, single file, behind Dawvid. The column moved across planted fields, heading towards the southeast.

"Why don't we use the road?" asked Naphtali.

"Sh-h-h," was the whispered reply. "I don't want our enemies to hear us."

Rivkah paled upon hearing her husband's words. An icy chill shot through her body and she halted for a minute, shuddering. Channah moved alongside Rivkah and slipped an arm around her mother's waist. Rivkah smiled faintly, but continued to walk.

The sun was receding in the west. Thin, wispy clouds overhead turned salmon-pink and then crimson. The lengthening shadows of hills stretched across the golden fields, and a cool evening breeze swept down from the high country.

They were all tired, particularly little Naphtali. Still they continued on, hour after hour. Feet were aching and strained with every step. Backs were sore and the sacks of food and blankets grew heavier by the hour.

The moon was rising in the east; a narrow curved band of white came to replace the golden sun. Pale, shimmering light played tricks upon the landscape. Cliffs turned into monstrous faces that dominated the black hills. Rocks appeared to be enemies ready to bar the way. The gusting night wind drove tall stacks of wheat into their faces and bodies. It was as if a thousand whips were lashing them, demanding that they end their forward progress.

Naphtali rubbed himself, trying to keep warm. Yosef pulled a blanket out of his sack and covered his little brother.

At last their leader came to a halt. "Follow me closely up the hill," whispered Dawvid to his wife and children. "There's a cave up there. Careful, don't dislodge any rocks. The slightest sound will echo through these hills and give us away."

A few minutes later they were safely hidden in a recess of a large, dark cavern. They bundled inside their blankets and lay close to one another to preserve body heat.

"We will rest for the night," said Dawvid, softly. "I know you're all cold, but we must not light a fire. We can't give them anything they can see."

"Papa," said Yosef, "can we speak now?"

"I know what you want to hear, Yosef. I will speak softly, so please listen carefully."

The bearded father looked at his family. He placed his left arm around Rivkah's waist and his right over Channah's shoulders, drawing them to himself. His brown eyes were sad and he bit his lower lip. Dawvid turned to Channah and took in her dark eyes and glum face. He saw the questioning look of little Naphtali, the pursed lips and raised brow of Yosef, and the half-opened, questioning mouth of his wife.

"We had to run quickly," he began again, "because the Assyrians are coming. They are as numerous as a cloud of locusts and are more horrible than you can possibly imagine. I saw their army coming from the north and the west on my return from Jerusalem. I had a full view of their numbers from the high hill just beyond our town. The sky turned gray just from the dust kicked up by their horses. The earth shook from their marching feet. It was just after I left that man... *Ribono shel olam* (Master of the Universe), I did not even bury him!"

"What man are you talking about, Father?" inquired Yosef.

"I don't know his name. I don't even know what city he came from. I only know that he was an Israelite and that the Assyrians had cruelly butchered all who fell into their hands. If you could have seen the poor wretch and heard the horrors he described... I can't even bring myself to repeat them... He died in my arms just before I felt the ground vibrating. Can you imagine what their numbers must be... to feel the earth shake from their marching feet before they are even visible? That's why we had to run. I had to keep us from falling into their hands. Since they are coming via the Jerusalem road, we have to travel cross-country, to the southwest across open fields."

"Do they kill everyone?" Channah quivered.

"No, only those who resist or who dwell in cities or towns that resist. But being taken into slavery in Assyria is hardly a desirable fate either."

Rivkah pulled her shawl tightly over her head as another chill shot through her body. Her face turned pallid, accentuating the darkness of her eyes. She looked to Dawvid, despairingly.

"But where can we run? Where can we hide from such a horde?"

"To Jerusalem," he retorted with strength in his voice. "Now let us all get some sleep. In a few hours we'll get started again – before sunrise. It's safer to travel by night and rest by day. Less chance of being spotted."

❖   ❖   ❖

For twelve days they traveled under the cover of darkness and hid from the sunlight. Silence was observed at all costs; a fall elicited a pained expression, but no words. At long last they reached the Judean hills and beheld the huge, straw-colored stonewalls of the Holy City.

"I had hoped to take you there," said Dawvid, "to attend a festival service during one of my happy trips to the Temple of the Almighty, but now Jerusalem shall be our home."

The Azuvels passed through the city gates under the watchful eyes of Judean soldiers who scanned every entrant carefully, looking for hidden weapons. The streets were crowded with people. They were in groups, conversing anxiously about the news from the north. They listened to stories of the Assyrians' atrocities. There were hundreds of terrified refugees from the northern Jewish state, wandering despondently and aimlessly through the city, repeating their woeful story to anyone who would listen.

With the massive influx of Hebrews from the north, quarters were not to be found at any price. Many of the refugees were forced to spend their nights sleeping in the street or, if a bit more fortunate, in the shelter of a half-covered alley. But Dawvid, having become well acquainted with a number of Jerusalemites during his many trips to the city, was able to persuade some friends, a family of six, to crowd themselves into a single bedroom, making their attic available to the Azuvels.

In the succeeding days, Dawvid busied himself in an effort to obtain commercial quarters for his spice business. Building owners, flushed with a demand for space that far outstripped the limited supply, were commanding sums that bordered on extortion and were far beyond Dawvid's ability to pay. His face grew longer each day as more and more of their few remaining coins were expended and no means of supporting his family seemed available.

Now living in Jerusalem, he went faithfully to the Temple each morning and sought guidance from the Almighty. A bearded priest approached him one day as the sad-faced Dawvid was murmuring a silent prayer. The priest reminded the glum refugee that the Temple's supply of *azuv* was running low.

Obligations to the Lord had to be carried out. Dawvid, after returning to his attic quarters, searched through their meager possessions, which had been carried away in such haste from their native land.He found a small packet of *azuv*. (Dawvid Azuvel was born in the Kingdom of Israel, one of the two Hebrew nations. Jerusalem was the capital of the Kingdom of Judea, as well as being the site of the Temple of Solomon.)

The following morning he carried the little sack, like a family heirloom, to the Temple. With a slight bow of his head, he handed it to a gray-bearded priest. Then Dawvid entered the court and murmured his silent prayer. His spirits were at low ebb. Despair hung heavily on his brow. When the service was over, he turned to leave.

Yoel ben Zakkai, a grain merchant and brother-in-law of the gray-bearded priest, approached. Dawvid recognized the corpulent, balding man, although he had barely exchanged a dozen words with Yoel in the past. Yoel's face was filled with overabundance, from the full nose to the puffed and reddened cheeks, to the heavy jowls only partially hidden by a graying brown beard. Still, it was not a harsh face. It was not the face of greed, either. Rather, it was a happy face – the visage of a man who enjoyed, not at the expense of others, but with others.

"I hear that you're seeking to relocate in Jerusalem," said the smiling merchant. "If you have a few minutes, I would like to discuss a proposal with you."

Obligingly, the surprised Dawvid followed the seller of grain.

The cheerful Yoel, his protuberant abdomen bouncing with every step, led the puzzled refugee to a storehouse some distance away, close to the west gate of the city. In an animated monologue, he suggested that Dawvid set up his spice business in a corner of the large building. Initially, there would be no rental fee. But if and when Dawvid's business improved, they would share expenses, with each contributing to the upkeep of the building in accordance with the amount of space occupied. With tears in his eyes, Dawvid tendered his profuse thanks.

"Please," insisted Yoel, "say no more. It's a business deal, pure and simple. It should prove beneficial to me, as well as to you. Customers coming to purchase your spices may stay to buy some of my grain and vice versa."

"But everything is in short supply. You could sell twice as much grain as you have here, and without the slightest difficulty."

"Now…" smiled the merchant. "But later…who knows? Shortages have a way of ending themselves with the return of peace and normalcy."

"I wonder, with the Assyrians pushing southward relentlessly, whether we'll ever have peace…or even survive."

"Your point is well taken. Look at it this way. With peace, there would be a return to the production of grain and to competition for its sale. So the presence of your spice business would help draw people to the building, potential customers for my grains. If however, perish the thought, those monsters overrun us, what good would the wealth be that I would obtain by overcharging in time of scarcity? And without Jerusalem, do all the riches in the world amount to anything?"

In the weeks that followed, the atmosphere in the Holy City changed from one of deep anxiety to one of near panic. Shrill, hysterical cries greeted every new report of the southward progress of the Assyrian army. The Temple was filled each day to overflowing, as desperate men pleaded for Divine assistance.

Then slowly, the mood of the city changed. Months went by with no further news of Assyrian movement in the direction of Judea. The monster had engorged himself with blood and booty and his stomach was full. His palaces were overflowing with captive Hebrews, new slaves for the Terror of the North. For the moment, Tiglath-Pileser was satisfied. And for the same moment, Jerusalem and the Kingdom of Judea were to be left in peace.

People returned to "business as usual" with barely a mention of the hundreds of thousands of their co-religionists who had been cruelly massacred or torn from their native land. The now-captive Hebrews, like the dead, would be silently remembered, but it was too upsetting to discuss their fate publicly.

In this regard, Dawvid was no different from the rest. He went about his business and soon was even more successful in Judea than he had been in his native Israel. The storehouse was enlarged to accommodate the expanding spice and grain trades. But on the anniversary of the day they had fled their home in Israel, he would always light a candle of remembrance for that poor man who died in his arms. It also served as a remembrance for the countless thousands of Jews who had been slain in those terrible days.

The state of uneasy tranquility did not last. A few years later, the residents of Jerusalem were again in a state of panic. For a second time in that generation, the city was being flooded with thousands of refugees, newly displaced from their homes. These new arrivals brought news that Sennacherib, successor to the throne of Assyria, was leading a mighty horde towards the Holy City.

One day Dawvid came home with news that the Assyrians had been spotted a day's march away from their city. He called Rivkah and the children together in the family room of their spacious home. The years had raced by in a blur since their flight from Israel under cover of darkness.

Channah was now a married woman and with child. She and her auburn-haired, stocky husband were occupying a room in the house at present time. They both turned pale on hearing Dawvid's report.

Yosef was now an intent young man of twenty, trying to find ways of using spices for the treatment of disease. He listened to his father's words with grave concern.

Naphtali, no longer a playful and untroubled child, looked worried.

Rivkah, now gray-haired and lined with age, was drawn back to the past. She was trying to decide what to take with them in their upcoming hasty departure.

All that work for nothing, she thought. *We build and they destroy.*

Yet Dawvid looked strangely peaceful.

"Listen," he said, "I know the news is bad, but we must remain calm."

"How can you say, 'Be calm,' Father, when the Assyrians are laying waste to much of Judea and are now marching on Jerusalem? Shouldn't we flee as we did before?" asked the perplexed Yosef.

"No," replied Dawvid. "We must have faith. Have you listened to the prophet Isaiah? Did you hear what he said? He said that the Assyrian army shall not enter the city. The Lord will protect Jerusalem."

"With what army?" inquired Yosef in a mocking tone.

"Never question the Almighty or His servants!" was Dawvid's reprimand.

"And what about King Hezekiah? (King of Judea, 2,700 years ago)," Naphtali wondered, aloud. "Is he staying or running?"

"He's staying," answered Dawvid. "And now we will go to the Temple – Yosef, Naphtali and I. We will pray that the words of Isaiah come true."

The Temple was filled that day and every day during the succeeding weeks with crowds too large to be accommodated in the huge building and its surrounding courtyard. The multitude that came to pray spilled out far beyond the Temple gates. They surrounded the House of the Almighty and formed a sea of wailing humanity. On their lips was a single plea: Divine intervention to save their city from a seemingly unstoppable foe.

The army of Judea mounted the walls of Jerusalem. They waited for the onslaught by the dreaded Assyrians. They were grimly determined to resist to the last, despite the realization that they did not possess the strength of arms to defeat so powerful an enemy.

Days and weeks passed. Each day the Jerusalemites gathered near the city gates, waiting for news – any news – good or bad.

They heard of the Assyrians laying waste to cities in the north, the west and the east. And then there was silence. No new refugees arrived, no news from any traveler.

Not a single soul approached the gate from the outside world. There was not even a stray goat to be seen anywhere – only the barren, straw-colored rocks of the Judean hills and wispy clouds floating languidly over the desert. Strange, dark birds, buzzard-like in appearance, circled the city from time to time. They seemed to be studying the faces of the people below. Like the patient, grotesque monsters that they were, they were watching and waiting for their hour to arrive and the feast to begin.

It seemed that all links to the outside world had been severed. For the inhabitants of Jerusalem, nothing seemed to exist anymore but their holy city and the vast, surrounding wasteland. Jerusalem was all that was left of the Holy Land after the devastation wrought by the Assyrians.

Fear gripped the city – but now it was fear of the unknown. People moved around less and less. They went to the Temple and lamented their misfortune; they ate and they drank, nothing more. No one went beyond the city gates. It was the paralysis of a sick man languishing in his chair in a darkened room, murmuring prayers, but without hope in his soul, awaiting inevitable death.

Dawvid, in strange contrast to most of his fellow Jerusalemites, carried on as if nothing had changed. Like the rest, he rose early each morning and went to the Temple. But after offering up prayers, he went to the storehouse to transact business. This, while others were returning to their homes to sit and do nothing. With all activity around him grinding to a halt, Dawvid proceeded to hire craftsmen to design and construct improvements in his place of business.

Many concluded that the spice merchant had lost his senses, but they were too concerned with their own anxieties to pursue the matter.

At long last, something appeared to change the scene. A soldier, standing atop the western wall, was the first to spot it, a speck on the horizon, atop one of the distant hills. It grew steadily larger, moving towards the city and assuming the shape of a man. The lone figure staggered in a zigzag pattern over the last yards separating him from Jerusalem. Panting with exhaustion, he collapsed ten feet from the city gate.

A shout from the guard did not inspirit the poor creature who lay there, chest still heaving out and in, head half-buried in the sand. But the cry did rouse some passers-by inside the city wall. Word spread quickly about the new arrival. Within minutes, hundreds were gathered near the western gate, anxious to find out what was going on.

Dawvid had been supervising the installation of a new ramp to support the heavier loads being transported into and out of his storehouse. The soldier's cry came just as Dawvid was shouting orders to the workmen, and so the spice merchant was unaware of what had happened.

But soon the noisy populace was filling the street up to the door of Dawvid's establishment.

Now, hearing the tumult, the spice merchant told the carpenters to stop what they were doing and await his return. He would be back as soon as he determined the cause of the commotion.

Dawvid made his way through the throng. "What's going on?" he asked when he reached the city gate.

"There's someone lying out there, on the other side of the gate," replied a man in the crowd. "The guard says that he's still breathing."

"Do you see anyone else out there?" probed Dawvid, looking up to the armed man standing atop the wall.

"No," was the reply.

"So why hasn't someone brought him in?" inquired the spice merchant with marked irritation.

"How do we know who he is?" asked a voice in the crowd.

"*Ribono shel olam!*" scolded Dawvid, throwing up his arms. "You hear that someone's out there, someone who needs help, and all the lot of you can do is stand here, doing nothing while the man dies!

"Open the gate and carry him in. When he's better, the Lord willing, you can ask him his identity."

After some hesitation, the soldiers on the wall and the crowd below went along with his demand. The gate was opened for the first time in weeks. A dozen men, impelled forward by Dawvid's scowl, moved out warily. They lifted and then carried in the half-conscious figure. The gate screamed shut with a final heavy thud.

Reaching into a pocket, Dawvid came up with a cloth. He dipped it in a pail of water held by a woman nearby, then moistened the stranger's sand-covered brow and wiped his pale, youthful face clean.

Nonplussed, but not eager to help, the Jerusalemites pitched in. They loosened the gaunt man's collar and dusted off his soiled tunic.

He was a fair-haired, slender young man, hardly more than twenty. His hands were soft, more attuned to writing and turning pages than to performing manual labor. His parched tongue moved over his now moistened lips and his eyes opened weakly, as if in a fog. He squeezed his lids shut and opened them again. The eyes were now clear.

They gave him drink until he would tolerate no more.

"You're in Jerusalem; it's safe now," said Dawvid, reassuringly. "Who are you?"

A hush came over the gathering as they anxiously awaited a response.

In a few minutes, the fair-haired lad regained his power of speech. He began to recount his story, halting frequently to catch his breath.

"I am Malachi ben Natan...a student...of Rabbi Yochanan...ben Raanan.... I am the only survivor...of the destruction of Bethel..."

The throng pushed closer in horror and waited to hear more.

The youth's face darkened as he recounted the events of the recent past.

"I was there when they captured our city...slaughtering everyone they found...even children... I hid...and prayed...that they would not find me... Then they put the city to the torch...to smoke out any hidden survivors... Squealing rats...flushed from their hiding places...attempted to flee... The Assyrians seemed determined that none,...not even rats,...should escape,... so they slashed at the rodents scurrying from the flames... The rats fought back...with claws and teeth,...but in the end...even they were cut down... My hiding place was a small storage shed...with walls of stone,...so the flames did not reach me. In the morning I looked around for signs of life... There were none,...only the charred ruins and baked bones." He halted, sobbing profusely.

Dawvid patted Malachi on the back, sympathetically.

At last the flow of tears ended and the sad-faced young man was able to continue. His respiration had slowed and the words flowed more easily.

"I left the city, creeping silently over a ridge past the leveled city walls. Tripping over a rock, I lost my footing and tumbled into a sandy ditch. To my dismay, I unknowingly had stumbled perilously close to the Assyrian camp...

"It was too bright outside to retreat. I would have been seen, for sure. So I buried myself in the sand, with only my eyes, lips and nostrils exposed to the air... Then I waited, baking in the scorching sun. My tongue was parched; it felt like dried wood. I watched the Assyrians and endured in silence. They were laughing the sickening laughter of butchers complimenting one another for having successfully carved up a carcass. They drank from huge leather pouches, probably filled with wine. They danced in a wild frenzy, bellowing strange, horrible sounds. They whirled in circles, each man employing one leg, like a scythe, to slice through the air while his other leg, in a continuous turn, hopped again and again.

"Suddenly, some of the dancers began to fall. Coughing, choking, they spat up blood and shrieked in terror. Men, turning blue, tore off their armor as they fell to the ground. They gasped and they struggled, reaching for air. They clawed the earth and crawled up the ridge, seeking higher ground. They fell, tumbling like so many sacks of wheat, down the incline. They convulsed and they puked up their guts. At last, their eyes turned glassy and they ceased to struggle.

"The rest of the Assyrians, mesmerized by the strange events, stood powerless to aid their fellows. But soon some of them were caught in the struggle for breath. By now, terrified, their entire army was in retreat. Running, stumbling, their weapons left behind, they attempted to flee some unseen force whose power they could not resist.

"I crept out of my hiding place and shook off some of the sand. Unable to believe my eyes, I followed the fleeing Assyrians. For the moment, all my caution was forgotten. Some of them, looking back, saw me. Yet none would pursue me. All they did was shriek and quicken their pace.

"I followed them into the darkness and continued 'til it was light. Unable to keep up with their maddening dash, I gave up the chase. Exhausted, I looked around me. The landscape was dotted with the bodies of Assyrians as far as the eye could see. Black as ants, they lay there motionless, half-buried in the sand.

"I wondered what all this could mean. There could be but one explanation. It was the power of the Holy One, blessed be His name, that destroyed our enemies."

(Modern scientists have proposed a second possible explanation: Bubonic plague may have wiped out the Assyrian army.)

Exhausted, Malachi ended his tale and sat there, staring at the faces of the Jerusalemites. The throng was silent; they were too dazed to speak.

Suddenly, someone in the rear shouted, "The Assyrians are gone! Praise be to the Almighty. Jerusalem is saved."

The crowd surged through the streets, spreading the news. All of Jerusalem now converged on the Temple to give thanks to the Lord.

In all this, the messenger was forgotten, save for Dawvid kneeling beside the young man. The spice merchant helped Malachi to his feet and escorted the fair-haired lad to the Temple of the Lord. After the service, Dawvid invited Malachi to his home.

By now, everyone in the Azuvel household had heard of the miraculous event. With the new arrival joining them at the family table, they ate heartily and chatted amiably. But even in that moment of seeming joy, Dawvid's heart was sad. He could take no pleasure in the deaths of others, even enemies as heinous as the Assyrians. Besides, it was the anniversary of the day when he and his family had fled their former home in Israel.

Dawvid lit a candle and uttered a prayer for the dead. He remembered the ten lost tribes in the north and prayed that they would someday be united with the rest of the Hebrew people.

(The Hebrew people were divided into twelve land-owning tribes plus the Levites who were the caretakers of the Temple. After the death of King Solomon, the Hebrew nation was split by dissension. The two tribes in the south, Judah and Benjamin, remained loyal to the descendants of King Solomon, who ruled in Judea. The ten northern tribes selected another man to rule over them in a state that was called the Kingdom of Israel. The Assyrians conquered the Kingdom of Israel and took the surviving Hebrews as slaves back to Nineveh and the other Assyrian cities. Hence, the Jews of Israel in the north were later referred to as the "ten lost tribes." Assyrian tablets indicate that these Jews were sent, in tribal groupings, to the distant reaches of the kingdom. Some scholars have concluded that these tribes later moved on to areas beyond the Assyrian kingdom and became the ancestors of Jews in the Caucasian area of Russia, Kazakhstan and the other Muslim areas of the Soviet Union, as well as in Afghanistan, India and China. It is believed that these Jews founded the city of Samaria as capital of a Jewish kingdom that existed for two centuries. They had named it after Samaria, which had been the capital of Israel. The name of that city was later changed to Samarkand, which is now the capital of the Uzbek state. The Manas people of eastern India are believed to be the descendants of the tribe of Menassah, and the Bnai Israel people of Bombay, the descendants of another tribe. There is evidence to suggest that the Panthan people of Afghanistan and Pakistan are also descendants of one of the tribes. It is further believed that founding members of the Jewish community of Kaifeng, China, came from the "ten lost tribes.")

THE INSCRIPTION

History had always been my best subject. Name any area in history and I could find something to say about it. When I was interviewed for possible admission by the Dean of Harvard Medical School he said, "I note that you were a history major. Is there any area of history that is of particular interest to you?"

"Yes."

"What might that be?"

"The history of the Jewish people."

I then proceeded to go through the history of the Jewish people over the past three millennia, in almost monologue fashion, employing my family history as an example of the Jewish experience. I came from a family who would not deny our faith, even when threatened with death. We had traversed the four corners of the world, not as adventurers seeking a new experience, but as a means for survival.

Bear in mind, there had been an unofficial quota on Jewish students at Harvard Medical School until the end of World War II. They were no longer asking the applicant's religious affiliation in 1949, and so it would be possible for an applicant to conceal his or her religious status. But I would have none of that. In this, the greatest nation on earth, I had to be accepted for whom I was.

Years later, I employed that same knowledge of history to tell of how my ancestors made their way from place to place.

"Out of Jerusalem shall go forth a remnant," said the Lord (*Isaiah* 27:32). So it came to pass two centuries after the fall of Israel to Assyria that a new and powerful enemy arose to demolish the remaining Hebrew state of Judea. Jerusalem fell to the Babylonians led by Nebuchadnezzar. The city and the holy Temple were razed to the ground and the children of Israel were sent into exile to raise their voices in heartfelt lamentation and pour bitter tears into distant pools of water. Thus began a separation of the Followers of

Moses from their Promised Land, which was to last seventy years for most of the Hebrew people. For the Azuvels, it was to be much longer.

The ancient world, like a huge caldron, was in constant turmoil. It seethed and boiled over as arid plains and life-giving waters were fought over by peoples who spoke a hundred different tongues. Might smothered right, victory went to the fiercest, and mothers wailed for the loss of their children. No sooner did an empire rise to devour its less martial neighbors than it grew fat and lazy, ending as prey to the primitive and wild. Empire succeeded empire, king replaced king, and waters ran red with the mingled blood of victor and vanquished. There were Babylonians and Chaldeans, Kassites and Hittites, Persians and Midians. Nebuchadnezzar and Belshazzar (successor of Nebuchadnezzar, king of the Chaldeans and ruler of Babylon) were replaced by Darius (King of Media) and Cyrus (King of Persia and son-in-law of Darius). Cyrus, in his day, became the mightiest of them all.

The ways of the Lord are mysterious. Why else should the ruler of a mighty empire that lived by the sword have shown such compassion for a small, defenseless people who lived by the Book? So did Cyrus permit the Hebrew people to return to Palestine and rebuild their Temple in Jerusalem.

Not all the Hebrews retraced the steps of their forebears to reenter the Promised Land in the days of Cyrus. While a large number followed the high priest Ezra back to Eretz Yisrael (the Land of Israel, the Biblical homeland), many remained in the land between the waters of the Tigres and the Euphrates.

In this land of exile, they were a small minority without a central Temple and a high priest overseer. The Hebrew people could no longer be content to be observers of ceremonies conducted by Cohanim and Levites in a single, central Temple. If the faith were to survive, it would be because every Follower of Moses carried his beliefs and his understanding within him. Knowledge was the key, knowledge of God's Word and the meaning of that Word. Thus did the exiled Hebrews maintain a great center of religious learning, a mighty tree of scholarship that later gave flower to the Babylonian Talmud. This island of piety and learning, surrounded by a hostile world of passion and violence, was in constant danger as new armies blackened the earth of ancient civilizations, and kingdoms fell before conquering swarms of warlike men.

Like lofty birds buffeted by air currents and storms beyond their control, the exiles sought to continue their celestial path above the darkness and cruelty of the world below. Here and there, a sparrow, fleeing the swirling eye of the tornado, was blown astray by the driving winds of turmoil and confusion. It sought shelter in a distant tree. The storm abated and the bird looked around at the alien land. Its compass lost in the gale, it had no way of getting home. And so the bird built a nest and sought others of its kind in the strangeness of the new surroundings.

So it was that in 331 BCE, the army of Alexander the Great conquered Babylon and continued on to India. Alexander, a Macedonian by birth, was carrying Greek culture to distant lands, to regions with traditions of their own. Ruling a vast empire with but a small Greek minority in an ocean of humanity, Alexander exhibited wisdom in showing great tolerance towards religious and cultural traditions other than his own. To the Jews of the Near East, he was viewed as a model ruler. It even became a tradition to name a second son in a Jewish family after Alexander.

Eight short years after the conquest of Babylon, Alexander returned to that land to die. The empire he welded together was dismembered by his hungry generals, with each seizing as much land as he could. Seleucus I was to rule in Mesopotamia. The new king sought to secure his power by bringing in immigrants from Greece and Macedonia, subjects who would be loyal to their Greco-Macedonian ruler. But regardless of how many Greeks and Macedonians arrived in the Seleucid Empire, they were still a small minority. Seleucid and his successors sought to Hellenize the kingdom, but to maintain their rule they would have had to avert revolts by the indigenous populations. One method employed to achieve this goal was population dispersal – the mixing of multiple ethnic groups in each region so that they would be less likely to band together to overthrow their Greek rulers. In line with this policy, Antiochus I transferred a considerable Semitic population to his newly founded city of Seleucia in 275 BCE. Beginning in 210 BCE, Antiochus III and Antiochus IV sent additional Jewish families to settle in Asia Minor.

Historian Dr. Abraham Galante had told Nathan Ausubel of his findings about the Azuvels in Asia Minor. In the twentieth century, archeologists uncovered the city of Sardis, which had served as the capital of the Lydian Empire more than two millennia ago. During the excavation they had come across evidence that a spice merchant with the name Azuvel was one of the many Hebrews transplanted to that city.

And so the Azuvels came to Asia Minor and made their homes in the city of Sardis (which had been known as Sfarda in Lydian and Persian). The term "Sephardic" probably came from the Jewish community of Sardis. They joined other Hebrews who had come there generations earlier. Sfarda had been the capital of ancient Lydia. At one time the Lydian kings had ruled a vast empire stretching from the Aegean to what is now Iran. Like cities throughout the ancient world, Sfarda knew many rulers. The Persians conquered the Lydians and, in turn, they became subjects of Alexander the

Great and his Seleucid successors. Generations later they became subjects of the Roman Empire.

On a midsummer's day in the third century CE, Alessander ben Avraham Azuvel sat at a table in the rear of his spice shop. His shoulders hunched forward as he studied the batch of hyssop resting on the table. A dark crinkly beard peppered with gray accentuated his elongated face. His dark eyes, half-hidden by sack-like lower lids, peered at the spice as the nostrils of his thin nose widened to take in the menthaceous smell.

Alessander looked up to see a bald-headed man dressed in a Roman toga enter his shop. The strong chin of the clean-shaven visitor jutted forward as if to announce that this was a man of position.

"Good day to you, Marcus Flavius," said Alessander. "Is there something I can do for you?"

"Good morning to you, Alessander." He paused and then added, "Alessander is all right, but why don't you take a Roman or at least a Greek family name instead of Azuvel?"

"Because, Your Excellency, we had that family name before the arrival of the Greeks and Romans."

"Well, have it as you like it," said Marcus Flavius with a wave of his hand. He turned and proceeded to navigate the circumference of the shop. He stopped at intervals to sniff the pots of spices.

"Are there any that meet with your favor?" inquired Alessander.

"Yes." Pointing in succession to a series of pots, he continued, "This one and this one and this one. Enough to last my household for a week. My wife will come by in a few days to select the rest."

"Perhaps she could stop in today or tomorrow morning," urged Alessander.

"No," thought Marcus Flavius aloud as he shook his head from side to side. "She has other things to attend to."

"But my shop will close tomorrow afternoon."

"I know it's your Sabbath. She can't come on the day after that. We have guests. There are too many things to attend to at home. But the day after that: That should do fine."

"But we'll be closed that day."

"What, another of your Jewish holidays? What is it this time? It wasn't too long ago that you were celebrating your Passover."

"Sunday evening begins the Festival of Shavuot. And you are right: it comes on the fiftieth day after the first day of the Passover which we call the Festival of Pesach."

"So what's the meaning of the name Shavuot?"

"Chag Shavuot means the Feast of Weeks. We count seven weeks plus one day after the first day of the Festival of Pesach."

"And what's its purpose? What are you celebrating? I know that your Passover celebrates the exit from slavery in Egypt. But what's this one for?"

"That's an interesting question. It commemorates the giving of the Torah at Mount Sinai…when we were traveling in the wilderness."

"It seems to me, as I recall from last year, that you Jews bring stuff to your synagogue on that occasion."

"Yes, we do. We are instructed to bring an offering of new grain to the Lord. And so two loaves of bread made from the finest wheat produced in Eretz Yisrael were brought to the Temple in Jerusalem, along with the first ripe fruits of the season."

"Any special connection between the Torah and the bread and fruit?"

"Rabbi Eliezer – he's a great Biblical scholar – recently said that it is necessary to rejoice with good food and wine because that was the day on which we were given the Torah."

"I knew there was something Roman in you Jews," smiled Marcus Flavius. "We always enjoy good food and wine. Why, we have a whole collection of gods whom we celebrate with feasts. It looks like every emperor becomes a god after his demise. If this keeps up, there'll be no work days."

"Well," said Alessander with a bow of his head, "our festivals are fixed. Three Biblical festivals plus the Festival of Chanukah – that one is post-Biblical."

"Well," the Roman smiled again, "you see, you can add a festival or two to your calendar."

"But we are no longer in our homeland," sighed Alessander.

"Yes," nodded Marcus Flavius. "It was that dreadful revolt, the second one, in fact. You people must realize that it is Rome that enables you to live in peace here in Sardis and around the world. And Rome cannot tolerate revolts."

"We are aware of that," nodded Alessander sadly.

"You may not know it, but I've read the Josephus account of *The Jewish War*. He was taken prisoner by Vespasian – the Roman general in command – who later became emperor of Rome. Vespasian had Josephus brought back to Rome to be executed there. Josephus told the Roman commander that there was greatness in store for the Roman commander. The Roman commander then spared his life in order for him to write a history of that war.

"It's quite interesting, written in Greek, you know. You people were quite something. But your people did not learn a lesson after that revolt was crushed and your temple was destroyed. You had to revolt again. It was Bar Kokhba, I believe, who led that final revolt in Judea. It took twenty legions to subdue the revolt, *twenty* legions. Rome had to draw away legions from all over the Empire to do so. That left whole regions unprotected. Well, we can't have that sort of thing: a disturbance of the Roman peace."

"I know that all too well," nodded Alessander again, sadly.

"Yes. Well, that's the reason your people were brought back to Rome as slaves, to serve as a lesson. Those who disturb the Roman peace will pay the penalty: a loss of Roman freedom. And look at Palestine now: virtually devoid of Jews, new Roman cities and a whole new people dwelling in the land. And a Roman peace."

"Yes," replied Alessander with his head bent forward, "a Roman peace."

"Well don't look so sad. Look, there are thousands of Jews here in Sardis. You people work, you tend to your shops and you live in peace – a Roman peace. And you thrive. That's the benefit of Rome. We punish a few unruly children as a lesson and the peace is maintained for the many."

"Yes," nodded Alessander, avoiding the Roman's eyes.

"Well, so much for that...By the way, look what's happening here in Sardis as an example of the benefits of Roman peace. A completely new center of the city is going up: a gymnasium, a civic center with gigantic marble-columned buildings rising to the sky."

"And how will all this construction be paid for?" inquired Alessander.

"By taxes, of course. Those who will benefit most from its construction must pay for what is done. The people of Sardis enjoy the benefits; the people of Sardis pay."

"And the glory of Rome is enhanced?" added Alessander.

"Well, of course," agreed Marcus Flavius. "We plan inscriptions on many of the great buildings. For example, there should be one commemorating the visit of Emperor Lucius Verus. You may not know it, but he actually came to Sardis; it was before either of us was born."

"Inscriptions," mused Alessander. "It is interesting how much value men place in having their names inscribed on a slab of marble."

"How else is one to be remembered? A man whose name has been inscribed in a hundred places must be a great man. An emperor whose bust has been placed in a hundred places must be a god."

Marcus Flavius paused and then said, "Well, back to the spices for my wife. I suppose my wife can send a housemaid with a list tomorrow morning. Arrange for the delivery before you close tomorrow afternoon."

"Thank you and good day to you, sir," replied Alessander, with a half bow as Marcus Flavius turned and exited the shop.

The shadows of early evening dimmed the light in the spice shop. Alessander lit a candle and went on with his work.

Sounds from the front of the shop drew his attention. Alessander rose to greet the new arrivals. Jochanan and David Aurelius, Jacob Sabbatios and

Samuel Theoktistos, all dressed in white Roman togas, approached. In contrast to the bearded Alessander, these men were all clean-shaven. Alessander held out a greeting hand to receive them.

"*Shalom*," said Alessander.

"*Shalom*," replied the new arrivals.

"And to what do I owe this visit by so many distinguished members of our community?" inquired Alessander. "Is it spices you are seeking? But I sense from the fact that you have all come at the same time, that it is not."

"You sense correctly," retorted Jochanan. His thin lips parted momentarily with a smile. Light coming in through the doorway reflected from his bald head as his brown eyes glanced past a few pots of spices and up at Alessander. "Not that you do not have the finest of spices. I have come here on so many occasions that my respect for the quality of your materials should not be in question. But we are here on other business."

Jochanan paused, his strong jaw firming ever so slightly.

"Yes?" pursued Alessander.

"It's about a synagogue," interjected David. With these words, his eyes brightened and his face rounded with a hint of excitement. He smoothed back his dark brown full head of hair and he turned to Jochanan.

"What about a synagogue?" inquired Alessander. We have one already."

"But it is too small for the size of our community," insisted Jochanan. "We have some 2,000 Jews in a city of, perhaps, 100,000 inhabitants. The synagogue can accommodate no more than a hundred or so at most."

"But there's no room for an expansion," observed Alessander.

"Precisely," interjected Jacob, his brown head of curly hair nodding in agreement. His clear blue eyes darted to Samuel as if waiting for some word.

"So where do we build a larger one and how do we get permission from the authorities?" questioned Alessander.

"I have the very place in mind," smiled Samuel. His wavy gray head of hair flew upward for a moment as his chin asserted itself in a forward direction. His hunched back strained to straighten itself and he pointed his walking stick towards the rear of the shop. "Here in the center of the city, next to the gymnasium."

"But all the space has been allotted. They're building a huge civil basilica on the main avenue, just behind our shops. Then the gymnasium complex will be complete. I know of no other available land."

"So what about the civil basilica?" Samuel smiled again, accentuating the wrinkles below his narrow eyes. His shoulders hunched forward again as he rested his weight on his walking stick.

"What about it?" questioned Alessander. "Are we to place a *Sefer Torah* in a non-religious building with people parading through while we are conducting a service?"

"No," replied Samuel with a twinkle in his eye. "We must ask permission of the authorities to convert the structure into a synagogue."

"And why, pray tell, should they agree to that?" questioned Alessander.

"Look at us," said Jochanan as his chin jutted forward again and his hand held proudly to the front edge of his toga. "We are all upright members of the Sardis community. True, our people make up but a small proportion of the total population, but we make up a significant portion of the business community. Look at all the shops here in the city: See how many of them are owned by Jews. We are loyal citizens of Rome and pay substantial sums into the Empire's coffers. And with a smile and some donations in the right places, we can relieve the city of the expense of completing the construction of the building. The building of the gymnasium complex – the grandiose plan for the center of the city – shall have been completed and the Roman citizens of Sardis shall have been spared from the taxes that would have been imposed to complete the project."

"Spared the expense?" puzzled Alessander. "You mean for the civil basilica turned synagogue?"

"Yes," nodded David.

"I doubt that it would suffice to persuade the governor to give up the basilica," replied Alessander.

"And some gold coins placed quietly in the right palms. Why not?" said David.

"Because if anything goes wrong, the Jews will be accused of attempting to bribe Roman officials. Then the entire community will be in danger."

"So what's the alternative?" questioned Jochanan. "No new synagogue?"

The faces of the four visitors appeared troubled.

Alessander's right hand slid down his beard as he contemplated the situation. At last his eyes brightened. "I have a solution."

"Yes?" said the four visitors anxiously.

"We will make a donation."

"But you just said –" David's voice trailed off into silence.

"We'll make an outright donation," said Alessander.

"A public gift to individuals? And they would accept the money under such conditions?" wondered Samuel aloud, his rounded shoulders arched forward as if to conceal themselves beneath the front of his toga.

The four visitors stared back in amazement. At last, David broke the silence. "Do you know the kind of money you're speaking about – the cost of the synagogue plus the cost of the rest of the complex?"

"You're talking about a sum far greater than we had in mind," noted Samuel.

"Look," replied Alessander. "I realize that the sum will be large, but not as large as what you are thinking. I do not propose that the Jewish community pay the entire cost for the construction of the gymnasium; only that we make a substantial contribution towards the cost of its construction. Then everything will be open and above board. And think of the additional benefits of that donation: the respect our community will receive for funding much of the project."

"Respect?" puzzled David. "Not envy?"

"There is that possibility, of course. But that will be balanced against saving the non-Jewish populace from some of the taxes that would otherwise be levied to pay for all the marble construction. When they learn that they're being relieved of a substantial portion of the tax burden, they will not care much about the fact that we'll also be building a synagogue."

"And how do we raise all that money?" inquired Samuel as he hunched one shoulder up in puzzlement.

"We'll dig deep into our pockets. And we'll give honors to contributors of large sums."

"Honors?" wondered Jacob aloud.

"Honors. Inscriptions on the wall. People will oftimes dig down deep to have their names recalled by the future generations who enter the building."

"And you?" smiled Samuel.

"I'll dig down deep," replied Alessander, "but not for an inscription. The Eternal does not need an inscription to know of my contribution."

"Then no inscription for you?" inquired David. "But why not?"

"Because of the history of this city."

"The history of this city?" puzzled Jacob.

"Yes, the history of this city. I speak of a time long before the arrival of the Romans. I speak of when Sfarda was the capital of a vast and wealthy empire. Did you know that there was so much gold here in this city that the minting of coins began here?"

"I was not aware of that," nodded Jacob.

"Nor I," added each of the other visitors to Alessander's shop.

"I speak of the time of the Mermnad Empire, before the Persians conquered the region. And the final and richest of the Mermnad rulers was Croesus."

"I've heard of him," interrupted David. "But what has he to do with a synagogue? I was not aware of a Jewish community here before the arrival of the Persians."

"Well, Croesus was very wealthy. In fact the expression 'rich as Croesus' refers to him. The story goes that an Athenian philosopher named Solon once came to the court of Croesus. And Croesus gave the distinguished visitor a grand tour of the palace. He feasted with the Athenian and had him observe the grand entertainment, which the king afforded as a routine. Then he asked Solon whom he considered the happiest of men. The king fully expected the philosopher to reply 'Croesus.' Instead, Solon mentioned the name of an

Athenian named Tellus. Now Croesus had never heard of this Tellus and so he inquired as to whether Tellus had as much money as Croesus, or could afford the food and entertainment to which Croesus was accustomed, or whether he ruled some mighty kingdom. And the Athenian philosopher replied that Tellus had had only a long and happy life, but a good death as well.

"Croesus must have viewed his Athenian visitor as a sort of crank. But years later, the empire of Croesus fell before the might of Cyrus, king of Persia. Cyrus ordered that Croesus be burned on a pyre. Cyrus was there when the flame was lit. Croesus then cried out Solon's warning – that no man could be said to have lived a happy life until he met a good death."

"And so Croesus met his end by fire?" asked David, with dismay.

"No. Not by fire. For Cyrus must have been deeply affected by the words of Croesus. He must have considered his own mortality. And so he ordered that the pyre be extinguished. Croesus was saved."

They all stood silent for a while. In the end, Jochanan broke the silence: "So what's the point? A good death is the key to a happy life? But what has this to do with our synagogue."

"Nothing and yet something. For we as Jews are taught something more about death. Do you recall the words of Rabbi Akiva when the Romans were torturing him to death? (Rabbi Akiva, 50-135 CE, was one of the most outstanding teachers in Jewish history.) He continued to teach Torah in defiance of a Roman edict. In consequence of this, he was arrested and tortured to death by the Romans who employed iron combs to tear the flesh from his body. He welcomed his martyrdom as a unique opportunity of fulfilling the precept 'Thou shalt love the Lord thy God with all thy heart and with all thy soul...even if you must pay for it with your life.' He said that he was happy that he had been put to the test and that he had proven his loyalty to the Almighty. To Croesus, before that pyre, a happy life had meant wealth and self-indulgence. To a Jew, a happy death does not require that the individual suffer torture, nor does it require that he have great wealth. We should have learned from Croesus that wealth is fleeting. To a Jew, to have lived a happy life should mean that he had led a *meaningful* life. The building of a synagogue would add meaning to all our lives, worth more than the wealth of Croesus. And so we have our lesson: Our wealth as mortals will turn to dust; but a synagogue in which future generations may lift their voices in prayer will be a more fitting monument to a happy life. For the many, an inscription will encourage a larger donation, and so it serves a purpose. As for me, there will be no inscription to serve for self-glorification."

The synagogue of Sardis, when completed, measured 60 by 390 feet. It was the largest in the ancient world. It was big enough to accommodate more than a thousand people at a single service. There was an entrance colonnade at the eastern end with three entry gates. The building had a magnificent mosaic floor and its walls were richly adorned with frescos and mosaics. At the western end, a mosaic depicting the water of life and two peacocks adorned the apse. A marble table was situated before the apse. A pair of lions of Judah flanked it. A marble tablet fronted the table with carved eagles bordering Greek inscriptions. The names of eighty donors were written on the central tablet in Greek.

While evidence was uncovered indicating that an Azuvel had made a major contribution to the building of the great synagogue, nowhere is the name Alessander ben Avraham Azuvel to be found on the building itself.

AN APOTHECARY IN EPHESUS

In the second century BCE, Sardis was a city whose gigantic, marble-columned buildings stood like mighty swords daring the heavens to shake them. It was to learn, like Osymandias, that stones are but congealed sand in the desert that crumble in the heat of the sun. It was to learn that man is but clay in the hands of the potter, molded and crushed and molded again. Only the idea and the word survive. So, too, did Sardis fall before the bubbling anger of earthquakes and the bloodstained weapons of invading hordes.

The Azuvels took wing, fleeing the destruction and the pestilence; they found sanctuary again in a new tree. Ephesus was a mighty oak, the grandest of the Ionian cities of its time. (There were twelve cities of the Ionian league, which was located on the Aegean coast of Asia Minor. These cities were mutually independent, but formed a confederacy for common purposes. Greek colonists who came to Asia Minor and married Anatolian women founded them. Thus the population was part Greek and part Anatolian in ancestry.) Its main street, the Marble Way (given that name because it was completely paved with marble), was dedicated to the splendor and power of its inhabitants. Like a radiant magnet, the city attracted the rich and the mighty, but it also attracted the craftsmen and men of commerce who require peace and stability for their work. Some 40,000 Jews had made their way to Ephesus and formed one-fifth of its free population. All week long the Followers of Moses busied themselves in their shops and offices. On the Sabbath they rested from their labors to pray in the synagogues of the city.

The city stood like a peaceful oasis amid the surrounding turmoil, yet the Jews of this metropolis were far from happy. Israel, their ancient homeland, was under foreign rule. The Hebrew nation, reborn under the Maccabees (a priestly family who led the revolt against the Greek King Antiochus IV), had been destroyed by the Romans. The Jews of Ephesus, like Jews in a hundred places in the Diaspora (Jews living outside of the homeland), had sent aid to their brethren in Eretz Yisrael during the revolts against the Romans in the first and second centuries. Heavy were the hearts of the exiles in Ephesus when they learned of the monstrous slaughter that had taken place in Palestine when the legions of Rome crushed the heroic resistance of the Jews.

Bar Kokhba, leader of the Final Revolt in Judea (132-136 CE), was dead and the survivors of the carnage had been carried off to Rome. Slavery was the Roman response to the yearning of a people to be free. A similar fate had befallen the great Jewish center in Alexandria. Pagan Rome simply could not understand or accept a people who would not bow before idols.

In exile, the descendants of the Israelite slaves in ancient Egypt, who had become warrior tribes that conquered Canaan, had been slowly transformed into birds that soared with the spirit of the Lord's ways. They lived in the land, but were not part of it. Having shed their claws of war, they had become birds of peace, whose plumage was study and the refinement of the mind, the analysis of Torah and the meaning of its message. They had abandoned the blade and the armor of those around them.

They pondered over the Commandments of the Almighty; they wept and they prayed to the Lord in their synagogues and in the quiet of their homes. To the outside world they were shopkeepers and craftsmen and men of commerce, busy making money and gathering wealth.

Early in the sixth century, more than a thousand years after the Babylonian exile of the Hebrews of Judea, Naphtali ben Avraham Azubel was getting ready for a Passover Seder, a home service held on the first and second nights of Passover. During the Seder, the story of the Exodus from Egypt is retold. (The "b" and "v" sounds are pronunciations of the same Hebrew letter. In transliteration into the Greek alphabet, Azuvel became Azubel.)

Traditionally, this was to be a night of rejoicing, a night when Jewish families gathered around a table to celebrate the miracle of freedom. Yet, Naphtali's face betrayed uneasiness. He shrugged it off with an "Oh well, maybe it will turn out all right," muttered under his breath. Then he went about his duties. Naphtali had closed his apothecary shop early to attend to the holiday preparations. He scanned the table carefully – the glistening brass candelabra with its burning-bright candles, ruby red wine in its opaque container, the sparkling central dish on which rested the food symbols of the holiday, the bowl of seemingly-clear water, and the beautifully-embroidered, square-shaped case with the word "*Matzoth*" (unleavened bread eaten on the Passover to recall the bread baked in haste for the hurried departure from Egypt) woven in its center, encircled by seven place settings; all resting atop a clean white Sabbath cloth. Aloud, he said, "Everyone to the table. Let us begin."

His wife, Sarah, and their four children joined Naphtali. Naphtali, a son to either side of him, stood at the head of the table. At the opposite end, Sarah waited for the festival service to begin. A dark shawl with an embroidered border covered her head. She was dressed in her holiday finery, consisting of a floor-length brown dress and matching jacket covering a white blouse embroidered at the neck. The edge of the jacket was scalloped and braided. A bronze chain, which encircled her waist, was partially hidden by the jacket. Two large shield-like bronze discs were linked at the front of the chain on either side of the midline. Her almond-shaped eyes shifted towards the fidgety girl standing to her right. Sarah half smiled as she observed Rachel shifting from one leg to the other.

Rachel, a plump girl of ten, had a pinkish, round face and happy eyes. Her outfit was a smaller version of the one her mother wore, except that the daughter wore no shawl. Flowers of many colors crowned her soft brown hair. Rachel's lips opened and closed repeatedly, while her hands moved impatiently from waist to back of chair to waist again. The conflict between obedience to her father and her hunger for food was heightened by the scents of roast poultry and meat that wafted in from the kitchen and filled the air.

Opposite Rachel was her sister Rivkah – slender, dark and intense. Her long, braided hair, containing but a single yellow flower, extended down the middle of her back. Her disdain for Rachel's continuous movement was obvious. Rivkah's clothing was clean and bright and simple; hardly dramatic, though not inappropriate for a holiday meal. Her blouse, hinting at the first blush of womanhood beneath it, was pure and white. It hung loosely over a long, dark linen skirt. Rivkah was thirteen – an age when girls became aware of the strange and marvelous changes taking place within their bodies. There was a feeling that grew inside her, of being transformed from an awkward caterpillar into a soaring winged butterfly. And so her chin inclined itself upward and her eyes looked away from the restless impatience of childhood represented by her younger sister.

Eliezer, the eldest of the children, stood between Rivkah and his father. Eliezer's face was long and serious, with elongated, twisting sidecurls. The first intertwining hairs of a straggly beard exaggerated the solemnity of his dark, thoughtful eyes. Yet, there was something more in those eyes, a sort of whimsical sneer behind the pensive look…there was a yearning to ruffle feathers hidden behind his austere facade. Half his face was hidden in shadow, the half farthest from the candelabra. His visage was capped by a wrinkled, cone-shaped *kippah* (skullcap worn for religious purposes) that covered the undulating waves of brown hair. The bodylines continued past a sunken cheek beside his full nose, down to the dark gray of his clothing. Slim shoulders and a drawn body made him appear taller than his medium height. He was austere and tense, like a cello string waiting to resonate at the first touch, yet an elfin smile crossed his face fleetingly as his eyes darted across the table to Shlomo, the youngest of the siblings.

As Eliezer was pensive, so Shlomo was the model of good cheer. Brown hair flopped exuberantly in all directions from beneath a cylindroid skullcap, tilted so precariously that it seemed ready to fall from its perch. Full brows and long lashes highlighted his bright, dancing eyes; his red cheeks exuded holiday delight and his rounded lips glistened in the candlelight. His small, soft body was dwarfed by the height of the chair and so he pulled himself up to his tiptoes, grasping the back of his chair, to catch his father's eye.

Naphtali dusted off his knee-length white tunic and the floor-length black and white striped woolen robe beneath it. He adjusted his skullcap with his hand. His fingers then slid down the luxuriant, curly hair on his crown, into the long, flowing beard that reached the center of his chest. He winced for a moment. He shook his head and bit his lower lip. *Mustn't do that. This is a Festival,* he thought. He regained his composure quickly, hoping his look had not been observed. His searching, narrow eyes, half hidden between bushy brows and puffed lower lids, now did a last minute recheck of everything on the table. A longish, straight nose scented the air. He was satisfied. His full lips parted now in a forced smile. But the grin quickly vanished. "Where is the basin?" he inquired with concern.

"Over there," said Sarah reassuringly, as she pointed to a vessel resting on a small copper-colored wood cabinet at the side of the room. "Use the cloth next to it to dry your hands."

Naphtali filled the cups, positioned at each setting, with wine. There were seven place settings, one for each member of the family plus one for the stranger. "Let all who are hungry come in and eat," said Naphtali in a loud voice as he filled the seventh cup. "Eliezer, unlock the door."

"To let the Prophet Elijah in?" asked Shlomo glowingly.

"And all who will share our Seder meal."

Naphtali chanted the *Kiddush* and then sipped some wine. Following this, he left the table. He immersed his hands in the basin at the side of the room, dried them, and then returned to his place at the head of the table. Naphtali nodded and they all took it as a signal to sit down.

Shlomo gave a sigh of relief. He would no longer have to stand on his toes to keep abreast of the events. The child now flopped onto his pillowed chair with a thud. Naphtali smiled kindly at the boy.

"You looked troubled before," said Sarah to her husband across the length of the table. "Is there something wrong with my preparations?"

"What?" replied Naphtali, appearing distracted. "No! Of course not. Come. Let's go on with the Seder. The parsley, please."

They each took a piece, dipped it into a bowl of water and ate without comment, except for Shlomo who made a comment about the water being too salty.

Naphtali slipped a hand into the embroidered *Matzoth* case and removed the greater part of one of the slabs of unleavened bread. "Shlomo," he said, turning toward the little boy, "Will you ask the questions?"

The lad beamed as he rose. The flush on his face appeared all the more pronounced against the fluffy white robe that covered his body. "I'm ready," he said eagerly.

"So begin," responded his father.

Shlomo recited the four questions, following which Naphtali read from the *Haggadah,* giving the traditional response. (The *Haggadah*, read on the eve of Passover, is the book recounting the story of the Exodus from Egypt.) Eliezer, his head bobbing up and down with the words, joined in the reading. They retold the history of the suffering of the Hebrews in bondage in Egypt and the story of the Exodus from the land of the pharaohs under the leadership of Moses, 2,000 years before them. Although the events had taken place in ancient times, each Jew, through the generations, is told to retell the story as if he were present during those events and was among the Hebrews delivered from bondage.

Although the children were all thoroughly familiar with the story, they listened attentively to the answers, as if hearing them for the first time. When the retelling of the epic events was completed, Sarah rose to bring in the food. Rivkah eagerly assisted her mother in that task. Mother and daughter returned, carrying dishes of fish. Portion after portion, course after course was consumed and washed down with deep-red wine. Rachel savored every dish and devoured large chunks of food with gusto. Finally she stopped to loosen her dress, exposing the white blouse beneath. She uttered a sigh of relief.

"You oughtn't to eat so fast," commented Rivkah reprovingly. "You do the same thing every Passover. Why don't you save some of your appetite for the rest of the year?"

"You finished your food just as fast as I did, Rivkah, but I guess there's more room in there," responded the little girl acidly, staring at her sister's waist.

"Why you –" began Rivkah.

Naphtali, anticipating a verbal duel between the girls, or even worse, interrupted. "Now children, it's Passover. We may eat too much of the wonderful food that your mother prepared for the festival meal, but, in a way, that too is part of the Seder."

"Why so?" asked Eliezer.

Naphtali looked at the questioning eyes of his son and smiled. "Because, Eliezer, a slave usually goes to bed hungry, but a free man is privileged even to overeat."

"And then they have to come to you for something to settle their stomachs," retorted Eliezer in a matter-of-fact fashion that failed to conceal the barb in his comment.

The father's face blanched for a moment. After a while, it regained color. He turned to his son and looked him straight in the eye. His voice was firm, but there was no harshness in it. "Now, Eliezer, don't make fun of the apothecary. He is a member of an honorable profession. Your ancestors have been apothecaries for generations. There is an art to the mixing of herbs and spices to heal men's ills. As for the Seder: I do not think of enjoying a Passover feast as a source of business."

"I'm sorry, Father. I didn't mean to offend you. I guess I was just trying to be funny... Forgive me, but I have always wondered how much good those powders and leeches really do."

Naphtali winced as if again perceiving a sting. He adjusted his position on the chair, hunching his shoulders forward, then arching them back like a soldier gearing up for serious matters. His eyes narrowed as if studying something beyond what others could see. At last, he relaxed and smiled softly. His lips parted expectantly as if awaiting the proper moment, the moment in which he would reveal all.

"Well, Father," said Eliezer impatiently, "you look like you're going to say something... What is it?"

"You ask whether what we do is of value. Since this is a night for questions, that question too, deserves an answer. Eliezer, I believe we do some good. The good comes in two forms – the science and the art. When a man is suffering with the torturous pain of a rotting limb, the powder I extract from the opium poppy will often relieve the pain. That is the science of our work. But there is also the art, the art of giving someone hope and confidence. I have seen pain, real pain, relieved by nothing more than a salt or sweet packaged into a tablet. It works, provided that the receiver is convinced that the tablet will relieve his pain."

Eliezer's eyes opened wide. Disappointment, tinged with a blush of embarrassment, was clearly visible in his face.

"Father," he inquired scoldingly, "isn't that dishonest – giving someone a false potion to relieve his pain? How does the apothecary differ from the conjurer when he engages in pretense?"

"Eliezer," chided his mother, "show some respect! You're speaking to your father."

"It's all right, Sarah. The question is a good one: It shows perception. I do not take offense at his asking it." He turned his head towards Eliezer and continued. "To begin with, I cited the example of the salt or the sweet, not to indicate that this is the correct medicine for real pain. Rather, I wished to point out that we must take into account, when we assess the value of any potion, the reaction of the patient's mind to the potion. A person may sometimes feel better if he is convinced that the medicine will help him. But this is not always the case. To determine whether the preparation does any good on its own, we should compare its effect with that of the salt or the sweet. If it helps many more people with the condition than does the salt or sweet, then the preparation has value. That, my son, is the science. But I must still stress the art of our work. The will to get better and the confidence the sick person has in his therapist and the medicine prescribed are all of great importance. Even the best of medicine will fail if there is not the will on the part of the afflicted for it to work; he must want it to work.

"And now I should like to tell you something that will amaze you all. But first I must extract a promise. You must each pledge never to repeat any of this to another living soul."

"Why do you ask this?" asked Eliezer. "Is what you are about to tell us so evil?"

"No, I would not ask you to conceal some foul deed." He paused for a moment and then went on: "You spoke to me before about the possible similarity between the practitioner of medicine and the conjurer. I would prefer to think of the physician or the apothecary as being something like a general. He is the one responsible for organizing an attack on the affliction and overcoming it.

"It is easier to understand what I mean if I cite an example in an entirely different field and setting. The brightness of the sun can better be appreciated when looking at a star."

He continued, "When Alexander the Great met the Persian armies on the field of combat near Arbela, he had less than one-twentieth as many soldiers as did his adversaries. Before the battle, he told his men that victory would be theirs. He spoke without hesitation in his voice. He addressed them with absolute conviction, as if there were not the slightest doubt in his mind about the outcome of the titanic struggle about to begin. His army charged into the Persian forces with such swiftness that the enemy fled in panic. And so the smaller and more confident army was victorious. Now suppose that before the battle, Alexander had told his troops that they were up against a force more that twenty times their size, and that it would take a miracle for the Macedonians and Greeks to win. The likelihood is that his soldiers would have advanced cautiously. Each Greek and Macedonian would have been looking warily for an escape route just in case the battle went against him. The charge would not have been as strikingly swift and overwhelming. In short, history would not remember him as Alexander the Great, but as Alexander the Loser.

"So it is sometimes in treating the sick. When the strengths and weaknesses are clearly exposed to the patient, it may leave him with a feeling of insecurity. Without the yearned-for assurance, he will have less confidence in the ultimate success of the treatment. Therapy is more likely to fail under these circumstances."

"I get the point, Father," said Eliezer with restless impatience. "It's about someone you treated with one of those mysterious concoctions. With a piercing look you convinced him that the bubbling brew would cure him. And now the cripple is dancing in the streets, happy and healthy...and appreciative."

"Please!" replied Naphtali with obvious annoyance. "I know that you dislike my long-winded introductions, but they do have a purpose. As to your most recent critical remark, I was not about to discuss one of my patients. The story concerns a place, far from here, where treatment has helped thousands. If the secrets behind the success were made known to the outside world, the treatment might lose some of its value. It might even result in the failure of the therapy. People who might respond to the regimen would, in their doubt, not improve. Skepticism and a hesitancy to cooperate – which can be disastrous in this form of care – would ultimately destroy the very fabric of the institution of healing and result in its downfall. Therefore, I must insist that each of you pledge never to reveal the secrets you are about to hear: The well-being of thousands who might seek care there in the future depends upon it. Now do I have your word, Sarah?"

"You have my word. I'll say nothing."

"Good. And you, Eliezer, my clever one with words that sting, you are my sharpest critic. You seek nothing but the unvarnished truth. You serve as the looking glass that follows me, faces me, forces me to examine myself – my virtues and my failings. What do you say?"

"I'll keep the secret."

After eliciting a positive response from his other children, the father paused, studying the impatient eyes of all around him. Then he began: "Have you all heard of Pergamum?"

"I've heard of it, Father," volunteered Eliezer. "It is a great city almost the size of Ephesus. It is the city where they treat the sick...at the Temple of Aesculapius. Isn't that the temple at whose gate they have the sign that reads, 'None who enter shall die?' I always thought it sounded a little too cock-sure."

"I see you know it well," smiled his father. "But what you consider 'cock-sure' has a purpose. It's the reputation possessed by the temple, known throughout the world and carefully read by every patient who enters it. It's a mystique that both attracts and reassures. People come from as far away as Rome to be healed by the priests, confident that if allowed to enter, they will be saved and their maladies will be cured. And, in a way, I'm part of it."

"What?" began the startled Eliezer.

"Let me go on," insisted his father. "As I was saying: in a way I'm part of it – not there, but here. One of the priests of Aesculapius makes frequent trips to Ephesus. He comes to my shop to obtain potions for use at the temple. You see, I do have something of a reputation in my field. That's how I came to learn the secret.

"Several weeks ago, he invited me to Pergamum to visit the temple. I went with him. You remember, it was the week I was away collecting supplies for my work. I learned that at the Temple of Aesculapius they combine much art with the little science we know today about sickness. The sign at the entrance to the temple reads, as you said, Eliezer, 'None who enter shall die.' But many of the arrivals are hopelessly ill. The priests who stand at the gate will turn away anyone who has the smell or look of death about him. For that person, there is nothing they can do.

"Inside the temple complex they have all forms of therapy – some for the body and many for the mind. These include giving the patients herbs and spices appropriate to their ailments. Their steaming mudpacks relax the muscles and relieve spasm;hot baths do the same thing, while the cold baths cause the body to tingle. There is a huge library on the grounds and the patients are encouraged to read and to pray. This serves to relax their minds. Now we come to the final therapeutic modality that I will characterize as a form of induced trance. Each patient is given an opiate, which soon puts him into a twilight sleep. The patient is then directed to lie down on a bed in the basement of the Temple of Telesphorus. (It is one of the buildings of the complex.) The patient does not know it, but there were tubes hidden in the walls during the construction of the temple. These connect the individual beds in the basement to the upstairs. There, the priests who minister to the sick study the chart of each patient, his complaints and the findings on their examination. A priest tells the foggy-headed subject, through the tube, that he will get better, that his sore back (or whatever else he previously told the priest was sore) is getting better and better.

"'When you awake,' says the priest, 'you will remember nothing of what you have just heard, but you *will* be well again.' Lying in bed, in a drug-induced twilight zone, and knowing nothing of the hidden tube through which he hears the voice of the priest (properly altered by a cloth over the tube used to produce the strange, eerie sound), the patient is convinced that the words he hears come from the spirit world, powers beyond the understanding of man, the voice of God. The patient is now certain of a cure."

"It's a fraud!" cried Eliezer. "The whole course of treatment is sham pretense. They don't really help anyone."

"Now calm down, Eliezer."

"But –" persisted his eldest son.

"Look here, I understand that you disapprove of supernatural pretense. I feel the same way about it. It goes contrary to our religious teachings. But I disagree with your assertion that it doesn't help anyone with the treatment. Suggestion does have the power to relieve symptoms in some patients. Let me give you an example.

"Two men are each stuck with a needle of exactly the same size and sharpness. The point is driven into their flesh at the same speed. One cries out in pain and is unable to function for some time. The other winces for a moment and goes about his activity with hardly an interruption. If, by suggestion, we can turn the former into the latter, we can get a person who is better able to function, despite his obvious pain.

"Suggestion does not cause a swollen knee to resume its normal shape, but it can make the afflicted feel better. As a result, the patient is better able to live with his malady.

"We should also remember that not all maladies have a physical basis. Some can be imagined. Such an individual derives the greatest benefit from a suggestion that he will be all better when he awakens.

"So don't sneer at the Temple of Aesculapius as being totally useless. Some day we will have better ways to treat the sick. There will be less need for suggestion as a means for making them feel better. In the meantime... there's Aesculapius."

He paused and then added, "At least for a while."

"For a while?" puzzled Eliezer. "You mean until we learn better methods of treating the sick."

"Not quite. I mean that the Temple may be brought to an end by the Romans."

"But why," questioned the son. "Are they dissatisfied with the care?"

"Not that. It is a change brought about by religion. Since the days of Constantine, the religion of the empire has been Christianity. The Greeks and Romans dedicated the Temple of Aesculapius to a pagan god of healing, worshipped long before the time of Jesus. The healing at the temple is not based upon faith in the Christian church, but upon the actions of the priest-doctors who minister to the sick. It is likely that the authorities will force a closure of the temple. But for the present, they carry on."

"Are they always successful in their treatment?" wondered Eliezer aloud. "Surely, there are conditions that can not be healed by suggestion alone."

"True, though nothing is said about it officially. I was told by one of the priests at the temple in the strictest of confidence – not to be repeated by you, of course – that occasionally there is a death of a patient. The body is then buried without any marker."

"Are the relatives informed?" asked Eliezer with dismay written on his face.

"No. No one is notified. Thus the mystique of the temple is maintained: 'None who enter shall die.'"

Eliezer sat back on his pillow and thought for a while.

"You have a point, Father. But, to me, it's just a point and not a long-term answer."

"That *is* something," smiled Naphtali. "When father and son agree – progress. You'll help me in the shop and you'll learn. And one day you'll discover new ways to help people. Then there'll be no need for what you call 'Pretense.'"

The hour was late. The Passover Seder was over. One by one, the children went off to sleep.

"Something else is wrong, isn't it?" said Sarah to her husband in the quiet of their bedroom, "your face, earlier this evening..."

"Don't trouble yourself. Things have a way of looking better in the morning. It's late. Go to sleep. There's an early service for me tomorrow and you have another Seder for which to prepare."

"But if there's something I've done wrong," she persisted, "it should be corrected."

"You? – Done wrong? – What are you talking about? The preparations were perfect. The Seder was perfect. It has nothing to do with that. Please go to sleep."

Sarah was not comforted. She remained awake, silently watching his silhouette twisting itself in the darkness. She was convinced that there was trouble on the horizon. There was something Naphtali sensed but had not puzzled through, and the uneasiness it had produced had been visible in his countenance earlier that evening. Whatever that something was, it was bad.

❖ ❖ ❖

The next few weeks were normal in Ephesus. It was getting warmer. Summer was fast approaching. But June came and there was trouble in the city.

Late one Saturday evening, Naphtali summoned his family to the dining room. His face was long and somber. He directed that they all be seated at the table to hear what he had to say.

"Sarah, I bring grave news. We all know that a fever has struck the city. I saw the first cases of it, even before Passover. But now it has reached tidal proportions. Hundreds upon hundreds have come to my shop, seeking a potion for the fever. But I have no remedy for it and the power of suggestion will not help its victims."

Eliezer leaned forward intently in his chair. "It's easy to see that the city is in trouble. There's panic in the streets. You hear whispers and even cries of anguish, but no one seems to have answers. What's this fever like?"

"For a few days, before the worst of the fever, the victim seems to feel that something isn't right. There may be a backache. He may feel sore all over. He may even feel a bit feverish. It's nothing you can put your finger on. Then one day, he starts getting the chills. Each attack is unbearable: No number of blankets seems to relieve the coldness of the afflicted. His entire body is convulsed with a tremor, from the chattering teeth to the quivering arms and legs. The skin turns blue with an icy chill and the patient feels as if his body will never warm up. But in an hour or so it is all over. Now the poor soul feels as if he's baking in an oven, his face flushed and drenched with sweat and his head throbbing with intense pain. They cry and they scream and say strange things." Naphtali paused, holding his head as if overcome with the symptoms he was describing.

"Are you all right?" asked Sarah, concerned.

Naphtali's mind was elsewhere. He shook himself, trying to clear his mind. "Oh...I'm all right. It's just that I was thinking: So many are dying. The stench of rotting flesh fills the city even though carts carry away the dead every morning. There's a sound heard throughout Ephesus: the mournful cry of the widow and the orphan; the wail of the father who has lost his child; this, together with the ear-piercing shriek of the delirious, burning up with fever, and the groans of the dying. It is the sorrowful echo of a lost civilization, a city without hope."

"Is this some sort of Divine punishment?" inquired Rivkah, not really expecting an answer.

"Who knows? The Lord told Noah that He would never again use the waters to destroy the earth. On the other hand, Sodom and Gomorrah were consumed with fire and brimstone because of their wickedness and that, of course, was long after Noah. Does Ephesus fall into this category? There is slavery here in Ephesus. Is the Lord of Hosts punishing the people of the city for allowing it to continue? The evil of slavery should be ended, but is this the reason for the fever? Such matters are beyond me and so I am considering another possible explanation more to the level of an apothecary's comprehension."

Eliezer's ears perked up upon hearing his father's words. "What explanation?"

Naphtali rose from his chair and made his way to the window. The Marble Way was bathed in moonlight. He looked out at the pristine marble buildings. Their blinding columns of white rose above the clear stone like the flashing teeth of a proud warrior, daring the heavens to do their worst. He studied the broad street intently with its beautiful shops, the sturdy pillars and the great monuments. He tried to lock them firmly in his mind, as if he were a son committing to memory the face of his mother left behind as he began a long voyage, perhaps never to return. It was a city of grandeur, a city of splendor, an exalted city of stone. It was the crowning glory of man's vanity; it was a city smitten by a fever; a proud Goliath being struck down by a stone. It was the ultimate proof of the Lord's words: "From dust thou art, and unto dust shalt thou return" (*Genesis*, 3:18). Naphtali thought long and hard and then turned to face his family.

"For years, the Aegean Sea has been receding, and Ephesus, which was built by the sea, is becoming an inland city. The mosquitoes come earlier and heavier."

"And the mosquitoes cause the fever?" wondered Eliezer aloud.

"That's my idea."

Surprise and even shock spread across their faces upon hearing Naphtali's words. Eliezer, alone, seemed to perceive some wisdom in his father's words.

Naphtali nodded in appreciation towards his eldest son and then turned to Sarah. "Don't look so doubtful. It has happened before. In fact, Ephesus has been moved twice, centuries ago, it's true, but moved nevertheless. The first – I know not why. The second – when the Greek general Lysimachus blocked the drainage systems, with the result that the city was flooded."

"Why would he do something so foolish?" asked Eliezer.

"Vanity. A Greek temple – the temple dedicated to the pagan god Artemis had burned down. (Artemis was the Greek huntress goddess, but in Asia Minor she was regarded as the symbol of fruitful nature.) It was in the time of Alexander the Great. Alexander wanted to provide the funds for the rebuilding of the temple, but the proud citizens of Ephesus wanted to rebuild the temple at their own expense. Alexander died and his general Lysimachus decided to build a whole new Ephesus around a temple of Artemis that would be one of the wonders of the world. To force the people of Ephesus to abandon their city and help construct his new Ephesus, he blocked the drainage system of the old city."

"But that was a long time ago. Right now we are faced with a dying city."

Sarah's face darkened. "What's to be done?"

"Leave," replied her husband simply. "We'll move towards the sea."

"But we've lived here all our lives," cried Sarah. "Your family and my family – they've been here for generations."

"Precisely. Let it be said that we lived here, not died here. I know whereof I speak. The fever is deadly. It comes when the water no longer runs freely. If we stay, it will destroy us."

"Where shall we go?"

"To Smyrna. It's a substantial city and the population is large enough to afford another apothecary. It's on the Aegean and, hopefully, will remain so for many centuries. It's a good city, full of warmth and cheer."

"It's not Jerusalem," Eliezer reminded him.

"No, it is not," agreed his father sadly, "but it may do until we return –" Naphtali broke off, twisting his lower lip in pain.

"And what of our friends?" inquired Sarah with concern.

"I presented my conclusions to the rest of our congregation earlier this evening after the service. In fact, I pleaded with them. Many are following my advice. As for the rest, may the Almighty help them."

The next 24 hours were spent packing for the journey. What was too heavy was sold or simply given away. Haste was the key word. Each additional day of delay was a day of risk. Sarah gathered up her kitchen utensils; Naphtali, the instruments of his profession, and a few family documents, and for each of them, including the children, a bundle of clothing.

On Monday morning they loaded their assembled possessions onto an ox cart and left the dying city. There was no time for tears. Farewells were brief.

A few days later, the Azubels were in bustling Smyrna on the shore of the great blue sea. They were beginning life again in a new place, just as their ancestors had done so many times before – one home in exile replacing another.

Fourteen centuries later, in the year 1960, I met my cousin, Nathan Ausubel, for the first time while serving as resident physician at Mt. Sinai Hospital. Nathan described to me what he believed to be the ancestry of our family. From Dr. Abraham Galante, a leading authority on the Jews of Asia Minor, Nathan had learned of the Azubels of Ephesus, apothecaries over a period of several centuries.

In 1972 my wife and I traveled to Turkey. I planned to visit sites where, according to Dr. Galante, our distant ancestors had lived. We visited the archaeological team working at Sardis and viewed the ruins of the largest synagogue in the ancient world. We went through the remnants of the Temple of Aesculapius at Pergamum and studied the secret air ducts leading from the upper to the lower levels of the huge central building of the complex. Then we traveled to Ephesus to behold the magnificent remains of that dead city. Finally we came to Izmir, the Turkish city formerly known as Smyrna.

In a travel office in Izmir, we sat patiently waiting our turn. It was the halfway point on our trip and we were anxious to complete arrangements for several side-trips. At last, the couple ahead of us left. A dark-eyed, chubby middle-aged woman, her olive-skinned hands shuffling through a series of brochures, sat behind an old, worn, dark-wooden desk. Her dress was dark, but its repetitive floral pattern and short sleeves contrasted sharply with the all-concealing blackness of the attire of most women of that Islamic city. She looked up and suddenly gasped in surprise. The pack of brochures tumbled from her hand. Her mouth half open, she studied my face – my hair, my eyes, my nose and my mouth, as would a detective comparing the features of a man seen on the street with a composite drawing hidden in the recesses of his mind.

"You're an Azubel," she said with the certainty of a mother spotting the telltale birthmark on a long-lost son's face.

She went on to relate the story of the family, the Azubels of Izmir. They were neighbors and friends of hers. The Azubels had continued to dwell in Izmir even into the twentieth century. Tombstones in the Jewish cemetery, some hundreds of years old, bore the family name.

Her story was interesting, fascinating in fact, but I was in a hurry. I needed to make travel arrangements and didn't have time to visit the Jewish Quarter or the cemetery that day. She gave me a card on which she scrawled her name and address. She was Esther Russo and the street listed on the card was one I had not spotted in my walks through the city.

"It's near the synagogue," she added, urging me with her eyes to visit the ancient ghetto of the Jews.

A few days later, we returned from the interior of Anatolia. My wife wanted to buy a hand-woven silk carpet, and so we went to a carpet store. The owner of the shop did not speak English and neither my wife nor I spoke Turkish. The shop assistant, a slight young woman with dark eyes and dark hair, spoke both languages and served as translator. We went through hundreds of carpets and came upon one "Tree of Life" woven in a beautiful rainbow of colors. I asked the price. It was 240 dollars.

My wife and I whispered for a moment.

"I'll take it," was my quick reply.

To my astonishment, the young woman whispered, "Offer him 120 dollars."

I acquiesced. The young woman then spoke to her employer, presumably relaying my offer for half the asking price. The owner waved his hands wildly and replied in a near roar, as if to emphasize the absurdity of my offer. I felt uneasy. Had I gone too far in following the shop assistant's directions?

A few minutes later, the young woman relayed the owner's altered terms. He would accept 220 dollars. Again, she softly reminded me not to offer a cent more than 120 dollars.

Again, I followed her directions. The shrieks and angry fist-waving gestures of the shopkeeper frightened us. My wife nudged me to give the man what he was asking, if only to save us from seeming violence.

But the shop assistant's silencing shake of the head kept me from responding. There were quick gestures and a machine gun's rattle of words – the shopkeeper's almost threatening proposals and the assistant's almost instant translations, each ending with a muttered, "Stick to the 120."

The price came down by fives and tens. There were now pleas for a starving family and harsh, grating grunts of something that might have been "How could you? Look at the workmanship."

The shopkeeper slid the carpet material across his face, caressing the soft material. Finally, he shrugged his shoulders in disgust as his hand flew upward and then sank to his side. He walked off, saying nothing.

"What happened?" I asked the young woman. "Why did he walk away?"

"He said that you can have it for 120 American dollars," she responded quite seriously.

The shop assistant carefully packed the carpet for shipment. In appreciation for her efforts, I reached into my pocket for a twenty-dollar bill and slipped it to the young woman.

"Don't give me anything," she said, fending me off. "Your family would be furious with me if I allowed you to overpay for a carpet."

I smiled a puzzled smile and responded with a question. "Have you been to the United States?"

"No."

"Then how do you know my family?"

"Because you're a Jew and an Azubel." There was not a hint of uncertainty in her voice.

"What made you think of that? Did you see me check in at the hotel across the street or did you speak to someone at the hotel about me?"

"Of course not," she responded indignantly. "What do you take me for? Can't you see: It's your face. It's the face of an Azubel."

By now I was determined to meet these Azubels and see for myself whether or not there was a resemblance. "I assume you know the Azubels of Izmir."

"Of course. I know several of the men and women of the family, the children as well."

"Then take me to them," I insisted.

"I can't do that," she replied. "They have returned."

"Returned to where?" I asked, puzzled.

"To our homeland, Eretz Yisrael. For them, the wandering is over."

THE PASSOVER CONSPIRACY

THE WORLD IN the Middle Ages had much in common with a beach. Men, like children playing in the sand, built civilizations: cities of dull-brown mud, drying in the noonday sun; stately, bright golden-brown castles (adorned with graceful towers climbing to the sky), whose powerful walls, like the shoulders of a 300-pound wrestler, dared the stranger to come near; moats – endless lakes of water that none seemed able to cross; flags flying from the summit – built to last a thousand years, only to be swept away by the next tide. Nations were born, grew powerful – white shining teeth and clenched fists challenging those around them – and then vanished like the ancient hulk of a punch-drunk boxer who had been crushed by the blows of an upstart.

The parched sands of deserts and the barren, icy, wind-blown hills gave birth to new tribes who were restless and thirsted for the sweetness of fields of grain that others planted, the sheep that others tended, and the cities that others built. Fearless and hungry, knowing the sword but not the pen, capable of splitting a man in two with a single blow, but understanding little of the art of mending, horde after horde swept out of the cold north of Siberia, the harsh mountains of Central Asia, and the alternately burning and frozen sands of the Gobi. They descended onto the plains of the Middle East, Europe and Africa, crushing everything in their path.

These were the Turks of Central Asia, cousins to the Mongols of Genghis Khan. Slashing, stabbing, piercing, trampling, they sliced their way from the steppes of central Asia through the more fertile valleys of Anatolia (the Asian part of modern Turkey) and across the angry waters of the Bosporus (the strait of water separating Europe from Asia) into Europe.

Enveloping, trapping, sieging, overrunning, they brought the Byzantine Empire to an end. From the crumbling walls of Constantinople to the very gates of Vienna, nothing could withstand them. By the sixteenth century, all of Europe south and east of Vienna (capital of the Hapsburgs, the most powerful rulers in Europe) lay beneath the hooves of their horses.

Yet, once in command, the Turks were not the worst of rulers. Knowing more of the art of war than the craft of governing, they employed slaves called Janissaries who converted to the Muslim faith and were freed to run the empire. Within their domain, subject peoples were able to travel in relative freedom. One of the Azubels of Smyrna (now called Izmir by the Turks) was David ben Yosef, a practitioner of the healing arts. David traveled to the newly conquered territories of Central and Eastern Europe, caring for the army of Selim I, known as Suleiman the Magnificent.

With the death of Suleiman in 1566, David ben Yosef Azubel settled in Budapest, in the Jewish quarter of Buda on the west bank of the Danube. The city was under Turkish rule at the time.

Like the sea that had overrun the beach and was now smashing relentlessly against the rocks guarding the redoubt that was Vienna, the Turks seemed ready to roll, wave-like, over it. But with a change in fortune, they were forced to retreat like the falling tide, running off into their shrinking ocean. Here and there, a puddle of Ottoman domination, disconnected from the main, disappeared, sinking beneath the rising sand of Europe.

The Jews of Budapest had prospered under Turkish rule. They specialized in the manufacture of decorative braids for uniforms. Some of their number, including the Azubels, were famous for their knowledge of medicines, and one served as physician to the pasha of Budapest. The Jews of Budapest sided with the Turks in their war against the Austrians. Consequently, the Jewish quarter was pillaged and the Torah scrolls burned when the Austrians captured the city in 1686. More than half the Jewish community died during the siege of the city, and Jewish residence in Buda was now prohibited. And so the surviving Azubels of Buda fled to the Kingdom of Poland.

Like shells washed up on the beach, unable to return to the sea, the Azubels found themselves stranded, living in a new milieu: Christian Europe, with new rulers – the Christian lords, princes, kings and emperors – had replaced the Muslim Ottoman Sultan. They also found themselves part of a new community of the Followers of Moses – Jews who spoke a strange Germanic dialect called Yiddish, which they had brought with them from the Rhineland. Their ancestors had fled eastward to escape the murderous assaults of the Crusaders in the eleventh and twelfth centuries. The Azubels learned to speak Yiddish and live within the stark, confining walls of the ghetto that locked Jews in, and sun, out.

For a decade or two, they might live in relative tranquility with only an occasional beating at the hands of the surrounding Christian communities. They paid their taxes to the local lord and wished nothing more than to be left in peace to study the Torah and practice their trades and crafts. But at any time, a sudden change in the wind could bring disaster. A regional epidemic of any disease or mysterious death of a local Christian could be blamed on the Hebrew people and lead to the slaughter of dozens, hundreds or even thousands of them. The preaching of a local priest declaring the Jews had murdered Jesus might likewise be followed by mob assaults on the ghettoes, with plunder, rape and murder.

Easter, coming close to Passover, was a particularly hazardous time of the year. A Jew who ventured beyond the ghetto walls on Palm Sunday took his life in his hands. In the grumbling world of unhappy people, rulers often found it expedient to unify their subjects by turning them against the Jews. Troops would then join the drunken mobs in ravaging the Jewish people. Yet through it all, they somehow survived.

In the eighteenth century, the gigantic Kingdom of Poland was home to the largest Jewish community in the world. It extended from the borders of the Germanic Holy Roman Empire in the west, to the Dnieper River in the east (later to be in the heart of Russia); from the gates of Riga in Latvia, not far from St. Petersburg in the north, to within a hundred miles of Odessa on the Black Sea in the south. It included all of post-World War I Poland, Lithuania and White Russia, as well as much of Latvia, Moldavia, Czechoslovakia and the Ukraine. Within this kingdom dwelt the European Azubels, the branches of the family tree of David ben Yosef Azubel who had left Anatolia two centuries before. They had remained in Christian Europe after the decline of the Ottomans, and had scattered across the southern reaches of the Polish kingdom from Galicia in the west, to as far east as the Ukraine. One of the branches, traveling close to the ground, produced shoots that took root in the rich, dark soil of Galicia in the southwestern corner of the kingdom.

On a cold and dismal early Saturday morning during the onset of spring of 1750, Avrum Azubel, a gifted silversmith, cautiously made his way between the puddles in the gray slush of an unpaved street in the ghetto of Dzikow, a modest-sized town in the province of Galicia. A large, circular hat of dark-brown foxtail that surrounded a black cloth cap covered his head, which was bent forward against the wind. The fur maintained its shape, despite the volume of rainwater that had fallen on it, which ran off onto Avrum's long, black coat. His right hand gripped the lapels of his outer garment tightly to keep out the chill. Avrum's long, crinkly beard of honey and straw-colored strands was soaked and dripping, adding to the considerable volume of water that had soaked his clothes through to the skin. An icy blast whistled through the narrow street and sent a shudder through his lean body. Quickly he raised his left hand to his head to keep his hat from flying off. All the while, his eyes remained directed towards the unsure footing ahead of him, rather than at the drab buildings along the way, which varied from one another only in their size and shade of gray.

A "Hello" coming from a doorway surprised Avrum, causing him to look up. It was Stanislaus Wojewski, the *Shabbos Goy*, a sandy-haired teenager with crossed eyes and an eager though somewhat twisted mind, who emerged into the dull light that filtered through dark clouds onto the winding, lusterless pathway. The rain had given his fine hair a flattened-down look. The stream of cold water running down his face had turned his cheeks almost chalk white. His brightly colored tunic seemed out of place amidst the gray of the homes and the black of the outer garments of the Jews of the village, for whom he performed, for a fee, the service of lighting their lamps and adding wood to their fires on the Sabbath. (The Ten Commandments require that the Sabbath be kept as a day of rest and prayer. Hence, Orthodox Jews will not perform work, including adding wood to the fire or lighting lamps on the Sabbath. They will employ a *Shabbos Goy*, a gentile to whom the Sabbath is not holy, to perform such necessary tasks.)

"Stanislaus," said Avrum in gentle reprimand, "you really should put something on your head. It's cold and raining, and you're liable to catch a chill. I would not want your mother to blame us for you getting ill."

"I don't mind the rain," the lad replied, expanding his chest to give a manly appearance. "Don't worry. I'm strong... Say, I guess you'll want an extra log or two on your fire in this weather. I'll be over to your house later this morning."

The youth's eyes widened with eagerness as he added, "By the way, it's the time of the year you people bake those flat bread cakes."

"*Matzos, matzos,*" (unleavened bread) interrupted Avrum instructively.

"Well, whatever. But I'd be glad to clean out the place where you make them...eh...for a fee, of course...eh...if I could get paid in advance."

"That won't be necessary," replied Avrum.

"Why not? It's full of dust after not being used for a year. I know. I saw it through the window. It's hard work cleaning up all that."

"That's not the point."

"I don't get it. You people pay me to light lamps and put a couple of small logs on a fire on Saturday – work a six-year-old could do – and yet you won't hire anyone to do even hard work the rest of the week. Now this *matzos* place – it must have a few inches of dust covering the equipment. You could afford to pay someone to clean it. You make enough, God knows, in your shops."

"It has to be one of our people who cleans it. That is the custom, you see. Certain rituals must be observed during the cleaning, and you have to be trained in the ritual."

"Hmm... Secret stuff. I hope it's not what I've heard... Some of my friends warned me against working for you people."

"I assure you there's nothing to be afraid of."

Stanislaus hesitated, reaching into his pocket. "By the way," he added, "I could use some money. Could you..." He shook his head. "I forgot. It's Saturday. You Jews don't carry money on Saturday."

"That's right. Now I must be off to the synagogue. Good morning."

The bearded Jew turned the corner and disappeared from the young man's view. Stanislaus stood there motionless, his mind elsewhere, while a steady runoff from a nearby arch continued to drip on his clothes. Another blast of wind sent a torrent of icy liquid down on his head, awakening him from his meditation.

Darn it, he thought. *What a rotten day. And nothing to do for the next few hours. It's so dead in the ghetto on Saturday – no shops open, no music, no excitement. Wish I had some money to buy a drink in the tavern on our side of town. Well, I'd better get out of here.*

Following the Sabbath services, Avrum made his way between the angular, dark outlines of buildings beneath the arches of the ghetto streets. The storm was over. With it went the last of the winter snow, washed away by the gushing waters. But there was still a near-frigid chill in the air. He held his coat lapels tightly against his neck and smiled as he pictured Sarah and the children, a glass of wine and a fine meal of roast chicken and boiled potatoes, near a warm crackling fire. He looked forward to the vibrant conversations in the geniality of a Saturday noon in the *shtetl* (the villages and towns where the Jews lived in Europe) with the world in harmony.

The door opened. Sarah, shivering and wrapped in a black shawl clutched tightly to her small, slender body, greeted him with a look of distress. Her pallid face was long, her forehead, lined with concern. Beyond her, the table, save for the graceful silver candle holders of unusual design, was otherwise bare – no browned, tantalizing roast chicken, no steaming pot of boiled potatoes, and no delicious aromas rising to fill the air. It was cold and damp in the house. Avrum was reluctant to remove his coat.

"I'm sorry," she began, "but Stanislaus did not show up. So the house is unheated and the food is cold."

"Strange, that he didn't come," he thought aloud, frowning. "He was around early this morning." The bearded head of the household watched his sons, Moshe and Yitzchak. They were short, slim lads of twelve and ten. Their long, golden sidecurls flew back and forth with each waving movement of their hands and bodies. They were busily fanning the smoking embers into flame. "He was so anxious to get additional work – hard work – yet he couldn't even remember to perform a simple task."

A week later, hands bound together behind his back, Avrum stood in a large, rather bare room with a high ceiling, huge fireplace and stone floor. He was in the castle of the Tarnowskis. His dress was that of a religious Jew of substance of his period – the *streimel* (foxtail hat), the long black coat of fine wool, tied at the waist with a sash of black silk, with the garment extending down to just above his knees. Visible below the bottom of his coat were black, woolen britches meeting long white stockings. The shoes were black and of fine, sturdy leather. Avrum was plainly uneasy in his surroundings. His deep, anxious eyes, half-hidden in the shadow of his foxtail hat, glanced fleetingly at the huge crest of the Tarnowskis – in the form of a shield – that dominated the dark, stone wall above the fireplace. The crossed axes hanging beneath it sent a chill through his slim body as he remembered that in Dzikow, the will of the Tarnowskis was law, the only law, the final law.

His eyes shifted from the wall to the only piece of furniture in the room. It was a high-backed chair of dark, polished walnut. The person occupying it was Countess Tarnowski. One might have pictured her as Brunhilde in *Der Nibelungenlied* (a folk epic about Teutonic heroes, written in the twelfth century).

She was tall, handsome rather than beautiful, and full-chested. She was dressed in a stately, yet pretty, floor-length red-velvet gown with a high neck and puffed sleeves. Her outer garment was embroidered exquisitely with black, silver and gold thread. Twin braids of golden hair were wrapped crown-like around her head. The noblewoman's face was strong, with clear, unwrinkled skin, high cheekbones, a straight nose and firm jaw. Her cold, bluer than blue eyes stared right back at him.

She studied the strange looking figure before her. He was a Jew, with the beard and sidecurls of a Jew and the clothes of a Jew. Yet there were things about him that just didn't fit her image of a Jew. She had been taught that they were sinister, crafty, oily, mysterious, brooding creatures from the Occident who bowed before, but did not revere their masters. These were supposed to be people who paid taxes (as little as they could get away with), yet held back enough to fatten their coffers. Her grandfather had advised her to tolerate Jews as a necessary evil, but never to trust them. But this Jew... his hair was too blond, his eyes too green, his posture too erect. He was not your average Jew. He was more like a nobleman. For what Jew would dare look the countess in the eye – and with his life hanging in the balance! *Take away the beard and the sidecurls. Take away that ridiculous coat and what do you have?* she thought. *A handsome man who could grace any court.*

Her thoughts were kept hidden behind the cold, polished marble of her face. "Very well," she said aloud in an officious manner, "so you didn't do it. But who did?"

"Did what?" he retorted without flinching.

"I took you for a man. Now you're being sly – like a Jew. Well then, I'll have to treat you like a Jew.

"I have ordered the arrest of the ten leaders of the Jewish community of Dzikow. You, of course, are one of them. I'm sure nothing of significance could take place in the ghetto without one of you knowing about it. Now you, at least, look as if you have a sense of honor – not like that dark, shifty bunch." She halted, analyzing his features. "Are you really the child of Jewish parents? I mean your hair, your eyes, and your manner. Those evil people could have kidnapped you from a good Christian home and then brought you up. Then you would not have to stand accused with them."

"Your highness, I do not wish to stand accused of anything, but I am a Jew. My parents were Jews, my grandparents were Jews, and all my ancestors – as far back as I am aware of – were Jews. The color of my eyes and the shade of my hair have nothing to do with it." He paused, but on observing out of the corner of his eye the armed guards drawing closer, their fists tightened as if to strike him, he began again, "Your grace, I was not trying to be sly, clever or anything else. What do you want to know?"

"The boy. Stanislaus – or whatever his name is: Who killed him?"

Avrum's face blanched. His forehead furrowed with the weight of the news. "I'm saddened to hear it. I liked the lad and gave him employment. But where did he die and in what manner?"

"Again, you're being clever. That's what I want to know! Where did he die and in what manner?" There was rising anger in her voice.

"Please," said the bearded man as the guards placed rough hands upon him, "I want to help. The news of his death comes as a shock to me. I saw him just a week ago, on the Sabbath. Aside from standing outside in the pouring rain without a hat – which I cautioned him against doing – he looked fine. That's the last I saw of him. He promised to stop at my house later to put a log or two on the fire, but he never showed up. When did he die?"

The countess's voice grew louder with her growing impatience. "See here, we don't know when he died. He disappeared last Saturday. As far as I can tell, you were the last person to have seen him alive. That makes you a prime suspect – unless you can point out some other person or persons who were responsible for his murder. Now, where's the body? If you don't know, then question your people. One of them must know." She paused. Her face hardened and she began again in a clear, emphatic tone: "Be sure of this. If the ten of you do not come up with the name or names of the killers, all ten of you will die."

"Where's the body?" Avrum repeated incredulously. "If no body has been found, how can you be sure that Stanislaus is dead, no less murdered?"

"Because we know all about the Passover conspiracy!" she shot back in a ringing voice.

One of the guards, a tall, muscular, bald-headed man, grabbed Avrum by the hand and began twisting it until the Jew fell to his knees. Avrum's face was distorted with pain and he cried out in agony.

"You'd better not contradict the countess," growled the huge hulk of a soldier.

"I think he has gotten the point." The golden-haired noblewoman smiled nervously at the guard. "You can let him up now. And leave him to me."

Avrum rose to his feet holding his pained hand in the other to which it was bound.

Looking at the bearded Jew, the countess continued. "You fail to realize that I am thoroughly acquainted with Jewish ritual. I *know* that Jews require blood to make their *matzos*. It's not your fault. It's the fault of your sick beliefs and your failure to accept Jesus."

"Your Highness," the Jew began, making every effort to appear polite and respectful, "I will not attempt to debate the relative merits of Judaism and Christianity with a noblewoman of your vast scope of learning. But I must humbly beg permission to correct those misimpressions about Judaism that have resulted in the deaths of all too many of my people in the past. There is no blood ritual in the preparation of *matzos*. You say that you are thoroughly acquainted with Jewish ritual. That so, you know I'm sure that Jews are forbidden to mix dairy with meat. Now how could we possibly eat *matzos* with dairy meals if there were even so much as a drop of blood in them?"

"What are the dark spots in the *matzos*, if not blood?"

"The product of baking, nothing else. Does not bread turn brown with baking? Since *matzos* have an irregular surface with only some parts touching the floor of the oven, only those spots turn darker brown."

"Then why all the secrecy in their preparation? From what I hear, no Christian has ever been present during their preparation. There must be some dark reason for all this."

"Nothing dark. Nothing sinister. On the contrary, it is our concern for insuring the purity of the *matzos* that causes us to do it all ourselves."

"Purity? That's an odd word to use. Are you suggesting that Gentiles are unclean?"

"No, your highness. I'm not suggesting anything of the sort. It's only that Gentiles would be less likely to care if some impurity got into the *matzos*." Seeing the frown that now appeared on her face, he continued, "Let me explain myself. *Matzo* is unleavened bread. It recalls, as you know, the fact that our ancestors left Egypt in haste and had no time to wait for their bread to rise on the morning of our departure. We Jews take great pains to see to it that there is no leavening in the *matzos* we are baking for the Passover. The wheat is carefully guarded from the time of the harvest. It is kept dry so that it will not be changed. We follow strict guidelines in the baking of the *matzos*. The entire operation – from the mixing of the dough to the completion of the baking – must be completed in less than twenty minutes. Even our rolling pins must be frequently shaved down to make sure that no leavening takes place in dough adhering to the surface of the pin. If so much as a speck of *chametz* (food that is forbidden on Passover) falls into the dough, it must all be discarded. We could not expect a non-Jew to follow Jewish ritual with such exactness."

"You talk about purity. And what of the Passover blood?" she inquired, like a card player trumping her opponent's play.

"If you refer to the first Passover night in Egypt, you have only to review the relevant passages in the Bible. I'm sure you've read them carefully in the past. The blood smeared on the door posts of the homes of Jews – as a sign for the Angel of Death to pass over those houses – was the blood of a lamb, not the blood of a human being."

"Ah," she shot back scornfully, "you would have the world believe that the Jews do not practice human sacrifice. Why, your whole religion began with human sacrifice. Abraham and Isaac: do you remember?"

"Your grace, permit me to point out most humbly the significance of the event that took place on Mount Moriah, the event which played so important a part in changing the course of world history. The Almighty put Abraham to the greatest test of faith a person could be ordered to partake in – to slay his own son as an offering to the Supreme One. Abraham passed the test, but did not kill his son. The Merciful One, blessed be His name, never intended to allow the sacrifice of Isaac or any other child. It was a ram, caught in a thicket that was to be offered up. From that day to this, and forever more, no Jew will ever be called upon to slay any human being as an offering to the Almighty for any reason. This too, is part of the meaning of that event. It should be recalled that the world in which Abraham lived was a world of idol-worshipers. In that world, the sacrifice of people, children in particular, was commonplace. The greater the request made by the pagan of his idol, the greater the sacrifice the pagan thought his idol required of him. To this idolater, a good crop or a victory in war necessitated giving up something of great value – even his son. That type of pagan behavior ended for Abraham, Isaac and their descendants. Therefore, to say that the murder of innocent people is part of Jewish ritual is untrue. It is contrary to every teaching in the Bible."

The tall, stately noblewoman looked sad and thoughtful. After a few minutes – which seemed an eternity – she commanded: "Guards, leave us here alone, the Jew and me."

"But my lady –" began the bald-headed henchman.

"Wladislaw," she interrupted, "give me your sword. My father taught me the use of the blade. I'm as skilled in its use as any man in the kingdom. So fear not. I can protect myself against him if he tries anything. In fact, untie his hands. I dare him to so much as move a muscle without my command."

The guards obeyed. They bowed and then withdrew from the room.

The door slammed shut with a dull thud. The noblewoman's eyes moved quickly from the door to Avrum. "See here, you do not understand my position very well. And you certainly don't appreciate what I've done for your people."

"I must confess that I'm at a loss to understand what you're referring to."

"I'm referring to the fact that not a single Jew has yet been killed."

"Then you say that we should be grateful to be alive, even when threatened with death for something we have not done?"

"Yes." Indignation was written on her face. "In the days of my great-grandfather, every Jew in Dzikow was put to the sword after a similar accusation. Now, I dislike crude violence, but I am ruler here. I would not be in command for long if I were to display weakness in such a situation. My husband is dead. I have several male cousins, each of whom would like to rule in my place. All I have to do is stumble once, and they'd have their excuse to take my place. So I *must* show a firm hand. When the news of Stanislaus's death spread through the region, and the age-old accusation of blood in the *matzos* was repeated from the pulpit in Dzikow, and in Holy Week of all the times for this to occur, the peasants became enraged. They were ready to charge into your ghetto and slaughter every Jew in the town. Under these circumstances, I did what I thought was most humane. I asked myself, 'Why punish every Jew in Dzikow for a crime committed by a few?' So I gave the order to have the ten leaders of the Jewish community arrested – you included. All you have to do is point out the guilty one or guilty ones or have the criminals come forward and confess their guilt, and the rest of you can all go free. The guilty will be executed and that should still things for the moment. You can then resume your occupations. After a time, the peasants will forget all about the incident and things will return to normal."

"But your Excellency," Avrum interjected, "there's no proof of a crime – no body, no blood, nothing. Isn't it possible that Stanislaus is still alive, and that he left Dzikow? And if a crime were indeed committed, there is no indication that it was done by a Jew. How do you expect someone to confess to a crime he did not commit?"

"Avrum, I summoned you here as a spokesman for those arrested. I did so because I thought you were above the rest. I thought that you could comprehend beyond your narrow religious views. So listen carefully. If Stanislaus wandered off, he is probably dead. From what I hear, he was none too bright. I do not see how he could get along on his own, away from his native town. You ask for proof. Just look at the faces of the peasants; look into the eyes of the village priest: that's all the proof you need. To them, there *is* a Passover conspiracy. And if I do not do something about it, they will. The difference is that when they get finished, there won't be a single Jew left alive in Dzikow.

"Things being as they are, I can not afford to procrastinate. What must be done has to be done quickly. That is why you and the others were arrested. Suppose, as you say, no crime has been committed. You may believe it and I may believe it, but the Polish people out there will not accept any explanation other than ritual murder. Only a living, breathing Stanislaus Wojewski would convince them that the Jews had not murdered him. If I were to set the ten of you free, without a live Stanislaus to disprove the accusation, and without someone waiting to be executed for the crime, my enemies would use that as a sign of weakness. They would destroy me, and shortly thereafter, all of you. That's the real point.

"Avrum, there is a way out of this. Select some old man, crippled, sick, but still able to use his hands so that it will appear believable, someone who might wish to be let out of his misery. Have him confess to the crime. He will be executed and the rest of you can go free."

Avrum had listened intently to her words. Seeing that the countess had finished speaking, he replied in a measured but firm tone of voice, with not a hint of hesitancy: "I cannot. We cannot. No man should be asked to confess to a crime, any crime, especially murder, that he did not commit. You say that the choice is between one dead, several dead, and all dead. But the decision involves much more than that. It involves something more than individual human life. It involves a belief in the Almighty. To admit that murder is a part of Jewish ritual is to blaspheme the Holy One, blessed be His name. Even to save lives – as you term it – that is not permissible. Furthermore, for any Jew to confess to so monstrous an act is to perpetuate the fiction for which, as you, yourself, pointed out, so many have died in the past.

"No. The way to fight a vicious falsehood is not to give it credence in any way. Not a single human being should be offered as a sacrifice to this pagan altar, to this idol of ignorance. Rather, it is essential that we speak out against the lie. As Abraham was prepared to give up that whom he held most dear to prove his faith in the Almighty, so we must be prepared to give up our most cherished possession – our lives – for our faith.

"As for your position: I'm sure that you are a devout, as well as a scholarly, woman. Where does it say in the Bible that innocent people are to be sacrificed to preserve a ruler's image? In which text are we told that false confessions are acceptable, to be forced upon people? Is that the purpose of a Messiah?"

The forehead of the countess's strong, smooth face became lined with anxiety. It was the outward sign of the struggle that was taking place in the convolutions of the brain behind it.

"You deal in morality," she replied, "to the exclusion of self-preservation. That is an option open to the powerless. But I must take other factors into consideration before choosing a course of action. I am a woman in a man's world, a noblewoman. I had to scratch and claw my way to the top, to my present position, to my *rightful* position – ruler of all the land as far as the eye can see. I did so because I was stronger in mind and stronger in determination than all the men who stood in my way. It was *my inheritance,* and I would allow no one to take it from me.

"When the Count, my husband, was alive, everyone thought that he ruled. But behind the scene, I wielded the power. When I think of it, what I endured to rule..." She paused, studying the strange look in the Jew's eyes. "You look surprised. Well, don't be. He was a drunken sop and a lecher on top of that. Oh, he was handsome all right. He was a fine figure of a man. He rode a horse well. He had good breeding: son of a duke, third son though, with two healthy older brothers, so there was no chance of a dukedom for him. But out of bed he was weak. Yes, I said weak. No backbone. No fire. And he was dull. Oh, so dull and dim witted. He had trouble getting past three sentences. Can you imagine having to spend the rest of your life with one such as him!" She sighed, and then grew firm again.

"I suppose I ought not to complain. I knew he was weak before I married him."

Avrum raised his eyebrows, quizzically. His right hand moved, involuntarily to his bearded chin. He appeared troubled. It was not so much that he disapproved of what she had said; it was that he pitied her. *That one could lead so shallow an existence for the sake of power,* he thought.

87

"You do not approve," she continued. "I can see it in your eyes. Don't give me that holier-than-thou look.

"It was, after all, *my* inheritance. Did you expect me to marry some cocky fellow and give up the throne, so to speak, and make sweet sounds like some fat contented peasant's wife? Just because I wear a dress? Why should a man rule me? I knew everything about him before I married him – his weakness for liquor, his dim wittedness...

"You listen intently in silence, but you seem to know so much. And you wonder why I'm telling all this to you. I would never dare say any of this to one of my own. Too dangerous. But you, a Jew, you couldn't do too much with the knowledge. To whom would you tell it? Who would believe you? You know, just the same." Her voice grew soft, her manner almost pleading. "Try to understand. I had to marry someone I could control. I needed a husband who would be viewed as a ruler, and who would give me an heir. (I do not want my domain thrown into turmoil when I pass from this world, with cousins battling one another over the succession.) As for his infidelity, it kept him conveniently out of the way so that I could conduct the affairs of state. I couldn't stand drunkards anyway. Can you understand how painful all this was to me? Having intimacy with such a man? With his death, I assumed power in name, as well as in fact. Well, actually, in my son's name, he's too young to direct affairs.

"Believe me, I sought not power as an end in itself, but as a means to effect change in the way things are done. But to wield power, one must accept the responsibilities of authority. The first obligation of a ruler is the preservation of authority. A man can fail many times; a woman gets no second chance. That's the cruelty of the world we live in. But let me assure you of one thing more: It takes absolute power to keep the peasants from doing what they wish to do now – massacre all the Jews. And so, to preserve my authority and avoid violent confrontation, I must give them something – someone on whom they can wreak their vengeance.

"Listen to me. Don't sacrifice yourself. It would be tragic to waste such a mind." She paused, and then added with almost gentle affection, "I haven't been lectured by any man since my father died. I could find it interesting to listen to you from time to time. Be sensible. Let some simpleton take your place."

Avrum's head sank to his chest. "Please, Countess, do not ask me to falsely accuse anyone." His head rose again and he looked at her, pleadingly. "Think of the great teachers in your own faith who have counseled charity, mercy, compassion – and then spare ten innocent men."

"Must you be so stubborn?" she cried. "What will sacrificing yourself accomplish? Will the world be altered?"

A strange clearness of purpose had gradually overcome Avrum and completely stilled the anxiety he felt when he entered the room. He was aware of everything that was said and the meaning of it all. He had listened to the invitation to escape a dire fate and leave the dying to others. He truly wanted to live, but each sentence of the exchange seemed to cut away another strand of the rope onto which he was holding, suspended from a cliff, above a deep, black abyss from which there was no return. And now it seemed as if only a few weakened fibers were all that kept him clinging to this world, to his wife and children. But there was nothing he could do. There was no way he could give a different answer to her questions. It was as if a higher authority were guiding her lips and forming her words to test him, so that there was but one answer he could give if he chose to be true to his faith. And that very faith now became his protective shield. It was like a light that shone in the dark to lead him down the narrow path of purity and away from the jackals of temptation that howled on both sides of him. That faith made his voice resolute when it would have been only human to tremble. That faith gave him the strength to say that which he believed to be right, rather than to surrender to the natural weakness of the flesh.

Avrum was Abraham on Mount Moriah; he was Akiva before the Romans; the Almighty was testing him, and the moment of truth had arrived. The question had to be answered. Did he love the Lord, his God, with all his heart and with all his soul, even if it meant the loss of his life? He had paused after the countess's last inquiry, not out of doubt, but to marshal his words so as to be persuasive without breaking faith. He wanted to be true to his convictions, yet not lock the door to his mortal existence. He did not wish to sever those last strands that bound him to life. He stood erect, his bearded chin held high, his eyes sad but clear, and began:

"We live in hope, in hope that we shall survive a while longer, in hope that you will change your mind, but failing that, in hope that our lives and what we do now will have some meaning after we are gone. Yes, we do hope for the future and in that way, perhaps, we Jews differ from all other peoples."

"How so?" she wondered aloud, half curious and half annoyed.

"For Christians, the greatest period in the history of the world is the time in the past when Jesus walked the earth. For Muslims, the era in which Mohammed lived is the most important in world history. But for the Jew, that time is not in the past. It is not with Abraham and Isaac on Mount Moriah, nor with Moses and the Children of Israel in their flight from bondage. Rather, it is in the future. The prophets speak of it. Isaiah tells us of it. It is the period when 'they shall beat their swords into plowshares and their spears into pruning hooks.' It is the era when 'nations shall not lift up sword against nation, nor shall they learn war anymore' (*Isaiah*). We work; we try to live our lives in such a manner that we shall be considered truly deserving. We pray to the Eternal One looking down on His loyal servants, that He will be moved to hasten the day when mankind can live in true and permanent peace. Perhaps, just perhaps, what we do this day will help... At least we hope so."

The noblewoman shook her head sadly from side to side while she cast her eyes on the cold, dark stone floor. She seemed unable to reply. After a while, she looked up. Her previously icy blue eyes had melted and were swimming in their tears. She reached for a handkerchief and wiped them. She blew her nose and cleared her throat, then spoke.

"Such stubbornness," she sighed. "Such pride. What a waste that someone with your will, your gift for language, should die for naught. What a shame that so fair a head should be food for jackals.

"Look! Alive, you could help me. You could advise me. We could make this a better world, even for *your* people. Is that not important? Is that not worthy of sacrifice?"

Again she halted. Her eyes smiled sadly at Avrum. Here before her, stood her conscience. He was her John the Baptist and she was Salome, a princess in a shimmering robe, yearning for approval. She desperately wanted him to tell her that what she was doing was right. And she desired more than that, more than she dared admit to herself. Her mind was caught in a war between desire and duty, between the needs of a woman and her perception of the obligations of the countess. Her face became distorted as the battle raged.

The battle ended abruptly. She looked suddenly different. Her lips were now rounded and moist as if pleading to be kissed.

"You're a silversmith, are you not?" she inquired gently.

"I am, your grace," he nodded.

"Let me see your hands," she asked with continued softness.

The countess studied his outstretched hands, soft yet gentle.

"I hear tell," she continued, "that you fashion objects of wondrous beauty, crowns with jingling bells and towers of fine filigree."

"Crowns for the Torah and spice boxes in the shape of towers for religious use. And other things – breastplates for the Torah and candle holders for one, two or three candles. I also make seven-candle menorahs like those in our ancient Temple in Jerusalem that was destroyed, and nine-candle menorahs that we light on Chanukah. That is the sort of artwork I do." (The Festival of Chanukah commemorates the victory of the Maccabees over the Syrians in the battle of the Hebrews for independence. When the Jews recaptured the Temple of Jerusalem, there was but a tiny bit of holy oil for the lamp in the Temple. Yet, the lamp burned for eight days, until fresh oil could be obtained. Eight candles represent the eight days, plus another candle used to light the others.)

"Could you fashion the form of my body in silver?" she asked, looking admiringly at her own figure where the robe clung close to her body.

"I could not, your highness," he replied, lowering his eyes to avert a direct view of her magnificent body.

She spotted this and pressed forward with continued passion. "Could not? Surely it is not that you lack craft?"

Avrum looked pained. "It's just that I never fashion human form. There's an injunction against graven images in the Commandments. We have interpreted it to inhibit such effort."

"Graven image!" she laughed. "So you picture yourself worshiping my body when you run your fingers over the curves and across my..." Her laugh changed to a grin and then to a frown. "I've heard tell that your women all wear wigs, and that beneath the wigs they are shaven as bald as some of our gentlemen are. But the wigs of Jewish women are plain and drab, whereas our gentlemen wear handsome ones, powdered white to add to their appeal. The clothing worn by your women is simple and coarse. They seem to try as much as possible to make beauty, plain, and plain, ugly. They never wear garments such as those I am wearing, even if they can afford them." She paused reflectively. "I suppose the intent is to make them less appealing to their neighbors' husbands."

"It is not proper to have a woman distract other men. There's enough weakness of the flesh without it. So modesty is becoming and right for us."

She studied his face again. *A fine face*, she thought, *even with the beard and the sidecurls. Those honey-golden locks, those gentle cheeks, pale from lack of sun, lips not too narrow or full, lips meant for... Yes, he's a Jew, but he's also a man with the handsome beauty of a gallant warrior.* She smiled a benevolent smile. "Kneel before your ruler," she said aloud.

Avrum knelt before the countess.

"You've missed much," she went on in a soft appealing voice. "Look at me. Look at my hair: fine-spun gold to run your hands through. My lips: Do they not entice you? My body: Does it not erase from your mind all thoughts but one?

Avrum's face was lined with anguish. He looked down at the cold stone floor, rather than at the countess. "I beg of you," he implored, "do not ask me such questions."

"Come closer," she commanded with caressing sounds. The sword fell from her hand as she extended it towards the bearded Jew.

He raised his hand to his bowed head that turned from side to side in distress. "I cannot."

"But I command it," she insisted closing her eyes in anxious anticipation. There was a momentary silence, with only heavy breathing audible.

"No, gentle lady. Let me respect you from the distance."

She sensed his pain and murmured almost tearfully, "Please."

Avrum remained motionless. The countess fell to her knees. She seized his hands.

"I must not," he cried with pained determination as he sought to free himself.

"You must," she begged.

"No!"

The words burned like a dagger driven into her chest and twisted to heighten the pain. The cold steel of it awakened her to reality. Her hands retreated and hardened into bared claws. The heavy sighs changed to a hiss as her full sensuous lips narrowed and pursed with seething fury.

"You'll die for this – and by fire. The last thing you see will be me. Think of the folly of your refusal as the smoke burns your eyes, as the flames are lapping at your body, as your flesh bakes and chars."

All the while Avrum's eyes had been directed towards the ground. Now he raised them and fixed them resolutely on the countess. "Then there is nothing more for me to say," he nodded sadly.

"No," she replied with regained composure. The noblewoman tilted her head towards the door, seemingly ready to call for her guards, but a thought held her back. "Well, one thing more. I will not go back on my word. If, within one week, you or any of your group of ten, or any Jew in Dzikow, points the finger at a member of the Jewish community and says that person committed the crime, or if anyone, no matter how unlikely he appears as a candidate to have committed such an act, by word of mouth or written confession or even a nod, admits he is guilty, then that one alone shall suffer death and all the rest will go free."

The Jews of Dzikow were desperate to save their fellow Jews, their leaders. They sent a delegation to Israel ben Eliezer, the *Ba'al Shem Tov*. (The *Ba'al Shem Tov*, 1698-1760, was the founder and the first leader of Hasidism, a religious movement within Judaism that emphasizes devotion to God through joyous song, dance and happiness in a mystical ecstasy. The movement began in Eastern Europe.) The delegation set out on the journey to Medzibuz in the Ukraine, hoping that this spiritual leader could do something, perhaps bring about a miracle to save ten pious Jews. Spring floods had washed out many of the roads they planned to take. It took several weeks to reach their destination. When at last they were brought into the presence of the founder of the Hasidic movement and had presented their plea for divine assistance, the *Ba'al Shem Tov* told them they were too late.

The ten men were dead. They had been brought to the bank of the San River and were tied together in a circle atop a huge pile of wood. The sky was dark and threatening and a bitter wind bit at their faces. But not for long. Thousands of Polish peasants had gathered along the riverbank with their numbers spilling over into the forest. They had come to witness the event.

The countess, herself, raised the torch that was to light the flame. "Behold," she declared in a booming voice, "the torch in my right hand. As they murdered our child, Stanislaus, for his blood, and baked the blood of his pure body in an oven, so shall their bodies be consumed by flame as punishment and as a warning to all others that those who transgress against the sons and daughters of the Church shall pay dearly for their crimes."

There were prayers, then cries of pain as the flames licked the bodies of the ten trapped men. At last, their voices were stilled and they were consumed into ashes. During all this, the noblewoman's eyes were glued to the fair-haired Jew with the beard of straw and honey. At the same time, his eyes were directed to the heavens.

"Look at me!" she screamed to no avail. His eyes and his spirit were elsewhere.

The flames died down. Nothing was left but ashes and charred bones and embers. The noblewoman's anger could not be stilled. He had not surrendered, even in death.

"Here," she declared, lifting a handful of ashes, "are the ashes of those who would murder our children. I cast them into the river, cleansing our holy soil."

A gust of wind came up from out of nowhere. It blew the ashes she had just tossed in the air, back into her face.

She cried out in pain, "I can't see! I can't see! Avrum, you did this to me!"

Guards rushed to her assistance, pouring gallons of river water on her head and into her eyes. Her eyes were still icy blue, but they stared blankly at a darkened world.

"Abraham, Isaac," she continued, "I didn't mean it. Save me! Save me, Jesus. I couldn't help it. Help me! Help me!"

Her tears and her pleas were in vain. There was not a blemish on her eyes, yet she could not see. She had to be led away from the riverbank and back to Castle Tarnowski to live and rule in blindness.

A year later, a messenger arrived at Castle Tarnowski with news that Stanislaus Wojewski had returned. Where had he been during that tragic year? With

Gypsies. A band of Gypsies had come through Dzikow on that Saturday in 1750 when stormy rain had melted the last of the winter snow. Bored with his life in a small town, Stanislaus had joined the band, leaving no word of his departure. But traveling from town to town and sleeping in the back of a wagon or on cold damp ground, soon lost its appeal. When the Gypsy band neared his home again, he crept away in the quiet of the night to rejoin his mother.

"Then there was no death, no murder, no crime," the noblewoman concluded with a heavy heart and voice to match. "I must make amends to the families of the ten. Perhaps then my vision will be restored."

Sarah Azubel refused to accept anything from the countess. She had learned from her husband before his death of his conversation with the ruler. "She did not simply execute ten innocent men," Sarah explained to the families of the other victims. "She murdered ten men she knew to be innocent."

After that, none of the widows or orphan children would accept "blood money" to ease the noblewoman's conscience.

Countess Tarnowski, weighed down by the gravity of her crime, issued a decree. It stated that from that time on, she and her heirs – as long as there was a House of Tarnowski – would supply all the firewood necessary to heat the synagogue of Dzikow.

But she remained blind for the rest of her life. It was a life spent in prayer and doing penance. Her long, never-ending night was filled with terrifying images. One image overshadowed the rest. It was that of a bearded face looking up at the sky as flames enveloped it. Words were remembered. "The last thing you see will be me." Only that sentence, uttered by her lips, had been cast upon herself. For his eyes were directed at some higher power, while hers beheld him. He was the last human being she saw before her sight was taken from her. The flames to which she had condemned the Jews in her anger were now trapping her and singeing her flesh. Her cries in the night that echoed throughout the castle would interrupt the scene, only to have the images return in her fitful sleep. There was no rest for her until death came to relieve her of the burden of life.

Her heirs continued to supply firewood to the synagogue each year, in accordance with the directions laid down by their ancestor. The tradition continued, generation after generation.

In the frigid winter of 1927, the head of the House of Tarnowski, living in the Republic of Poland, decided that enough was enough. Ten lives, he concluded, had been more than paid for in wood. The story of the Passover Conspiracy had to be finally buried and erased from memory. And so the donation was ended.

A NAME

AT TIMES, some who have asked about my nationality have commented that my name sounds German.

I reply to them: "My name may sound German, but I am not German; I am a Jew. My real family name is Azubel. In fact, Ausubel was an insult name."

"An insult?"

"Yes, an insult. Let me tell you the origin of my name."

A Jew learns to live with tragedy: He has no other choice. He returns to his work when the *shivah* (seven days of mourning following the burial) is concluded, resumes the toils of life and the cares of the day. He suffers in silence, but he remembers – in the quiet of his home or during the sanctification of the Lord in the *Kaddish* prayer. (A prayer recited by mourners to sanctify and glorify God's name. It does not mention death.) To the outside world this may seem indifference, but the Lord of Hosts knows better. The Omnipresent hears the hushed wail of the widow and sees the choked tears of the orphan. He perceives the questioning eyes of the faithful. "How long, O Lord?" they ask. But there is no answer.

So did the Azubels carry on. The sons learned the craft of the father – turning beaten silver and gold into religious objects of beauty in praise of the Almighty. The boys grew to manhood in Dzikow, a town too small to support two such craftsmen.

Moshe, the elder of the two sons, decided to leave. He bid a tearful farewell to his mother and brother and moved on. The year was 1760. Poland, despite its basic weakness – a weak central government – was still a land that stretched so far, a man could ride in a straight direction for more than a week and still not reach the other end of the country.

In the town of Rozwadow, not far from where he had started, Moshe found the environment conducive to his needs. He met and married a local Jewish girl and settled down in the town to raise a family in the faith of his fathers.

There were but thirty Jewish families in the town. All worked as craftsmen or tradesmen under the protection of Prince Georg Lubomirski, commander of a royal Polish regiment and ruler of the area. They sold their wares to the Polish peasants and an occasional nobleman in the surrounding area on the two market days of the week, Tuesday and Thursday. They paid their taxes to the Prince, their lord and protector.

Moshe, with his knowledge of precious metals and precious stones, turned to earning a living as a *luftmensch*. Literally translated, it means "air man." The occupation was one in which he was to procure something a buyer agreed to purchase at a specific price. To achieve this he had to locate a seller and buy the item from him. For example, if Prince Lubomirski desired a tiara with certain gems – each of a specific size and quality – to present to his wife, he and Moshe would agree on the price the prince would pay for it. Moshe would then travel to a place where such an item could be obtained and purchase it. A keen knowledge of market conditions in many places was necessary for his survival. Failure to deliver the promised goods was unthinkable. His handshake was his solemn word and could not be broken, even if it resulted in substantial monetary loss.

The occupation had its dangers. Travel in those days was hazardous. There were brigands frequently waiting in hiding at any roadside. When on the road, Moshe usually dressed in shabby clothing to divert attention from his person. He would conceal the money or valuables he was carrying in the lining of his tattered garments.

In eighteenth-century Poland, Jews did most of this type of work. They were willing to take great risks for a much smaller profit margin than were their non-Jewish competitors. It was not that they thrilled at the idea of engaging in perilous activity; it was simply a question of facing the reality of their condition. Barred from safer occupations, prohibited from owning land outside their ghettoes, and driven from country to country, the Jew had learned to live by his wits and take greater risks to survive.

Moshe eagerly looked forward to his stays at home. They provided him with respites from the dangers of the road; from the difficulties in obtaining kosher food; and the loneliness that was part and parcel of his separation from his wife and children. He longed to sit at his desk, reviewing the Scriptures and the Commentaries. His sons, Judah and Samuel, would sit at his feet and listen to their father as he told them stories from the holy books and from the post-biblical period.

When in Rozwadow, Moshe would rise early and take his sons to morning services. The small Jewish community had no rabbi and, in view of his considerable knowledge of ritual and the Scriptures, Moshe would lead the prayers and chant the portions from the Torah and the Prophets at the service. In the late afternoon he would return to the synagogue for further prayers. The two boys were particularly proud and attentive when their father chanted from the Torah.

It was a day in the fall of 1772. Moshe, now a gray-bearded man with deep-set, thoughtful eyes, sat at his desk. He was reviewing the Talmud with concentrated intensity. A question of law confronted him: Jewish law. He needed to consult the sages of old. There was no *Beit Din* (a Jewish court of law) in Rozwadow or in any of the nearby villages, and so the members of the Jewish community had sought Moshe's scholarly views.

"What was to become of Leah bat (daughter of) Hershel?" he asked himself.

A young man, handsome in the eyes of some, rogue in the view of others, had come to their town some years before. He had dazzled Leah's parents with his winning ways and had proposed to marry their daughter. The parents had readily accepted the young man and entrusted him with the family's savings to be used to start a new business. The young man went off with the entire sum, ostensibly to purchase merchandise with which to begin the enterprise. Three years had passed and he had not returned.

"Killed by bandits. What a tragedy," thought those enamored with the young man.

"Bandits should have gotten him before he ever set foot in Rozwadow," concluded most of the others. "The scoundrel's made off with a family's savings and left a fine young woman in limbo."

What to do? How long must he be missing before being presumed dead? In the meantime, Leah, who never cared a wit for the young man in the first place, was getting older. And no Jew would think of marrying a girl betrothed to another unless she received a *get* (a divorce or cancellation of a betrothal). But how could she obtain one from a man who wasn't there?

Moshe had his own views about the young man, but they did not matter here. Decisions could only be based on law, and in the Jewish community the laws of the Scriptures prevailed. To consult the local civil authorities was unthinkable. And so he sought advice from the writings of the Talmudic authorities Joseph Karo and Johanan ben Zakkai and Rabbi Josse. The disturbed expression on his face suddenly disappeared, giving way to unconcealed joy as he came across a passage on the next page.

"She's not betrothed at all," he announced to an empty room.

He read on feverishly. Sentences, paragraphs and pages were chewed up and gulped down with the zeal of a hungry man drinking from a bowl of soup after a week of starvation and thirst in the desert.

A few minutes later, he had finished. His mind and his stomach were at ease. He closed the weighty volume on a marker and looked up. His head nodded up and down from time to time as he carefully reviewed the facts in his mind, trying to be sure of the basis for his conclusion.

Betrothal would only have occurred, he thought, *after the young man made his proposal to the prospective bride and a token of that proposal was received and accepted by her. But he hadn't proposed to Leah. How could he? She detested him. And no token was offered, or kept. Hence, there was never any betrothal. Leah is free. In fact, she's been free all along, but nobody realized it. Her family has been defrauded of their life's savings. Too bad. But there's no reason to compound the misfortune by ruining a young girl's life.*

With a rush of excitement, he rose to get his jacket. Hershel had to be informed of the good news.

A loud knock on the front door interrupted his happy state. The pounding continued. He went to the front door and cautiously began to open it. Eliezer ben Shmaya HaLevi literally forced his way in. Fear, cold numbing fear, was written on Eliezer's face. His cheeks were devoid of color, an ashen white, as if all the blood had been drained from them. Eliezer's eyes, icy pale blue, were staring wildly, as if they had just seen something horrible. The whole of his small body trembled with alarm.

"Rev Moshe, the Austrian army is marching into Rozwadow! What are we to do?" ("Rev" is short for "rabbi." It is a term of respect when addressing a man of learning, rather than denoting that the man was a rabbi.)

Moshe placed an arm on the shoulder of his excited friend. "Calm yourself, Rev Eliezer. I don't think they will do anything to us. Besides, there's nothing we can do about it."

Eliezer's face changed from one of excitement and terror to an appearance of confusion mixed with annoyance. "I don't understand. You sound as if you knew something about this beforehand. How else could you be so calm? Don't you realize that this means war? When Prince Lubomirski brings his regiment here to drive out the Austrians, we'll be in the middle of a battle." His mind raced wildly. "Maybe we should get our families out of the town. We can hide in the countryside until the smoke clears. Maybe –"

"Rev Eliezer," interrupted Moshe, with his right hand raised vertically like a judge ordering silence in the court, "please, sit in that comfortable chair, the one with the pillows. I'll pour you a glass of whiskey. Then we can talk in a relaxed manner."

Moshe went to the cabinet in the corner of the room. He opened it and withdrew a bottle of clear amber liquid. Then he filled two small glasses and handed one to the now-seated Eliezer. Finally, Moshe slid calmly onto his chair near the desk and sipped from his glass of whiskey. Eliezer finished his drink with one quick gulp. His Adam's apple rose and then fell as the fluid rushed down. He cleared his throat with a low growling sound, but said nothing. Moshe's glass was still half full, but he placed it on his desk.

"Rev Eliezer, I had gotten wind of something like this about to happen, but I did not know for certain until you arrived with the news. Last month I was in Krakow. While there, I heard that Poland's neighbors were planning to help themselves to pieces of Poland."

Again, Eliezer's eyes widened with astonishment.

"Don't look so shocked," continued Moshe. "It's an age-old story. The strong gobble up the weak. Poland is weak, and Austria, Prussia and Russia are stronger, particularly when acting together. Like jackals, they tear at the flesh of their wounded sister state as she hemorrhages to death. The speculation was that Austria would seize Galicia. Now it's no longer speculation."

"Rev Moshe, who told you this?"

"Is it important that you know? – Well...it was told to me, in confidence, by an Austrian with whom I have had dealings."

"And what will Prince Lubomirski do? After all, he's got a lot of soldiers. Do you think he'll give up without a fight?" Eliezer paused and then added tremulously, "A-a-a-and what will happen to us?"

"The prince will do nothing. He'll still be a prince and still have the same land. But the soldiers will not wear Polish uniforms, only the ones with the royal blue of Austria. It doesn't change the system, only the name of the monarch and the location of the capital. As for us, we'll be as we have always been...under someone's thumb. Only it will be an Austrian thumb instead of a Polish thumb."

Eliezer listened attentively to Moshe's words. His face slowly lost its appearance of agitation and became more placid. *His logic is undeniable,* thought the tavern-keeper. *For a Jew, nothing has really changed.*

Eliezer rose. Aloud, he said, "Thank you, Rev Moshe, for the whiskey and the information. I'd better get back to my tavern." Smiling, he added, "These Austrians may want food and drink."

The next few weeks were quiet ones for Moshe and his family. The peasants in the surrounding countryside were initially in a state of panic. But as time passed without any meaningful change in their condition, they resumed their normal activities that included trips to the town to buy wares on market days. Moshe was involved in a few local sales of property, but he had not received any orders for unusual items. There had been no requirement for travel. He kept hoping that the change in rulers would not make life worse for his family.

A few months later, Moshe learned that their new ruler, Kaiser Joseph, was making changes that affected the Jews in particular. There were new rules. The right of Jews to sell liquor in rural communities such as Rozwadow was severely restricted. His friend, Eliezer, found his tavern empty much of the time. The Kaiser commanded the Jews to engage in farming, but he did not give them land to cultivate. Jews were forbidden to enter certain occupations. Last and most devastating, poor Jews were ordered deported from Galicia. The idea of being driven from their homes and pushed across the border into Lublin (a province in the Kingdom of Poland, lying to the east of Galicia later seized by Russia) or, worse still, Russia, brought terror to the hearts of every Jew in the province.

One day, the Jews of Rozwadow, men, women and children, were ordered to go to the town hall. Moshe, his wife Esther and their sons, Judah and Samuel, lined up along with the other Jews of the town. Moshe wore a pale, brave smile as he tried to reassure his anxious wife who stood fidgeting with her dark wig. Her forehead was lined with consternation at the thought of an encounter with the Austrian authorities. The boys, their eyes wide with curiosity, had not yet learned to fear contact with the authorities the way their elders had. To the adult Jews of the community, nothing good could come of such a meeting; only new burdens and new forms of oppression. To Judah and Samuel, it was a chance to look at those funny "tin soldiers" standing in front of the town hall.

Moshe watched the boys' joyful playing for a while and then called a halt to their activities.

"It's best not to attract too much attention in front of *them*," he said in quiet rebuke, his eyes looking toward the Austrian soldiers guarding the entrance to the building. "They sometimes find it annoying to see a happy Jew. So save your playing for when they're not around."

Hershel ben Yaakov entered the village square and looked with troubled curiosity at the long line of Jews. Upon seeing Moshe, he rushed over.

"What do they want of us?" he inquired.

"They want to give us names, all of us, including the children."

"What a strange idea," puzzled Hershel. "We all already have names." A smile suddenly appeared on his lips. "By the way, I have good news. We have – I mean Leah has – Leah is betrothed...to Rev Isaac's son Motel." Nodding his head as if to indicate approval of his own words, he added, "It's better that a girl marry someone from the village, someone she's known all her life. Strangers are not to be trusted. Don't you agree?"

Moshe's face blanched ever so slightly. "I was once a stranger in Rozwadow."

"Oh," replied Hershel without the slightest change in expression to hint at comprehension, "that's different. You're one of *us* now."

"Rev Hershel, forgive me for pointing out that you can have seen a person a thousand times and have lived in the same village as he has all your life, and never really have known him; or you can know someone who was a stranger just a few weeks ago. The sages tell us that every man is presumed to be honest until shown otherwise. Yet, we each should try to act wisely and show caution, lest we be made the fool. Presume a man's honesty, but let his actions, not his looks or wit, show whether he is worthy of trust."

"Well then," smiled Hershel, "Motel's actions certainly seem worthy of trust. The little we've been able to give as a dowry could hardly be the attraction. Then again, with his looks..." Hershel's right hand went to his cheek as his mouth opened in laughter.

"He's a fine young man, Rev Hershel," said Moshe, trying to bring a halt to the howling laugh. "I'm sure they'll be happy together. Don't you think that's what really matters, not the place of his birth?"

"Of course, of course... All this talk about fools and sages, neighbors and strangers – it's way over my head. And you shouldn't take offense, Rev Moshe. How can you compare... I mean how can you think...when I spoke of strangers... I mean you... You bear the name..."

"The name?"

"You know what I mean... Your father. I mean Rozwadow is not so far from Dzikow. Everyone in Rozwadow has heard about him."

"Because my father died a martyr – that makes me acceptable? Lord of the universe!" Moshe's right hand rose to his bearded cheek and his mouth remained open in consternation.

After a moment, he went on, "Rev Hershel, David's goodness did not guarantee Absalom's fidelity. It is true that we should do what we can to preserve our parent's good name, but a good father is no guarantee of a good son. Each of us makes his own way in the world."

"I don't understand what you're saying. Surely a person's background counts. Why, look what happened to us when we tried to have our daughter marry two notches above us. Now that we've fallen flat on our faces, we can't go farther down. So our daughter will marry someone from the bottom, a man with a big nose and a little jaw, the son of a tailor. And she'll be content with that."

"Content?" said Moshe, annoyed. "She accepted the betrothal, so she must *want* to marry him. And please don't look down on his features or his father's occupation. Did not the Lord tell us to not look on outward appearance, but to the heart (from *1 Kings*: 16:7)? Did he not choose even a king from the sons of a humble man? If we followed your logic, David would have remained a shepherd playing a harp and never become king of Israel."

"But that was the Bible," insisted Hershel as he found no relationship between the discussion and the quotation.

"The Bible is what we base our lives on. That's what makes us who we are."

"Rev Moshe, it's just what I said. You must be descended from the prophets. All those nice words. It's like the Haftorah portion; filled with all those phrases no one can understand... But I must rush home to get my family. If they want to give us names, we'll oblige them. God be with you, Rev Moshe."

Hershel rushed off, while Moshe and his family moved forward slowly.

Group by group, the families entered the town hall through the main entrance and left by the side door.

"I'm afraid Hershel hasn't learned much," commented Moshe aside to his wife. "He still judges people by their names and their faces."

"Motel's a fine fellow," commented Judah, overhearing his father. "At least he's been nice to Samuel and me."

"That, my son, is more important than his looks. And Leah accepted the betrothal. She must see something in him, something meaningful that her parents have missed. At least now they will have a chance for happiness."

"Did Rev Hershel really give away all that money?"

"Judah," interrupted Moshe, "what they lost was money...not that foolishness with money is to be complimented. But at least no life was lost. And their intentions were good. If we learn from these mistakes so that they become fewer, some good will come of it yet. Remember: Feel with your heart, but think with your brain. If you're lucky, they may agree."

Another family entered the building and the Azubels moved up again.

Eliezer ben Shmaya and his family exited the town hall via the side door. Seeing Moshe, Eliezer turned. He signaled his family to wait and then approached the Azubels.

"*Reich*" (rich), they named me," said the tavern-keeper laughing bitterly.

"With all the restrictions they've put on my inn, *Arm* (poor) would be more appropriate."

Eliezer then rushed away to rejoin his family in crossing the village square. They disappeared into the tavern.

A few minutes later, it was the Azubels' turn to enter the town hall. Moshe looked around with an appraising eye as he walked. Two Austrian soldiers stood, stiff and silent, near the entrance. Their rifles were held tightly at their sides. You had to look hard to see breathing, to detect signs of life. "Samuel is right," thought Moshe, "they are tin soldiers."

Inside were several army men, two officers, as well as several soldiers in the ranks. One soldier pointed to a desk at the far corner of the room.

An Austrian captain sat behind the desk. He was dressed in a fancy uniform with a stiff collar and shiny gold buttons. The officer was fondling his sand-colored moustache with one hand while adjusting a monocle with the other.

Moshe had met such men before – vain, supercilious, self-centered men, who looked not at you but through you, at an imagined mirror in which they could admire their own likeness.

He remembered a galloping rider, a nobleman he presumed, on the road to Krakow. The man was impeccably dressed from the handsome cap on his head to the fine woolen jacket that whistled in the wind, to his firm leather riding boots. The rider struck his horse again and again, seemingly just for the fun of it. Man and horse came closer and closer. Moshe suddenly realized that they were headed straight for him. He ran to the left, but the horse changed course and kept heading in his direction. The rider's laughing eyes were glued to his target. At the last second, Moshe dove off the road, down into a gully, to escape certain destruction. The nobleman kept riding, his gleeful howl carried on the wind. He never looked back to see whether the shabbily dressed Jew were dead or alive.

Moshe's reflections left the road and moved to a big city. He recalled a scene – a sidewalk cafe. There were faces, white, dull red and gray, in the shadows, illuminated by the flickering light of candles. Moshe was sitting at a small table in the corner of the room. Opposite him sat a merchant planning improvements in his shop, in a drab monotonous voice. But Moshe's eyes were elsewhere, having been drawn away by a loud exchange between two men with boorish faces. Both were army officers. One was bragging of female "conquests," while the other roared his approval. Mug after mug of beer was downed between coarse descriptions which brought waves of nausea to Moshe's lips.

The captain sitting behind the desk in the town hall withdrew a handkerchief from his pocket. He blew onto his monocle and then proceeded to clean it with the handkerchief. He seemed indifferent to the Azubels standing before him. His head turned and he muttered something about "being tired of dealing with these oily people" to the lieutenant standing some distance away. The junior officer sneered his agreement.

The sound of paper being shuffled caught Moshe's attention, and his eyes moved to the right of the officer. A soldier with the stripes of a sergeant sat there beside his captain. He held a quill in his right hand and was rear-ranging several sheets before him with his left hand. To Moshe, he was like hundreds of border guards and minor bureaucrats he had encountered in his time – men who recorded names and places without seeing faces, men who learned to write, but not to comprehend. They had their function, he thought. What it was, he was not sure.

Whatever the reason, the tin soldiers, the supercilious captain, the lieu-tenant and the officious sergeant – they were here in control. In their view of the universe, a Jew was some dark, conniving creature from the underworld, slimy and slithering, a snake without feelings. Moshe was determined not to grovel before them, but he had no wish to provoke their anger. He would take the middle road – respectful silence. Moshe removed his cap, revealing a skullcap covering his salt and pepper hair. He took another step towards the captain's desk, cap in hand.

"Well," said the captain sharply, "what are your names and occupa-tions? It's for the census. You Jews don't have family names, so I'll give you your occupation as a family name if it sounds right to me... Don't look so surprised. It has a purpose. We're assigning family names so as to know who has paid his taxes and who has not, who is to remain in Galicia and who is to be pushed across the border. We can't have fifty people each named Abraham son of Jacob.

"Well then, what are your names and occupations?"

Moshe tried hard to appear respectful in front of the Austrian officer. He nodded his head in a slight bow and replied:

"Your Excellency, I am Moshe ben Avraham Azubel, a *luftmensch*. This is my wife, Esther and these are our sons, Judah and Samuel. My wife cares for our home and my sons study Torah."

The officer looked puzzled. "Moshe what? I've heard some of you Jews call yourselves Cohen or Levi, but A-zu-bel? What kind of name is that?"

"Your Excellency, it has been handed down from generation to genera-tion and has some religious significance, as do Cohen and Levi."

"Never mind," snapped the captain impatiently. He looked to the sol-dier beside him and added, "Sergeant, we'll call him Moses Ausübel – 'Moses out of evil.' That's a good name for a Jew. Call his wife Esther Ausübel and the two children Judah Ausübel and Samuel Ausübel. Mark it down.

"Next."

Moshe and his family, somewhat perplexed, slowly filed out of the town hall and returned to their home.

As they entered the house, Judah looked up at his father and asked, "Why did he call us Ausübel – out of evil – Papa? Do we have to keep such a name?"

"Judah, a name is what you make it. The name Azubel has stood for something, something meaningful. Ask the people around here: they'll tell you. Now we are to be called Ausübel. If we lead good and honorable lives and hold steadfast to our faith in the Almighty, that name, too, will be remembered with honor. We will keep the name Ausübel, but we shall not forget our past."

Two hundred years later, in 1977, the name Ausübel is no longer to be found in Rozwadow or anywhere in Galicia. The Holocaust erased the name from the province like a killer tornado sweeping up people and homes and even tombstones.

The descendants of Moses Ausübel live on in the United States, Canada, Australia, Switzerland and Israel. They have become scientists, physicians, dentists, oral surgeons, lawyers, psychiatrists, psychologists, architects, social workers, writers, teachers, accountants, hospital administrators, leading economists, prominent environmentalists, movie producers, successful businessmen, and even a Nobel Prize nominee. They have not dishonored his name.

THE MARRIAGE OF AN INDEPENDENT JEWISH WOMAN

In the *shtetls* of Europe, the place of women was in the home. In childhood, girls were taught to cook and clean and to raise children. The boys went to *cheder* (Hebrew school), and the scholars were then to go on to the *yeshiva* (academy for higher Jewish studies). Schooling for girls did not exist.
But there were exceptions, and I am the descendant of one such exception.

Each spring the dark earth is recalled to life by the sound of raindrops. Nature blossoms forth with an orchestra of color – green and gold, red and violet. Summer's warmth, like the mellow trumpet, brings spirit and vibrancy to the budding world. In the security of a warm nest, baby sparrows listen to the chirping of their elders, preparing for the day when they, too, will soar into the blue and seek mates to share a home of their own.

A chilling autumn wind plays deep notes on the eternal cello, heralding the retreat of youth to age. One burst of color remains: the final glow of the flame before the fire of life goes out, and then…the long winter's darkness.

We are born; we live and share this earth; we die. But we leave something behind – some word, some mark, some little change from what had been before. And the history of the world is the sum of those tiny transformations.

The century that followed the arrival of Moses Azubel in Rozwadow saw many changes take place in the town. The name "Poland" disappeared from the map as greedy neighbors dismembered a nation that was too weak to resist. In the division of the spoils, Rozwadow became part of the Hapsburg Austrian Empire, just a few miles from territory that was annexed by Russia. The town became a major center of commerce and trade for the northeastern part of Galicia. The Jewish population of Rozwadow increased from thirty families to over 1,500 people, through natural increase coupled with new arrivals fleeing the land of the Tsar. Some Jews prospered in trade, but most remained small craftsmen and storekeepers. For the Followers of Moses, the religious center of the town was its two synagogues. There was but a single rabbi to guide the two congregations.

A son, Judah, was born to Moses and Shindel Silber Ausübel in 1871. Moses was sexton of one of the two synagogues of Rozwadow. Judah was the first of the fifth generation of Ausübels in the town.

Little Judah loved to visit his grandfather, Avraham Ausübel, and sit at the foot of the gray-bearded old man, listening to tales of long ago. The scenes Avraham depicted were diverse. They ranged from tiny villages to bustling towns and even big cities. There were Rozwadow and Dzikow and names of strange far-away places from beyond the mist of time. People appeared before Judah's eyes as words flowed from his grandfather's lips – dark-bearded sages and comic characters, good, simple people and demonic oppressors who hadn't a single redeeming feature in their characters. Bodies and faces took shape and the little boy could see them as clearly as if they were standing close enough for him to feel their breathing. Such is the nature of an oral history. Time is but a dimension, adding depth to the present.

One day, Judah took in his grandfather's winged words and was carried back to a scene in Avraham's youth. There, in the synagogue, stood the great *tzaddik* (righteous man), Rabbi Naphtali of Ropczyce. A wrinkled dark skullcap covered the rabbi's bald head. Thick bushy eyebrows stood like gray canopies above his deep, dark, piercing eyes. Long gray sidelocks, a walrus moustache and a great, flowing white beard covered his wizened face. Little Judah could see the rabbi raise an arm from under the black and white prayer shawl and point a bony commanding finger at the assembled congregants.

"*Tzedakah*," declared the rabbi in ringing tones, "is not something you give away from leftovers, after you have attended to all your needs and all your pleasures. It is a commandment, a duty that may not be avoided. As long as one of your brethren is in need of food or clothing or shelter, as long as there is one homeless widow or one hungry orphan, you are forbidden to look the other way. Find them and befriend them. Dig deep into your pockets and help them, for they are, in the sight of the Lord, the flesh of your flesh, your brothers and sisters, your parents and your children, *His* children. Follow the ways of the Lord of Hosts and He will be your shield and your provider. Fail to do so and no army and no gold will save you." (The Jewish belief in *Tzedakah*, "charity," which is derived from Hebrew words for "righteousness" and "justice," is based not simply on pity for the needy, but the principal of justice. It is based on the belief that we are all God's children and should therefore help one another.)

The boy's eyes glowed with the light of the message, even as the darkness of evening was enveloping them.

"It's late," said Avraham, smiling that wistful inner smile of spiritual joy. "Time for you to go home..." His face turned strangely sad as he went on: "And give your mother a hand... She looked so frail when I last saw her."

"I will, *Zeide*, (grandfather)," the boy replied as he reached for his dark jacket. "I'll see you in the synagogue, Saturday."

"And we'll listen to Rav (Rabbi) Moshe," said the old man with resumed cheer. "He's Rav Naphtali's grandson."

"Oh what a horrible sight it was," cringed the old man one day as he pictured the terrors of the Revolution of 1848. "The peasants hacked off one of those swollen fingers to get at his ring. He was an Austrian and an army officer, a symbol of their subjugation, but he was a man, a human being just like them. I'm almost certain he was dead already, but his body was jolted by the blow from the ax and bounced up as if his soul were crying out against the desecration of his mortal remains.

"I hid under the hay there in the barn, not daring to move, afraid even to tremble."

"But what had you to fear, *Zeide*? You weren't a soldier or even an Austrian. The Polish peasants were not being oppressed by you."

"Judah, a Jew always has something to fear. It's the length of your hair or the darkness of your clothing. Whatever. It has no relationship to reason, only to blind hatred. And the more aggressive they are, for whatever reason, the more you have to fear."

"Things don't seem so bad here," objected the lad.

"Today!" replied Avraham with emphasis. "But what of tomorrow? The Austrians understand this all too well. In Galicia they play us against the Poles in order to keep the power in their hands. Elsewhere it's the Hungarians pitted against the Rumanians. It's all the same except that the Jew is something special. They can all hate the Jew."

His *Zeide* was dead. His mother was dead and his father had remarried. Judah was not yet thirteen and the heaviness of the world was pressing on his shoulders. To the new woman of the house, Moses's second wife, the five children of Shindel were a lot of extra trouble. After all, Moses was a sexton, a position with religious significance but without any commensurate financial reward. Besides, she wished to have children of her own. How were her little ones to compete with five older siblings for the little there was on the Ausübel table?

Judah, the oldest, was the first to be sent off. There were no funds to send him to a *yeshiva* and so, on the day after his Bar Mitzvah, he said his farewells to childhood and to his brothers and sisters. He was not even five feet tall, but he would have to stand as a man. Judah packed a tattered bag with his clothing and a few other possessions. Sadly, Moses led the lad down the street to the carpenter's shop. Judah's new place of residence was only a few hundred yards from his former home, yet it was a world apart from the house in which he had spent his childhood. Judah was now to be an apprentice, learning a trade.

The boy looked up encouragingly at his father. Even one so young knew what it meant to his father – a man born to scholarship – not to be able to keep a son at home while the lad went to school.

"I'm looking forward to it," Judah smiled bravely. "I like to work with my hands... And I will see you every time you pass the shop... I hope the master will let me go to the synagogue... I'll make up the time. We can meet and pray together."

For the next six years Judah was an unpaid worker and domestic servant. He slept next to the stove and was responsible for keeping it burning during the cold winter months. Once, the flame went out and he was punished severely. It did not happen again. As an apprentice living in the home of his master, Judah's food was meager. It was limited to the scraps and leftovers in a land where even master carpenters and their families had barely enough to eat.

Judah's stature remained small, though his musculature expanded. He grew to manhood, short but powerful, with broad shoulders and strong arms that could support and balance enormous loads. He was a quiet man, a gentle man, not given to heavy drinking or intemperate speech. His demands were small, never voiced above a meek request, and his pleasures, simple: a warm fire on a cold night; a kind word at the end of the long day; a gold and red sunset; or the gaiety of a local festivity, a wedding or Bar Mitzvah. These were the things that evoked a smile from the little man. He was devout, never failing to pray early each morning and again each afternoon and evening, and he never missed a Sabbath service. Despite his short, squared beard, his face had the look of softness and tranquility. Puffy lower lids gave his eyes a sleepy, contented look, like that of a pet puppy whose chin had just been stroked. His nose, like his face, was unobtrusive, and his smallish mouth was almost hidden in the woolly, brown beard that covered the lower half of his countenance. From the moment he rose in the darkness of the early morning hours, to the darkness of the night when he went to sleep, a small black skullcap covered his dark-brown hair. When the weather permitted, he would work out of doors, his long brown sidecurls wafting in the breeze.

By the age of nineteen, Judah was thoroughly skilled in his craft. Still, the master carpenter kept delaying Judah's release. Finally, having passed every test of skill with which his master challenged him, the gentle young man was declared a master craftsman.

Judah opened his own shop in rented space. He now saved what he could from his scant earnings, after first providing funds for his younger siblings' education. At last, he accumulated enough money to buy an inexpensive piece of land away from the center of the town. With his two strong hands, and using whatever lumber he could spare, he built an enlarged home for his father. This served to reduce pressure on his brothers and sisters to leave, as happened to him.

The next task was a home and shop of his own. Another parcel of land was purchased. With loving care, a building was constructed. He had long pictured it in his mind – every board, every nail, the squares and the triangles. And now the dream became a reality. As the wood and the metal gave substance to his dream, he planned anew – the chairs and the table, the bed and the bureau, the objects that make a house a home.

Judah moved into the new quarters, eliminating a rental expense. He continued to devote his evenings to the project. Sturdy oak was carved and polished into quality furniture.

Prince Lubomirski, passing by his shop one day, observed the quality of his workmanship. He subsequently employed Judah's services on many occasions. Then too, the mere fact that the prince had employed Judah's services induced others to give the little craftsman employment. Judah's increased earnings allowed the purchase of those furnishings no carpenter could make. At last, the house was completed and furnished. The little carpenter was now ready to talk to his father about a matter of great importance.

"Papa," said Judah in a quiet, almost apologetic tone. "I'm ready to get married."

"A good point. I was about to bring it up myself. I've been talking to Motele the shoemaker. He has a daughter –"

"Excuse me, Father. I know that marriages are to be arranged by the parents, and that I'm not supposed to meet the bride until we're together under the canopy, but...you see...I already know whom I want to marry."

Moses's eyes rose in disbelief. He gripped his chest as if to steady a racing heart. Then he cleared his throat, uneasily. "Do you mean to tell me that you've discussed marriage with a girl?" He shook his head back and forth, refusing to accept that possibility. "You couldn't have. It would be a scandal... Who is she, anyway?"

"Papa, calm yourself. I didn't discuss marriage with her. I've never even spoken to her."

Moses's hand relaxed and fell to his side. He sighed in relief.

"But I did see her...from the distance," Judah added. "She's Chaya Sarah, daughter of Jacob Korn, the shipbuilder."

"Well," smiled Moses, almost unconsciously. "You have large ideas..." His cheeks reddened with embarrassment. "I didn't mean to make fun...of her height...or yours. I mean... Well. I couldn't afford to send you to the *yeshiva*... I mean...times were hard...You know what I mean. You're a carpenter, a man who works with his hands, and she's...Her father's a prosperous man and a scholar. He might want... Well, we can't expect a dowry."

"Papa, forget about the dowry. I don't want anything except her."

Moses's eyes moved far off as he ruminated. Then he looked at his son and began again.

"There are things you should know. Word of them has probably not come to your ears. How shall I put it? I'm told she is a very strong-willed young woman. I say woman, for she is older than most girls getting married these days. And perhaps that is no accident. For as eligible as she is, with a prosperous father and so forth, most of the fathers of eligible sons have avoided approaching her father."

Judah looked puzzled.

"You see," Moses went on, "she has expressed opinions to some of the women in Rozwadow, opinions that have shocked them. I don't mean that she is not an observant young woman, far from it. But I'm told that she discusses portions of the Torah and such, and comments on things said in the synagogue with which she disagrees. She spoke of the place of women in society: that there were women such as Deborah who led the Jewish people." (Deborah was judge and prophetess during the period detailed in the *Book of Judges*. She led the tribes of Israel in their war of liberation against their Canaanite oppressors. She was one of seven prophetesses of the Bible.)

"So what's wrong with that? There have been women who led our people in times gone by. As for opinions expressed in the synagogue – have you not, on occasion, disagreed with conclusions others have drawn?" asked Judah.

"That's different. I am a *man*.

"It's just that women are not trained in such things. They are supposed to learn to cook and clean and care for their husbands and children. Oh, they should know some prayers, to light the Sabbath candles and so forth.

But to debate scriptural material? A man is the head of the household; that's the way it's always been. Can you imagine a *yeshiva*-trained scholar coming home and having his wife debate with him on scripture? Next thing you know, she'll question his decisions. There would be no tranquility in the home."

Moses reflected again for a while and then added, "That's what becomes of Jacob Korn having his daughters educated by a home tutor."

Judah looked up at Moses. "If she's had an education, so much the better." He paused for a moment and then added, "I mean no disrespect, but do you not sometimes follow the dictates of your wife?"

"Dictates of my wife?"

"Yes. Such as when you sent me off to become a carpenter's apprentice and when you did the same with Shulum (Moses Ausübel's second son by his first wife). Joseph was much younger. He, too, would have been sent off to become an apprentice after he became a Bar Mitzvah, if not for the fact that I provided the funds for him to study at the *yeshiva*."

Moses flushed with embarrassment. After a while, he said, "I'm sorry... I guess you're right. I'm sorry that we did not have the resources to further your education or to send Shulum to the *yeshiva*. You're right about wives. We men may delude ourselves into thinking we are the masters of our households when, realistically, women are running the place."

"I didn't mean to cause you embarrassment. And as for Chaya Sarah being a strong-willed woman, I would honor the advice of a woman who is both a wife and a scholar."

"Honor?"

"Yes, honor."

Moses ruminated briefly with his hand firmly gripping his bearded chin. Then he said, "I'll handle the matter. I'll try. But Judah, don't tell a soul that you even set eyes on her. It wouldn't look right."

Chaya Sarah sat at her desk, reading Rashi's *Commentaries on the Torah*. Her eyes were luminous, glowing with the marvel of what she was reading. After a while, she closed the book on a marker and held the volume to her chest. She breathed deeply as if to draw in the words and the pages, the logic, the concepts, the inspiration.

How wonderful it would have been to study with him, she thought. *But that was 800 years ago. I don't know whether or not he taught girls the Torah.*

It was an early fall day. The bright light of the sun, coming through the window, fell on the pallid face of the tall, willowy brunette. She had dark, pensive eyes. Her face had a haunting beauty, austere, yet sensitive. But hidden within were her finest qualities: a brilliant mind and a passion to experience all the beauty, all the wonder that the world had to offer. The warm rays of the sun gave her a sense of tranquility.

Her eyes wandered from the closed book to the window and then to the river beyond. A barge was moving slowly down the San River. It passed just a few hundred yards from the window. Its deck was piled high with lumber. She pictured the barge leaving Galicia, gliding down the San to the Vistula, passing the villages of Russpolant (the Russian-ruled part of Poland) on the way to Germany. Chaya Sarah imagined the vessel arriving at the port of Danzig on the Baltic Sea. She pictured gleaming spires and bustling streets against a blue sky and blue waters. She saw ladies of fashion and hawkers of wares, men who were anticipating voyages beyond the horizon as they stared out of offices facing the harbor, and scholars who contemplated the meaning of it all. Her arms folded across her waist. She hugged herself with joy as she imagined traveling on one of the barges her father built, and arriving at distant shores. A half smile appeared on her usually serious face. The barge passed and she could see Rozwadow on the far side of the river. There were a series of puffs of smoke on the other side of the river, which were coming closer to the town.

It must be the train from Krakow, Prague, Vienna and places beyond, she thought happily. *I would love to go to Vienna someday and visit the concert halls, the theaters and the museums. It's not hard to get to Vienna now that there's a railroad linking Rozwadow to the capital.*

Suddenly she was distracted by the sight of the ferry that was just arriving at Branwica dock from the Rozwadow side of the river. Her father stepped off the ship, along with the other passengers. Tall and slender, clothed in the dark clothing traditional to the Orthodox, he headed towards their home. He came closer. She observed a smile on his face.

What's he up to? she wondered.

Jacob knocked at the door. Chaya Sarah quickly opened it. She threw her arms around his shoulders and kissed his cheek.

"Papa," she said, "I'm so happy you came home just now. I've been thinking."

"Yes, Chaya Sarah, I've been thinking too –"

"Papa," she interrupted hastily, "your barges go down the San and the Vistula with lumber and other goods that the Danzig Merchants ship to Germany. Do they also take passengers on board to see Danzig and the other cites along the route?" (The Danzig Merchants were a small number of members of the Jewish community of Rozwadow who were involved in trade with the Germans in Danzig. They bought up lumber and grain in the surrounding district and shipped those commodities by barge down the San and Vistula Rivers. They were the wealthiest Jews.)

"No passengers. The merchants of Rozwadow travel to Danzig by land."

"Papa, have you ever thought of going to Vienna for a visit? You know I'm twenty and have learned my lessons well, but I could study and learn even more in Vienna."

"I thought of going to Vienna...a long time ago. But let's not discuss that now. You're twenty. My little girl has blossomed into womanhood. There are things we must talk about, things that should concern a grown woman... But first, for a little while, I'd like to speak to my little girl."

Jacob removed his dark felt hat, revealing a black skullcap. He took off his knee-length dark coat, exposing a dark suit. Then he walked to his favorite chair and sat down. His taut, fine-boned face was enveloped in a sea of brownish hair – the beard and sidecurls of an Orthodox Jew. The skin was tanner than his daughter's, the product of weathering air and water. The nose, thin and not overly long, bore the freckles of prolonged exposure to the elements. His soft, brown eyes looked pleasantly at his little girl, now grown so tall.

"What did you study today?"

Chaya Sarah's eyes widened and she responded eagerly.

"Papa, I was reading Rashi's *Commentaries*. He makes a most interesting point."

"Which one are you referring to?"

"The meaning of the word 'recognize,' Papa.

"In the story of Joseph and his brothers, you remember that Joseph was sold into slavery by his brothers (except for Benjamin), and that Joseph was later able to interpret the Pharaoh's dream. As a result, he became an important man in Egypt, the right hand of the ruler of the Nile. When the seven lean years he foresaw came to pass, Joseph's brothers were sent by their father to Egypt to buy grain. They bowed before Joseph, now the Egyptian overlord. It says in the *Book of Genesis*, 'And Joseph recognized his brethren but they recognized him not.' Rashi points out the dual meaning of the passage. The simple and obvious interpretation is that Joseph saw them and recognized their features. Joseph had been beardless when his brothers sold him into slavery and now he had a full beard and wore the garments of an important person. And so his brothers did not recognize his features or his attire when they bowed before him.

"But there is a second meaning to the word 'recognize.' Joseph recognized his brethren, meaning that now that they were within his power, he recognized them as his brothers and took pity on them. He ended by treating them with brotherly love. By contrast, when Joseph, at an earlier time, had fallen into the power of his brothers, they had not recognized him as a brother and did not act towards him in a brotherly manner.

"I think that this second message has universal application. We are all God's children and should act towards one another as brothers and sisters. This holds true for Jews and Gentiles alike. When the Tsars of Russia send their Cossacks through the villages where Jews live – raping, robbing and murdering – they are not treating the Jews as fellow children of the Almighty. One of the key points of 'recognize' is to treat those you think of as adversaries in a brotherly manner, even when they fall into your power."

Jacob rose and approached his daughter. He placed his arm gently around her shoulder. She inclined her head towards him and he looked deeply into her eyes.

"Chaya Sarah, you are my eldest and, perhaps I shouldn't say this, my most beloved child. You have the ability to understand, to get to the deeper meaning of things. It is a wisdom few men can match...and none that I know in this district. You are a good daughter of Israel and will make a fine wife and mother –"

"Papa, I was thinking about going to Vienna," she interrupted.

"What are you talking about? What Vienna?" Jacob withdrew his arm, abruptly. "I've got to attend to the shipyard and the ferry. A girl can't just go hopping around to strange places. Not a Jewish girl. It's not proper.

"You're already twenty. To be truthful, I've been troubled by the fact that parents of young scholars are not approaching me with proposals for your hand in marriage to their sons. And when Menachem, the cloth merchant, had dinner at our home, you responded to his comment with a chilling rebuke."

"Menachem, the cloth merchant! He's a widower more than twice my age and with children older than I am. But that's not what bothered me. When he said that a wife should abide by her husband's wishes and never express an opinion to the contrary, I could not remain still. Women are not chunks of lox. They have minds with which to think. I could not picture spending the rest of my life as a silent wife, fearful of expressing an opinion."

"Well..." Jacob hesitated, "Menachem is certainly no scholar. It would pain me to think of your mind being locked up in such an environment.

"But it's time to consider the future. I'd like to keep you as my little girl, but that wouldn't be right. You're a woman now."

Chaya Sarah pursed her lips with anguish, and then looked at him pleadingly as she spoke. "Papa, what of the whole world? I want to be like you. I want to know and understand the Scriptures, medicine, music, art and history. You run the ferry line just as Grandpa Hershel and his father, Shmuel Zanvel, each did before you. But you didn't settle for that. You founded a shipbuilding enterprise.

"Even that was not enough for you. You wanted to do something more than just make money. You wanted to probe into the mysteries, to feel the pulse of the world, to understand, and to put that understanding to use. Parents bring little children to you, asking you to heal them... And you *do*. I remember the time you spent three days and nights at the bedside of a little boy who had a high fever and had difficulty breathing. They say the child's face was blue as the river water. You sponged the child and gave him medicine. You had the mother boil water 'til the air in the room was as thick as smoke. When the boy recovered, everyone said it was a miracle. I would like to have that feeling of accomplishment, that feeling of doing something beyond..."

Jacob's right hand went to his chin and he stroked his beard, thoughtfully.

"You love music," Chaya Sarah went on, "so you constructed your own violin. No one around here had done anything like that. You were dissatisfied with your timepiece, so you built a clock, starting from metal and wood. You have always clung to the belief that the ability to think and to apply one's mind to achieve was the Almighty's most precious gift –"

"Please," interrupted Jacob sadly, his right hand now held up before him, "don't continue in this vein. We must remember our responsibilities, our religious obligations."

"But you've always told me that the pursuit of knowledge would not destroy our faith in the Almighty. You assured me that it could only bring us closer to the Creator of the Universe. Why then should it bring us into conflict with our religious obligations?

"There is much out there to be experienced and absorbed – museums and libraries, concert halls and the university. I want to broaden my vistas. You, yourself, said that I possess wisdom few men can match. Am I now to wilt and die like a rose that flowers but for a few days in the sun?" Her head sank low and she winced with the misery she felt. "Is that what it's all about: A dream that can never come true?"

Jacob's face looked pained. He rose from his chair, shoulders hunched forward as if burdened by a heavy weight, and moved slowly towards a shelf of books at the side of the room. Jacob looked from volume to volume. He raised his hand as if to take a book and then let the hand drop. He retreated to his chair and sank into it. Jacob was plainly uncomfortable, one hand wringing the other, his shoulders twisting against some unseen resistance. He looked hard at Chaya Sarah for what seemed an eternity. Finally, he spoke.

"Chaya Sarah, responsibility comes first. If we fail to recognize our obligations, what good is learning? The Lord has blessed me with a large family and, with hard work, I have been able to provide for us all. Yes, I believe in the pursuit of knowledge. It was for this very reason that I engaged a scholar, gave him food and lodging and money, in return for teaching my children. If I had not done so, only the boys would have gone to *cheder*. The girls would have remained at home to learn cooking and cleaning, but little else. Was I so wrong to have exposed my daughters to scholarship?"

"But why tempt me with the sight of delicacies I could never eat?" she asked bitterly.

"Why? Why?... Because I believed that we all, women as well as men, should have an education. The stimulus of that exposure wetted your appetite for more and you probed deeply. You became a scholar...yes, a scholar without equal among the people of your age in Rozwadow. But who says that not traveling to Vienna or Danzig means an end to learning? Is all the wisdom of the world locked away in some distant city? Is that the only way to obtain knowledge?

"I do not set myself up as a model for prospective scholars. But if I'm to be the example, then review my sources of enlightenment. First and foremost, they are the Torah and the Talmud. There are the writings of the Sages, as well as the books that fill these shelves. And I am perfectly willing to buy any others you desire. I haven't gone to the secular schools in Krakow or Vienna, just to *cheder* and the *yeshiva*. I never had any teacher in science or mathematics or art or music, even though I provided one for you children. So if I'm to be your example, the trip is unnecessary."

"Oh, Papa," she wailed.

"Just a moment," he began again. "I'm not so foolish as to suggest that I've learned everything there is to know. Of course there is much that can be learned in a university setting. But there is much to lose as well. It was in this context that I referred to our religious obligations.

"Look around you here in Branwica and across the river in Rozwadow. Is there so much as a single Jewish boy or girl attending the government school? Have you ever asked yourself, 'Why?' It's that they would be forced to break the commandment, 'Honor the Sabbath.' Classes are held six days a week in the government school – Saturdays included. The Jewish child would be compelled to attend school and write on the Sabbath or face dismissal from the school. The Jews in our district are all observant Jews. None has ever agreed to send his children to a school that obliges Jewish children to violate the teachings of the Torah.

"Now, you speak of Vienna. What you refer to is not just a brief trip to the capital to see the sights. You're not given to such frivolity. Your interest in Vienna must be far deeper. You're contemplating a course of study at the university.

"I understand what you're going through. I know what it is to be gripped with the passions of youth, the thirst for knowledge that cannot be quenched by glib phrases or invocations to have faith, that all will be right in the end.

"Don't look surprised. I was not born with a beard. I, too, was once young. I, too, had the desire to travel, to study in distant places, to go to the university. And I, too, had a father who seemed to be throwing cold water on the flame of my desires. Oh, how I insisted...and pleaded. Yet, when I reviewed the matter calmly, with no one there to rail against me, I realized that he was right. I was, after all, a Jewish boy, the graduate of a *yeshiva*, not a *Gymnasium* (secondary school equivalent to our high school). In the eyes of a university faculty, I had received no formal education at all."

"But aren't there examinations that can be taken to prove that you had the background to enter the university?"

"Yes, there are." He paused, searching for a way to phrase his response. "And suppose I passed them, what then? Look at my face. The beard may be fuller now, but it had its beginnings when I was your age. And the sidelocks were as long then as they are now. I wore them proudly, dangling over my shoulders, not concealed beneath any cap. What a sight that would have been at the University of Vienna. I'd have been out of place, sneered at and scorned. But that's the least. Every Jew has had more than enough of that in his time. You get used to the sneers or the taunting.

"But what's worse is that I'd have been reprimanded for what they term an 'unkempt' appearance. I've heard tell of Orthodox Jews who were ordered to shear off their beards and sidelocks. And I would have been required to attend classes on the Sabbath or face dismissal from the university. So the price I would have had to pay was the violation of the Commandments.

"I'm not saying that there aren't Jews at the university. On the contrary, there are. But they're people who have forgotten or disregarded their roots and their responsibilities. Well, I'm not one of them and neither are you. If we are not who we are, who are we? If we deny what we are, what are we?"

"Is Judaism only to be practiced in a *shtetl* in Galicia? Is it necessary to give up the quest for knowledge in order to remain a Jew?" she grimaced.

"A Jew give up the quest for knowledge? Never!" His words became incisive, pouring out with vehemence she had not heard in her father's voice before. "We are the Children of the Book; we are the Children of the Commandment; and we are the Children of the Law. Study is essential to our makeup; without it we are but an empty shell. We would then become a people who have forgotten the link, and have broken the chain of learning."

"At least you attended a *yeshiva*. But what about me?"

"You're a woman and women are not allowed into the *yeshiva*. Perhaps at some future time it will be different, but here and now, a woman is expected to marry and, with God's blessing, raise a family. But you can still study at home."

"The maker of chicken soup, sneaking in a little reading when no one is looking," she commented bitterly.

"I have made it sound bad...harsh...but it is not really so. It's not a question of whether one approves or disapproves of women entering the *yeshiva*, it's the way it has always been; it's the way it is now. We each have our responsibilities. But bear in mind that the Jewish family is based upon the mother. It is from her that they derive their Jewish heritage."

"But why the rush for marriage?" inquired Chaya Sarah, earnestly. "One day I am a child with long, flowing hair lifted by the wind as I race across a field; the next day, a married woman shorn of her youth, a *sheitl* crowning my burdened head."

"Why the rush?" repeated Joseph. "It's the law of nature and the law of God. There is human desire; we believe that it should only be fulfilled in marriage, leading the man and the woman away from the dangers of unrequited passion. They can then direct their attention toward the spirituality that brings us closer to the Almighty. If a Jew is to remain what he is, a student of the holy word, a man in quest of understanding while he holds steadfast in his piety, he must be relieved of such hungering in a fashion that conforms with God's law.

"Then too, there is the product of that marriage – children. Fish lay a million eggs, birds, several, but humans have but one baby at a time. 'Why,' you may ask, 'is it so?' The fish have many enemies – the currents, the competition for food and, most of all, the other fish. Out of a million, perhaps one or two will survive. The bird, too, has many enemies; fewer than the fish, so out of a dozen offspring, one or two will survive to adulthood. The human has enemies, fewer than the bird; so he needs fewer offspring to ensure the survival of his kind. But the Jew is something special. His position is closer to that of the bird. He needs issue almost as numerous as the bird, just for his people to survive. For in addition to the dangers that other humans face – disease, hunger, cold and natural disasters – he faces a special enemy, persecution, aimed at the destruction of our people. And so without the large families that Jewish women have borne and raised, we might (God forbid) have disappeared as a people."

"Are we now to be compared to fish and birds? Is the sum of our existence to be having children?"

"No. We are not fish and we are not birds. But we do have a need to survive to fulfill our mission. Think of how many of our people have been lost. Those men, women and children must be replaced if we are to continue to exist. Look at your history books. Time and time again, powerful enemies have sought to extinguish the flame of our belief in the Almighty. The idolaters of Rome sought to impose their heathen rites upon us and to keep us from the practice of our religion. And when we rose in rebellion 1,800 years ago, they sent all the legions of the Empire against us. The Romans who carried their vengeance to every village and town slaughtered one million of the Hebrew people, the flower of our nation.

"Yet even after our small nation suffered so horrendous a blow, we persisted. We refused to give up our uniqueness, our faith. The Romans did not understand this. They could not comprehend that a people were prepared to die, rather than to give up something so seemingly intangible as a faith. They determined to snuff out the candle of Judaism by ending practices essential to our faith. And so they forbade ritual circumcision. When the Hebrew people resisted, the Romans went further. They tried to smother us with restrictions in order to douse the flame of our faith. This led to the final revolt in Judea led by Bar Kokhba. Twenty Roman legions, armies from as far away as Britain, converged on little Judea, determined not only to crush us but to destroy our will to resist. Another half-million Jews were killed. This time, the Romans decided to solve their 'Jewish problem' by removing the Hebrew people from their land and driving them into exile. Without roots, the plant was expected to wither and die.

"But we did not. We clung to the Book and the Commandments with a tenacity never before seen in human history. We wandered over the face of Europe, Asia and Africa, driven from land to land by blows from clenched fists and swords raised against us in anger. And for what? Because we would not give up that which made us what we are, the Children of the Book. Because we would not deny our faith in the Almighty.

"The Byzantines gave us a choice: conversion or a sword in the belly; the Crusaders offered us conversion or death by drowning; the Spaniards offered us conversion or death by fire; and the Tsars offered us conversion or death by pogrom. You would think that if what they had to offer was so wonderful they would not feel the need to beat, stab, burn and drown people as a mean of persuading them to accept Christianity.

"Some Jews gave into their fears and, as the dagger was held threateningly to their throats, accepted the Cross. Of these, some recanted as soon as their tormentors were gone. But others, out of continued dread of that horrible moment when they were threatened with violence and even extinction, remained Christians and were lost to our people. They were afraid to tell their offspring about their Jewish heritage, lest the children be tempted to return to that tradition. They even feared that the very mention, to some Gentile, that they were descended from Jews might subject their offspring to persecution.

"Some added themselves to our enemies list. These converts to Christianity went to the other extreme, perhaps in an exaggerated effort to assure the survival of their progeny. They became outspoken anti-Semites, adopting the worst aspects of the Christian world around them. And they taught this product of self-hate to their children. So it was that Torquemada, a descendant of Jews forcibly converted to Christianity, became the first Grand Inquisitor of Spain. In that position he instituted a policy that led to the deaths of tens of thousands of Jews.

"But despite all the threats and the savagery against us, the overwhelming majority of our people remained true to their faith, accepting martyrdom, rather than deny their Judaism. All in all, hundreds of thousands, no, millions of our brethren were butchered by these enemies in every possible fashion. But they *never* surrendered. And we, the survivors and descendants of survivors, must remain steadfast in our faith so that their lives may not have been lost in vain. We must multiply to survive, to overcome the efforts of our enemies who seek to extinguish the flame of Judaism."

Chaya Sarah shook her head in pain. "Papa," she cried out, "is this what you ask? That we give birth to generation after generation of children destined to become martyrs to an ideal, a faith?"

"No," insisted her father. "It will not be so forever. That is not what our Scriptures tell us. The day will come when the Children of Israel, scattered like sand across the earth, will return to the Promised Land. But until then we must carry on. And it is your duty as a Jewish woman to raise a family in the faith of our fathers and mothers. Your wisdom will not be wasted because you shall teach your children and they will be the better for your knowledge and your inspiration.

"Remember one thing more: always keep your bag ready for travel. For a Jew, there is no certainty, no matter where he is. Austria may appear to be a safe place to live in today. But tomorrow the Austrians or the Poles may decide to wipe us out." He paused, seeing a surprised look on her face. "Don't look so surprised. I meant what I said. You see how many of the peasants behave toward us: distrust and outright hate, often reinforced by what they hear in church. And as for the Austrians, don't think these Germanic people too sophisticated, too cultured, for such behavior. You have only to hear the words of their language to know that there is a strong undercurrent of hatred directed at the Jews festering within many of them. Have you heard them use the term '*Judenblick*?' (The literal translation is "Jewish look." In German, it is the term for "the evil eye.") When Jew-haters' phrases become part of a people's vocabulary, beware. So keep your eyes, ears open. Try to anticipate our enemies. If you see smoke, do not wait until you're trapped in the flames before making a decision to flee."

Chaya Sarah had listened intently to her father's words. Her face revealed the grief she felt as she reviewed the sad history of her people. When the narration was ended, she remained silent for some time. She then began to shake her head. At last she sighed deeply and her facial muscles relaxed. Finally, she spoke.

"Papa, you call me to arms as a soldier in the struggle of the Jewish people to survive. How can I compete with such logic? You have advised that I continue to study in silence, grasping every bit of knowledge I can. I will have to do so. The Scriptures shall be the core of my perception, my source of inspiration. I will have to settle for reading in the flickering light of a candle when my day's work is done. Someday, things will have to change: A Jew will be free to go to a university while still adhering to the precepts of Judaism; a woman will be able to broaden her mind and still raise a family. But now, if I can't achieve, my sons will have to for me – and I will help them do it!"

Jacob looked hard into his daughter's eyes. A faint tear formed above his lower lid and he quickly wiped it away. He felt choked and cleared his throat before replying.

"Chaya Sarah, I've always been proud of you, but never more than at this moment."

She, too, appeared on the verge of tears. But she did not give in to what she considered frailty. She bit her lower lip to counteract the pain. Then she pushed her small jaw forward with determination.

After a while, the solemn look on Jacob's face faded and the half-smile with which he came home, reappeared.

"Chaya Sarah, now that you are grown, parents should be approaching me with marriage proposals. It's customary for parents to make such decisions, but I feel that with your intelligence, you should make the choice." He paused reflectively and then added, "Now don't tell anyone that I discussed such matters with you. It would not seem proper."

Chaya Sarah studied her father's countenance, and then replied, "I take it that you're referring to a specific marriage proposal, rather than the concept of marriage in general. I noticed a smile on your face as you were approaching the house."

"You *are* observant, Chaya Sarah.

"I do have one proposal to discuss with you. Moses Ausübel has proposed that his son, Judah, marry you."

A perplexed look crossed Chaya Sarah's face. "Who's Judah Ausübel? I don't remember meeting him."

"He's a carpenter. You remember: He was assembling a cabinet he had constructed for my study a few months ago."

"Oh yes," she nodded. "I remember him. I thought he was looking at me that day. But when I turned towards him, his eyes looked away. But I'm sure he noticed me. There was a faint blush on his cheeks."

Jacob smoothed his beard between his right thumb and index finger. "Then it was probably the son who put the father up to the proposal. A fine kettle of fish! Sons telling their fathers whom they want to marry!

"But who am I to complain! I'm discussing the proposal with you. Now, let me give you the pluses and minuses of this proposal as I see them.

"Judah's mother is dead and his stepmother is less concerned with the dead woman's children than with the well-being of her own future family. That's a minus. But on the other hand, she would probably be less noisy in your household affairs. That's a plus.

"Judah was shipped off as an apprentice as a young child, with the result that he has had little education. That's a minus. On the other hand, he owns property purchased from his earnings. He built his own shop and house and has even furnished that home. It is proof of independence, as well as determination – a definite plus.

"Judah built a home for his father and step-mother, following the Commandment to 'Honor thy father and thy mother.' It is the mark of a Bar Mitzvah – an unequivocal plus.

"And his family are all observant people. He is a descendant of a Jewish martyr and many sages. His father is the sexton of the wealthier synagogue of Rozwadow,although the prosperity of the congregation has not, from what I hear, improved the sexton's financial position. There are scribes and *Sofers* (writers of Torah scrolls) in the family, a mark of scholarship. That is a plus. On the other hand, they are not people of wealth – no Danzig Merchants. That is a minus.

"I believe that there is some Sephardic ancestry in Judah's background. Judah's mother, Shindel Silber Ausübel, rest her soul, was a cousin of Motele Silber. Motele has told me that his ancestors came from Venice a long time ago. Before that they lived in southern Italy and even before that, in Spain. Her relative possesses a scroll telling the history of the family. That is not a plus or a minus.

"Oh, one thing more. Judah's father says that a dowry is not important. I thought it strange for him to say so. The prospective groom's parents usually insist that the bride's father agree to support the couple while the young man spends his days studying Scriptures. After that, they want the groom taken into his father-in-law's business or set up in an enterprise of his own. For me, the absence of a demand for dowry is a plus, but for you it may be a minus.

"So what do you think?

"Oh, I forgot. He's shorter than you...by half-a-foot or so... But you've seen him. You know." He paused and then added, "His father told me that Judah is well aware of your scholarly pursuits. Judah told his father that he would be honored to have so knowledgeable a woman as his wife and that he would be pleased to have your advice on all matters."

Chaya Sarah sat there, silent. She was weighing the plusses and the minuses in her own mind. She tried to picture not only the man, but also the inner man behind the description. At last she spoke.

"Papa, I've listened attentively as you enumerated the positives and the negatives. You described to me a short, independent man with an honorable background, but with little money. He's a son who honors parents who have not done well by him. He's a stoic plodder in a noisy world. But he's not totally silent. He did speak up for me. And he wants me for myself, not for my money. He is willing to work hard, to stand on his own two feet. If he lacks book learning, I'll teach him. I'll marry him, I'll encourage him and I'll draw out the wisdom in him. For there must be wisdom in a man who recognizes that women have worth above the tending of household chores. We'll raise a family and I shall be mentor to our children. They will have to achieve all that I dreamed of."

Jacob smiled and embraced his daughter.

"Then it is done," he said. "Do not think that his intentional omission of a request for a dowry will result in my neglecting your needs. I do not need a contract to tell me where my heart or my responsibilities lie."

The match was arranged and the wedding day came. It was Saturday evening after *Maariv* (evening service). Ausübels and Korns, relatives and guests, were gathered together for a wedding under the stars. The men, dressed in dark suits, were seated on one side of a field, with the women occupying benches on the other side of a wide median path. At the far end of the meadow stood a *Chuppah*, the canopy, which symbolizes the Jewish home, supported by four poles.

The rabbi, a solemn figure in black, made his way down the central strip, carrying a prayer book and the *Ketubah* (marriage contract which details the religious and legal obligations of the parties). He took his place beneath the canopy, facing the guests. Rabbi Zvi Hirsh Horowitz stood, in his flowing robes, awaiting the bride and the groom. A stranger, coming from a Jewish community thousands of miles away, and suddenly dropped on that patch of ground in Rozwadow, would have had no doubt as to Zvi Hirsh's position. That commanding presence had to be *the* Rabbi who, in the *shtetls* of Central and Eastern Europe, was the combination of teacher and mystical guardian of his flock, the heir to a religious dynasty, a man whose words were savored like rare wine and whose pronouncements were treated as if they came from the prophets. Zvi Hirsh had the thick bushy eyebrows of his father, Rabbi Moshe, and his grandfather, Rabbi Naphtali. An expansive brown beard and spiraled sidelocks covered his young face, giving it the look of age and wisdom. A black, squared skullcap rested atop his full head of hair, as if it were the miter of the High Priest of the Temple.

Judah arrived and was escorted to the canopy by his father and stepmother. The undersized groom appeared awkward and uncomfortable in his long, white robe. His trouser legs folded on themselves at the ankles, as if the wearer were a boy, presuming to robe himself in his father's attire. A shiny, new black top hat crowned his head. He lifted it and replaced it, trying to find a more comfortable position...but to no avail. Dark-brown sidelocks, drenched with perspiration dripping from under his unaccustomed head covering, glistened in the light of a hundred candles. A rippled brown beard extended from his chin, not so long and full as to hint of grandeur, not curved or shaped to conform to fashion, not so thin and straggly as to infer a poor soil for hair's growth, but rather simple, squared and firm, saying softly to the world that this was a Jew who worked with his hands and did not conceal it; this was a Jew who worshipped the Lord of Hosts and would not deny Him; this was a quiet and unassuming man, who nevertheless could be firm in his resolve on matters he considered important, without shaking the hills with bellowing sound. No mocking enemy would ever say that anyone was permitted to cut one hair of that beard without first inflicting a mortal blow to its owner. Judah moved his shoulder ever so slightly as he looked straight ahead at the rabbi. Then he turned slowly to face the center walkway between the guests.

All eyes shifted from the rabbi and the groom to the tall, dignified figure in white, who appeared at the threshold to the meadow. It was the bride, clothed from head to toe in snowy lace, her delicate features and brunette hair but hinted at behind the pristine veil of purity. There was a parent on either side of her, escorting her resolute steps. The three of them moved forward until they reached the canopy.

At this juncture, Jacob left her side, to be replaced by Judah's stepmother. With the two mothers attending her, Chaya Sarah circled the canopy seven times, in accordance with Orthodox Jewish tradition. (One of the many explanations for these seven circuits is that they represent a sevenfold bond which marriage will establish between the bride and groom and their families. This act also recalls the seven times that the *tefillin* straps are wrapped around a man's arm. Just as a man binds himself in love to God, so is his bond in love to his bride. The number seven represents the completion of the seven-day creation of the world. During these seven days, the earth revolved on its axis seven times. Since marriage reenacts the creative process, the bride's encirclement symbolizes the repetition of these seven earthly rotations.)

All the while she kept her eyes focused on Judah's face. Immersed in that sea of darkness – hat, hair and beard – was a small, pale, gentle face. Her eyes felt his softness; she smiled within. The outside world saw only her veil of solemnity.

Her circuit completed, Chaya Sarah took her place beside Judah under the canopy.

The bride and groom faced the rabbi and the marriage contract was read aloud. The assemblage listened intently to the words. In scattered locations, there were gasps of surprise at the absence of any mention of dowry. Eyebrows were raised, knowingly. Here and there, a face pinched with disdain at such doings. Then one by one, distinguished guests came forward to recite the blessing.

Judah repeated after the rabbi: "Behold thou are consecrated unto me, by this ring, according to the laws of Moses and of Israel."

He guided a band of gold onto Chaya Sarah's left ring finger. A glass, wrapped in a napkin, was placed on the ground before the groom, as a reminder of the lost Temple in Jerusalem. Facing the host, Judah crushed the glass. The ceremony was over.

Food and drink were ready and the guests returned, again and again, to fill their plates and glasses. Throughout all the proceedings, men sat on one side of the meadow, women on the other. As their first married act together, the bride and groom ate from the same plate, symbolizing the joining of their fortunes in life.

The musicians began to play. Moses Ausübel approached his daughter-in-law and said a few words to her. She rose from her seat. Separated by a single handkerchief, each holding on to one end of it, Moses and Chaya Sarah danced. Following this, other members of the families were honored with a handkerchief dance with the bride. Then Chaya Sarah seated herself back among the women and watched the remainder of the proceedings.

A group of men joined in a circle, their arms placed on each other's shoulders. They began to dance: One foot was raised and thrust forward, then back, following with the reverse done by the other foot. Faster and faster they pranced and flung themselves forward and back as the musicians quickened the tempo. Finally the song ended and the laughing men returned to their side of the meadow.

The women now rose and moved to the center of the field. They danced as couples, ballroom style, to slower music.

Wine and whiskey flowed until some had difficulty standing.

"So, Judah," commented one such staggering guest, his portly waist bulging with every breath, "you've taken on a *big* job." He roared with laughter at his own words, his surplus flesh rippling its approval. "I mean," he chuckled, lowering his hand and then raising it up high, "you and she... You'll need to make yourself a stool to stand on." He howled, unable to contain himself. He slapped Judah on the back.

The stoic groom did not flinch.

The musicians played on – wild joyous music, slow delicate music, happy tunes, sad tunes – and the dancing grew fast, then slow, then fast, then slow, until none had the strength to take to the floor.

Shortly after midnight, the newly married couple left the party. They retired to the home Judah had built. The wedding and the celebration were over. It was time to begin a new life together.

FOR WHOM SHALL I VOTE

From childhood, I recognized that I was living in a unique country, founded on the principle that our government derives its just power from the consent of the governed. Implicit in this consent is the fact that our representatives are elected, not for life, but for fixed terms. When, in the view of the people, a representative is no longer adhering to their wishes, he or she can be voted out of office. And so I have made it my solemn duty to vote in every election.

The nineteenth century brought winds of change gusting through Europe. The American experiment had, in a way, brought about a French revolution, but that country had reverted to imperial status.

Napoleon was defeated; however, the tempest unleashed by the French Revolution and its aftermath presented Europe with new forces with which to contend – nationalism and the yearning for freedom.

The venerable Hapsburg Empire was in a particularly vulnerable position. It was an anachronistic conglomerate, a state lacking the glue required to hold it together in the modern world. Peoples of the many nationalities – not one of which formed a majority of the population – were joined together by a German-speaking Kaiser whom few revered. A German-speaking aristocracy governed them. A series of revolutions and lesser upheavals had exposed the inherent weakness of the nation's structure. To shore up the state's crumbling foundation, a dual monarchy named Austria-Hungary was established, with the warrior Magyars as partners with the German-speaking Austrians. This concession only heightened the yearning of other nationalities within the empire for a say in their future. Finally, the Kaiser agreed to the formation of an elected legislative body in the Austrian half of the empire.

In 1907 free elections were to be held in Galicia for the first time, to select representatives to the Austrian Parliament in Vienna. The official nominee in the district of Charzewice (which included Rozwadow) was the Polish historian, Prof. Michael Bobrzynski. The Jewish youth of Rozwadow, stirred by their own sense of identity, put up an opposition candidate, Rabbi Gedalia Szmelkes.

Shortly before the election, Judah Ausübel, who had been busily engaged in doing renovations in the home of Prince Lubomirski, was summoned to the study of the nobleman.

The prince, a man of impressive dignity – tall, handsome, clean-shaven and outfitted in a neat waistcoat and trousers – stood facing a large bay window set off by flowering silk curtains. He looked with pride at the sloping, grass-covered lawn and the fine apple orchard in the distance. This was Lubomirski land. His family had owned it for centuries, as vassals who felt themselves almost the co-equals of the Polish crown. Now his land was under the aegis of the German-speaking Hapsburgs. But those were monarchies far off in the distance, and this was Charzewice.

He looked at the orchard in the same way that he looked at all the land in the district – as his. Although he felt possessive about the territory and its inhabitants, he also felt responsible. These were "his people." The Lubomirskis were not only rulers, they were guardians. Like parents, they had to make decisions, for they knew what was best for their children even when the children disagreed.

The business of elections presented a new and undesired wrinkle.

How ridiculous, he thought. *Why don't they simply invite me to Vienna? Or, if I choose, I'll send a delegate. Why the absurdity of having peasants and artisans selecting representatives?*

His lip twisted in annoyance.

We've lived through annexation, he mused within, *so I guess we can adjust to this. Maybe –*

The prince's eyes lit up. He turned from the window and moved past large oak panels that supported a row of portraits of his ancestors: some stern-faced, others half-smiling, but all with the regal touch that befitted a prince of the realm. He paused before shelves filled with gilded volumes at the side of the room. He searched for a specific book.

A gentle tap on the door distracted him. He turned in the direction from which the sound was coming.

"It's you, Judah…" He paused, somewhat puzzled, and studied the carpenter's face. "You look strange. Your face seems peculiar. What happened to you?"

"Oh. It's my beard, Your Excellency," replied Judah, embarrassed. "I lost part of it."

"Lost part of your beard? Was it caught in something and you had to cut off some of it? You should have removed an equal amount on the other side. That would even it out."

"I didn't have time to do so, Your Excellency. But I'll attend to it to-night."

"That's fine." The prince looked troubled. "Your one eye seems puffed and dusky. It's on the side opposite the missing beard. What sort of vice was it that you were caught in?"

Judah hesitated for a moment. "A...a few young men, Your Excellency."

"Young men? Ah... I see. They tried to cut off your beard." His head bent slightly forward and he shook it in dismay. "I wish they wouldn't do such things. It's so senseless. Serves no purpose." He straightened up and added, "When did this take place?"

"This morning. On my way here."

"This election thing," he mused, annoyed. "Was it any of my peasants?"

"Well... It doesn't matter, Your Excellency," replied Judah, bowing his head.

"From the appearance of your face, there must have been a struggle."

"I resisted. I'm afraid I hurt a few of them."

"So they fled."

"Not quite then. A scream scared them off."

"A scream?"

"My eldest son happened along. I had forgotten one of my tools and he was bringing it here. He saw them cutting off my beard and screamed. They fled."

"A child?"

"I told him it was dangerous being so far from home. Especially now. I had to lead him home. That's why I was a few minutes late."

"Disturbing business. I'll have to speak to the overseer. Must caution the peasants against such things... But please be seated," the prince added graciously, with a sweep of his hand.

Judah, a small man who had suffered enough to know his place, appeared uneasy at the surprise request. He held his cap nervously in his two hands before him. His head, covered with a rumpled black skullcap, was half bent. He surveyed the elegant period furniture of the room. A medallion-backed armchair characteristic of Louis XV stood before a moderate-sized desk inlaid with colored woods and tortoise shells, such as no craftsman in Galicia could duplicate. Straight-legged Louis XVI chairs with fluted decoration were covered with soft cushions encased in exquisitely embroidered tapestries. There were two narrow, tastefully designed sofas, one on either side of a pure white fireplace, into whose marble facing had been carved the figures of winged angels with puffed cheeks, blowing horns in the direction of the central crest of the Lubomirskis. Then he looked at his own soiled clothing. Finally, he replied respectfully:

"Thank you, Your Excellency, but my clothes are dusty from the work and this morning's happening. It would be better if I stood."

"Very well," said the prince. "I have a question to ask you. Are you one of those radicals working for this Szmelkes?"

The carpenter was taken aback and felt unsure of himself. Still, he had to reply.

"Your Excellency, I know Rabbi Gedalia Szmelkes. He is a good man."

Seeing the cold reception his words received, he quickly added, "But I have not been involved in politics."

The nobleman cleared his throat.

"Well, Judah, let me get to the point. I want you and all your family to vote for Prof. Bobrzynski. Now make sure that *all* your relatives vote for him. We want a near-unanimous vote in this district." He paused for a moment and then added, "It would help create good feelings. The people will feel united, under proper direction. It would reduce chances for a recurrence of the unpleasantness you experienced this morning."

The bearded carpenter bent his head even lower. His dark-brown beard was pressing against his chest. His hands gripped the cap they were holding even tighter. His eyes avoided the prince's face as he spoke.

"Your Excellency, I'm sure that the professor must be a fine man if you say so, and I'm sure he will win the election, but I can't promise that my family will vote for him."

"Judah," said the tall nobleman, now impatient, "you do not understand. I am convinced that you are a good person. I have given you lots of work inasmuch as you are a fine craftsman, but also because I believe that you respect authority. But I must be firm. If you disobey me in this, there will be no employment for you now or in the future. Now, if you promise me that you and all your family will vote for Prof. Bobrzynski, I will take your word for it and say no more. If you say 'no,' then take your tools from my estate and do not return."

The little carpenter slowly raised his head. His eyes met those of the tall prince. "Your Excellency, I would not lie to you. I have not decided whom to vote for, and I would not order my relatives to vote for any candidate."

The prince's cheeks blanched. He paused for a moment, mouth open. He appeared not to believe what he had heard. "Are you serious?" he asked incredulously.

"Your Excellency, I have spoken the truth."

The nobleman's face turned grim. "Then gather your tools and leave!" he declared reprovingly. After a moment he added, "You've made a terrible mistake."

The sad-faced carpenter left the study and returned to the room in which he had been working. He gathered his tools together and placed them in a sack. He left the great stone mansion, trudging past the green lawn and the blossoming orchard without noticing any of it, passing through the swinging iron gate and then down the long dirt road, home. His pace was slow and his back sank forward under the load of his tools. It was not so much their heavy weight that caused his back to sink; it was the emptiness of his pants pocket accompanying it. It was a warm summer day and the sun beat down unmercifully on his little body. Within half-an-hour he was swimming in his own perspiration.

It was mid-afternoon when he reached his home. His tall, delicately featured wife, Chaya Sarah was outside. She was washing clothes in a large wooden tub while humming a tune softly. Her face, ordinarily a soft pale pink, appeared brown and healthy. The song ended abruptly as footsteps approached. She was surprised to see Judah when she looked up.

"What happened? Did they attack you, again?"

"No," his head sank.

"Are you in pain from this morning?"

"Not from then."

"Why are you home so soon? I thought you had several days' work at the prince's house and would want to work late. You must be ill. Your face is so pale."

"No, Chaya Sarah, I'm not ill. It's just that... I won't be working for the prince anymore."

"What happened? The prince always liked your work."

The little man shook his head back and forth.

"It's not my work. It's just that I refused to promise that we would all vote for that professor instead of Rabbi Gedalia Szmelkes." Judah felt a burning sensation in his throat and attempted to clear it. "Aren't we Jews," he went on, "entitled to vote for the candidate we prefer? It says on the signs that this is to be a free election." And yet he could not end on so harsh a note. As one who had always tried to see the other man's point of view, he added, "Then again, he *is* the prince."

Chaya Sarah looked at her husband with disbelief. It was the first time she had ever heard this soft-spoken man express resentment – even with an attached apology for that indignation. Heretofore he had always been silent, suffering within when beaten, when others cheated him of his wages, or when callous folk spoke to him in barbed or mocking tones, mistaking his gentleness for weakness or stupidity. And now suddenly, something had aroused his ire. His voice had not risen, but the current of unrest was clearly discernible to her fine-tuned ears. She recalled his last words and asked hopefully, "Judah, will he put you back to work after the election?"

"No," he replied with resignation in his voice. "I can never work for the prince again... He said so."

If there were a momentary conflict between her desire for financial security and her craving for the recognition of human dignity, it did not show itself in her countenance. "Well, so be it," she said with grim determination. "It will be hard on us with the loss of the wages, but we'll manage somehow." She paused briefly and then added, "Please don't say anything about it to anyone, especially my parents. We don't want any handouts." She looked hard and deep into the somber, silent face of her husband. His countenance seemed to express guilt rather than anger. "You did the right thing," she insisted. "What are we that this should be demanded of us? Slaves? Servants? Faceless people who shuffle back and forth, and bow before our rulers? Are we supposed to accept beatings in silence and then say 'thank you'?" Her voice rose with indignation.

Judah's eyes widened. He was accustomed to hearing his wife offer sage advice, but always in gentle, even tones. Now she was furious, pouring out resentment.

Chaya Sarah sensed his alarm. Her face softened and she murmured, "I'm proud of you, Judah." She embraced her sad little husband. She was hesitant to let go. Time stood still. His bearded face buried in her arms and his soot-covered clothes pressed against her dress. Her cheek was tilted over his skullcap-covered head, hugging it, but he stood tall in her enfolded arms.

A child's voice came from within the house. They quickly released one another and went in.

A month later, the election was held and Prof. Bobrzynski was elected.

A few days after the election, a messenger came to Judah's workshop. He delivered a note summoning Judah to the prince's residence.

The carpenter had not had any work for three weeks and the family's funds were at low ebb.

Judah, his heart racing with excitement tinged with fear, rushed to the nobleman's house. An hour later, he was shown into the prince's study. The carpenter removed his cap, exposing his skullcap, and waited for the prince's command.

The prince was sitting at his desk, writing. He appeared unaware of the arrival of the visitor.

Finally, Judah cleared his throat softly into a cuffed hand to attract the nobleman's attention.

Without rising, the prince turned his head in the carpenter's direction.

"Your Excellency," began Judah, "I was told you wanted to see me."

"Yes, Judah," the prince replied pleasantly. "But where are your tools? There are still four more rooms to be redone."

"I... I didn't bring them. I thought you said –"

"Never mind what I said. The election is over. Let's forget about what I said."

The nobleman hesitated, looking at the little man's bowed head. For a moment, the regal look vanished from the prince's face to be replaced by an embarrassed blush.

"I'm sorry...that I pressured you. Please return to your work."

"Thank you, Your Excellency," replied the carpenter with a voice choked with suppressed tears as he moved towards the door.

"By the way, Judah," smiled the prince. "You were right."

"Right, Your Excellency?"

"Yes. You said the professor would win the election – and he did."

IT'S TIME

IN MY EARLIEST childhood, I was aware of the crisis facing the Jewish people. My father had warned of the dark cloud that had descended, threatening the survival of the largest segment of the world Jewry: those living on the European continent.

"Who am I?" I asked myself. "Who are we? Why had we been so mistreated, driven from place to place? Had we done something so wrong that we should suffer such unending persecution?"

I sought to learn the history of our people in the context of the history of the world. And so I became a student of history, combining the oral history related to me by my grandfather who was my roommate, and the written history, which I devoured with a passion.

Perhaps, by learning more of the lives of my father and grandfather, and why they came to the United States, I might better understand.

On November 24, 1894, a first child was born to Judah and Chaya Sarah Ausübel. They named him Adolph (Avraham in Hebrew) after Judah's grandfather. A second son, Harry, was born two years later, followed by a third son, Samuel, born in 1899.

On a warm day in May, in the year 1900, Chaya Sarah busied herself in the kitchen of their home, washing little Samuel. The brown hair of her youth was not to be seen. It had been supplanted by a *sheitl*. She wore a simple, long gray dress, which, together with her somewhat drawn face, made her appear older than her twenty-seven years. Despite all the effort at concealment, the delicately etched porcelain beauty was still there. As soon as Samuel was clean and dry, she bundled him in a blanket and cradled him in one arm. She picked up a basket of freshly washed clothing in her other arm and walked outdoors. She rested the baby in his blanket on the dry grass, and set the basket nearby. Then one by one, she draped the wet clothes over a clothesline. When the task was completed, she returned to the kitchen with her son. She lowered the boy gently in the center of the room.

"Play, Samuel, play," she said affectionately to the seated infant while stroking his head. She smiled happily when the child uttered a sound of contentment.

"Lots to do. Must get started," she sighed to herself as she turned away. Chaya Sarah placed a bowl on the table. She dropped in the contents of several fresh eggs she was cracking. She added baking flour and stirred the mixture into pasty dough. Next, the busy mother set about peeling and boiling potatoes, cutting and stewing onions, mashing the boiled potatoes, and then mixing the mashed potatoes together with the stewed onions while adding some oil. Her arms were in constant motion – adding a pinch of this and a drop of that with her left hand, while tasting portions of the mixture, using a spoon held in her right hand. At long last, she halted and smiled.

"The *perogen* (small filled pockets of dough, a dish eaten in Eastern Europe) will be just right," she murmured softly.

Chaya Sarah removed the doughy mixture from its bowl, rolled it and cut it into rectangular sections. She placed portions of the potato-onion mixture on the rectangles and folded the dough around the mixture. The *perogen* were set in a pan and heated over a low flame.

The dish was ready now. She set the table with plates and eating utensils, stopping briefly to attend to her crying child. Her duties temporarily over, she washed her hands and face, then sat, for the first time in hours, waiting for Judah and the older boys to come home for dinner.

Ten minutes later, the house was a beehive of activity. Adolph and Harry were back from playing in the fields and Judah had returned from his work. They washed and then seated themselves at the table. Judah recited the blessing, and hungry mouths were soon devouring the results of several hours of labor over a hot stove.

"Judah," said Chaya Sarah mildly, "I was thinking it's time for Adolph to go to school. You know he'll be six years old."

"He's been studying with the *melamed* (Hebrew teacher)," responded Judah, straightening up his chair. "What do you have in mind? Surely, you're not thinking of his going to a government school. Those teachers compel the children to write on the Sabbath."

"No," replied Chaya Sarah, looking very serious. "I was not thinking of that school. I was thinking of a different school – the Baron de Hirsch School that's going up here in Rozwadow. In it, a Jewish child will have the opportunity to acquire an education without violating the tenets of our faith."

"How did this all come about?" wondered Judah aloud.

"Baron de Hirsch is a wealthy Jew. He is a fine human being who has given large sums of money to be used to open schools for our people, throughout Austria. His intent is that Jewish children receive a broad education. Most Jewish families can't afford both a *melamed* and a private tutor knowledgeable in areas of learning other than the Scriptures. Now their children will have the opportunity to study Arithmetic, the Sciences and History, as well as Torah and Talmud. I have spoken to Mr. Spinnrad who will be the headmaster. He is a good man, an intelligent man, and his background is excellent. He has been educated at the university as well as in a Talmudic academy."

The mother's eyes now focused on Adolph who was listening intently to all that was said. "What do you think of that?" she asked encouragingly.

"Will they teach me all the things you were telling us about?"

"That and much more." Her eyes lit up as she spoke. "There are so many marvelous things in the world to which you have not yet been exposed. I want you to learn as much as you can about all the new knowledge, as well as the old wisdom. This school is only the beginning; but you have to walk before you can run.

"When I was a young girl, I dreamed of going on to study at a university, of having the opportunity to use the libraries and museums of a large city such as Krakow or Prague or Vienna to further my knowledge of the arts and sciences, of experiencing great music in the concert halls that abound in those great cultural centers and..." She paused, sighing sadly, then added, "But it was not to be." Her eyes now became intent as she spoke with determination tinged with a sense of joy. "But now I have you; I have three sons; and (God willing) we will have more children. Let my children achieve that which I only dreamed of."

Adolph's brown eyes widened like saucers as he tried to picture it all. "I'd like to go to school, Mama. I'd like to do everything you said." There was excitement and enthusiasm in his voice.

Chaya Sarah's gaze returned to her husband. "Well Judah, what do you say to Adolph's going to school?"

The carpenter smoothed back his beard thoughtfully. "You know that I always follow your recommendation. He will go to school."

And so Adolph was enrolled in the first class to enter the Baron de Hirsch School. In the years that followed, more and more of the Jewish children of Rozwadow enrolled in the school to be exposed to secular learning, as well as to God's word. It was a small school, measured against those in Krakow and the other cities of the empire. The faculty consisted of a headmaster and two assistants. But Mr. Spinnrad, Mr. Tewinger and Mr. Komita had brought to the Jewish community of Rozwadow the progressive educational principles followed in Vienna.

Adolph adapted quickly to the twentieth-century education and was particularly proficient in history and literature. He was gifted with a bright, inquiring mind, but what set him most apart from the other boys in the school were a quiet sensitivity and a love of nature. He was a dreamer in a harsh world of reality. While most of the young boys were participating in sports, he was writing poetry.

> *Lying on a bed of dew-soaked grass,*
> *Inhaling the scents of a blooming carpet*
> *All green and red, violet and yellow,*
> *Birds singing, butterflies emerging, shimmering*
> *In the filtered light of leafy trees*
> *Spreading their branches to the sky,*
> *I saw her...*

(Translation of excerpt from *Phantasie im Walde*, "Fantasy in the Woods." It was written in 1908 by thirteen-year-old Adolph Ausübel.)

He sat at his mother's feet, his head resting against her knees, reading his poem in the genial quiet of a late spring afternoon. She stroked his soft, brown, wavy hair and listened. There was a silent bond between mother and son. It was an affinity of dreamers. When seeing barges floating lazily down a river to far-off places, they yearned to be there when the vessels arrived at some distant port. It was the kinship of romantics. They would watch a train puffing its way across the countryside – its sleek gray body etched against golden fields and a bright blue sky, with dark balls of smoke rising from its engine to vaporize into a gray mist and disappear into a few white cotton clouds above. They heard the vibrant voices of actors performing a Johann Schiller drama in a theater in Vienna, or pictured a gallery in Munich filled with paintings by Reubens and Rembrandt and Raphael, or imagined themselves sitting in a moonlit cafe in Budapest, with a Gypsy violinist charming a haunting melody from within his instrument. It was the vision, common to poets, in which a field is a pageant of color, glowing in the light of a life-giving and life-restoring sun, with flowers swaying in harmony with a chorus of winged travelers overhead.

Adolph dreamed, but he also worked. At thirteen, he became apprentice to the town attorney. He continued his schooling and worked in the lawyer's office after school. Up to that time, none of the Jewish children of Rozwadow had ever gone on to a college. Adolph had his mind set on going to a university when he completed his secondary school education. He was intent on becoming a lawyer or writer.

The onset of World War I dramatically changed the lives of the people of Rozwadow. After several Austrian defeats, the town fell into Russian hands. Chaya Sarah had wisely followed her father's past advice, and had "kept her suitcase packed and ready." When the Russians neared their town, Judah, Chaya Sarah and their children fled in the direction of Vienna.

Vienna, in 1915, was filled with refugees from the East. The Ausübels found an apartment where they could stay. Judah had been turned down by the Austrian army because he was half an inch too short to meet their minimum standard. With so many men away at war, Judah readily found work as a carpenter. Adolph, too, was rejected by the armed forces. He had an inguinal hernia (a hernia in the groin).

With the scarcities brought on by the demands of war, inflation was rampant. One person's income was insufficient to pay for the needs of the family. And so Adolph put aside all thoughts of further education for "the duration of the war." He went to work in a shoe factory. Harry was drafted into the army and the younger children – Samuel, Charlotte, Jozef and Anna – remained at home with their mother.

Months later, the Ausübels learned that the Russians had been driven back and that Rozwadow was again in Austrian hands. Chaya Sarah cautioned her husband: "Let's remain in Vienna, at least until the war is over. They drove us back; now we're driving them back; tomorrow, things may be reversed. They may recapture Rozwadow and then..." She gulped painfully and then continued, "You know how the Russians treat Jews. So it would be far wiser for us to stay here until hostilities come to an end. Judah, as long as Adolph and you both have jobs, we can get by."

Judah, as always, was convinced.

Chaya Sarah directed the education of the younger children. Each day, they waited impatiently for the mail, for word that Harry was safe.

During the next few years, the newspapers were filled with news of German and Austrian victories. But food was getting scarce, and the only soldiers who returned were in the truckloads of wounded on route to hospitals. The old Kaiser, Franz Jozef, died, and a new Kaiser took his place. Younger and younger teenagers, boys who had not learned to shave, were taken into the army. Still there was no end to the war. The Russians, exhausted from years of battle and torn by internal dissension, withdrew from the conflict. And still the war went on with the remaining Austrian troops battling Italians and Serbians. It was the battle of Armageddon. What had been lost in the battle was any thought of right and wrong. Survival was all that counted. By 1918, ninety percent of Austria-Hungary's seven-million-man army had been killed, maimed or taken captive on the blood-soaked battlefields in the war that saw inches of territory paid for with stacks of corpses, only to be lost again. The will to fight on was gone and the nation surrendered to the Allies. The tattered remnants of the Austro-Hungarian army came home.

During the war, Adolph had steadily advanced in position. By 1918 he was manager of the Saltzer Shoe Company, one of the largest shoe manufacturing concerns in Austria. Harry returned from the war and went to work in the shoe factory, managed by his older brother. He became a designer. Samuel followed his father and became a carpenter.

Vienna was now the capital of a small country. It was no longer the seat of power in a large empire. The people were dejected. Staying alive was all that mattered. The city had swollen with countless German-speaking people who had fled from the newly liberated provinces, as well as Jewish refugees from Galicia, Bukovina and Hungary. The population of Vienna in 1919 was larger than necessary to conduct the affairs of a sprawling empire that was no more. It was now far too large for a city that, while rich in culture, was poor in industry and commerce. Food, clothing and habitable quarters were scarce in this city, packed with displaced humanity in a loser nation that had suddenly been shorn of its agricultural provinces.

Men competed for the few available jobs and salaries were low as a consequence. Optimism was gone. Trust was gone. Everything had to be paid for in hard currency. It took the combined earnings of Judah and his three older sons to keep the family of eight financially afloat on the sea of distrust and despair that prevailed. Under these circumstances, it was better to keep a job that paid good wages than to endanger the financial security of the family by starting all over again after years of college. And so Adolph remained at the Saltzer Shoe Company and held in check his yearning to attend the university...at least until things improved.

In the winter of 1920, the mood of the Austrian people turned ugly.

Chaya Sarah sat in the kitchen of the Ausübels' apartment, awaiting the return of the workingmen of the household. Charlotte, Jozef and Anna sat at the table, doing their homework. The mother was anxious, tense and impatient. Her next-door neighbor, Mrs. Goldschmidt, had just left after relating the shocking news that her husband was in the hospital. The poor man had been beaten senseless by a mob of wild-eyed, violent men, urged on by a chorus of women screaming, "Kill the Jew!" His sidecurls had been cut, his clothing torn to shreds, and a score of bones, broken. His face was almost unrecognizable – a distorted mass of red and purple with dark slits in bulging heaps of clotted blood masking his eyes. The mouth, twisted and swollen beyond belief, had hissed out the story of violence between the jagged edges of his broken teeth. He had survived only because his attackers thought he was dead.

Chaya Sarah's concern for her neighbor only heightened her fears for the safety of her husband and sons. "Where can they be? It's getting late."

"Can we eat, Mama?" asked Charlotte with impatience written across her face. "I'm hungry." Seeing her mother's worried look, she became silent again.

"Where's Papa?" wondered Jozef aloud. "And why are Adolph and Harry and Sam so late?"

"Please, children," replied Chaya Sarah. "Enough with the questions. I don't know." Her face turned gray as she spoke the last words. She raised a hand to her chest to still her racing heart. Regaining her composure, she began again, "Lotte, go downstairs. Stand near the door. Keep a sharp eye on everyone who passes. But don't show yourself. If you catch sight of Papa or the boys, call up to us. If you see signs of trouble, get right back up here."

Charlotte, obeying her mother's instructions, headed for the door.

"Remember," added Chaya Sarah with emphasis. "Stay in the shadows."

Charlotte exited without a word.

Chaya Sarah stared at the door for a while. Then she resumed her role as organizer of the household. "Anna, put the books away – yours, Jozef's and Lotte's. After that, take out the brown tablecloth, the dishes and the silverware. We must get ready for dinner."

"Yes, Mama."

Turning to her youngest son, Chaya Sarah continued to issue instructions. "Jozef, you have good eyes. Stay near the window, just behind the curtain. Watch to see if anyone is coming. Call me as soon as you see anything."

Chaya Sarah and Anna set the table. The mother stepped to the window, looked out nervously and then returned to the table. She sank heavily into a nearby seat, and then stared at the sideboard across the room. A large clock rested on it. She listened to its ticking in the oppressive silence of the room. She watched the slow inexorable movement of its hands. Fifteen minutes seemed much longer. Hearing Jozef move, she turned towards the window and looked at the boy expectantly, waiting to learn what lay in the darkness beyond him.

"Could that be Papa?" Jozef cried.

Chaya Sarah and Anna rushed to the window and peered outside, their faces pressed against the glass. The street was a faintly shimmering blackness, reflecting the weak light of a cloud-covered moon combined with the pale rays emanating from the flickering lamps, half-hidden behind windows. In the distance, Chaya Sarah saw a small figure walking briskly in their direction. She strained her eyes to define the image. It was a man – a dark suit silhouetted against the glistening jet of the city street. A head came into focus, a dark, brimmed hat atop a bearded face. Chaya Sarah sighed with relief. It was her husband.

"Now where are the boys?" She asked anxiously. There was no reply.

A few minutes later, Charlotte was joyfully galloping up the stairs, two at a time, while Judah ascended behind her, at a slower pace. The little man appeared at the door. Chaya Sarah rushed to embrace him.

"Where were you so late?" she asked when she felt able to speak. "Out there," she added, pointing, "They're beating up Jews. You with your beard and skullcap, they could have crippled you – God forbid – the way they crippled poor Mr. Goldschmidt."

"I was working late. But what's this about Mr. Goldschmidt? Are you talking of our neighbor, Ezra Goldschmidt? Who attacked him?"

"The poor man – God should help him now – was in the center of the city this morning. The streets were dark and angry with grumbling men gathered in groups, discussing the issues of the day. Ezra didn't know what they were talking about, only that their faces turned ugly at the sight of a beard or skullcap. Suddenly, a shout came as if from nowhere. 'Kill the Jews!' rang horrid in his ears. Before he knew what was happening, he was thrown to the ground, his head and body suffering a hundred blows delivered by vile hands. The next thing he knew, he was in a hospital bed, wrapped in blood-soaked bandages and barely able to discern images through his battered eyes." She paused to catch her breath, and then added, "Where are the boys? It's getting so late!"

"Be patient!" rejoined her husband. "It's only seven o'clock! Calm yourself! This is the Fourteenth District, not the Ghetto. There are so few Jews in this neighborhood; the hooligans will probably be looking elsewhere for victims. What's more, the boys are not noticeably Jewish. They have no beards or sidecurls and none of them wears a skullcap when traveling in the city. Look – Sam's shop is not near the center of the city, so he's not anywhere near the trouble. He should be home soon."

A few minutes later, Sam arrived home, and Harry, shortly thereafter. Each was embraced by his father and mother and greeted joyfully by his siblings. News of the riot had spread and so the boys had taken circuitous routes home.

"Now where's Adolph?" the mother asked with a tremor in her voice.

"He left the factory early to meet Jacob Schwartz, I think," replied Harry. "But I thought he'd be home before me."

"The Second District!" cried Chaya Sarah, shivering. "That's where Jacob lives (in a district largely inhabited by Jews)."

All their faces darkened with dread. There was an urge to do something – to check with all the hospitals, to call the police, to cry out to the heavens – but all they could really do was wait...and hope. The clock ticked and the family sat, waiting. No one ate. Eight o'clock, nine o'clock, ten o'clock. They took turns, two at a time, keeping watch at the window. The street was empty. No one spoke.

The sky turned angry, with blackness hovering menacingly overhead. Cold gray darts of rain came pouring down, sending rivers of dark water running down the street. Jagged bolts of lightening crossed the violent sky and booming thunder resounded like the roar of Russian cannon. It was Rozwadow again and the enemy was approaching; it was an ominous warning of the death and destruction to come. The resounding boom and the echo ended. This was followed by a silence interrupted only by the sound of rain against the window. The rain-streaked panes glowed a reflected rainbow of color in the shimmering light of a nearby lamp.

Chaya Sarah stared through the glass intently, hoping against hope that her son was safe. Houses and streets had taken the shapes of figures in a surrealistic painting; all elongated and distorted, curling and swirling in the shifting streams of water. The wind-swept wintry shower beat a tattoo on the glassy drum as whirling gusts moaned their way down the street. Eleven o'clock and the street was empty. Twelve o'clock. The rain had stopped and the street was still empty, silent and empty – a devastating silence.

Shortly after midnight Samuel cried out, "It's Adolph! I can see him. He looks fine."

"Thank God," said Chaya Sarah with relief as she rushed back to the window. It was indeed her eldest son.

Harry and Samuel ran down the stairs and escorted their brother up to the apartment. In a minute, Adolph was through the doorway. He threw his arms around Chaya Sarah and hugged her for dear life.

"It was terrible," he shuddered, unwilling to let her go. "You heard about the riot?"

"Yes," replied his mother, sighing. "What happened to you? Why are you so late?"

"I was caught in the middle of it. I had gone downtown to buy myself a shirt. Later, when I was sitting in a trolley, alongside Jacob Schwartz – you know him. Jacob lives in the Second District – we heard a lot of noise and some shouting in the street. The trolley came to a halt and a mob of young thugs, some carrying sticks, others, knives, boarded the trolley and went charging through the car. They passed Jacob and me. In fact they didn't trouble anyone in the car. But they were looking all right, looking for beards, looking for sidecurls, looking for skullcaps. I knew because after they left the car and the trolley started up again, I saw them chasing an old Jew with a beard. I couldn't see what happened to him; the car had rounded the corner. But I could hear the screaming. Jacob looked at me and I at him. What could we say? What could we do? We said nothing, but we felt a dreadful sense of shame. Maybe we should have stopped the trolley and rushed to his aid."

"Could you really have stopped them?" asked Chaya Sarah, rhetorically. "There would only have been two more battered Jews lying in the street."

"I guess you're right... But you can understand how we felt."

"Of course," replied his mother, nodding sadly. "I know all too well." She waited for Adolph to continue. When he remained silent, head hung low, she asked, "But what happened after that? What did you do from so early in the afternoon until after midnight?"

"Jacob and I got off the trolley, some distance from where he lives. We figured they'd be suspicious of anyone getting off too close to the district. Then we started to walk towards his home, using side streets wherever possible. Every time we saw some of those hooligans, we tried to avoid appearing anxious. Most of the time they just ran past us, waving their knives or wooden clubs or lengths of pipe in the air. One group of them stopped to study us carefully. I stared right back and pretended I was annoyed. Then one of them said, 'They can't be Jews. Let's get moving.'"

"Thank God," murmured Chaya Sarah. "But why did you choose this time to go to the Second District? Were you oblivious to the danger?"

"Jacob's my friend," appealed her son with pain in his eyes. "It just didn't seem right...especially after what happened in the trolley... I just had to..." His voice trailed off into silence. There were tears in his eyes.

"Of course," replied Chaya Sarah, comfortingly.

Adolph stared at the floor.

"Go on," said Judah. "Tell us what happened."

Adolph reached into his pocket and came up with a handkerchief. He dried his eyes, swallowed the last salt of his tears and then began, "I'm all right now."

"So what happened?" asked Charlotte impatiently.

"Two of those glaring monsters seemed about to strike us when that fellow called them off. I think the only thing that saved us was the stare I gave them. A Jew is supposed to cringe and bow his head: At least that's the way they reason."

"Gosh," said little Jozef, "weren't you scared?"

"I was scared all right. My chest felt like someone was sitting on it. But I was not about to let them know it."

144

"That's a lesson worth remembering," interjected Chaya Sarah. "Never let your enemy think you're afraid of him... But go on, Adolph. How did you finally get out of the mess?"

"Well, every time we got close to the Second District, we saw barricades. There were more thugs brandishing their weapons, standing beside the mounds of rubble and overturned carts. They were like an army laying siege to a city. This was what one of them called the *Judengegend* (Jewish neighborhood). They were checking all those who attempted to enter or leave. I didn't see them beating anyone, but I heard a few of them brag about beating up Jews. Jacob and I decided not to chance passing the barricades."

"Why didn't you both come here at once?" Chaya Sarah asked.

"I guess we should have. It's just that he was worried about his family and I wanted to stick with him."

"Did you ever get through?" questioned Samuel.

"We did."

"How?" asked Judah, stroking his beard.

"The soaking rain was what saved us. It drove most of them to seek shelter. We crossed over an unmanned section of the barricade in the darkness. It was eerie once we got into the district."

"Eerie?" puzzled Chaya Sarah.

"Eerie... To walk along those quiet streets – not a bit of rubble, every door and every window in its place – you'd never have guessed that anything bad had been going on..."

"So go on," said Charlotte.

"I accompanied Jacob to his house, then turned and came home. And that's the whole story."

There was a long pause as each of them reflected on the events of the day.

"You're home," said Judah, breaking the silence. "Safe and sound. That's what counts... Now I, for one, am not hungry, but the little ones probably are. Why don't we all sit down and have something to eat?"

Anna looked up, as if by reflex, upon hearing the word "food," but she still appeared troubled. "Why were they doing such things? We never hurt them."

"Because there's blindness and the genuine hate," replied her mother. "It's been there all along. Yes, this is the city of Freud and Herzl, of Schoenberg and the Adlers. Yes, Jews have contributed greatly to the cultural heritage of this city, but we're hated and despised all the same. At this moment they're angry over losing the war, so they blame the Jews. Right now they can't get jobs, so they blame the Jews. They feel a need for a scapegoat, so we're the logical choice. But we wouldn't be the 'logical choice' if that contempt had not been simmering all along beneath the surface."

"Why do you draw such a conclusion?" queried Charlotte. "I can understand the war and the jobs, but have they really hated us all along?"

"Lotte, it's there and it's been there long before we came to Vienna. Until now it's been a loathing for Jews. And that loathing has even become part of their language – *Judenblick* (literally translated as the "look of the Jew") stands for 'the evil eye.' It was always reflected in the snide remarks about 'dark, oily bearded people who cheat and corrupt the city'; it's been the job discrimination; it's been the requirement for registration. Do you think that being registered as a Jew has no significance? Why do you think Gustav Mahler accepted baptism? Do you think they would select a Jew to conduct the orchestra?" (He had to convert to Catholicism to secure the position of Conductor of the Vienna Court Opera.)

"But the Viennese are not like that," insisted Anna. "They're good people."

"And these *good people* had a Karl Lueger for their mayor," replied Chaya Sarah acidly. "What do you think he preached all those years before we came here: Love thy neighbor? They called themselves the 'Christian Social Party.' Their idea of being 'social' was to drive out the 200,000 Jews who live here. (Karl Lueger, 1844-1910, was leader of the anti-Semitic Christian Social Party and mayor of Vienna.)

"Now they're hungry, so their words turn to violence. Tomorrow their bellies may be full and the weapons may be sheathed. But the darkness and the hate will still be there, ready to burst to the surface at any time."

Again there was silence.

"Wonder why they never entered the Second District?" inquired Charlotte, breaking the silence. "Instead, they chose to blockade the area. Adolph, do you think they really meant to do harm? Or were they just beating their breasts to make noise?"

"It wasn't just breast-beating," replied Adolph, bitterly. "It was blood on their weapons. If they kept out of the ghetto, the reason was not concern for the Jews; it was out of concern for themselves. They knew that the Jews would greet them with rocks and bottles thrown from windows. So their assaults were limited to those occasions where they outnumbered the Jew, ten to one, with all the weapons in their hands."

"Listen everyone," interrupted Chaya Sarah. "It's time."

"For dinner?" questioned little Jozef.

"Dinner?" his mother smiled faintly. "Well, we can have that too." Her face turned deadly serious as she continued. "I mean it's time to leave. We must pack our bags and get out of Austria."

"But where shall we go?" asked Charlotte, unhappily. "And Mother, we all have friends here."

"Friends we can have elsewhere. As for where we're going, we're going to America. My mother is there. Most of my sisters and brothers are there. We must make arrangements to join them."

"But Mama," said Adolph, pleadingly. "I have a good job. I'm already a factory manager. And if I keep saving, I'll have the funds to open a plant of my own... I mean a factory of our own. Harry, I'm sure, will join me. Sure there are a lot of Viennese who despise us and even hate us. But that's not all Viennese. The saner people will realize how much Jews have contributed to this city. A logical view will eventually prevail. Look, if we leave Vienna now, all that we've accomplished thus far shall have been for naught. We'll have to start all over again." Adolph studied his mother's resolute face. She would not be swayed from her decision. Nevertheless, he continued to plead. "Mama, the police will stop all the rioting. It won't go on forever."

But Chaya Sarah insisted. "No, Adolph. The handwriting is on the wall. I don't think we should wait until we're all like Mr. Goldschmidt, in the hospital or, God forbid, even worse happens to us." She turned to her husband and added, "What do you say? Do we stay or go?"

Judah shook his head sadly. "You're right. We must go. But America is far off and getting there will be costly. We don't have enough money to pay for eight tickets."

Chaya Sarah thought for a while and then replied. "We have enough money to pay for two tickets, if the price has not changed radically from what it was two weeks ago. Adolph and Harry will use them. Judah, you and Sam will continue to work here. We can live on your two salaries if we scrimp and do without. When Adolph and Harry get to New York, they can stay with my mother. They'll get jobs. They'll save as much as they can. We can count on both of them to do that. When they've accumulated a large enough sum, they'll buy two more tickets. Then Judah, you and Samuel will join them. Then with four working and saving in America, we'll soon be able to follow. That's how it will be."

I THANK GOD

I HAVE BEEN viewed as a workaholic all my life. In addition to an active career in medicine for more years than most people ever dream of working, I have been involved in a dozen different projects and have continued to work on each of them.

What drives me on? Perhaps it was from observing my parents and grandparents. If you saw how my father struggled for the survival of his family and his people, beyond anything that a frail human body should endure, you will understand why I view the burden placed upon me by my workload as but a feather, for which I thank God.

On the twenty-first day of May 1921, two young immigrants stood on the deck of a ship in New York Harbor. Like so many millions before them, they looked with awe at the Statue of Liberty across the bay. The warm, late spring sun illuminated their faces. Adolph, the older of the two, leaned against the rail, his full head of wavy brown hair fluttering in the breeze. The ocean spray wet his smooth, fair, handsome face and flushed his cheeks pink. His gentle brown eyes, slightly puffed at the lower lids, narrowed against the breeze, and his mouth, half open, drank in the salty air. With his gaze still directed at the statue, he thought aloud in his native tongue:

"Harry, the light of the torch is for us. With God's help, we've seen our last beating."

Harry inclined his head towards his older brother and nodded, "I guess Mama was right."

A few days later they were boarding with their grandmother, Martel Hobler Korn and Aunts Brena and Bella in the Lower East Side of Manhattan. They were eager to learn about this strange new land as quickly as possible. Here, people rushed back and forth, almost without stopping. It was a pace unseen in the villages of Galicia, where little changed from year to year, or in continental Vienna which rested on a Strauss waltz and past imperial glory.

The transition was made easier by a host of familiar faces. Seven of their mother's eight brothers and sisters were already in New York. Scores of old friends from Rozwadow, drawn by the lure of the *Goldene Medina* or uprooted by the violence of the World War, had come to America before them and now greeted them with warming bear hugs, advice and encouragement. (*Goldene Medina* literally means the "Golden Land." This was a reflection of the golden opportunities many immigrants believed were available in the United States.)

Within a few weeks they were both working with restless energy in a shoe factory, but at the bottom of the ladder. Adolph spent his nights studying the English language, as well as writing to his family in Vienna. The written word was a reflection of his soul, and so he wrote long narratives in which he poured out his feelings and his experiences. And he waited eagerly for responses from the mirror image of his inner being, his mother.

At work he would converse only in Yiddish or, as the occasion arose, in German. He wanted to be certain of his command of English before he employed that new tongue. Reserved and sensitive by nature, it pained him to hear barbs directed at others. Adolph wished to avoid embarrassment. He had witnessed the snickers and, even worse, the mocking laughter that so often were the response of Americans to the imperfect phrasing in English by Greenhorns (an expression employed by Americans to refer to immigrants who were unschooled in English and the ways of Americans). He and Harry saved every penny they could. They denied themselves everything, short of food and a change of clothing, so as to hasten the day when their family would join them.

A year later they had saved enough to purchase two tickets to America. Judah and Samuel joined them. The more workers, the sooner the family would be reunited. The four Ausubel men (the *umlaut*, two dots above the letter "u" used in German in the name Ausübel, was dropped in the United States.) rented an apartment in the Williamsburg section of Brooklyn. Within a year they had saved enough for the passage of Chaya Sarah and the three younger children.

"Lotte, Jozef and Anna should go to school and learn to be Americans," suggested Chaya Sarah to her husband one day, shortly after her arrival. "The older boys will continue to work and I'll study English with them at home. We'll need the income if we're to send at least one of the children to a university."

Judah nodded his agreement.

"And what about you, Judah: Will you learn English?"

"It's beyond me. I'm an old man." He lowered his eyes, ashamed. "You know I never had any schooling." He raised his eyes and tried to smile. "The whole area here is teeming with people from the *shtetelech* (plural of *Shtetl*) who understand me, so I'll do my best with Yiddish. It's the quality of my work that they should be interested in."

Chaya Sarah replied with an affectionate arm placed around his shoulder as she smiled, sadly.

Samuel worked as a union carpenter while his older brothers continued as employees in the Barnard Shoe Company. As for their Yiddish-speaking father, opportunities were limited to the odd and distasteful jobs that others declined. His appearance (the "funny-looking" long white beard and dark clothing) made him look strange and perhaps even frightening to those unfamiliar with Orthodox Jewry. His inability to communicate in English was equated with weakness and, even, stupidity. Under these circumstances, the potential for exploitation of the elderly Jew was considerable. He was low man on the totem pole – the last hired and the first fired. And when he did find work, even at low wages, his pay envelope often contained only a small portion of the promised compensation.

On one occasion he was employed in the construction of shelving. From Sunday through Thursday, he put in eleven hours of work each day. He paused only a few minutes for lunch. On Friday he arrived at the workplace at 7 AM and worked until 3 PM. He had to leave early to prepare for *Shabbos*. The pay envelope was waiting for him. Judah opened it. He stared hard at its contents – a five-dollar bill. He knew the number and the picture. It was ten dollars short of the fifteen he had been promised. Perplexity and sadness were written across his face. He had so hoped for something special for the Sabbath – a few dollars to set aside for Jozef's education or a new dress, at last, for Chaya Sarah. He looked up questioningly, pleadingly, at his employer, holding the envelope and the single five-dollar bill in his hand.

The pudgy-faced, stocky employer glared at Judah fiercely and snarled around his cigar in staccato English: "Your work wasn't good enough. Besides, you're cheating me out of a half-day's work. I wasn't born yesterday. Take it, Mockie (an insulting term for an illiterate immigrant), or you won't get a cent!"

Judah did not wait for a translation. The man's eyes told him everything. Judah's response was not tears or a cry of outrage or a raised fist. Rather, it was only the look of resignation so familiar to European Jewry, and a silent prayer to the Merciful One to lighten the load of His servant.

Slowly, he made his way home. His legs moved heavily as if they were dragging a weighty load. But his steps became faster and lighter as the thought of the approaching Sabbath clouded out that twisted, bulging face, the harsh sound of that voice and the saliva spewing out from around the cigar. It would soon be *Shabbos*. There was no time for unkind thoughts. He had to wash and change and get to the synagogue.

A meal on the Sabbath had a special joy of its own. Amid the geniality of Yiddish conversation and singing, Adolph asked, "How was your new job, Papa?"

A dark look crossed the old man's bearded face. It left its mark, even as he urged the others to continue the singing.

"What did he pay you?" Adolph insisted.

"Five dollars," was the glum reply.

"He can't do that to you. He promised fifteen. Did you finish all the shelving?"

"All."

Adolph's face turned grim with determination. "I'm going to talk to him. There must be something... This is America." The years of work in a law office in Rozwadow loomed before Adolph's eyes. He planned his moves step by step, from polite request, to firm insistence as to his father's rights, to vigorous complaint to the authorities.

"Let it be," replied Judah, softly. "We're strangers in this land and want to stay here. If they don't pay us from time to time, at least they don't beat us. This man's not a human being. He snorts fire. All we'll get for our effort is trouble."

"But Papa," pleaded Adolph, "didn't you once stand up to a prince?"

"Leave it as your father says," interrupted Chaya Sarah with finality in her voice. "A man who does such a thing is not going to back down. What proof do we have that he promised your father more or that he did not give him the fifteen dollars? None. Just a Yiddish-speaking old man's word against a big shot with money and influence. It would embarrass your father and he still wouldn't get his wages. The Lord will punish the wicked in His own time. And as for us, we'll manage."

There was silence around the table as father, mother and six children absorbed the implication of her words. Then Chaya Sarah smiled softly and turned to her youngest son.

"And how was school this week?" she asked.

❖ ❖ ❖

"I've been promoted. In charge of the fitting room," Adolph reported to his mother the following week. His face showed his delight.

"And Harry's a designer," smiled Chaya Sarah. She was silent for a moment and then, as in a remembered dream, she burst out, "I had such plans, such hopes for you – the university, a law degree... My Adolph in a factory – the Barnard Shoe Company instead of a law office. The Almighty works in mysterious ways. Who are we to question His wisdom? I once even imagined going to the university, myself... So Jozef will become a professional and you – you and Harry will save part of what you earn and put it aside."

"We'll give it to you," Adolph insisted.

"No. You'll bring home half and put the rest away. One day, when you've saved enough, you'll have a factory of your own – with your brother as a partner.

"It's the family. It's the future of our family that counts. We must work together. Your sons will go to the university, the Lord willing. And your daughters as well. I hear that women go to the university in this country. Keep in mind: Life is a continuum. If your children and grandchildren achieve, you achieve." She looked into his tear-filled eyes. "What am I telling you this for? You know it already – every thought in my mind, every feeling in my heart."

Judah returned from work early one day to find his wife lying on her side in bed. She was moaning in pain. Her face was pale and drawn, her hands pressed against her abdomen, her legs flexed and moving as if she were unable to find a comfortable position.

"Ruler of the Universe," he cried, "what has happened?"

"Oh, Judah," she groaned, "I don't feel well. Call for a doctor."

The bearded man rushed out of the room, to return a few minutes later.

"Did you find a doctor so quickly?" she asked hurriedly, continuing to twist back and forth.

"No," he responded rapidly as he reached for her hands. "I asked Mrs. Jacobs, next door, to go for one... When did you get the pain?"

"I've been getting attacks for months, on and off, but never as bad as today. It feels like it would get better if I could only pass some gas."

"Did you eat anything special before you got the attack?"

"No," she moaned. "My appetite has not been good for some time. I didn't even take a bite of food today."

"I'd better not ask so many questions. You seem to suffer more when answering them," said Judah anxiously, biting his lower lip. "The doctor is sure to be here soon."

He pulled a chair to the side of the bed and sat there, covering her hands gently, comfortingly, with his. His usual tranquil look was gone. He watched her uneasily, his brows drawn together and his mouth twisted in pained empathy. Beads of perspiration swelled on his forehead like huge glistening tears. Weighted down with sadness, they rolled down to disappear into his gray beard.

The doctor was clean-shaven and looked stately and severe, dressed in the quality of dark fabric that Judah associated with importance. Judah was asked to leave the room.

The pale little husband went into the kitchen where he waited, hands clasped together, twisting one palm against the other. From time to time he would raise the left thumb of his clasped hands to his lip. He paced back and forth.

Finally, the doctor came out of the bedroom, carrying his black medical bag. His grim face hinted strongly of bad news.

"Mr. Ausubel," said the physician professionally, "I gave your wife an injection to relieve the pain." His Yiddish was clear and direct.

Judah stared obliquely at the physician, from a bowed head. The bearded man waited apprehensively for further news.

The doctor placed his bag on a chair. He carefully removed the stethoscope from its position around his neck and folded it neatly into his bag. Then he removed his glasses and wiped them with a handkerchief, taking particular care at one corner of a lens. Each slow, methodic movement added additional weight of tension to the hunched shoulders of the bearded man. Judah's heart quickened in the silence, but he said nothing.

Finally the doctor continued: "She is very sick. Her belly is soft now, but it was in spasm. She needs tests. I would prefer to admit her to the hospital, but she wants the tests done in my office. However, if the pain gets worse, I will want her in the hospital." The doctor extended his fingers, revealing a vial. "Here are some pills. Give her one every three hours if she has moderate pain. Have an ambulance take her to the hospital if the pain gets severe. Otherwise, I'll expect you to bring her to my office tomorrow morning at ten to begin the tests. Here is my card."

"Thank you, doctor," said the sad-faced old man as he escorted the physician to the door.

After the doctor had gone, Judah went into the bedroom. Chaya Sarah was still lying on her side, but she was not thrashing about. She raised a hand that Judah promptly reached for and kissed.

"Don't say anything to the children," she said softly. "Maybe it won't be so bad. But..."

"But what?" asked her husband.

"But I think it's not so good," she answered with her face sinking. "I used to watch my father helping sick people back home. When they kept getting this kind of pain, they didn't last long."

Tears flowed as Judah held tightly to her hand with both of his.

The next two weeks were spent going to doctors' offices. There were blood tests and x-rays. Tubes were inserted and specimens taken. Finally, they knew. It was as bad as Chaya Sarah had feared. Her illness was fatal and she probably had no more than a few months to live.

It was a Friday evening, late in the winter of 1926. In the purple darkness that comes with the passing of day into night, Chaya Sarah rose, with difficulty, from her bed. Her face now was darkened and wrinkled and her cheeks, sunken. The quiet, tall woman put on a clean Sabbath dress and her plain, dark wig. She moved uneasily through the room, resting momentarily with her hands on the bureau as she took a few deep breaths. The frail, shadowy figure entered the kitchen and headed for a hanging cabinet in the corner of the room. Again she halted, holding on to the cabinet doorknob as her chest alternately rose and sank with labored respirations. Summoning her last ounce of strength, she opened the cabinet door and removed a candle, which she placed in a holder on the kitchen table. Lifting her hands before her, she recited the prayer for the lighting of the Sabbath candle.

A key turned in the door, but she did not hear it. The door slid open silently and her son, Adolph, entered. He looked with concern as he spied the skeletal figure swaying, silhouetted in the pale flickering candlelight.

"Mama, what are you doing out of bed?"

"It's the Sabbath," she sighed. "I was lighting the candle."

"But you ought to rest. The girls should do that." He surveyed the shadows. "Where are Lotte and Anna?"

"They must be over at friends and probably didn't notice the time. They'll be home soon, I'm sure."

"Then come, Mama. Let me help you back to bed. You can rest there until dinner."

Adolph supported her haltingly back to her bedroom. Her wasted body barely dented the mattress as she sank into it. He sat at the edge of the bed and held her hand gently, reassuringly. Chaya Sarah tried to keep a smile on her face, but a pained expression kept coming back to it. She studied Adolph's countenance. He appeared serious, yet there was something in his face that did not quite fit with that picture of solemnity.

"Mama," he burst out, "I have good news."

"Good news?" repeated Chaya Sarah, her eyes brightening a bit. "What's happened?"

"Nothing has happened yet. That is, nothing except that Frances said, 'Yes.' I'm going to get married! To Frances Einwohner. You met her. Her mother is from Galicia and her father from Lublin."

A weary smile came to her emaciated lips. "I'm happy for you, Adolph. I remember the girl. She's a nice girl. I remember her mother. You may have forgotten. Her mother stayed in our house on her way to America when you were quite young. She's a distant cousin." Then reflecting, she added, "Did you tell your father?"

"No, Mama. You're the first to hear it."

"Well...we'll have to make plans...with her parents." She paused, contemplating a whole series of necessary arrangements – the rabbi, the hall, the caterers, the invitations, how many to invite and where to seat them. "It's not like the old country," she reflected aloud, "where parents told the children whom they were to marry. But it's better this way. Now the question is: Where will they want the wedding and how many do the parents invite?" To herself, she mused, *There's always someone who feels left out. But you can't invite the world.*

"Mama, it's decided." There was finality in his voice. "We'll be married here. The apartment is small, so we can only invite the closest relatives. Now don't argue with me. I don't want you feeling sick, trying to run around at the wedding. So it will be here. We'll move the furniture out...except your bed. They can bring the canopy into the room. We'll open the windows and let in the stars. You can rest where you are now and see the whole thing. We'll get married in two months."

The old woman glowed within. Her cold, thin fingers gripped his hand more tightly and she murmured with feeling, "You really want me there."

Adolph bent his head towards her and kissed her hand. She could feel warm drops falling on her forearm, the tears from his eyes. He kept his head buried near her hand and spoke in a cracked voice, choking on his tears.

"We really want you there. You'll be there. You'll be fine."

❖ ❖ ❖

In the spring of 1926, Adolph and Frances were wed under a canopy in a bedroom in Brooklyn, New York. Chaya Sarah watched from her bed. She did not have the strength to escort the bride in the traditional circling of the canopy. Her withered body had grown even weaker in the two months preceding the wedding. Her face was as wrinkled and sunken as a prune, yet her eyes, bulging from hollow sockets, exuded only happiness and contentment.

Chaya Sarah knew that it was the last wedding she would ever attend. Shortly before the wedding, she spoke to her eldest son. "Adolph, you know that my time here is short. Your father is a good man, but this family needs a leader who knows the outside world. You have the understanding to be that leader and so I pass my mantle to you. When I am gone, it will be up to you to care for your father and all your brothers and sisters. When I was a girl, I dreamed of going to the university. But circumstances did not allow it. And so I dreamed that my children would attend the university. The Lord knows you had the brain to go on to greater things. A war intervened and we had to flee for our lives. In Vienna we needed an income to survive. You took up the mantle and provided for us all. If you ran a company, you saw to it that Harry had a good job. Then came the anti-Semitic riots and I sent you to America as the torchbearer who would bring our family to these shores. You gave up a good position without hesitation because we were depending on you to save our family. Again, you performed magnificently, and so now we are all safe in a free country. At every step, you were the son I hoped to have.

"I realize that it is a heavy burden that I now place on your shoulders just as you are about to begin married life. But again, you have to be the guiding light. See to it that Harry has employment. He is a good worker, but he does not possess your talent. Sam has learned carpentry from your father, so he'll make his way in the world as a carpenter. I know that you will see to it that Jozef completes his university education and the girls marry respectable men. And now I have one more favor to ask of you as the head of the family: Take your brothers and sisters along on your honeymoon – all except Lotte. She and your father will take care of me here. The younger ones already recognize you as the leader, and so being with you on your honeymoon will enable them to have some enjoyment instead of the pain of watching their mother dying. Frances is young, but she already comprehends family responsibility. I pray that Frances will show the understanding to accept the burden I have placed upon both your shoulders."

The warm rays of the June sun came, but Chaya Sarah had to appreciate them from the distance. She was no longer able to rise from her bed. She would take a few tablespoons of nourishment, but no more. Her skin was almost separated from the wasted frame.

She looked up one day to see her little husband. The pained expression on her face disappeared and was replaced by an almost angelic glow.

"Judah, I thank God for having lived to witness the marriage of our firstborn. I will not be here to see a son graduated from the university, but you will. And Adolph has assured me that he will look after you and the children when I am gone." Her sunken eyes firmed a bit. "Adolph, Harry and Sam are grown men, too old to begin again as students, but Jozef is still young. He must continue his studies, Adolph will see to that. And one thing more: Jozef is taking his tests this week. Keep him, as best you can, from knowing how sick I am. Let him confine his thoughts to his studies. He must get good grades. I'll stay alive 'til he finishes his exams."

And she stayed alive until the exams were over. On July 24, 1926, Chaya Sarah passed away. Following Jewish tradition, she was buried before sundown on the following day.

With a small down payment, Adolph and Frances bought a piece of property – a six-family apartment house in the East New York section of Brooklyn. They used one of the four-room apartments as their home. To reduce expenses, Adolph served as the janitor, getting up early each morning to fill the stove with coal. He also did whatever repairs were needed to maintain the property. He followed a new schedule... For five days a week he worked at his job in the shoe factory. On the weekends, he would do the repairs. Frances served as charlady, getting down on her knees to wash floors in the hallways and on the staircases.

One by one, Judah Ausubel's children were married off, until only the two youngest remained with their father. Their crowded apartment of yesterday was now occupied by only Judah, Jozef and Anna.

A son was born to Adolph and Frances and they named him Marvin (Moses, in Hebrew, after his great grandfather, Moses Ausübel of Rozwadow). A *Pidyon HaBen* was held thirty days after his birth, as is customary in Judaism for the firstborn son of the mother, and Marvin was repurchased from the *Cohen* for five silver coins. Marvin was a seventh-generation *Pidyon*

HaBen, the firstborn son of a firstborn son of a firstborn son, back to Moses Azubel, born in Dzikow in the eighteenth century. The coins were then exchanged for paper money and set aside, to be used for an eighth generation. (*Pidyon HaBen* means the redemption of the firstborn son. The firstborn son, who is not descended from a *Cohen* or *Levi*, would be dedicated to the service of the Almighty in return for the sparing of the firstborn in Egypt. The father redeems his son, when the child is thirty days old, by the payment of five shekels [silver coins] to a *Cohen*. All *Cohanim* are direct paternal descendants of Aaron, who was the older brother of Moses and the first priest of Israel.)

Adolph and Harry worked hard in the shoe trade and saved as much as they could. They were hoping to start a business of their own. With the $5,000 they finally amassed, they purchased machinery, and a shoe factory was opened. It was named the Marvin Shoe Company, in honor of the first of the new generation of Ausubels.

Then a daughter was born to Harry and his wife, Dinah.

With the Ausubel brothers struggling to get their new business on its feet, finances were tight. And so when Frances became pregnant again, Adolph and his wife knew they could not afford a hospital for the delivery of the child. Their second son was born at home. They named him Herbert (Chaim Yaakov in Hebrew, after Adolph's grandfather, Jacob Korn, the boatbuilder and scholar).

Adolph paid a visit to his father one day. He presented him with an offer. The young man's face was earnest, his eyes gentle and appealing.

"Papa, come and live with Frances and me. Joey and Anna will come too. Joey is going to school and Anna is a young girl who would rather go out on dates than stay home to cook and clean like a housewife. With us, you'll all have a home. It will be crowded, but it will be family. You can watch your two grandsons grow to manhood. Besides, Anna will get married one day and who will care for you then?"

The old man puzzled, rubbing his beard. "Adolph, you live in four rooms with a wife and two children. Where could you possibly put three more people? After all, this is America, not Rozwadow." He halted, searching for words – words to convey his deep-felt appreciation for the offer and for the love behind the offer. He felt a heavy warmth in his bosom, more than vintage wine could produce. *But it was impossible*, he thought, *well intentioned, but too many complications stood in the way*. Aloud, he went on, "What about your wife? She took a whole family along on your trip after the wedding. Does she now want to be saddled with the care of your father, sister and brother? You may want more children. Where will you put them? On the roof?"

The son pursed his lips, twisting them, biting them. Tears welled in his eyes and rolled down his cheeks. He responded in a choked voice. "Papa, you've had a hard life. You're entitled to have your children care for you. You've worked since you were thirteen. You were the oldest of your mother's five children. She died when you were all still young, and you had to make your way in the world as soon as you became a Bar Mitzvah. Yet, what did you do with your first savings? Buy land and build a house for your father. Are you not entitled to that which you did for your father? I am your son as you are your father's son. We are commanded to honor our father and mother. Having been a dutiful son yourself, how much more are you entitled to be cared for by dutiful sons! As for my wife, Frances was born in this country, but her parents were not. She was brought up in a home where they show respect for parents. She will make a home for you and care for you. As for my future children, God willing, the Almighty will provide. We'll work harder and we'll manage. Times are hard now with the depression...but they'll get better. When we need more room, we'll get more room."

And so Judah, his son Jozef and his daughter Anna moved into the four-room apartment, joining Adolph and Frances and their two sons.

It was a crowded and busy home with no place in which to sulk. But there was always room for a party with two dozen guests wedged together, like sardines, around the single rectangular dining room table. They might have been assembled to celebrate Jozef's winning of a school competition or to welcome a newcomer from Europe or a visitor from Israel. That one dining room table was to serve as desk for Jozef who was going to college, for Marvin and Herbert who were attending elementary and then high school, and for Adolph who composed poems or wrote letters to relatives and friends who were spread across four continents.

Anna married and moved from the apartment. A daughter born to Frances and Adolph replaced her. They named her Corinne (Chaya Sarah in Hebrew, after her grandmother). Jozef became an architect, married and moved to an apartment of his own.

Years passed. Judah's beard was now a snowy white. His already small body became even smaller, as the bones of his spine wore down with age. He loved to talk to his grandsons in the bedroom they shared. Conversation went on into the wee hours of the morning. He would tell them of the

Old World and its villages, about weddings and births, about sickness and suffering and death, about his generation and the generations that preceded him. As his grandfather Avraham had narrated to him, so did Judah retell the history of his people.

Herbert, at an early age, developed a passion for history. At a time in life when other children were reading comic books, Herbert was reading history texts. And when his grandfather related a story, Herbert would try to identify the period during which the events took place.

It was a living history that they shared. These were real people, Judah's people, and Herbert's people. These were real events, as real as if they were happening that very minute. The Revolution of 1848 was not just a chapter in a book, whose pages were turning brown with age; it was Judah's grandfather, Avraham, with terror in his eyes, hiding from the enraged mob of peasants; it was the convulsing body of an Austrian officer being struck, blow after blow; it was the Polish peasants quarreling over the disposition of the spoils – the rings on the officer's fingers and the clothes on his back. The stories each night were new, vital and exciting. The telling would end only when Frances entered the room and appealed for silence. "Please," she implored, "go to sleep. The boys have to go to school in a few hours."

These were hard years for the struggling family in East New York. The Great Depression may have begun to fade on an economist's chart, but in the home of Adolph Ausubel, it continued and even worsened. Orders for shoes were hard to obtain in the buyer's market that prevailed. (A buyer's market is an economic term for periods in which there are more goods offered for sale than are desired by buyers. The result is a fall in price.) When a pair of shoes was sold, it was often at below cost, just to keep the employees working and hoping. Rents had to be paid and utility bills met. Adolph would come home at night, often past midnight, heartsick, embarrassed. A whole day had been spent going from store to store, and Adolph had nothing to show for it. Late at night, little Herbert could hear the sobs of his father who was too proud for charity and too human not to feel the pain. Not even Grandpa's story could drown out the sobs. Adolph sat in the kitchen, unable to sleep, and poured out his heart on a scrap of paper.

Go away, you wretched gloom. Leave forever, ne'r return.
Give me reason to sing, that my tears may cease to burn.

(Translation of an excerpt from *No More Gloom* written in Yiddish by Adolph Ausubel in 1936.)

To add to his misery, there was the building in which they lived. Property values had fallen drastically. The mortgage on the property was significantly greater than the market price of the building. Taxes, coal bills and the like had to be paid. Rents had to be slashed to keep the apartments occupied.

Some advised Adolph to simply default on the loan. But he would not. He worked all the harder. He was now a painter and a plasterer, a roofer and a plumber...anything, rather than to announce that he had failed.

"Besides," he said to Frances, "where would we live? Here, at least, we have a roof over our heads. Things are bound to get better."

But not everyone recognized his financial difficulty.

"Your carpets must be getting thicker," remarked one of the tenants, "to store all that money we pay you in rent."

"It's a pity I don't own a carpet," smiled Adolph palely in response.

Samuel Ausubel asked for a family meeting. Judah sat with his three older sons in his bedroom late one evening. Marvin and Herbert lay on their beds, quietly following the proceedings. Frances observed from the doorway.

"As you know," Sam began, "my wife has hay fever. Summers are terrible for her. I would like to buy a summerhouse in Bethlehem where the air is free of the pollen that troubles her. It's a resort town in the White Mountains of New Hampshire. We can rent out some rooms to boarders to cover the costs of the property. So it's a good business proposition. What I need from you all is help – money to get us started. What can you each give me?"

Judah reached for his bankbook, hidden under the mattress. "I have a little over 2,000 dollars. You can have it. I'll keep the rest so the account can stay open."

Samuel next looked to Adolph. "And you?"

Adolph looked at him uneasily. "I can't say just yet. I'll have to see."

"But I have to know how much, soon. The property won't wait forever. And the smaller the mortgage, the easier it will be for us to manage it. You've got a business...and property, too."

Adolph caught Frances' angry look. "I'll let you know in a few days," he said.

Samuel turned away in annoyance. Then he looked at Harry.

"Adolph knows what we have in the business account. And you know I've had problems. We have Dinah's mother to care for. We have an apartment with rent to pay..."

"Well, it looks like a working man can't expect any help from manufacturers," concluded Samuel, bitterly.

Sam and Harry said their good-byes.

Adolph and Frances sat in the kitchen after they were gone.

"You know my feelings on this," began Frances. "Why didn't you tell him straight out? You don't have any money to spare."

"How can I? He's my brother."

"He's your brother. Harry's your brother. And you're not their father. They already have one."

"Let's not have another argument. My father and the boys will hear us in the next room."

"Your father won't understand us in English."

"But the boys..."

"We can't talk in our bedroom. Have you forgotten? Corinne sleeps there."

"Look, we'll talk another day. When you're calmer."

"It's always another day, Adolph. All our married life it's been that way. Someone will hear. We've never had a place we could call our own, even a place to argue – in private."

"What are you saying? We didn't have my father and Annie and Joey living with us when we got married. It was only later, after mother..."

"After she died. But your brothers and sisters came along on our honeymoon! Who ever heard of such a thing? We couldn't even have privacy on our honeymoon!"

"But my mother was ill and dying," he pleaded. "I wanted them to share our joy, to be distracted for a few days from the sadness at home."

"And me?" she replied acidly, "Didn't I count?"

"Of course you do. You're my *wife*. Let's stop arguing now."

Her voice rose. "No. We haven't gotten to my point. You should tell Sam the truth! The only money you have is the money you owe others. And you're not going to borrow additional money to give Sam so he can borrow less. It's about time you let them all worry about their families and you paid attention to yours."

"And I don't worry about my children?"

"Of course you do. But you're also always acting like the father to your siblings. You think you've got to worry for them even though they're all grown up with families of their own. And you act like a father to your father as well."

"My father took care of his father. The least I can do is be a dutiful son. Would you want me to set a bad example for our children?"

"I'll tell you one thing: I never want to be a burden to my children... Oh! Oh! Oh!" Frances cried.

"What's the matter? Is it another of your attacks?" His voice conveyed fright.

"Such waves of pain. Give me a glass of tea. Oh! Oh! Oh!"

Herbert heard his mother's cry. He ran into the kitchen to find her doubled up, lying on the floor, her hands clutching her abdomen.

"Mama, what's the matter?"

"Go to sleep. It's just some gas. It will pass. I've had it before." She saw his frightened look. "Don't worry. I'll be all right."

The next evening, Frances was waiting in the kitchen when Adolph arrived home late. As soon as he entered, she began, "Well, did you tell Sam?"

"I didn't call Sam. I was with customers 'til late."

"But you're going to tell Sam what we spoke about?"

"I'm not sure. I'll have to see." His eyes evaded hers.

"It's your wife you're talking to, not a stranger. I should have a say in it."

"He's *my* brother."

"He's *your* brother. He spoke of *manufacturers!*" Frances shouted, angrily. "Union members know that when they work they get a pay check. But if there's nothing left, the bosses go home empty-handed. Did he ever think of that? Does he know that you sank what little savings we had back into the business? And this 'property' of ours as he called it: The mortgages are bigger than what you could get for it. Even with all our hard work, we don't see a penny from it. Does he know that? When his Gertrude was pregnant, she delivered in a hospital. Well, my son was born in this apartment. We couldn't afford a hospital!"

"Please," insisted Adolph. "It's family business...between brothers. Don't mix in."

"Who takes care of your father? Your sisters? Sam Ausubel's wife – Gertrude? I do. If I'm good enough to take care of your father, I should have a say."

"The truth is," continued Frances despite Adolph's insisting on a truce, "whatever we have, it's as much mine as it is yours. It was money the both of us saved before we married, and money we saved after we married which you sank in the business when it was going down – not your brother's money. I cook and I clean. And now I'm a charlady scrubbing floors to keep the building going. Well, I have children to worry about. I should have a say!"

"And I don't do a thing? I work day and night, weekdays and weekends – never a stop. What are you saying?"

"That we do all this together for *our* family, *our* children. Your brothers and sisters, I can love them all, but they're all grown up. They're responsible for their own lives now. You're not their father."

"You keep saying, 'their father!' What does this father business have to do with Sam buying a house?"

It's not just Sam buying a house, it's the whole damn thing: you and your family. Look, when things went bad in the business, you still made out paychecks."

"You mean in the Gramercy Footwear?"

"No, the Marvin Shoe Company."

"Yes. But you have to pay the men."

"I'm talking about you and Harry, after you paid the workers."

"So?"

"So Harry cashed his checks, but you didn't cash yours."

"What sense would it make for me to have cashed them? There wasn't enough money in the bank to cover them."

"Well then, why couldn't it have been smaller checks for each of you, which together would have equaled the checks Harry cashed?"

"But they *were* small checks. And Harry needed the money. He had rent to pay and a mother-in-law to support."

"And you? You don't have expenses? Your father is paying for his up-keep?"

"Of course not. He's my father, not a boarder."

"Don't you think I know that? It's just that partners should be partners. If there's no money for two paychecks, then there's no money for one."

"So I didn't cash my paychecks. So what good does it do to bring it up now? Harry never told me not to cash my checks."

"Yes, but he *knew* you didn't and he cashed his. Did he ever suggest that it wasn't right – one partner to take pay, the other not? But that's not the worst."

"Look, let's not rake over those coals again."

"Rake over those coals? You not only didn't cash your paycheck, you took savings – *our* savings – and sank them in the business, week after week."

"I was trying to keep the business going."

"And did Harry sink in his savings, week after week?"

"Harry has no savings."

"Harry has no savings! Harry has no savings!" she said angrily. "How do you know?"

"I know. He's my brother..." Adolph pleaded to end the discussion. "Let's have dinner and call it a night. I've got to get up early. There are customers to see in the morning."

"But we've settled nothing. I *will* be heard. I'm filled up to my throat. I could bust."

"So be heard if you must," he replied resignedly. "But it does no good."

Frances stopped to catch her breath and then continued. "And when you emptied out all our savings, you borrowed money to sink into the business. Now the Marvin Shoe Company is gone, but you're still left with debts to pay. You alone – not Harry."

"It wasn't his idea. He was ready to quit; I refused to give up. His paycheck was only a small part of the expenses. There was rent and the workers..."

"But he knew all about it. He didn't object to taking a paycheck realizing it came from your pocket. If the business survives he receives 50% of the profits, but if it sinks, he doesn't pay back a nickel of the losses."

"Those were loans I made. I gave my word. I'll pay them back – every penny."

"You know, you never asked your father for a penny, even though he lives here and we supply all his needs. Doesn't that trouble you? And sometimes, when your siblings who don't take care of him come here for a visit, they'll say: 'Why don't you get him a nicer suit?'– accusing us. We're the providers for your father. But when they need money, they come to him for money and quick as a wink, he gives out every penny he has to his name to *them*."

"My father has a right to give his money to whomever he wishes. God knows he's worked hard enough for the little he has. And I told you, he's my father, not a boarder."

"But even in times of need, when we were desperate, from others you could borrow, but not from your father?"

"My father gives. He doesn't lend."

"You mean like to Lotte and now to Sam."

"He's a good man. He gives with a full heart. When Lotte needed money to buy a farm, he gave her everything he had saved, all except a few dollars to 'keep the account open.' Now, after he has had a few years to accumulate a couple of thousand, he's giving it all to Sam, all except the 'few dollars to keep the account open.'"

"So Lotte's farm and Sam's country house are important, but our being choked with debts is not."

"We'll manage. I'm paying off the debts, am I not?" He put a hand on her waist.

She shook herself loose. "You're too proud to ask for help when you need it."

"Where's the comparison? I have survived without asking for help. Lotte wouldn't still have a husband with her if my father hadn't bought that farm for them."

"You mean when she and her communist husband came back from Birobidzhan, he would have left her if he didn't get the chicken farm?"

"He would have dropped my sister and her baby like hot potatoes. As for his being a communist, the fact is he's the biggest capitalist you'll ever meet."

"Why do you say that? He's never owned a factory or a business. In fact, as far as I know, he's never employed anyone. And he went to Birobidzhan in Russian Siberia. So how does all that make him a capitalist?" (Birobidzhan was a province in Siberia in which the Soviet Union proposed to establish a Jewish homeland. Some Jews moved to the province, but the vast majority of the inhabitants were Siberian natives.)

"As for journeying to Birobidzhan, he went there because the communists sold him a bill of goods about a 'workers' paradise for Jews.' He's not a religious Jew, or even a believer – and he was a worker at the time. Their propaganda offered him more, so he went. And a wife close to delivery was not going to delay him. So off he goes to Russia, to the workers' paradise. And his wife gives birth on a train trip to Siberia...with no doctor in attendance. So the infant is born with the cord wrapped around its neck, with no blood going to its brain. And there's no one to help my sister cut the cord.

"So the baby ends up retarded and now he's saddled with an *umgluck* (misfortune). Well, the communist paradise half way round the world to get to turns out not to be such a paradise. The ground is frozen and does not yield easily to the spade. And the workers' quarters they gave him were cold. Rushing back to America, he comes home to us with a problem: He's got a wife and a retarded child and no source of income. Buy him a chicken farm and he'll take care of the two of them.

"It was the height of the depression. I hadn't a penny to my name and I couldn't borrow a penny more. So my father gave them the money."

"And when we visited them, Adolph, do you remember what you saw? Lotte waiting on him hand and foot and keeping the child out of his way. And she 'yeses' everything he says. He plays the role of a big shot. He's a farmer, admiring his *famegens* (property). The only reason he tolerates our visits are that they give him a chance to spout off about his accomplishments and because we bring presents worth far more than any of his food we might eat."

"I'm afraid that if, God forbid, Lotte became ill, he would sell the farm, take the money and leave her. That's the kind of capitalist he is: Hurrah for himself and to hell with the rest of the world."

"I understand what you're saying about Lotte. But I still say: I wish you'd stop playing the role of their father."

"Please stop saying that. I'm not their father. They have a father."

"So you're not their father, you're the mother hen... Yes, that's it. Your mother, may she rest in peace, directed the household and your father always listened to her. You were her firstborn – the thinker and the writer, and the scholar – just like her. So when she died, you took her place as the real head of the family."

"Please! Calling me their father or their mother solves nothing. I'm the eldest. I do what I have to do."

"But comparisons can be important if we are to understand, if we are to solve our problems. You're still the mother bird protecting her chicks who are no longer chicks. They're grown birds with nests and chicks of their own. Even a mother bird stops feeding her chicks when they're big enough to fly on their own."

"So who stops them? Did I stop any of my brothers or sisters from leaving to get married? I certainly did not."

"No, you didn't do any such thing, but you still are trying to shield them from responsibility. Look, if you were a millionaire, giving Sam some money wouldn't matter. But you're not. So if he wants to buy property, it's his responsibility to decide if he can afford it and can pay the interest he would have to pay on the debts to finance it. You've got no business saddling yourself and us with debts to shield him from responsibility for his decisions. And the same is true with Harry. He's your brother and you've insisted that he have an equal share in the business,even though he doesn't take equal responsibility."

"But he does his job inside the factory."

"Inside the factory? Look, he's supposed to be a designer. But you do the designing. And you're the salesman. And you're the one who worries how the bills are going to be paid. Harry just cashes his check and he knows that if something is left over after the bills are paid, he'll get his share. Always, you're the mother bird shielding him from the rain coming down."

"He works hard."

"So do other workers. But they gave up being partners in the business. And now they get paid as workers and not as partners if there's a profit made. You should have done the same with Harry. He doesn't take on a boss's responsibility. He has a worker's mentality. When it's five o'clock, he goes home and forgets about the business. And when Friday comes, he expects a paycheck. You, on the other hand, take the business home with you when you leave. When the chips are down, he doesn't risk his own savings. He should be treated as an employee. If he's a good worker, then he should be paid as such."

"Can you imagine how he'd feel? Me a boss and he a laborer? He's my brother, not a stranger."

"He's a grown man, you're a grown man, and the rest of your brothers and sisters are grown-ups. You can still get along, but each should take care for his or her own nest."

"But all this talk about my brothers and sisters just adds to the heartache." Adolph paused and then went on: "Forget the dinner. I'm not hungry anymore. Let's go to bed."

"No. I'm not going to bed. Not until you agree it's time you stopped being the parent to your siblings. You're paying off those loans; you're not to borrow any more money to give your brothers so they can have paychecks or a house in the country."

"Have it your way. I'm too tired to argue any more. Let's go to bed."

"Not until you have dinner. You'll need your strength."

Adolph looked at his wife for a long, hard minute, and then said, "You weren't this way when we got married. You were such a softhearted person. You gave your life's savings to your parents so they could buy a house. What changed you?"

"I was a girl then. I'm a woman now with children of her own, a woman who's lived through heartaches."

The depression did pass, only to be replaced by a horror, far worse. A colossus strode across Europe, crushing everything in its path, most of all, the Jews. Adolph watched and read, soberly, bitterly, of an *Anschluss* (the joining together of Germany and Austria. In actuality, Austria was seized by Nazi Germany in March, 1938), a Munich Pact (a pact between Nazi Germany, Great Britain and France, in September 1938, sanctioning the dismemberment of Czechoslovakia. The German army seized the Sudetenland and, subsequently, much of the rest of Czechoslovakia), an invasion of Poland, and a *Blitzkrieg*. (*Blitzkrieg* means "lightning war." The lightning conquest of France by Nazi Germany in 1940 was the result of a *Blitzkrieg*.)

As early as 1923, Adolph had feared for the survival of European Jewry. In his Yiddish poem, "A Dark Cloud Has Descended," he expressed his concern. That Jews had been oppressed in Tsarist Russia was of no surprise. Enlightenment had yet to penetrate that country. But when anti-Semitic violence began sweeping through countries such as Germany and Austria, which had long been considered "enlightened," then the dark cloud that had been there for centuries was now descending, and this threatened the very survival of the millions of Jews living on the European continent. Adolph urged European Jews to leave before it was too late. For those strong in body and spirit, emigration to Palestine afforded the opportunity to rebuild the ancient Jewish nation. For the rest, the lamp of the *Goldene Medina* beaconed. The United States was a land that had as the reason for its founding, freedom – including freedom of religion. It was a nation that offered the golden opportunity to worship as you chose and also to achieve up to your ability and your willingness to work hard.

Now, scores of relatives and friends were trapped in the flames as the lightening from that dark cloud set Europe aflame. Adolph spent many a night filling out affidavits to bring some of them to America. And he spent hours and days persuading others to join in the effort.

"I can't afford to support an immigrant," said one man, resisting Adolph's plea to become a sponsor.

"You can't afford not to," was Adolph's reply. "You speak of money while I speak of lives."

More and more, Adolph became convinced that a Jewish state in Palestine was the only long-term answer. The Hebrew people had been driven from country to country. Sometimes they were one step ahead of the enemy, but all too often they were trapped and slaughtered by the Haman of the era. (According to the Scroll of Esther, Haman was an official in the court of King Ahasuerus of Persia. Haman sought to exterminate all the Jews of the kingdom. In subsequent eras, those who have attempted to destroy the Jews as a people are referred to as the spiritual descendants of Haman.) A land of their own, their ancient homeland, was the only solution, their assured place of refuge.

The United States geared up for war. The war came.

There was now a seller's market in the shoe industry. Adolph could not possibly fill all the orders forced upon him by pleading shopkeepers. In these conditions, he had a sense of honor. He had his own sense of purpose. He refused the cases of whiskey, lavish lunches and the vacation trips that were offered him. Instead, he wanted his customers to give to the many causes for which he pleaded. He raised money for HIAS (The Hebrew Immigration Aid Society was an organization which assisted Jews in coming to the United States and in getting settled in this country, thereby helping Jews escape Nazi persecution). Adolph enrolled hundreds of members in the Zionist Organization of America in order to swell the cry for a Jewish State in Palestine. He raised thousands of dollars for the Jewish National Fund, which bought land in Palestine for new settlements, and the *Haganah* (the Jewish underground army in Palestine, which was formed to protect Jewish settlements that were being attacked by Arabs in the period before World War II. It later became the army of the State of Israel.).

These were eventful years, terrible years. Things *had to* be done. In Adolph's mind there was no excuse for not staying up until midnight and beyond in the effort to help his fellow Jews. A weakened body, swelling bags under his eyes, wrinkles upon wrinkles upon wrinkles on his forehead, heartburn, chest pain: None of these were acceptable reasons for him to stop, even for a moment.

> *Awake world! Listen. Hear them crying.*
> *Men, women, children dying...*
> (An excerpt from *Rozwadow, What Have They*
> *Done to You?* by Adolph Ausubel, 1943.)

These were dramatic years with much sorrow. But there were also reasons for celebration, like warming rays of sun peeking through the dark clouds of a turbulent sky. With the shoe factory running at capacity, the family was able to move to larger quarters.

Judah now had a room of his own. More grandchildren were born. He looked forward to the quiet, happy moments, as well as to the noisy greetings at the Passover Seder, when many of his children and grandchildren would join him.

To Adolph, as long as the Lord blessed his father with years, his father would sit at the head of the table. Soft-spoken and even-tempered, Judah might have gone unnoticed in a crowd of elderly Jews – a little, bald, white-haired man with gentle eyes, who in his almost nine decades on Earth had never been heard to utter an epithet against a fellow human being. He savored his joys quietly: A single cigarette puffed on the occasion of the marriage of one in his family, or a sip of whiskey to celebrate the birth of a new grandchild. He suffered his misfortunes in the same way – reciting the *Kaddish*, and then taking out a little wooden stool on which he would sit for the mourning period. On the table lay the letter that had just informed him of the death of a brother in Europe – three years before its arrival.

Judah was not a passive member of the household. He shared their joys and sorrows, as well as their meals. And he constantly sought ways to improve their lot. At eighty, he decided to restructure all the closets in the house. Half a year later, he finished the project and began another. He set about to lengthen the garage so as to accommodate the new larger cars. A year later, he put the finishing touches on the doors and wondered, "What next?"

The synagogue needed refurbishing, thought Judah. This was an expensive proposition. The old man – a stranger to wealth – approached his rabbi with a proposal.

"If the temple members will supply the materials, I will rebuild all the woodwork in the synagogue."

The rabbi studied the wizened face and the little body of the carpenter. "How old are you, Judah?" he inquired with seeming concern.

"Eighty-two," was the reply. "But I can still do a good day's work," Judah was quick to add.

"Then the Almighty will surely not interrupt such a labor," the rabbi concluded with a half-smile on his face.

Three years later, Judah mitered and glued the last piece of wood into place. The project had been completed.

Judah saw his grandchildren grow to adulthood. He was there in attendance when Harry's daughter, Maxine was married. He lived to see his firstborn grandson, Marvin, graduate from Harvard Law School and practice law; his grandson, Herbert, graduate from Harvard Medical School; his granddaughter, Corinne, graduate from Barnard College; and many other grandchildren attend colleges and graduate schools. Marvin and Corinne were now each betrothed, and Judah looked forward to their future weddings.

But age and disease were catching up with him. His grandson, Herbert, now a physician, discovered that Judah had a fatal illness. Judah longed for the company of his family. His body grew weaker and he required transfusions to sustain him. Herbert would bring home bottles of blood and insert a needle into Judah's arm to allow vital red cells to flow into his grandfather's veins. But their effect was transient. Soon, the old man was too weak to walk. Herbert would now carry his grandfather to the tub, each evening, to bathe the old man's frail, worn body.

As the months went by, Judah developed a terrible itch. He would scratch and scratch, but to no avail. Pills and salves failed to relieve his distress. One evening, as Herbert was starting up another transfusion, Judah looked up. "Why do you bother? Why do you torture me? Let me die."

Herbert, tears now welling up in his eyes, replied, "No. I won't let you die."

The words had come forth from the mouth of a grown man, a physician, but the voice was that of a child who refused to let go...of his grandfather.

It was the evening of the Festival of Passover. Herbert dressed Judah in a dark suit and carried his grandfather to the cushioned chair at the head of the dining room table. Judah, his eyes grown small with advancing years, looked around at his family, his children and grandchildren. He knew it was his final Passover on this earth. There was an inner joy in knowing of the love they all bore him. He went through the reading, his frail hand shaking as he turned the pages. Adolph, who sat at his right hand, slowed the reading so that his father could keep up with him. Finally, Judah begged his son to continue the reading while he listened. Adolph finished the *Haggadah* and Judah was carried back to bed.

On June 4, 1955, Judah lay in a hospital bed. The shadows of approaching evening darkened his face. His feeble, shriveled body moved ever so slightly. The little, bald head, with its squared beard, rested on a pillow. His eyes, now dark and sunken, pleaded as he looked at Herbert, seated at the edge of the bed and clothed in a long doctor's coat.

"Herbert, go to the wedding. I will not die before the festive occasion is over."

Herbert kissed his grandfather on the forehead and then left to attend his sister's wedding.

True to his word, Judah did not breathe his last breath until the wedding was over. His body was laid to rest beside that of his beloved wife, Chaya Sarah.

As the years went by, the Ausubels continued to prosper in a modest way. Adolph had moved his family earlier into a house of their own. And then to an even larger home. He never ceased his love for writing and, as old age approached, he occupied himself more with writing and less with business. He contributed a poetry column to the Yiddish language newspaper, *Der Tag*. The column was titled "The Crooked Mirror," and in it he poured out his love for God and the universe He had created. (*Der Tag*, meaning "The Day" was published in New York City.)

A son was born to Marvin and Marion Ausubel. The child was named Eric (Yehudain Hebrew, after Judah Ausubel). Adolph took out the five silver coins that had been used at the *Pidyon HaBen of* Marvin. They were used for the redemption of this eighth-generation, firstborn son in the Ausubel family.

Adolph loved to have Marvin visit him, and he was particularly pleased when Eric came with his father. The grandfather would take the boy to the synagogue and place a skullcap on his little head. They would sit toward the rear of the house of prayer. He would tell Eric about the synagogue and the service. The slender, bright-eyed little boy with honey-colored curls flopping over his face, listened intently, but he understood more of the gleam in his grandfather's eyes than the details of the sections of the service.

A second grandchild was born and Adolph went to the synagogue to give her a name. It was Nancy Federman, born to daughter Corinne and her husband, Dr. Jay Federman. Marion gave birth to a third grandchild, Warren, and Corinne to his fourth, Daniel. Adolph's middle child, Herbert, married and Adolph looked forward to enjoying his advancing years with the luminous eyes of more grandchildren to behold.

One November evening in 1963, Adolph stood before a ranch house in Long Island, sniffing the cool wind. He looked up at the twisted limbs of a sycamore tree reaching to the sky. One branch seemed to be pointing a strange crooked finger down across the moon, like a final umpire announcing, "You're out!" The tree swayed in the strong breeze, shaking the last crumpled leaves to the ground. The stars, for the most part, were hidden behind dark clouds faintly silhouetted in the moonlight. Adolph shivered, his face paling for the moment. Then he tugged his coat a little tighter, perceiving the change in the seasons – the faintly glowing autumn candle being snuffed out by winter's icy blast. The thinning hair on Adolph's head had turned gray with age, and now it swirled in the raw gusts like a sparsely planted wheat field being manhandled by a storm. A recession of his hairline had lengthened his furrowed brow, giving it a concerned cerebral look. The muscles slowly relaxed, but the furrows remained. The bags below his eyes sagged like the wrinkled breasts of an aged woman, but the eyes were now filled with cheer. He turned towards Frances who stood beside him, bundled in a gray woolen coat.

"With God's help," he said expectantly, "we will have two more grandchildren soon. Marion must be in her eighth month and Stephanie is not far behind her."

Frances laughed. "You always did like large families."

"I wonder why there's no light in the window. We *were* invited to dinner tonight. It's not like Stephanie and Herbert to forget."

"Ring the bell," she insisted, "instead of getting excited. They could be in the kitchen and have forgotten to turn on a front light."

Uneasily, Adolph pressed the doorbell and waited. The door opened. Stephanie's eager eyes, glistening in the pale moonlight, greeted them. Adolph studied the silhouette from the long flaxen hair on her head to her full waist. After a friendly but brief exchange, Adolph and Frances walked in, arm in arm.

"Happy birthday, Dad!" was the joyous cry of many voices coming from the darkness.

The lights went on. Adolph stared, open-mouthed, at the faces he saw. Tears came to his eyes and tumbled down his cheeks. He looked at his sons and daughter and their respective spouses. He had come expecting a quiet dinner and had found a family assembled.

"Am I ill?" he suddenly asked, concerned. "In sixty-nine years, I've never had a birthday party."

"No, Dad," responded Herbert, embarrassed. "It's just that we've been too neglectful all these years."

They showed Frances and Adolph to seats on the couch. One of Herbert's neighbors took pictures of the family in snapshots and movies. Adolph sat there, beaming, and absorbed it all. Drinks were served, along with an assortment of cheeses and fish. No one seemed in a rush to do anything but talk.

At one brief lull in the conversation, Herbert asked curiously, "Dad is there something you really wanted in life, but never got?"

His father mused for a while and then smiled. "I could have been rich – maybe even a millionaire. Mind you – not that I would have objected. But around me I have all the riches that count – a loving wife, children (and grandchildren) growing strong and healthy in mind and in body, and the pleasure of seeing new life swell within you, Marion, and you, Stephanie. I am thankful, every day that I have awakened to experience the wonders of His world, and I am thankful for the pleasure of seeing you all.

"I would have gone to the university and become a lawyer or writer or both, if war and the struggle to keep a family together had not postponed it and then made it impractical. But I have children who have accomplished all this. No," he concluded thoughtfully, "there's nothing material that I miss terribly…only people."

His eyes moistened with sad reflection and he reached for a handkerchief to dry them. They all felt the impact of his words and sensed his emotional response. Adolph Ausubel was a strong man in many ways – strong in spirit and determination. He was a man who could push his not-so-powerful body beyond the limits of normal endurance. Adolph was also a sentimental man who loved his family and his people far more than any worldly goods. He could remain strong in purpose and in action at the center of a crisis, or break into tears, remembering his father or mother, a relative who died in the Holocaust twenty years ago, or a friend he had seen yesterday, lying in a hospital bed, suffering from an incurable disease.

"The family," he began again, "we should be as one. Separately, we can be broken as twigs. Together, we can be strong. Hold on to the family. I tried. My sisters, my brothers…" His voice trailed off. Tears rolled profusely from his eyes. He reached for his handkerchief again. He wiped his eyes, and then added, "I was thinking of Lotte and Sam."

He fell into silence.

"Sam, I know about," said Herbert. "But what happened with Lotte? I remember her on her chicken farm from years ago. Then I never saw her again."

Adolph wiped his eyes, but seemed unable to speak.

"Because they sold the farm," interjected Frances, "and moved to Florida. Then, one day, your father got a telegram from her husband. Lotte had died. The husband said he knew she would want to be buried near her family, so he was shipping the body here by train. The body arrived C.O.D. Can you believe it? Send your wife's body C.O.D. He didn't even show up for his wife's funeral and we never saw him again. Your father and his brothers and sister made all the arrangements quickly and she was buried."

"Where was I at the time?" inquired Herbert.

"You were on duty at the hospital. We didn't want you to miss your work."

"She had a daughter, I remember. What happened to the child?"

"God knows.Lotte's husband moved and no one in the family ever heard from him again. He probably placed her in some home before he took off." She paused and then added, "But this is your father's birthday, so let's not dwell on such matters."

Adolph sat silent.

Trying to distract him, Stephanie wondered aloud, "We know how much you love your family. But could you really have become a millionaire?"

Adolph's face brightened. The tears were gone. "I think so," he mused. "Years ago, when you were but a baby and I was making shoes, I thought: Some short women would like to look taller without having their feet arched so far forward by a gigantic heel that would cause them to practically fall on their faces as they walk. What could be better than a soft cork platform, between the insole and the sole of the shoe? It could raise them several inches above the ground, yet they could still walk comfortably. I went to the cork company and showed them my design. I asked them to make a few dozen pairs in various sizes to be used as samples.

"A few days later, they had the platforms ready. The fellow from the cork company thought it was a good idea. He refused to charge me for the order, then asked if I would mind if he made some for other customers the following season. After he had refused to charge me for the order, and with our having a season's head start on our competitors, I felt it only right to reciprocate. So I agreed.

"Now if I had taken out a patent on the platform and was receiving a royalty for each pair of platform shoes made today, you can imagine what kind of money I would be collecting."

"I never knew that," smiled Stephanie. She focused on her father-in-law again and inquired eagerly, "Were there other times you missed making a fortune?"

"Yes," he reflected, nodding his head. "It was during the Second World War. One of my customers – Sommers, whose store was on 57th Street in Manhattan – told me of his difficulty. The landlord of his building had died and left the property to a charitable organization that, in turn, had placed the property up for sale. Sommers was fearful that a competitor would buy the building in order to get his store. His lease would soon be up and he would be left in the lurch.

"I asked how much they wanted for it.

"When I learned that they were asking $36,000 for the property, I sensed that it would be a good investment, 57th Street being one of the most prestigious shopping streets in the country. Immediately, I called the attorney for the charity and asked whether the property was still for sale. Learning that it was, I told him that I would be over to his office that very day with a certified check to bind the sale at his asking price. Then I assured Mr. Sommers that his lease would be renewed as soon as I owned the building.

"Two hours later, I sat in the law office with a certified check in my hand. The red-faced attorney was apologizing profusely for his error. I was now informed that I. Miller Shoes had placed a binder on the property the previous day. Another attorney in his firm had accepted the binder from I. Miller and he had not been aware of it when I called. He assured me that I could have the property at that price if the I. Miller deal fell through. It didn't. You couldn't touch that piece of property today for a million."

"Too bad," sighed Stephanie.

"Not really... It was not so intended."

"Do you really believe that?" asked Stephanie, doubtfully.

"It's the story of our people. The Almighty did not intend for it to be made easy. A man who has too much, obtained too easily, may lose the ambition to do more. 'By the sweat of your brow, shall you eat bread,' the Almighty told Adam. And for the Jews, that's the way it's been. If God intended our people for riches, He would have left Abraham in Ur, in what is now Iraq, sitting on a sea of oil. The Torah tells us that Abraham was a prominent man with many subordinates, a sort of Sheik, if you will. As Abraham's descendants, we could now be wallowing in the splendor of palaces, through no effort of our own. Instead, what did the Lord do? He directed Abraham to travel across the desert to a land of figs and nuts, to a land of dry plains and hot sun, where the descendants of Abraham, Isaac and Jacob could work and think. He gave us ideas, principles and books of law instead of riches. My mother taught me that our greatest achievements were those of the mind, not monuments of stone or bronze, not palaces of gold and polished wood, and not a large empire with subjugated peoples. You want to see pyramids? Go to Egypt. You want to see a desert made to flower? Go to Israel. You want to see the splendors of an empire? Go to Rome and visit the Coliseum. Sit there and picture humans being thrown to lions. But if you want to learn of morality and law, read the Torah and the Talmud.

"When we were forced from our land by the Assyrians, the Babylonians and then the Romans, and when we were driven from country to country by oppressors, we had to live by our wits. In all this suffering, we never forsook our codes. We emphasized learning – the acquisition not only of knowledge, but also of wisdom. We sought not only to know, but also to *understand*. For we are the Children of the Book, and we are the Children of the Law. (The Jews considered themselves "the Children of the Book" – the Five Books of Moses. The Books of Moses are also books of law. The Jews, through the Bible and post-biblical writings, follow a prescribed system of law.)

"It is such a background that spawned an Einstein and a Freud, a Maimonides and a Rashi, and so many others. This is the background that has produced more Nobel Prize winners in science, relative to their numbers on this globe, than any other people, with not even a close second.

"As we studied, analyzed and debated the meaning of His words, we produced legal scholars, philosophers, historians and writers in every major area of human thought. Locked in the ghettos, no fields to play in, the Jew had to derive pleasure from that which he could develop in his mind and hand in a confined space. From this confined background – the ghettos and impoverished villages of our exile – came the great musicians, singing of our sorrows or attempting to buoy up our spirits, like David did to Saul.

"A Jew knows what it is to be scorned, hated and oppressed. Who better to champion the rights of those who feel themselves wronged than one who has both suffered from those evils and has been trained from childhood to think, to analyze and to debate! From this background we have you, Marvin, not simply as a lawyer, but as a man of the law, capable of counseling attorneys and arguing persuasively before the highest judicial bodies.

"The wounds we have suffered in the past have taught us to have understanding and compassion for the pain others feel, and we are the better for having survived it. When Herbert cares for a poor afflicted patient, he will remember what it was like to be poor and hungry. He will remember what it was like to hear a father crying because he had searched all day for work, day after day, and had not been able to earn a single penny. Herbert was reared in a house where age was respected and honored. He will convey that feeling to the elderly he cares for.

"And you, Corinne, my baby, a teacher and as well as a mother – when you raise your children, like the grandmother for whom you were named, you will raise them to be strong and wise... I've talked too much..."

His eyes glistened again. He wiped them.

"Come to the table everyone," Stephanie broke in. "We haven't lit the candles yet."

It was after dessert. Stomachs were full and the people at the table were leaning back in their chairs, waiting for the bloated feeling to subside.

"You know," said Herbert, looking at his father, "there's one thing I could never figure out."

"What is it?"asked his father.

"It's the Rozwadower *Chevra* (Brotherhood)."

"The *Chevra*? What's so puzzling? It's an organization of people from my town who came to this country. It was a place where a newcomer to America could seek out old friends, an island of the Old World in a strange new place. But you should know that. You went to those Saturday night meetings with me often enough."

Herbert fidgeted a little and then said, "I know that. But what sometimes amazed me is why you kept going there. I mean long after the immigrant days..." He paused, looking for the right words.

"But the *Chevra* still does good. There are still newcomers to America. Should they not receive the same greeting that we did? And we raise money, money for Jewish charities, money to help *landsleit* (countrymen) in Israel and elsewhere. You know there are Rozwadower groups in Israel and even in South America."

"Dad, I know all that. But there are other things." He paused and then went on, "Look, you're a sensitive person and we all know that. So how could you stand some of the members? They're so coarse. They insult one another. They insulted you! They can't discuss an issue without calling those who disagree with them '*dumkopfs*' (dumb-heads) and worse. Then, ten minutes later, they're having *arbus* (chickpeas) and beer together and playing pinochle. I tell you, I wouldn't stand for it. If people cannot be civil, I'd have nothing to do with them."

"But those are just expressions. They don't really mean them."

"But *you* don't use them," pursued Herbert. "You don't use invectives when you respond to such insults. And they hurt, despite what you say now. I remember the nights you went home sick after such meetings, and the sleepless nights that followed."

"I know what you mean. And I don't excuse the language. I just learned to live with it. I learned to appreciate the worth of people, despite the foolish and sometimes terrible things they say to one another. Look, Herbert, you've learned to live with the same thing, haven't you?"

"What do you mean?"

"I mean, didn't you used to tell me how some of Jewish doctors at Mt. Sinai behaved at medical meetings, as compared with the way the doctors behaved at the *Goyishe* (Gentile) hospitals? Didn't you describe the way they sometimes insulted one another and then acted like the best of friends five minutes later? And these were *educated* men, people who were respected as leading experts in their fields. Now in the *Goyishe* hospitals – I remember you telling me – they could put a dagger through your heart with polite phrases. So is that better?

"What can I tell you? I wish Jews didn't talk that way, but I can't keep a permanent *broiges* (animosity) over it."

The hour was late. Frances and Adolph rose to leave. Each member of the family shook Adolph's hand, hugging and kissing him before he left.

"You know, Frances," he said as the door closed behind them, "I have a lot to be thankful for. Tonight, before going to sleep, I'll write a poem about it."

❖ ❖ ❖

On January 11, 1964, a granddaughter was born. Marvin and Marion named her Lauren. On the following Sunday morning, Adolph went to the synagogue to give the girl her Hebrew name. Upon leaving the synagogue, he sustained a heart attack and was rushed to the hospital. Pale and weak, he looked up at his sons. Then he closed his eyes for the last time.

On the following day, in accordance with Jewish tradition, he was laid to rest. At the funeral, his final poem was read. It had been published in *Der Tag* on the day of his death (January 19, 1964), and was entitled *A Dank* (A Thank You).

I thank God for having been born,
For having been placed on my feet.
He gave me eyes and ears
To sense, with wonder, the grandeur of the universe.

I thank God for letting me live.
I am grateful because I understand Him.
He granted me the freedom to choose my way of life
Though no one can always be right in his choice.

I thank God for lovely children,
For the health of my wife and children.
I thank God especially for my grandchildren.
I have sufficient reason to be grateful.

I thank God every morning
For waking me from the night's sleep,
For freeing my mind from the troubles of the day,
For giving me the faculty to comprehend His world.

God, as we are already in this world,
Leave us here for many more years, in good health and comfort.
And if You agree to that,
I will be grateful to You for this as well.

But if You choose to end my days
Before the light of morning comes,
Then thank you, God, this one last time
For all Your wonders and for all the smiles.

IN THE LAND OF THE TARTARS

VIRTUALLY ANYONE brought up in the modern world has learned of the Holocaust. Most have heard of the Spanish Inquisition. Many are aware of the Pogroms in Russia. They even may have heard that Jews were persecuted in many countries in Europe, being labeled as "Christ-killers." But then we get to the "lesser slaughters," where "only" thousands of Jews were sent to their deaths. Tragically, there were many such slaughters over the centuries, and because members of my family were among the victims, I must bear witness to those occurrences.

On a Sunday morning in June 1914, a young Bosnian student on the streets of Sarajevo assassinated the Archduke Francis Ferdinand, heir to the throne of Austria-Hungary. The chain of events that followed was to dramatically alter the lives of millions of people throughout the world. The little town of Rozwadow was not immune to the tragedy that befell mankind. Armed giants fought to determine which ones would dominate Europe and the world.

On a midweek afternoon late in June of that year, Isaac Ausübel sat at his worktable, carrying on an ancient Jewish tradition. Before him was a parchment onto which he was carefully transcribing, letter by letter, word by word and inflection by inflection, the words of the Torah. To one side of his parchment lay the Torah from which he was copying. He took great pains not to make a single error that might result in a need to destroy the parchment and begin again. He knew that tradition did not permit for a single change, and that every Torah scroll must be an exact duplication of that first scroll written down by Moses at the direction of the Almighty, over 3,000 years before.

The air of the room was sultry and oppressive. Beads of perspiration appeared on his forehead and trickled down his brow. Isaac paused to dry them. As if by reflex, the handkerchief glided over his soaked, wavy brown head of hair now gray at the temples, forcing him to readjust his skullcap. The long sidecurls had to be squeezed dry in his handkerchief, and the short crinkly pointed beard patted to remove excess moisture.

He rose from his seat, walked to the window and then stood there, silhouetted against the blue sky above and the buildings across the dirt-covered street below. He was a tall man by the standards of his day: tall and lean. His forehead and the corners of his eyes were lined, but not unduly so for a man past fifty. His nose, somewhat full, yet unobtrusive, bathed itself in the warm yellow glow and he wet his lips as if to test the air currents. The bright summer sun was irritating to his deep, brown, perceptive eyes. He extended a bony hand so as to shade them from the glare. He stood there a while, surveying the thoroughfare.

His five-year-old son, David, was running down the road. A smile came across Isaac's face as he watched the lad trying to catch a butterfly. To his father, the little boy was the picture of youth and health. Long brown curls flew from under the lad's cap. His eyes were bright as only the eyes of a child could be. What fascination they held in them at the sight of a gold flower or a jumping frog or a butterfly.

A slight breeze coming through the half-opened window felt good as Isaac continued to gaze down the dirt-covered street. In the distance he could see Bertha and Mindel headed in his direction, arm in arm. Bertha, at ten, was the eldest of his children living at home. She was a vibrant, happy girl, with her figure a shade plump, yet pleasing. The breeze seemed to lift her long brown hair, exposing her cheeks which appeared more flushed than earlier that morning. Mindel, a nine-year-old, was the more frail of the two. Her slender body had the appearance of delicate china, fragile to the touch. Her cheeks were somewhat sunken, but at this moment they looked fine. Both girls wore happy smiles as they skipped down the dusty road.

They must have been wading in the San, thought Isaac as he spied dirt sticking to their bare feet below the long dresses. *I warned them to be careful of the currents and to take along rags with which to wipe their feet.*

The girls spotted David and joined him in chasing butterflies.

His energy replenished, Isaac arched his shoulders back to loosen the joints. Then he returned to the table to resume his labor. He bent over the parchment, his eyes moving back and forth between the parchment before him and the Torah scroll positioned to its side, looking for the place where he had stopped. Finding the spot, he slid into his seat.

"Ah yes," he murmured inaudibly. "I was up to that line."

Just as he reached for his quill, his wife, Faiga, entered the room, with a glass in her hand. Her wig-covered head, thin, sallow face and sunken eyes made her appear much older than her forty-one years. A plain, long dark dress hung limply over her slender body, and unpretentious, low-heeled black shoes barely emerged from beneath the dress.

"What is it, Faiga?" he asked pleasantly.

"I brought you a glass of water from the well. It's so hot today," she replied with gentle concern.

He thanked her, rose to receive his glass and savored the cooling drink. Then he inquired: "What have you been doing?"

"The wash...at the river bank...while watching Bertha and Mindel. I know you don't like them wading, but really, Isaac, they only went in a few feet. And besides, it's brutally hot."

"I'm glad you were watching them." Then he looked at her tenderly and continued, "Faiga, you ought to rest. You don't look so well today. Leave your work for another time...and have the girls help you."

Faiga's cheeks flushed with pleasure and she turned appreciative eyes on her tall, thin husband. She surveyed his face from the wavy hair on his head to his deep brown eyes, to the small, pointed beard on his chin. How happy she was to hear him express concern for her. Faiga smiled within as he placed his arm on her shoulder and kissed her forehead. A feeling of security stole into her soul.

To have Isaac and his love, she thought. *What more could I ask for?*

She had loved him as far back as she could remember. But he was her cousin, an Ausübel. When Isaac's first wife passed away, his father, David, and his uncle, Samuel, arranged for the marriage of their children. Faiga had assumed Isaac would be a good husband, but she never dreamed that he would love her as much as she loved him. But here he was, both a good and loving husband. She kissed his cheek, blushed and left the room hurriedly.

Isaac stared at the door for a long while. Finally, he returned to the table.

"Now where was I?"

A few days later, Isaac was seated at his worktable, transcribing on a parchment. The door flew open and Bertha rushed in. She was puffing like a steam engine and her eyes were widened with excitement.

"Papa, Papa, come see the soldiers!"

"Now, Bertha," he scolded, "how many times have I told you never to come charging into my room? You could have caused me to make a mistake. I might then have to destroy valuable parchment and start all over. Now please don't do that again."

Isaac observed how Bertha's cheeks reddened at his reprimand. As if suddenly remembering her words, he added, "What was that you said about soldiers?"

"I'm sorry, Papa. I should have knocked. It was just the excitement of seeing all those men in uniform! The whole Austrian army must be here."

Isaac put his work aside. He left with Bertha to see the new arrivals.

It was true. Thousands of men in battle dress were marching down the road through the town, heading in the direction of the river. There were infantry and cavalry; there were wagons with supplies, and cannons being pulled by horses.

Suddenly Isaac was seized with cold panic. He rushed down the street and grabbed little David by the waist.

"Don't stand in the street," he scolded. "You could, God forbid, be trampled by those horses."

By this time the Ausübels had been joined by hundreds of other villagers watching the soldiers with the military band that accompanied them. Men and women, in groups, were talking excitedly. Many were waving banners and shouting encouragement to the marching men. Peddlers soon joined them and began hawking their wares. The tavern was opened, its owner hoping for business. Rozwadow had not seen so many people and such pageantry in as far back as any of them could remember.

Faiga emerged from the kitchen to witness the spectacle. Her face showed curiosity mixed with concern. She threaded her way through the crowd to her husband's side. Isaac slipped his arm around her as they watched.

"What are they cheering about?" said Isaac gravely. "Do they think war is a happy occasion?"

"But, Isaac," responded Faiga, hopefully, "they say that Austria and Germany will defeat Russia in a few weeks."

"God knows," he ruminated soberly. "Whichever way it turns out, it can't be good for us. The Russians are only a few miles away, just beyond that thin ribbon of water." His face turned dark. "What if the Russians win? Have you listened to those Jews fleeing Russia tell of how they treat our people in that country? Pogroms!"

By nightfall it was quiet again. The soldiers had passed through on their way to the front. The peddlers had taken away their carts with their wares. The tavern was closed. And the crowd had dispersed; people resumed their everyday activities.

During the next few days the distant sounds of guns and cannon were heard. After that, the thunder of war ceased. A cavalryman, riding through town, brought news of Austrian victories. The Kaiser's forces were advancing.

"You see, Isaac," said Faiga, reminding him, "they told us that the Russian army would melt away like butter over a fire."

"Wait, Faiga, wait," he cautioned. Isaac was not ready to cheer.

Soon the town was a major center of traffic that now moved in both directions. Fresh troops moved through the town on their way east to the front. Their steps were not as jaunty as those of their comrades-in-arms a few weeks earlier. No marching bands accompanied them on their journey. Occasionally, a company of soldiers paused at the tavern for refreshments, for a last song and laugh before they entered the fray. But the laughter was hollow: A pall had spread over the land, cold and damp as a winter's fog. One look out the window told it all – wagon after wagon grinding westward through the mud, carrying the dead and the wounded back from the battle.

"You see, Faiga," Isaac's face lengthened. "War is nothing to cheer about."

By September, the picture in Rozwadow had changed. The traffic was now all one way. News spread that the Austrians had suffered defeat. Hundreds of the Kaiser's soldiers were crossing the San in Jacob Korn's barges, then marching westward, away from the front. Some walked erect, in formation; others limped along, using their rifles as makeshift crutches; still others required human support.

Hours later, the Austrians were no longer marching; they were running. It was each man for himself. The strong – a torn garment here, a small flesh wound there – sprinted. Some wounded – battered heads wrapped in blood-soaked bandages, mangled arms and legs, exposed fat and muscle – hobbled or crawled. But the weakest – limbs missing, deep cavernous wounds pouring out blood and bile – just lay, gray with despair, in the village square where they had been abandoned. Their pale, glassy eyes were directed towards a darkening sky.

The distant blast of exploding shells was heard again and the firecracker sound of guns returned.

Isaac returned to his house from a walk along the San. His face was pale and uneasy.

"Faiga, it looks bad, very bad. The Russians are coming. Branwicza, across the river, is in flames. The Austrians are running; the people of Rozwadow are running; maybe we should start running, too."

"But what about my father?" she replied anxiously. "He's too weak to run. It's better that we stay and care for him." She shivered for a moment, rubbing her arms. Then she added without much conviction, "they'll be too busy fighting to bother with us."

Night brought a rainbow of color to the sky – the glow of bursting shells and burning buildings, first on the other side of the river and then in Rozwadow itself. Night also brought new sounds. There was the boom of cannon coming closer and closer. There were the ear-piercing shrieks of the wounded as houses exploded, sending pieces flying in all directions. There were the wails of women and children who saw the lifeless forms of their loved ones.

Isaac, Faiga and the children huddled together in the cellar, hoping and praying while the building above them vibrated repeatedly, sending showers of dust down on them.

By morning, all had become still. The sounds of war had gone again.

Isaac emerged from their underground shelter into a house filled with broken glass and chunks of rocky debris. He looked out of a shattered window and saw Russian soldiers coming down the street, rifles at the ready, with fixed bayonets. Before he could do anything, soldiers smashed through the door and charged into the house.

"You there, you the Jew," shouted one of the soldiers, commandingly, "who else is in the house?"

The soldier's Polish was imperfect, but Isaac understood his meaning well. "Only my family," responded the Jew anxiously, trying to conceal the paralyzing terror he felt within.

"All come out. Quick! Quick!" demanded the Russian.

Isaac called down to his family. They rushed up from the cellar. Then the Ausübels moved slowly and unsurely into the street. A look of terror crossed Faiga's face as she saw the bayonets.

"We'd better raise our hands," Isaac advised his family. "Don't want them thinking we have weapons."

"This way," said the soldier as he pointed his bayonet in their direction. "Everybody to the village square."

There were several hundred Jews assembled in the town square. Russian troops, with their spear-ended rifles, surrounded the frightened men, women and children. With a melancholy look on his face, Isaac moved among them, stopping to speak to some.

"They're just checking for Austrian soldiers," hoped one man, aloud. "When they're finished looking, they'll let us return to our homes. After all, it's the eve of the Day of Atonement. They won't trouble us on the holiest day of the year." His voice rose with feigned conviction. "Those who ran away will be sorry they left. Who's going to stand guard over their possessions?"

"I fear you have too high an opinion of the Russians," Isaac responded. "Don't you see what those soldiers are doing?"

As the horrified Jews watched, the Russians soldiers systematically loot-ed their homes. The flashing steel of enemy weapons kept the Followers of Moses from leaving the square Then the Tsar's men set every Jewish home afire, being careful not to inflict damage on any Polish residence. As their world was being consumed into ashes, the Jews in the square were informed by the Russian major in command that the Tsar considered Jews too untrust-worthy to be allowed to remain in a town near the battle zone.

"No Russian fighting man wants a Jew at his back," he declared in an imperfect Polish. "Therefore, you will all be removed from the war zone and taken to Zakilków on the Vistula. The march will begin immediately." (Za-kilków was a town in Russian-occupied Poland located alongside the Vistula River.)

"But we're not dressed for such a trip. Our coats and boots are back there in the burning houses. And some of the people are old and weak," said Isaac, plaintively, to the Russian officer.

"March or die," responded the Russian major with seeming indiffer-ence. "No stragglers will be tolerated."

The rain came down relentlessly, adding a chill to the morning air. Fog covered the ground. A group of people sat in the open field, their bodies barely visible through the mist. The oldest, Samuel Ausübel, tried hard to cover himself with the thin jacket he was wearing. A soggy cap covered his bald head. His sunken brown eyes looked at the ground with a vacant stare. A long, straggly beard hung limply from his ashen face. Suddenly, a fit of coughing overtook him. He pulled off one of the rags covering his legs and covered his mouth with it.

"Papa," cried Faiga huddled next to him, "you look very ill. We must find some shelter."

"Faiga," retorted Samuel, "it's no use. They beat and shot Shulem Katz yesterday when he tried to leave." Seeing the distressed look on his daughter's face, he added, "Maybe it will be better in Zakilków."

Isaac sat hunched over, between Faiga and the children, with one arm around Bertha and Mindel. David was resting on his father's lap with Isaac's body partially protecting the lad from the rain. Isaac looked at his father-in-law and uncle, Samuel. He knew the old man was in deep trouble. Samuel's nostrils were spread wide and he was breathing more and more rapidly. The fits of coughing came closer and closer together. Finally, Isaac could see the blood-splattered phlegm that Samuel was spitting up into a rag and hear the frightening, high-pitched stridor that came forth as the old man sucked air into his lungs between the fits of coughing. He touched the old man's head, then whispered to Faiga with alarm: "He's burning up."

"Get up, Jews. It's time to get moving," was the command in Polish that came from a Russian soldier, whose outline was barely suggested through a veil of fog. "You there, old man," he shouted, his bayonet now clearly visible and pointing menacingly ahead, "do you hear me?"

Isaac tried to raise Samuel to his feet. Faiga helped in the effort. Isaac looked at the soldier and appealed to him: "Can't you see he's ill? He needs a place to rest...and a doctor."

"We have no time for laggards," the soldier explained. "March or be shot: those are my orders."

They were all up by now. The children moved ahead easily. Isaac and Faiga supported Samuel between them as they trudged across the field, grinding onward through the thick, dark mud. They strained with every step as feet and calves and knees sank deeper and deeper into the numbing mud that seemed to be sucking them into the bowels of the earth.

It grew harder and harder to support Samuel as his steps grew weaker and weaker. Soon, he felt like dead weight and his legs were no longer moving. His lower limbs, covered with congealed mud, seemed fused together into a brown fish-tail which was being dragged along behind a silent body slung between their shoulders. Isaac looked at the old man. Samuel's mouth hung open. He was not breathing as rapidly as before; he was not breathing at all. He was dead.

"Why are you stopping?" cried the soldier, darkly. "Remember: I warned you that I would shoot stragglers."

"Save your bullets," responded Isaac. "They can't hurt him now. He's dead." Isaac stared at the soldier for a long moment, trying hard to contain the bitterness he felt. Then he asked, "May we bury him?"

The soldier appeared upset. He hesitated for a minute and then replied haltingly, "I... I don't know... I'll have to ask the sergeant." Then, backing away from the Jews, he added, "Don't any of you move from this spot while I go and ask him."

The Russian returned. He informed them that the sergeant had granted them thirty minutes to bury the old man. Having no shovels, they scooped out a shallow grave with their bare hands. Samuel was laid to rest, and his body was covered with the muddy earth and a few dull-gray stones. The family stood beside the grave, their hands, their faces and their bodies covered with the mud of the fields, the mud of the grave, the mud of their sorrow. And they silently recalled the mud pits of Pharaoh where their ancestors toiled – those pits of endless suffering and death. There was gloom on their faces, but not despair.

"O Lord," said Isaac, in Yiddish, as he looked up at the dark-gray sky, "We commend to Your loving care the soul of Your servant, Samuel Ausübel. He was a good man and walked upright in Your ways." He paused and looked searchingly into the eyes of each member of the family, one at a time. Then he went on: "Children, remember this man, your grandfather. Here he lies in a field, in the province of Lublin, in Russian Poland. No monument will be erected to record his passing. He was a Jew being force-marched from nothing to less. But his memory will stay bound to our hearts and minds as long as we draw breath and have the power to think and feel."

Faiga, too grieved to say anything, held tightly to her husband, the rock of support in her time of loss.

Isaac chanted the mourners' *Kaddish*, following which they left the gravesite. Heads hung low, they trudged on slowly in the mud.

The following day they came to the site of a recent battle. The ground was a series of craters and mounds as if giant hands had gouged out the earth. Spent shells and fragments of torn clothing, as well as rusting metal and fragmented wood of broken weapons littered the earth. Here and there, a body lay, half-covered by the settling dust.

"Cover your eyes," directed Isaac. "The jackals have been here," he added bitterly as he spotted a human form stripped of clothing. "Some people have no respect for the dead."

"Here's an Austrian boot for you," said one gruff-faced Russian soldier, in Polish, as he tossed a dark leather overshoe into little David's open arms. "It can keep your foot warm...or you can sell it." He laughed heartily and then moved off.

David looked at the strange object.

"Papa, it's got something in it!"

Isaac seized it from the boy's hands. He shuddered for a moment as he dropped it to the ground.

"Leave it," he said firmly.

"What was it?" inquired Faiga in a loud whisper.

"A foot," replied her husband. His eyes flared. "We're not animals! We don't steal from the dead!"

After several more days, the survivors of the march from Rozwadow arrived at Zakilków, to be joined by thousands of Jews from the other villages and towns of Eastern Galicia. There were Jews from Ulanów, Nisko, Rudnick, Lezajsk and the many other hamlets they all once called home. Friends and relatives greeted one another, glad to have survived. But the joy of being alive was overshadowed by sadness as they described to one another how the Russians had driven them from their homes. They learned who had fled to the south and west and who remained to be ensnared by the Russians, who had been killed in battle and who died on the road to Zakilków.

Isaac and Faiga spoke to many people from different villages. They looked for relatives and found a few. Shulem Ausübel was there along with his wife and children, but so many others were not. One reported seeing Judah Ausübel and his family fleeing in the direction of Vienna. Another told them that Faiga's brother, Mendel, was spotted headed in the direction of Krakow. Repeatedly, Isaac was heard to say with concern: "I hope they made it safely."

While their parents were being made sadly aware of the common fate of the Jews of eastern Galicia, the children remained cheerful. Bertha constructed a doll out of rags and thread and used it in playing house with her sister. David continued to exude the spirit of joy while chasing butterflies, the crowded conditions not withstanding. Nothing seemed to alter the brightness of his eyes. He knew that Grandpa Samuel was dead, but it was not all that real to him. It was as if his grandfather had gone on a trip and would return in a few weeks.

All the Jews had been herded into a barren field. Their Russian captors offered no food to them. Whatever coins they had on their persons had to be used to purchase food, at inflated prices, from Polish farmers in the area. All transactions took place across barbed wire, with Russian soldiers keeping a watchful eye to see that none of the Jews escaped. For six weeks, the growing mass of Jewish humanity remained near Zakilków while disease and exposure "weeded out" the old and the infirm. The stench of death was pervasive and many followed Samuel Ausübel to unmarked graves in unknown places. The crispness of autumn was in the air and people rubbed hands together to keep warm. At last, the waiting was over and they were ordered, group-by-group, to board boxcars that would take them away from the war zone, to Jewish communities in the east. At least, that is what they were told.

Isaac, Faiga and the children filed into a crowded boxcar, together with sixty or so other Jews. Isaac had wisely purchased two loaves of bread that morning. The Ausübels ate one loaf at lunch and the other for dinner. Isaac and Faiga sat on the floor of the car, close to one another, in an effort to preserve body heat. Their backs rested against the car wall. The children napped with their heads resting on their parents' laps and their feet flexed against their bellies in a fetal position.

By nightfall, the children were restless.

"When will we·get to where we're going?" asked Bertha.

"I don't know," rejoined her father. "Whom shall I ask? There are no soldiers in this car."

The next morning came and they were still locked inside the moving train. The children were hungry but there was no food.

"When will we eat, Papa? I'm hungry," was David's plaintive request.

"I wish I knew," wondered Isaac aloud.

By this time, the Jews had organized a system to take care of the necessary functions. There was one large garbage can, which they placed in one corner of the car. When one of their number needed to relieve himself, a group of men and women acted as a curtain, standing with their backs to the individual using the can.

That afternoon, the train came to a halt. After a few minutes, the door of the car slid open. Two Russian soldiers stood in front of the opening, holding rifles with fixed bayonets. The blades were pointed in the direction of the Jews in the car.

"Nobody leave!" shouted one of the soldiers, menacingly, in corrupted Polish. "Sergeant to come and collect money. You want bread, water, you pay. Gold fine. Silver fine. Austria money fine."

The Jews huddled and reached an agreement. Some had coins, some, bills, and others, no funds at all. They would pool their meager assets and share their food until they arrived at the unknown destination. The money was given to the sergeant when he arrived. The food they received in return was divided. The Ausübels gathered in their allotment – two loaves of bread and a pail of water.

"Eat only a little at a time, children," directed Isaac. "I don't know how long we will be stuck on this train."

An hour later the train was moving again. Isaac had asked a soldier where they were going. He was given an "I don't know" for an answer. Through the openings in the wall of the car, Isaac could see forests and empty fields. He wondered: *We've been traveling for a long time. What sort of place are they taking us to?*

Hours passed. It was night and they were still moving. It was getting colder and colder in the car. The Ausübels huddled closer and closer together to stay warm. Morning came and they were still traveling. Through the cracks in the wall, Isaac now saw snow covering the ground.

They ate a little bread and sipped a little water. It was getting colder and colder. The Jews now placed their hands inside their shirts or wrapped rags around their fingers to keep warm. But the cold cut through their clothing like a knife. Still the train kept moving, hour after hour.

The train stopped a few times, but the doors were not opened. The Jews, locked within its walls, sensed that something terrible was in store for them.

"Why won't they open the doors? What are they going to do to us?" asked one frightened man.

No one answered.

And still the train kept moving. The boxcar now felt like an icebox. Not only families huddled together to keep warm: groups of families were now bundled together to keep from freezing.

David tugged at his father with pleading eyes. "Papa, can I hide inside your jacket? I'm so cold."

Isaac bundled the boy in his lap and hugged him tightly.

What evil people these Russians are to do this to us, thought Isaac.

And still the train rolled on, taking them farther and farther from the world they had known.

On the morning of the fourth day, the locomotive came to a halt. The door of the car slid open and the Jews were commanded to come out. They had arrived...but where?

The exiles from Galicia filed out of cold, dark freight cars, escaping at last the stench of caked sweat and frozen excrement. Then they stood on the platform, looking around, puzzled.

"Where are we, Papa?" asked Mindel.

"See those people there," said Isaac as he pointed to one end of the station. "We must be in the land of the Tartars."

The people they saw appeared Asiatic. Many had slanted eyes and flattened bridges of the nose. The Ausübels had seen pictures of such people, Eskimos and Mongols with long moustaches, clothed in warm fur-lined coats and hoods, but they had never met any until now.

To the Asiatics on the platform, this group of new arrivals must have appeared even stranger. The Mongols peered at them with questioning faces, as if to ask, "What sort of deranged people are these to come to icy Siberia in winter dressed in summer clothing? And what kind of parents exhibit such callous disregard as to bring children lacking gloves and coats to places that are 30 degrees below freezing?"

To these clean-shaven Asiatics, their moustaches not withstanding, the bearded Jews with the funny hats on their heads, must have been a sight. They must have thought these Europeans to be insane to expect skullcaps to keep their heads warm.

The Jews of eastern Galicia had arrived in Siberia in November. They had come to a land that has but two seasons – a two-month summer and a ten-month winter. It was colder in Siberia in November than it would have been in Rozwadow in mid-winter. Even with rags wrapped around hands, fingers became numb within minutes.

"Well, don't stand there, waiting. You're free to go...anywhere but back." The words of the Russian commanding officer were stated with ringing finality. And yet, there was something more in his voice. The words were conveyed with a mocking twist of his mouth. It was as if he were calling to someone he had just pushed off a cliff, laughing as he shouted, "Have a pleasant journey."

But Isaac had no time to dwell on such sad thoughts. His limbs were turning to ice so he had to start moving. There was a need to act quickly if his family were to survive. He had some familiarity with Russian writing and this enabled him to read the sign on the platform. Then he turned towards Faiga and informed her: "We are in Tartarsk. Come Faiga, come children, we had better find a place to stay before we freeze to death."

Isaac turned to a few friends from Rozwadow standing nearby, advising them each to seek shelter and to do so with great haste. One by one, the Jews on the platform left in bewilderment. They were not sure what to do or where to turn. They walked down the snow-covered dirt street, wondering what act of providence could have brought them to this place.

Tartarsk was a city much larger than the town of Rozwadow or the other small hamlets of eastern Galicia. One- and two-story houses fronted the streets for blocks in every direction from the station. Isaac noted a sign on a two-story building near the station. *This must be a hotel*, he thought. He led his family into the lobby, grateful for a chance to get indoors. He was not too skilled at speaking Russian and so there was difficulty in communication. But in the end, he realized that there was one insurmountable barrier to his procuring a room for his family: He had no money.

"Why are we leaving?" asked little David as his mother tugged at his hand.

"Because your father says so," she replied.

"But it's so cold out there," the boy pleaded.

"Don't you think I know that?" said Isaac sadly, as he turned to his son. "They won't allow us to stay here. And in this country, what they say – goes."

The Ausübels trudged down the road through the town and then out of the town. Along the way, some of the town folks came out or stopped to stare at the odd group of Europeans, but none invited them in or offered any help. It began to snow, more and more heavily. Great blinding flakes fell, covering their faces, their bodies and the landscape. The wind was icy cold and it was growing dark. Their bodies were frozen from the tips of their noses to the soles of their feet.

"Papa," cried Mindel, "aren't we going to have a place to stay? My feet won't move. I can't go on."

"Just a little farther," said Isaac encouragingly. "This way. Let's take shelter in that barn."

Cautiously, he opened the creaking door and looked around the lofty wooden building. Cows were hitched to a rail. "Look," said David, excitedly, pointing to several bales of hay. "Can we sleep there?"

"Yes, David," replied his father. "Bertha, Mindel, help me push the bales in a circle. Then we can sleep bundled in the center. Let each of you cover himself with some of the hay."

"But Isaac," interrupted Faiga, "what will the owner say? He may chase us out into the cold or call the soldiers."

"Let us pray that he is too comfortable in his bed to be checking the contents of his barn on a cold night like this," was Isaac's thoughtful retort.

That night they slept hidden beneath the hay. But even that blanket could not insulate them from the icy air. In the morning, a ray of pale, wintry sunshine, coming through a crack in the wooden wall, awakened Isaac. He felt cold and stiff. The bearded Jew rose and stamped his frozen feet as if to reassure himself that they were still there. The sound of stamping feet woke Faiga and the children. Isaac instructed them to remain in the minimal warmth of the barn while he made an effort to secure food and quarters.

Exiting quickly, he shut the barn door and looked out on the limitless expanse of white snow and gray sky. Occasionally a bush or dwarfed tree, half hidden in the snow, interrupted the undulating sea of white. To the left, he spotted a house completely hidden by the great white waves, but for the dark-gray puffs of smoke rising from its chimney. He waded through drifts of shimmering white crystals in the cold, clear morning air. Each exhaled breath was a cloud of vapor, which was quickly transformed into falling, glimmering slivers of ice. Within a minute, his beard had been converted into a series of sparkling, curved icicles, like a waterfall that had been frozen in mid-fall. Finally, he reached the house several hundred feet away and knocked at the door.

A clean-shaven, gray-haired old man, who seemed more European than Asiatic, opened the door hesitantly just enough to view the bearded Jew. The look in the old man's eyes was a cross between curiosity and fear. He studied the bearded stranger from the skullcap on Isaac's head to the thin, fall clothing covered with hay and snow, down to the shoed feet that sunk deep into the snow. The old man's arms held the door firmly to keep the stranger from entering the house. They stood there for a few moments, the clean-shaven old man and the bearded Jew, uncertain as to how to proceed.

Finally, Isaac broke the silence. He managed somehow to convey to the old man the fact that he and his family had slept in the barn. Isaac pleaded to be allowed in. The door was suddenly shut from within, leaving the Jew in despair, and then opened again, slowly. The old man, a rifle now plainly visible in his hands, beckoned Isaac to enter.

The Jew stood before the fire trying to rub the cold out of his hands and stamp life into his frozen toes. At last he felt able to continue. He pleaded for work, any work, in return for food and shelter. The old man replied warily, insisting that he had no money and that food was scarce. However, he would allow Isaac and his family to sleep in the barn if they, in return, would care for the cows and deliver the milk to his customers. He warned Isaac against stealing any milk and threatened to call the police if as much as a drop of milk were missing.

"And what about food?" Isaac appealed.

The old man said there was not enough food to feed Isaac's family, but that they were welcome to all the leftovers that the old man threw out and all the milk that his customers did not buy. Isaac thanked him and assured the old man that he would not regret the arrangement.

In the days that followed, the Ausübels busied themselves caring for the animals. They milked the cows, collected and stored the manure for fertilizer and cleaned and fed the animals. Isaac and Faiga were happy in the thought that there was the possibility of survival. They wore every bit of clothing they had with them, layer upon layer. Yet with all that, they were still numb to the bone.

The old man kept a careful eye on them. At first, he would count the number of pails full of milk produced and the numbers sold, and estimate the quantity of hay in the barn at the beginning and the end of each day. He would inspect the animals and check the stored manure. But as time passed, with a satisfactory accounting for the milk and supplies and with the 60-degree-below-freezing temperatures of Siberian winter, his appearances at the barn became fewer and fewer.

The leftovers were very meager when there were any at all. And there was little, if any, milk that was not quickly bought up. But at least they were alive. Their thin waistlines became even thinner that winter; their faces, pale and drawn; their bodies, continuously cold. They felt numb all day and through the night. Each day they went through the city as scavengers. They would hunt through piles of trash, looking for almost anything – a rag that might cover a hand or foot, a newspaper to use as insulation inside a shirt, a piece of wood to add to the fire or a potato peel or hardened crumb to eat. They also sought odd jobs, even for the most meager reward. The Ausübels almost never were paid in money; at best, their wages were the first crack at going through the garbage.

Somehow, they survived that winter. But not all their fellow Jews were as fortunate. The "weeding out" process continued as Jews died of untreated diseases, frost and starvation.

In April of the following year, the Ausübels were cheered by their first good news. A bearded man whom none knew had come to Tartarsk. His mission was to seek out the Jews in exile. From him, Isaac learned of the progress of the war. The Russians had advanced into Austria after having captured Galicia. They had gotten as far as the Carpathian Mountains before being turned back by the German army. The Russians then had fled, leaving Galicia back in Austrian hands. The information was pleasing to Isaac, but it was not too useful to a cold and hungry family several thousand miles from their native town with no way of getting home. The bearded stranger had a second bit of news that was of more immediate use. He had been sent by a Jewish relief organization and was to give every family some money to help them survive. It was very little, but it was all he had. The man told Isaac that he would return from time to time if he could and bring additional funds.

Isaac returned to the barn that evening. With his eyes lit up, he told his family of the bearded stranger who had come and gone.

"Who is he?" asked Bertha, almost unbelieving.

"I don't know," replied her father, seriously. Then he smiled. "But the coins are real," he added as he opened his hand, exposing the shiny pieces of metal. "They may be the key to our survival." Faiga and the children excitedly counted the few coins. It was the first hard money they had seen since their arrival in Tartarsk.

"Faiga," said Isaac, turning serious again, "this may be a long war. The coins in my hand would not buy food for long. We cannot depend upon the scraps received from the old man or recovered from the garbage in the city to carry us through another winter. Our children must have food each and every day. And we must acquire sufficient funds to pay for warm clothes or we'll freeze to death next winter. To do this, we must find a way to earn money on a steady basis."

"But how, Isaac?" asked Faiga, exuding frustration. "There is no demand for Torah scrolls here."

"Cigarettes, Faiga. Cigarettes."

"Cigarettes?" repeated Faiga, perplexed.

"Yes, cigarettes. Many of these people, the Russians as well as the Tartars, smoke. Let us use some of these coins to buy tobacco and paper. We'll roll cigarettes and then sell them. There is a surplus of starving Jews willing to do anything just for a morsel of food to stay alive. So for work, these Russians and Tartars give you only garbage. But for cigarettes, that's another matter. For that, they'll pay hard money."

❖ ❖ ❖

The Ausübels now had two occupations. They cared for the animals and helped in the fields in the summer months in return for the privilege of sleeping in an unheated barn in mostly subfreezing temperatures. They were also the makers and sellers of homemade cigarettes. Money was scarce, as times were hard, and it was more common to sell a single cigarette or even half of one than to sell them in quantity.

They survived the next two winters, still in exile in Tartarsk. Their mysterious benefactor had returned twice during this period, with small sums of money for each of the exiles. But times grew harder and harder. Russia was losing the war. From whispered words and an occasional newspaper, Isaac pieced together the picture of Russian defeats. Although this news was secretly pleasing to a people who had been forcibly removed from their homes and driven into exile in an icy land by these same Russians, it was also a source of hardship to Isaac and his family. Russian soldiers took away more and more of the little there was to eat. Animals were slaughtered for food, leaving fewer cows to provide milk. Isaac and his family had to take turns standing guard over the animals. They had to fight off scavengers who sought to steal the old man's cows or milk. By the spring of 1917, the state of the Ausübels exiled in Tartarsk was at low ebb.

It was a moonlit Siberian spring night, but it felt like winter. It had been so long since they had experienced a real spring...three years – the three years they had been in exile from Rozwadow. To Isaac and Faiga, Rozwadow was home, still strong in their minds; to Bertha and Mindel, it was but a memory, a fond memory of carefree days long, long ago: To David, it was almost like a dream, like an illusive butterfly that he thought he had caught between the palms of his hands after much effort, only to find it gone.

Isaac, Faiga and the children bundled together beneath the straw, trying to keep warm. The children, their scrawny bodies covered with patchwork clothing and assorted rags, were asleep. Isaac lay on his back, looking up at a pale ray of moonlight that came through a jagged opening in the barn roof. Faiga stirred, just a bit. Her eyes opened and she drank in the thin, strong face of her husband. How it had aged in just three years. The full head of wavy hair and the long crinkly beard were now almost totally gray; the forehead, cheeks and corners of the eyes were now heavily lined. Isaac looked gravely concerned.

"I saw you wash your hands outside when you came home," she whispered in a melancholy voice. (It is customary in Judaism to wash one's hands outside the house after returning from the cemetery.) "Who was it this time?"

"Moishe Katz," he replied, nodding his head, sadly. "It was just a cut. But there was no medicine, nothing with which to disinfect the wound. From a persistent sore covered with nothing but filthy rags came poisons that filled his body, turning him pale and weak. His leg assumed strange colors. The blackness ascended from the cut on his toe to the instep and then up his leg. Some tried to help him in vain. In a week, he was gone. We buried him in the same field with the rest."

"Oh," sighed Faiga. "First his wife, then his daughter, then both his sons and now Moishe – one by one, all have gone. Not one left." She bit her lower lip in pain. "The world is getting emptier and emptier. The Katzes, the Schwartzes and so many, many others."

Mindel began to cough, a harsh, grating cough, again and again. Isaac and Faiga watched with helplessness and terror in their eyes. Then, trying to avoid waking the children, Isaac quickly but silently slid off his thin jacket and placed it over Mindel's wasted body. The paroxysm of coughing finally ceased and Mindel appeared to breathe more easily. Faiga gave a sigh of relief and then closed her eyes, trying to get some sleep. Suddenly, she began to shudder.

"Isaac," she whispered, "is there any hope for us?"

The gray-bearded man studied his wife's troubled face. He slid his arm around her. The warmth of his touch still evoked both joy and security in her bosom.

"There's always hope," he replied without much conviction, "as long as we're still alive." A lump rose in his throat. He could not continue.

Faiga's eyes grew misty. Tears flowed profusely but silently down her face and disappeared into the hay. Isaac held her caressingly.

"At least," he began again, "we have each other."

A week later, just when things were looking their worst, they received some good news. There was a new government in Russia with a man called Karensky at its head.

"He's supposed to be a Social Democrat," said Isaac to his wife, trying to say something positive.

"For the Russians he may be a Social Democrat, but what is his attitude towards Jews?"

"I don't know." Isaac nodded his head, thoughtfully, and became silent.

❖ ❖ ❖

"We can leave! We can leave!" shouted Isaac, joyfully, upon his return from Tartarsk.

What are you talking about?" responded Faiga. "There's a war going on. How can we cross the battle lines to reach Rozwadow?"

"We can't. But we can go to Ufa and wait there 'til things quiet down."

"Where's Ufa?" questioned Bertha.

"I don't know. It's just that they told me we could go to Ufa and that it's closer to Rozwadow," replied her father. But he added quickly, "There's a map in the station. Let's go there and see."

❖ ❖ ❖

A few days later they were ready to leave. Their scant belongings had been packed into a few tidy bundles to be carried by handgrip or slung across the back. They secured the barn door for the last time, said a few farewells, and then headed for the station. It took most of the coins they had saved from two years of cigarette sales to purchase the tickets to Ufa. Ufa, they had been told, was a large city in the Ural Mountains, considerably larger than Tartarsk. Their excitement made the train ride seem much shorter. Their destination was a city closer to home, if a few thousand miles away can be termed closer to home.

"You know," said Isaac as they walked through the city after their arrival, "it's even bigger than Krakow."

The children had never seen Krakow, the largest city in Galicia. They had never seen buildings four- and five-stories high. David looked with wonder at the tall buildings.

"Do they shake in the wind?" he asked.

"Not if they're built well," was his father's retort. Isaac's eyes went to his wife. "Faiga, we'd better find a place to stay – one that is not too expensive. There are no barns in a city as big as this."

They walked from building to building, looking for space for rent. Isaac had learned to speak an unpolished Russian during his three years in Siberia, good enough to handle simple business discussions. And so negotiations came quickly to the point. The little money they had was insufficient to meet the sums demanded for quarters. They were despairing of being able to find any place to stay, when one building owner advised them to go to a specific area – a less desirable part of the city – where they might find quarters within their means. An hour or so later, they had solved their first problem. They had rented a cellar of a shabby building. The room was dark and filthy with a dense layer of dust covering its bare stone floor. The ceiling sagged in an undulating pattern between rotting wooden supports that gave the dank cellar a maze-like quality. Two tiny windows, coated black with soot, allowed a trickle of light to penetrate the darkness. The wind seeped in through cracks in their glass. But with all the negatives, it was still warmer than the barn in Siberia.

During the next several days, Faiga and the girls set about removing the filth and turning the cellar into a home. Isaac and David went out foraging through trash, wherever it could be found, looking for anything useful. They found very little.

"We must start our cigarette business again before we run out of money."

And so the old Jewish way in the Diaspora continued: Eat less, live poorly and save your pennies. Buy something, put some work into it, and then try to sell it for a penny more. If you work as hard as you can and deprive yourself of all but the barest necessities, you may someday have a few more pennies.

By now David had joined the girls in selling cigarettes on the street. Papa and Mama stayed home and busied themselves making the cigarettes. They knew that the Russians were more likely to buy from children, not clearly delineated by their appearance as being Jews, than from a bearded man with the look of Moses or a woman with a dark wig on her head. Towards evening, Mama would prepare what little food they could afford, while Isaac joined a few fellow Jews in prayer.

Several weeks after their arrival in Ufa, Bertha came home with her face lit up.

"Mama, Papa, I've got a job...with real wages."

Faiga looked at her daughter with a half-pleased, half-puzzled expression. The mother in her realized that Bertha was now a blossoming teenager of thirteen. All the potentially undesirable consequences of an offer of employment immediately crossed her mind.

"How did you get the job? And what sort of job is it?" Mama asked.

"I was selling cigarettes...on the street...when this man approached me. Don't look so worried, Mama. He was an older man, old and fat." (The words did not have a soothing effect on Faiga's worried face.) "Anyway, he said there was a labor shortage – all the men away in the army, fighting. He told me I could do a lot better working...in a steady job, than I could selling cigarettes on the street. It is a factory job. They make fur hats. He showed me the place and he offered me twice what I'm making now. And I only have to work twelve hours a day. Besides, it's indoor work so I won't have to freeze outside in the winter cold."

"What kind of man is he?" pursued her mother. "Old and fat is no guarantee against evil intentions. You're so young. You can never tell what some strange man may have in his mind."

"Mama, the man seemed only to be looking for someone capable of doing a good-day's work. And I look strong. People take me for being older than I am... He didn't ask me my age." She paused, looking at her mother's still-troubled face. "Mama, I can take care of myself, so please don't worry," she added with all the confidence of youth.

Isaac interrupted the women with his concluding words: "Bertha is right. And we can certainly use the extra money. But please, Bertha, be careful. I'll have David wait for you at the factory each day. He'll accompany you home. They'll be less likely to bother the two of you together than one alone."

The Ausübels purchased just enough food to sustain themselves. Any improvements in their quarters that could be accomplished by labor or with the use of salvaged materials were made. But no funds were expended for such a purpose.

"We must save for the day when the war is over. We'll need enough money to pay for our trip home."

By autumn, Ufa was in turmoil. First there were rumors, and then definite news of revolts in the cities of Russia. In November 1917, Isaac heard that a group called the Bolsheviks had overthrown the government of Russia. By the following month, Russia had signed an armistice agreement with Austria and Germany.

But Isaac's hopes for getting back to Rozwadow were dashed by the civil war raging in Russia. Railroad lines were controlled in part by one side, and in part by the other. Civilians were forbidden to travel by train. And so they waited and worked and kept alive.

The year 1918 saw the World War end with the surrender of Austria and then Germany. Poland was reborn as a nation with Galicia as part of it. Isaac wondered what change this would bring to the Jews of his native town. But Rozwadow was thousands of miles away. And while the rest of the world was returning to peace, the civil war in Russia was increasing in intensity. There would be news one day that the White Russian Army (of the Tsar) was winning. The next day it was the Red Army (Communist) that had gained a victory. Isaac wondered when it would all end and whether he would ever get his family back to Rozwadow.

Another year passed in Ufa.

The gray-bearded Isaac sat hunched over on a chair in his basement quarters. He was rolling cigarettes on a rough table by the diminishing light coming through the little windows. A blast of cold air stiffened the back of his neck, causing him to look up. It was a fresh crack in the windowpane, large enough to put a fist through, that was the source of the frigid air. His eyes now moved to the stone floor and the shiny bits of glass lying below the window. Isaac cleaned up the debris and then stuffed the opening with some old newspapers. He looked out at the darkening sky of a cold November day. A howling wind outside produced a whining sound as it came through the cracked windowpane, so Isaac readjusted the paper until the sound was gone. Then he returned to the table, lit a candle and rolled cigarettes again.

Faiga stood near the stove at the other end of the room, preparing the evening meal. She took in the aromas of boiling potatoes and a small head of cabbage. It was to be a sumptuous meal by their exile standards. She had even put two meat bones in the pot. Her tongue could almost taste the marrow. But then she looked at the bones and thought the better of it. It would be better, she concluded, if Isaac and the children had first opportunity to suck marrow from the bones. If, by chance, there were anything left, she would try to draw it forth for herself.

The lighting of the candle by Isaac interrupted her thought of food. Faiga's eyes went to her tall, slender husband who sat bent over his work. "We have both potatoes and cabbage for our meal tonight," she said, smiling with delight. "And two bones."

"Very good," replied Isaac. He thought for a moment, then added, "I guess we can afford one good meal after five years in Russia."

"Oh, it didn't really cost anything. Not money, I mean. Mindel swapped a few cigarettes for the potatoes and the cabbage. As for the bones – Bertha's boss gave them to her. It was a sort of bonus."

Isaac stirred uneasily in his chair. "Bonus?" he repeated, frowning.

"For hard work," replied his wife, reassuringly. "Nothing else."

Isaac returned to his work.

Faiga lifted the cover off the pot, stirred its contents and again savored the rising vapors. Her eyes grew dreamy with a vision of the past – a country town with narrow streets lined with busy artisans, a cool river on a warm summer's day, a simple but comfortable home and happy children.

"Isaac," she murmured softly, "do you remember how David loved to catch frogs and study their faces – the frog making eyes at him and he at the frog?"

"And you were afraid he'd get warts," chuckled her husband.

She laughed a hearty, reminiscent laugh.

"The poor frog must have been frightened to death 'til David put him back gently in the stream. David would always wave good-bye 'til the frog disappeared from view."

Isaac continued to roll cigarettes but his mind, like Faiga's, was in another world. A few minutes later he looked up from the table.

"Faiga, we must prepare."

"For what?"

"For the return to Rozwadow."

She looked up excitedly, her face swelling with joy.

"Isaac, is there news? When do we leave?"

"No news," he replied thoughtfully. "But we should be ready in case it comes."

Her face sank a little and the smile vanished.

"What preparations should we make?" she asked.

"We'll have our pictures taken. We'll get identity papers; those are necessary for travel from one land to another. Then we'll wait."

Faiga returned to her cooking, and Isaac to rolling cigarettes.

They worked and they waited for a chance to leave. Their papers were ready.

Two months later, an epidemic broke out in Ufa and thousands became ill. Isaac, Faiga and Mindel were stricken with the disease and suffered with high fever and retching coughs. They were sick enough to expend funds for medical assistance. The doctor said they had typhoid fever. Within a week, all three were dead.

Bertha was now fifteen and David, ten. Both were now old enough to understand the finality of death; there was nothing either could do to change it. Five years of hope now gave way to despair; Bertha continued to work in the factory, toiling at a bench from dawn to dusk and even beyond; David would sell cigarettes until sunset, and then call for his sister. In the evening after returning to their cellar abode, they would roll cigarettes, go through the routine of eating, then collapse into their separate beds for a few hours of sleep. But the freshness of youth was gone from their faces. David would never again look bright-eyed at a butterfly or a frog or a golden weed. Bertha would never again feel overjoyed at dipping her feet in the river. They continued to function, almost mechanically. But they had given up hope of ever seeing home again. For even if they finally got back to their native town, who would be there? They had seen Rozwadow burned to the ground. They had heard of people fleeing to the south and the west. They had seen many of their relatives and friends taken to Siberia. And now they were alone in exile and had not seen a familiar face in more than a year.

Perhaps, thought Bertha, *they're all dead. Maybe, we too will die soon.*

Just as their spirits reached low ebb, they were jolted back to life and hope. A man came to their cellar home one evening and, after a series of verbal exchanges at the door, they allowed him in. He was from Rozwadow and had been searching for survivors of the Russian exile. He had been to Tartarsk and many other places and had stopped in Ufa on his way back to Galicia. As always, he had made inquiries. A hint here and a fortunate word there, and here he was in their abode. The man had located several other survivors and now he had found Bertha and David. Their fellow Jew from Rozwadow had come to take them home.

"But what's left of Rozwadow?" Bertha asked somewhat hopelessly.

"Rozwadow lives," was the answer. "Some of our brethren hid in the woods when the Russians came. After the Russians were driven out, the Jews returned. Later, others came back from Krakow, Prague and Vienna. Together, they rebuilt the town."

"What is it like in Rozwadow under the Poles?" asked David to display his knowledge of current events.

"It's a struggle," was the answer, delivered in a grave tone of voice. "When the war ended, Polish peasants invaded our town. They looted Jewish homes and shops, just as the Russians had done to us before. The butchers murdered and maimed scores of our people. They got drunk on wine looted from Jewish-owned taverns and they shouted, 'Long live Poland!' and 'Beat up the Jews!' The swine even poured wine down the throats of their horses. For eight days they terrorized us.

"Then some of the younger Jews – men who had served in the war – galvanized the community into action. We organized a defense force: Wolf Greisman, who served as an officer in the Austrian army, led us. We collected old rifles, knives, anything that could be used as a weapon. We drove those murderers out of the town. It was amazing. The monsters who looked so powerful when they were assaulting old, defenseless women, fled at the first shot aimed in their direction. They were ready to rape and plunder, but not to die fighting."

"But how did you happen to stop in Ufa? Did you expect to find us here?" asked Bertha, still too numb to appreciate it all.

"I did not know for sure that you were here. I'm part of a team of searchers. We had known for a long time that many of our brethren were in Tartarsk. We had sent money while the war was still on, hoping to keep as many as possible alive until the fighting ended and you could return home. And now we came to gather in the exiles. Many, unfortunately, had died, but a few remained. We searched through the surrounding area and found a few more. Then I heard that some had gone to Ufa two years ago. I came here while my comrades were escorting the other survivors home. I found two other families and had given up hope of finding any others until I heard of two Jewish children living in a cellar. I thought I'd give it one last try before returning home. And with God's help, I found you."

"But who organized it all? Who sent you?" asked David.

"The Jews of Rozwadow. We will never allow our brethren to be forgotten or abandoned."

And so Bertha and David returned to Rozwadow five years after that fateful Yom Kippur eve when the Tsar's army burned their home and drove them into an icy exile. They had left much in Russia. They had left a grandfather in an unmarked grave in a field; they had left friends buried beneath the Siberian snow; they had left a father and mother; they had left a sister; they had left their youth and the brightness of their eyes. But as the human soul somehow seeks to renew itself, a cry of joy came to their lips. Bertha and David saw their uncle, Mendel Ausübel, and ran to his outstretched arms. Tears flowed from Mendel's eyes as he hugged and kissed them. Mendel took them back to his house and the children dined on the best meal they had enjoyed in five years. Afterwards, they sat by the stove and the children told Mendel about Grandpa, Mama, Papa and Mindel and all the rest. Mendel wiped his eyes and then hugged them.

"When will it all end?" he wondered aloud. "When will they leave us in peace?"

The children now had beds of their own, soft beds, not those lumpy collections of rags and straw. And they had a warm house and food. Uncle Mendel wanted them to return to a carefree youth. But it would not work. They had seen too much and suffered too much to ever be children again.

On a Tuesday morning a few months later, Uncle Mendel brought news. Esther Plattner, Bertha and David's older sister in the United States, had sent a ticket for Bertha to come to America. Esther wrote, in an accompanying letter, that she was sorry she did not have enough money to send for David as well.

A few weeks later, Bertha bid a tearful farewell to her uncle and her brother. A new life lay ahead of her in a new country.

David remained in Rozwadow and grew to manhood. He moved to Krakow and was there when the army of Nazi Germany arrived, a generation later. Again, he was ordered to board a boxcar, along with his fellow Jews. The Nazis told them that they were being sent to a "new Jewish community in the East." But this car was not headed for Siberia. Instead, it took them to a concentration camp, for sorting out those who would work until they fell dead, and those who would be exterminated immediately.

In 1945, David was one of the few emaciated survivors who stared, almost unbelieving, at the allied soldiers when the camp was liberated. His hollow eyes had seen tens of thousands of his fellow Jews murdered within that barbed-wire-enclosed slaughterhouse.

David moved to Palestine where the sun's rays spilled warmth upon the earth, mending his sickly body. He met Ida, a fellow survivor of the Holocaust. They married and were there to witness the rebirth of the State of Israel, two thousand years after imperial Rome had driven the Jews into exile.

Ida bore him a son and they named him Isaac, after David's father. They had a daughter whom they named Rachael.

Isaac fought and died for Israel in the Six-Day War. He was nineteen years old.

Rachael grew to womanhood and married Jacob Rachmuth. In 1975, Jacob and Rachael named their first-born son Isaac. The name and the people *will* live on.

TO THE END OF THE EARTH

SEVERAL YEARS AGO, Stephanie and I took a second trip to China. This time, we intended to spend more time in the north of the country, going up to Mongolia. We traveled by bus to the Great Wall of China and marveled at this amazing structure that stretched as far as the eye could see, following the landscape up and down the mountainous terrain. I commented to our guide, "What effort it must have taken to build a wall several thousand miles long, wide enough on the top for a large army, accompanied by cavalry to move across!"

"Effort!" replied our guide. "The bodies of thousands who died during its construction are buried beneath it."

Then we walked for a few miles on the wall itself. "I guess the Chinese rulers felt it was worth it," I said to the guide. "To keep out invaders from the north."

"Worth it? It never worked. The Mongols crossed it. All you needed to do was to bribe someone. What was achieved was a great tourist attraction, nothing more."

I'd like to travel farther north."

"What for?"

"I want to see the area where members of my family traveled many years ago."

"What, are you a Mormon or something? I've heard they send missionaries up to Mongolia."

"No, we're not Mormons."

"Do you have family in Mongolia? I haven't heard of Europeans or Americans settling there."

"No. Our family members passed through this region a long time ago. But none of them are in Mongolia at present."

"Very well. There's a bus that goes in the direction of the capital of Mongolia. But I must caution you – that's not an area where many foreigners travel. You could end up with food poisoning or something. And the accommodations are not like those in Beijing or Shanghai."

"That's OK. We don't have enough time for an extended stay. We just want to experience the area."

The following day we took a bus to the north, past the Great Wall. We traveled for miles and miles, seeing nothing but dried yellow grass. As we gazed at the barren landscape, I said to Stephanie, "Can you imagine walking a thousand miles across this surface, your belly empty, never sure you would ever see the end of it?"

"So this is what your family endured," Stephanie replied with a sad look on her face.

"Yes. It was the trip of my granduncle Shulem, his wife, and their ten children. When I tell people about it, they hardly believe me. We, in United States, are amazed at the story of American pioneers crossing 3,000 miles of the continent in covered wagons, but 7,000 miles across Siberia, Mongolia and China, mostly on foot, is almost unbelievable. I can visualize it now..."

At the same time that Isaac Ausübel and his family were dropped off in Tartarsk, Shulem Ausübel stepped down from the cold, dark freight car onto the platform of the city of Tartarsk. A small boy was cradled in Shulem's right arm. His wife, Sheva, was soon at his side, grasping his left arm for security. Her right arm held an infant wrapped in a gray blanket.

Shulem was a dark-bearded Jew with a *streimel* covering his head, and a three-quarter length black coat covering his dark suit. His wife was a Jewess, dressed in drab floor-length clothing with a dark *sheitl* concealed by her babushka. The two adults stood there, studying the faces of the Asians before them. They were two exiles in a mysterious land.

Eight other children, ranging in age from the diminutive twenty-year-old eldest son, Avraham Berish, to the four-year-old Frumah, joined them. Frumah's small white hand clutched that of her oldest sister, Zivia. Zivia was an eighteen-year-old woman, whose slender frame was hidden beneath a long dark coat. A sack was slung across Avraham Berish's right shoulder. Berish hitched that shoulder as he shifted the weighty sack. He did so cautiously, so as to avoid striking his siblings with its heavy contents.

Other exiled Israelites descended from the train into the icy air of a Siberian winter. They all looked bewildered.

For a fleeting moment, Shulem caught sight of a kinsman, but the man disappeared from view.

"I thought I saw Isaac," he commented to his wife.

"Isaac who?" she questioned.

"Isaac Ausübel," he replied. "You know; my cousin, the *sofer*."

"Shouldn't you go after him?"

"Too difficult. We have ten children with us and he was moving fast. Our little ones could never keep up. We might get separated, and this is no place for us to get separated. It's icy cold. We'd better get off the platform and seek shelter before the young ones freeze to death. Perhaps we'll meet up with Isaac or some of the others."

"This way," Shulem directed with his hand pointing in one direction.

The family trooped down the snow-covered street in double file: father and mother in the lead, with Berish and his taller fifteen-year-old brother, Joseph, bringing up the rear. Here and there a patch of the dirt showed through the snow. One- and two-story buildings lined the street on which they walked; most looked as if they needed a new coat of paint.

"Papa," cried Frumah ahead to her father, "My feet feel like ice."

"I'll carry you," said Zivia as she lifted her little sister from the snow.

"We must find shelter," whispered Sheva to her husband. "The little ones cannot take the cold, especially with their thin shoes."

"Yes..." Shulem paused for a moment as he studied a sign in Russian. "This way," he began again. "It says 'boarding house.'"

They entered through the front door into a narrow foyer. A stocky, bald-headed man with a walrus mustache came towards them. Shulem signaled his wife and children to remain where they were as he approached the man seemingly in charge. The man spoke Russian, a language with which Shulem had limited skills. Shulem pleaded for the man to speak slowly, the bearded Jew struggling to find the right words.

Sheva and the children waited just inside the door. At last Shulem turned and went to his wife's side. "We can stay three nights, perhaps four. There is an attic in the building. It will do for all of us. No heat up there, but at least we'll be off the snow and away from the wind."

"How much will it cost?" inquired Sheva.

"We don't have enough to pay for it."

"You mean he took pity on us? How nice."

"Not quite," replied her husband. "I told him that Berish and Joseph and I were carpenters. I pointed to the tools that Berish is carrying. We can stay three or four nights, provided that we fix his roof and do a number of other repairs."

"In this weather – repair a roof? You'll freeze to death up there!"

"It will be hard, but there is no alternative. We'll work for an hour and then warm ourselves up for a few minutes. I think we can do it. When I can, I'll send Joseph away for a while to see what's to the west. The Russian officer said that we can't go home, but how can he stop us? It's a long, long way back to Rozwadow, but perhaps we can make our way home."

"It took us three days to get here by train," said Sheva with concern. "Do you realize how far from home we are? Can you imagine how long it would take us to make such a journey on foot? Besides, we have babies. How are they to survive such a journey?"

"Those are a lot of questions! I don't have the answers. But I do know this: The Russians have not sent us here for a vacation. We'll have to overcome enormous challenges if we are to survive. So let's go to the attic and get some rest. We'll need all our energy for the work and for the journey ahead."

"And what about food?"

"I have a few crowns. After that, we'll see."

"It's no use," said Joseph as he approached Shulem and Berish. "We can't go west."

There was a troubled look on Shulem's face as he studied his son. Joseph was a thin, brown-haired youth. Aside from a few twisted hairs on his chin, he was beardless.

"And why not?" asked the father.

"They've stationed soldiers to the west."

"They? You mean the Russians have stationed soldiers to the west of here just to keep us from walking back to Galicia?" He paused for a moment and then went on, "Did you see them?"

"No, Papa. But I heard and saw the results."

"What results?"

"I heard shooting. And I met Jews – men and women and even children – fleeing eastward. Several were bleeding from wounds. They said that they had been shot at by Russian soldiers. They said that others had been killed. It was a massacre."

"Why would the Russians care if a group of Jews were walking towards the west? Were these people approaching a military camp? Did the Russians fear an attack?" Shulem's face twisted back and forth in disbelief.

"From old men and little children?" interjected Berish. "It must be that they are making certain that none of us survives. It would seem that they want the thousands of Jews they are sending here to vanish without a trace, without anyone to tell their story."

Shulem thought for a long while. Then he spoke with determination in his voice. "They have sent us here to die in the frost. We should not go willingly to our deaths." His voice grew louder and his clenched fist rose above his head. "If we have to travel to the end of the earth, we will. " His arm returned to his side and he continued most softly, "That's our only chance for survival."

A biting wind drove snow on to their faces as they ascended the narrow path. The sky and the mountains had been as one – varying shades of white and gray. But now there was nothing but a blinding whiteness as the heavens poured down sheets of icy crystals. Their feet sank deep into the snow as they struggled ahead.

"We have to rest," pleaded Sheva.

Shulem nodded. "We'll all huddle together," he directed. "Berish and Joseph, heap up the snow around us to serve as a barrier against the wind."

A few minutes later, the twelve Ausübels were huddled together in a crouched position, body against body.

"Are you sure we are going in the right direction?" questioned Sheva anxiously.

Shulem thought for a moment and then replied. "I believe we're headed south. At least that's the way I figured from studying the sun's movements. It's winter and the sun should be to the south."

"But there has been no sun for days."

"But that was the direction of the road when we started out. We have to continue on it unless it comes to an end."

"Couldn't we have stayed in Tartarsk until the spring?"

"Where in Tartarsk? I stretched out the job at the boarding house for as long as possible. As soon as the work was completed, the man insisted that we either pay rent for our attic or leave. We exchanged carpentry services for food and shelter wherever we could. But there are no more jobs. I know. Berish, Joseph and I covered every house in the city and beyond. We simply did not have the funds to pay for food and lodgings – in the boarding house or elsewhere. So we had to leave. Heading south was the only logical choice. If we were to journey west, the Russian soldiers would shoot at us. Going north would have been absurd. If we went east, we'd be going farther and farther into the cold of Siberia until we reached the ocean. What sense would that make? To the south is China. It would be warmer. And, more important, we would be away from the Russian army."

"But what can we do in China?"

"Maybe go to America or something." Shulem looked around to the rest of his family and then continued:

"Time for us to get moving. We seem to be going higher in the mountains. One of the Asians who speaks Russian told me that after a while we should be going downhill. I would like to get into the next valley before nightfall. If we don't reach a town by the time it turns dark, we'll stop and rest for the night in the same manner as we did just now. Joseph, make sure none of our food falls from your sack. We have a long way before we can get fresh supplies, so we'll have to eat sparingly to conserve what we have."

Sarah was burning with fever. The next morning they dug a grave through the frozen ground. Five days later, her little brother, Schmuley, was gone and they had to dig again. Then Yechiel, then Rivkah, then Leah. The last to die was little Simcha. Each time, the parents could not give in to their agony. They had to keep the remaining children alive.

Four months later, the surviving Ausübels reached what appeared to be a town. Shulem and Sheva led the four remaining children – Berish, Joseph, Zivia and Frumah – down the single street, past the dried-mud walled circular homes.

The residents of the hamlet – Asians, each with almond-shaped dark eyes separated by a well-formed nose – came out to witness the strange sight. Rifles and swords held at the ready, they studied the emaciated bearded Caucasian who was dressed in a foxtail hat and tattered dark clothing, leading five other gaunt members of his race. From the looks on their faces, it appeared that many of these Mongols had never seen a European.

One of the residents approached. He was a stocky man with green eyes and a wispy mustache. He wore a thick sheepskin coat. A pointed light brown cap with black felt trim over a fur interior lining covered his head. He studied the faces of Shulem and the rest.

Shulem used his limited Russian to find out where they were.

"Ulaam-Uhl," replied the man in the same language. "You are not in Russia. This is Mongolia. You are fortunate. I am the son-in-law of the head man of the town and the only one who speaks Russian." He paused for a moment and then went on: "And who might you be? Are you Russians? I must warn you that the people here don't care much for Russians..." He studied the sacks carried by Shulem and his two sons and then added, "Why are you here? To trade?"

Shulem explained as best he could that they were Jews who had been sent to Siberia against their will. He described their journey to escape the Russians and how glad they were to be out of the grip of the Tsar's army. He detailed the loss of six children in four months. The sacks contained their carpentry tools.

"I'm sorry you were treated so badly," said the Asian, shaking his head from side to side. "It confirms what I have observed of them over the years. They have stolen the lands to the north and would not hesitate to steal more of it if these people didn't resist."

"These people?" wondered Shulem aloud. "Are you not one of them? And those green eyes; the other eyes I see are brown."

"I am not native to Ulaam-Uhl. The people here are Khalkhas." (Khalkhas are one of the five Mongol tribal leagues who inhabit Mongolia proper. The Ordos and Tsaktar are both of Mongolian blood. The Ouryanti and Darkhat are Mongolized Turks.)

"But," Shulem became silent.

"You're right. I am an Ouryanti – a mixture of Mongol and Turk – so to the European I look like them. My name is Abdul Çelebi. I was born north of here. The Russians seized that area before I was born. That's why I know Russian. I was conscripted into the Tsar's army. It was there that I met one of your fellow Jews. He, too, was a conscript. Those Russians made fun of him and even beat him. And our officer made him eat pork – mostly rancid pork. I know that it is against your religion as it is against the Muslim faith. But they never forced Muslims to eat pork; there were too many of us in the unit. One day, we Muslims decided to end this practice – forcing the Jew to eat pork. And so they stopped that disgusting behavior. So, you see, I know about Russians and Jews."

"So how did you get here?" asked Shulem.

"The Russian officer led us on a raid – to seize horses. He took me along because I speak the Mongol tongue."

"And what happened?"

"I told you; these people resist. Our entire unit was wiped out. They let me live because I was part Mongol. So I stayed here and married the daughter of the village elder, Timur." He turned and added, "And that is him – the older man with the shining sword. I will tell him about you and your family."

Abdul then went to the side of the village elder and spoke for a while in an animated fashion. Timur then spoke to the other inhabitants of the hamlet. The villagers went home.

Then Timur, accompanied by his son-in-law, approached Shulem. "He has invited you all to his home," announced Abdul.

A few minutes later, Timur and his guests entered a house in the town. A number of women and children rose as the village elder made his entrance. Shulem studied the faces of the inhabitants and then the construction of the building. It consisted of a light framework, outlining mud walls. The house had a domed top about ten feet high. A fireplace was in the center, with carpets covering the earthen floor around it. There were Oriental-faced statues positioned over the door through which they had come in. Each figure was about a foot in height. Household utensils were positioned on the circular wall, along with one hand-woven silken hanging of bright colors in a geometric design. Along the circular wall opposite the entry door, there were several beds, one after another, the long end of each against the wall. Each bed was positioned behind high corner posts that supported a frame with colorful hanging curtains. The curtains were held against the posts by rope-like pieces of material, but it was clear that they could be pulled shut to offer privacy to the occupants.

Timur spoke to the adult women in the residence. Then they prepared food while the Asiatic children studied their European counterparts. One Mongolian woman beckoned Sheva to observe her manner of preparation.

"I told my father-in-law that you do not eat meat. It was easier than trying to explain your kashrut," said the Russian speaker.

The Ausübels feasted on curds and milk. It was a better meal than any they had had since leaving Galicia. Their hosts consumed meat, as well as the milk and curd. Shulem and his two sons conversed with Timur and Abdul. Abdul served as the translator of statements made by the Jews in Russian and by his father-in-law in the Mongol language. After the meal, the Mongol children invited Berish and his three siblings to look around the hamlet. Facial expressions and hand movements conveyed their proposals and Abdul added an explanation in Russian.

"You will rest here and regain your strength," announced Abdul in translation of his father-in-law's words.

"My thanks for your hospitality," replied the smiling Shulem, as he bowed to the village elder.

Two months went by, with the Ausübels regaining something of their former appearance. Gaunt faces were now more rounded, and ribs no longer showed when Berish and Joseph removed their shirts. Joseph and Berish had taken to joining some of the Mongol nomads as they moved their herds of sheep, cattle and horses from the winter lowland pastures to the summer mountain meadows. Abdul would come along to serve as their guide and translator. The Jews learned something of Mongol culture and words of their dialect. Berish was the fastest at learning to speak the Mongol language. The Mongols, in turn, learned something about a people, of whom they had never heard.

In Galicia, Shulem and his sons had been carpenters with but a modicum of education. Shulem had attended *cheder* and was then apprenticed to a carpenter. Berish and Joseph attended the Baron de Hirsch School while doing carpentry work after school. Berish had graduated from the gymnasium and then became a master carpenter, but Joseph was still in school when the war broke out.

Now Berish resumed his interest in acquiring knowledge. More so than his parents or his siblings, he kept questioning all with whom they came in contact. He had brought some paper with him into exile. Now he took careful notes, written in miniature script so as to conserve his limited supply of paper.

The Mongols played a game in which a group of pieces from the anklebones of a sheep were tossed into the center of a circle of participants. Each participant received a turn. The positions of the several bones, as they landed on the ground, gave rise to an interpretation of what the bones foretold.

The Mongols survived as nomadic herdsmen. Farming was not possible in a land in which just a few centimeters of rain fell per year. They were obliged to move their flocks very often, to take advantage of the little grass that was available.

Berish and Joseph were invited to join the nomads as they moved their temporary camp to bring the flocks to new pastureland. When the two Jewish lads traveled with the Mongols, they slept at night in portable houses, which Abdul explained were called yurts. The framework was of curved wooden strips, which were carried on a cart drawn by double-humped camels. When they reached the site for the new camp, the framework was assembled to support the circular tent with its domed roof. The wooden slats were then covered with layers of white felt, which served as both waterproofing and insulation. The layers of felt were bound around the framework by ropes.

"How is this felt made?" inquired Berish of Abdul.

"To make the felt we used the natural-colored wool fleece sheared from our animals. Our women then beat the wool fleece with sticks. This separates the fibers more evenly. The resulting material is then immersed in hot water and agitated. The women remove the felt from the water and press it into sheets. These are laid out on a sedge mat. Three or more sheets of felt are pressed together to make the covering for one yurt. Everyone in the area helps kick and beat and roll the sheets together. It takes about two hours to do so. The matted wool is removed and rolled up again. The maker then presses it back and forth with her elbows until it is absolutely firm."

"Very interesting," commented Berish. "But what of the carpets that cover the floor of the yurt?"

"They are not carpets at all," replied Abdul. "Come, let me show you."

They entered a yurt.

"See," said the Turk, "these are not woven. They are made of felt, just like the outer coverings of the yurt."

"And the colors?"

"I said that the batches of wool are immersed in hot water. If one type of wild flower is placed in the water, its red color is transferred to that batch of wool. In this way, we make red, blue, brown, orange and white felt."

"But the patterns in different colors?"

"Do you remember the floor covering in my father-in-law's house?"

"Yes, it was a beautiful carpet. I mean..."

"It is a *shyrdak*, made for their wedding. Two sheets of white felt form its base. Colored felt is then cut into patterns to produce the bird's wing, ram's horn or raven's claw design. These are then sewn onto the white base, using horse hair thread or sheep's wool thread to quilt the pieces in place."

"You must waste a lot of wool; I mean, to cut out a pattern in blue and then discard the rest."

"Not at all. The residual was used to make a sister's *shyrdak* with the reverse pattern; blue where the first *shyrdak* was red, and red where the first *shyrdak* was blue. In that manner nothing is discarded. Now you've had your lesson for today. Come, let's take a ride."

By now Berish and Joseph had learned to ride Mongol horses. The orange-colored wooden saddles used by the Mongols contained projecting metal pieces that made sitting most uncomfortable. Berish and Joseph were therefore obliged to do as the Mongols did – ride in a standing position.

While all Mongols were expert horsemen, riding was not done simply for sport. They were managing flocks of horses and sheep. The bond between the Mongol and his horses was so strong that there was no need for fences to keep the animals from running off. The mares, milked several times each day, were the source of both milk and curd. These formed a major portion of the Mongol diet. The sheep provided the wool for the making of felt, and when slaughtered, provided skins as well as meat.

Abdul and the Jewish lads galloped across a landscape that consisted of undulating hills of dried yellow grass beneath a cold blue sky, traversed by an occasional cloud.

In the distance, they saw a Mongol horseman with a huge bird perched on one hand. "That bird – it looks like a falcon but it seems much larger," observed Joseph.

Abdul led them on a gallop until they were alongside the Mongol horseman. This horseman wore a dark coat with gleaming bronze buttons and a leather belt with a silvery buckle. A peaked hat, much like Abdul's, covered his head. But this horseman's hat had a white feather stuck in its peak.

"The bird is an eagle and the man is an eagler," said Abdul. "He wears a thick glove of animal skin to protect the hand on which the bird rests. The eagle is held by a rope around one of his claws."

"But what is the purpose of all this?"

"He sends the eagle aloft to hunt prey."

"So why should the eagle return once it has been set free to fly?"pursued Joseph.

"Because man and bird need one another. When game is plentiful, the man shares in the eagle's catch. When game is scarce, the eagle is fed a portion of one of the animals in the man's flock that is slaughtered to provide food."

Abdul spoke briefly to the eagler who then released the eagle from its rope. The great bird flew off.

"No point waiting for the eagle to return," said Abdul. It may be gone for hours.

Abdul waved good-bye to the Mongol and he and his Jewish companions galloped away.

"What are those animals?" asked Berish as he spotted a group of brownish horse-like animals that had the appearance of zebras without the stripes.

"It is said that animals like those were the ancestors of our present-day horses. Our forefathers tamed some of them and bred them to produce horses that were leaner and faster. That enabled the armies of Genghis Kahn to conquer much of the world. Later, these wild horses were hunted down until there are now very few of them. The men of our village follow Buddhist teachings. They do not hunt the wild horses, for these animals have as much right to this land as we do."

"There will be a feast today," announced Abdul to Shulem and his family one morning. "You should find the events quite interesting."

"What kind of events?" questioned Berish.

"Wrestling, archery, sword skills and others," replied Abdul.

"They're not going to fight with swords?" inquired Shulem, with his face turning long.

"No," smiled Abdul. "It's man against an enemy's head – a melon."

"Oh," smiled Shulem.

"And I'm going to wrestle in the tournament," added Abdul. "I haven't gotten far in the past, but I've been practicing."

"Please be careful," urged Shulem. "You don't want to get hurt."

That afternoon the Ausübels stood along with the inhabitants of Ulaam-Uhl, observing the events of the day. It was the finals of the wrestling competition. Abdul, clothed in a loincloth, was greasing his body. His opponent – a huge Mongol with powerful shoulders – was doing the same.

Timur waved a yellow cloth. The match was to begin. The two competitors circled one another, each looking for a weak spot. The huge man lunged at Abdul. The half-Turk sidestepped the charge and pushed his opponent to the ground with a slap on the back.

The Mongol rose, dust covering his oil-soaked frame. Again, the competitors circled one another, arms before them ready to seize the opponent.

Abdul dove at his opponent, feet first. His legs locked, scissors-like, on his opponent's right calf, and the half-Turk flipped him to the ground. After much twisting and turning, the Mongol extricated himself from Abdul's leg-vice.

The match continued. Abdul used dexterity against an opponent nearly twice his size, but he was unable to pin the huge Mongol to the ground.

After many lunges for nearly half-an-hour, the Mongol finally succeeded in grabbing hold of Abdul by the waist. He forced the half-Turk to the ground and smothered him with his huge body.

The match was over. The opponents rose and embraced, then bowed to each another. Timur gave the winner a congratulatory slap on the back, and then went to his son-in-law. After a few words, Timur signaled for the next event.

Abdul wiped his oiled body with a cloth and then approached the Ausübels. "I became careless," he said in the Russian language in which they communicated with one another.

"There was nothing you could really do," interjected Berish. "He was so much bigger than you."

"Size should not be the only deciding factor," insisted Abdul. "I was faster than he. He would have eventually exhausted himself with the lunges and the falls, and then I could have pinned him. I'll have to practice for next year."

One man stuck twenty spiked sticks in the ground, and then pushed a melon on top of each one. An archer took up a position some one hundred feet from the line of melons. He fired twenty arrows, one at a time, directing each at one of the melons. He struck seventeen of the melons.

"Excellent," remarked Berish.

"Good, but perhaps not good enough," retorted Abdul.

A second contestant replaced the first and he, in turn, was replaced by a third. The twelfth and last contestant took up position. No one had equaled or exceeded the number of melons hit by the first archer.

"Watch this man," murmured Abdul to Berish and his father. "He's been the best for years."

This contestant fired sixteen arrows without a miss. The seventeenth arrow missed its mark, as did the eighteenth. A few murmurs were heard in the crowd. Timur waved for silence. The contestant stretched his bow back and took aim. As he fired his arrow, his fingers became entangled in the string. His arm suddenly was pulled forward. The arrow missed its mark. The contestant grabbed his arm as he winced with pain.

"He's made a fine effort, but he'll have to withdraw," said Berish.

The contestant removed his hand from the pained shoulder and moved to another position some 90 degrees from where he had stood before.

"What's he doing?" questioned Berish.

The half-Turk raised a silencing finger before his lips.

The contestant took aim and fired his final arrow. It split one melon and went on to strike another. A roar of approval came up from the crowd.

"Unbelievable," commented Berish. "Two melons with one arrow!"

Timur gave a congratulatory slap on the back to the winner, being careful not to strike the injured shoulder. Then the village elder left the arena.

"Where did Timur go?" asked Shulem.

"For his horse. He is competing in the sword competition. Watch him. He's the best I've ever seen."

The twenty spiked sticks were moved to new positions so that they were at thirty-foot intervals. A fresh melon was pressed atop each spike. One by one, a series of competitors, each mounted on a horse, came charging at the row of spikes, slicing off the melons as he went by. Fresh melons replaced those that had been struck. But no competitor had succeeded in cutting all twenty melons. Timur charged last. He not only succeeded in slicing all twenty melons, he was able to twirl his sword in the air between slices. A roar of approval from the audience greeted the village elder as he climbed off his horse.

Several hours later they were back in Timur's house. The Ausübels were exhausted from the celebration that followed the completion of the sporting contests.

"I have a question to ask," said Shulem. "I hope I will not offend you by asking it."

"Please ask," smiled Abdul. "On such a good day all questions should be answered."

"Your eyes... They're green, the only green eyes in the village. I assumed they were from your Turkish father, but I had been told in the past that Turks have dark eyes."

"What you have been told in the past is correct. But my father's father had blue eyes and a great aunt had green eyes, rare colors in their tribe. Look at it this way: Many peoples have dwelt in the land. My father, a Turk, married my mother, a Mongol. Perhaps, in the distant past, some Turk ancestor took a bride of some other people who have many blue-eyed daughters. Who knows? We are probably all a mix of this and that.

"As I said: It was a good day," smiled Abdul. He paused for a moment and then continued, "Timur has made a proposal. He has seen your tools and the way you use them. We do not possess such tools."

Shulem looked worried.

"Have no fear," Abdul assured the bearded Jew. "He does not want to take your tools from you. They are needed for your occupation. What he proposes is that you remain here as his guests, and that you use your tools and your skills to help the village in the construction of a new temple. As you know, I am a Muslim. All the other inhabitants of Ulaam-Uhl are Buddhists. They follow Lamaist Buddhism similar to that which I'm told is practiced in Tibet. Incidentally, the statues above the door are household gods. But let me get back to the construction of the temple. Timur has long hoped that a monastery would be erected in this area. One problem has always been that it would have to be much larger than our homes. And it should be a fine building worthy of being the religious center of the area. Timur has drawn up a sort of loose general plan. It is based upon the appearance of various monasteries he has visited in the past."

He reached into his jacket and came up with a drawing on animal skin. He presented it to Shulem. The Jew studied it carefully.

"You know better how to support such a large structure," began Abdul again. "You and your sons have the tools and the skills to lead the construction of the monastery. The people of the town will do much of the work under your direction, and they will try to obtain whatever materials you need to complete the task.

"I know that you and your family would like to return to your native land. But how are you to get there? There is a vast Russia in the way. There is a war going on. Here in Ulaam-Uul, you are safe. You have added flesh to your bones. It will take some time to complete the project. You will have food and shelter throughout. Perhaps the war will be over by the time the temple is completed. Perhaps it will be safe to return to your homeland by then. In any case, if you desire to move on after the monastery is finished, I will personally escort you to Urga, the largest city in Mongolia. From there you can follow the trade routes to distant places. (Urga is the city of the Hutukhtu – the Living Buddha who is the hereditary theocratic ruler of the Mongol people. The city, subsequently renamed Ulan Bator Khoto, is now the capital of the

Mongolian People's Republic.) "I will not press you for an answer. You are the head of the family. In our culture, you are the one to make the decision, but it may be different with your people. You may want to discuss the proposal with your family. Let me know when you have come to a decision."

Abdul studied Shulem's face and added, "I ask but one thing. If you accept Timur's proposal, you will agree to stay until the building is completed, even if the war ends before that time, and even if it would be safe for you to return to your native land before the building has been finished."

"On that we are in agreement," replied Shulem. "If we undertake the task, we will stay until the work is done. And if I do not survive to see that day, my sons will be bound to continue the work."

The Ausübels withdrew to where the silken carpet hung on the circular wall. They spoke in muffled voices for a few minutes and then became silent.

"There is but one problem – a religious problem," began Shulem. "As you know we are Jews. We are forbidden to worship any but the Eternal. Avraham *Avinu* broke the idols of his father, Terach. Now I respect Timur and his people. They are good people. But no member of my family can be involved in the making of what we consider to be idols." (*Avinu* is "Our father." Abraham is considered the father of the Jewish people.)

"That goes without saying," assured Abdul. "I have never been involved in the making of such figures. The people here have respected my religious beliefs and they will respect yours as well. Is that the only problem?"

"I had thought whether it was right for us to be involved in the construction of a house of prayer not of our faith. But my son, Berish, reminded me that it was a Jewish architect, Niccolo Matas, who designed and oversaw the construction of one of the great churches of Florence, a city in Italy. And so we have concluded that it would be acceptable for us to be involved in the construction of a Buddhist monastery. So there is no other problem."

"Then it is agreed?"

"When do we begin?" he smiled.

Abdul turned to his father-in-law and repeated Shulem's statement in the Mongol tongue.

"A toast," smiled Abdul, translating Timur's reply. "You can all drink the liquor. My religion forbids me to drink fermented spirits, so I will drink another beverage."

Timur poured a milky liquid from an opaque flask into several glasses.

"What is this beverage?" inquired Shulem.

"*Kumys*," smiled Abdul. "It is fermented mare's milk. *Kumys* is a delicacy in this area."

The project was completed late in the fall of 1917. A great monastery dominated the barren landscape not far from Ulaam-Uul. All the people of the region were gathered to witness the opening of the monastery. Hutukhtu himself was present, along with the Da Lama (head of the new monastery) and several Miu Lamas (ordinary Lamas).

"It is a proud moment," smiled Abdul to Shulem. "Timur is honored that the Living Bhudda has journeyed here for the opening of the monastery.

"Much has transpired since you started the project. The war in Europe and even here in Asia continues. There is a revolution going on in Russia. Therefore, it would not be safe for you to travel back through that land. You can stay with us as long as you choose. I said to you, when I first presented Timur's proposal, that I would escort you to the big city if you desired to leave our town after the monastery had been completed. Tomorrow, the Living Bhudda is returning to Urga. I will take you along with his party. All the trade routes pass through that city. From there you can travel south to China and beyond. So what is your choice?"

The Ausübels huddled for a few minutes, and then Shulem addressed Abdul. "We appreciate your years of hospitality. Please thank Timur for all he has done for us. If we have, to some small measure, repaid his kindness with our labor, we are happy to have done so. But we should move on. And so we accept your offer to escort us to Urga."

The trip took several days more than was anticipated. A windstorm came up and frightened the horses. Seven pack animals were gravely injured when they tumbled down a ravine and had to be destroyed. Their burden was recovered and then placed on other animals. The Ausübels had to give up three of their horses, leaving three of the Jewish family on one horse and three on a second. Four of the Mongols were reduced to traveling on foot, so that their horses could be used to transport goods.

Urga may have been a major city in Outer Mongolia, but it was a minor habitat by Western standards, far smaller than Krakow in Galicia. They had arrived in the city at a most difficult time. While the Living Bhudda was away, Tsarist troops had seized the Mongol city and were now using it as a base for their fight against the Bolshevik enemy in Russia.

Some Russian soldiers eyed Shulem and his family suspiciously as Hutukhtu's party entered the city.

"I think we are in danger," whispered Shulem. "One of those Russians has run into the large building over there, perhaps to tell his superior of our presence."

"Stay here with me," replied Abdul, his rifle now held at the ready.

The Russian soldier reemerged from the building, along with an officer. The soldier pointed in the direction of the Jews.

"You," shouted the officer in Russian. "Come here!"

Abdul raised a cautioning hand in front of Shulem and his family. Then he approached the Russian officer. Words were exchanged, following which Abdul returned to Shulem's side.

"Strange man, that Russian officer. Defeated by the Germans from without and the Bolsheviks from within, he has to worry that a few Jews might have escaped his grasp. So I told him that you were from China and were returning to Shanghai. He appeared perplexed but accepted my word, perhaps because he saw my hand on the rifle trigger. But he will not be held back for long. We had best withdraw from here. I and my men will lead you to the road to the south, but we will not accompany you beyond that point."

"But..." said Shulem anxiously.

"I do not mean to abandon you. Rather, I will stay just south of the city. Several of the Mongols from Ulaan-Uul will remain there with me. When the Russians see that we're well armed and that we intend to block their way south, they will know better than to follow you.

"I would give you horses for the journey, but sadly, we lost so many on the trip here. We are now woefully short of pack animals with which to bring goods back from Urga."

The party of Mongols and Jews left the city center and headed south. "The road is long. There will be a few watering places along the route. My men have packed as much food as they can for you to take with you. Let Allah be with you," said Abdul as they parted.

Four weeks later, all of their food was gone. They had consumed all the water in their leather pouches, although they had filled them at a watering hole. The ground was dry. The Jews had taken to eating dried grass, roots and all, wherever they could find some. Ice, melted in their hands, was their major source of water.

Their steps grew shorter. Each day they walked for as many hours as possible. At night they rested from the icy winter wind, huddled together under a blanket.

"Frumah can't go on," whispered Sheva to her husband.

"We can't just sit here. If we do, we'll all die," he replied. "We'll take turns carrying her. It's the only way."

"But how far?"

"To the end of the earth if needs be," he replied, grimly.

They kept trudging, day after day. Each day the distance they covered became shorter and shorter. They kept going, as if by reflex. Their eyes no longer focused on the terrain.

A week later, a Mongol band approached on horseback. They studied the strange band of Caucasians who were crossing the seemingly insurmountable Gobi Desert that stretched for a thousand miles. One rider moved his horse close to the Jews. He quickly touched Shulem with one hand, as if to make sure it was not a mirage. Then he reached down into a saddlebag and withdrew a chunk of dried curd, which he threw down to Shulem. The other Mongols did likewise, filling the open arms of the Ausübels with chunks of curd and pouches of water. Then the band galloped off without a word.

"Praised be to the Almighty," declared a happy Shulem.

"And to the Mongols," added Berish. "In the history books we read of them as barbarians who conquered much of Europe. But these Mongols are far more decent than many of the Europeans we have dealt with in the past."

They all nodded in agreement.

An icy winter wind blew in from the north. They ate and drank as best they could. Flat bread gifts from passing Mongols would be consumed slowly over a period of weeks. Dried grass had to do when nothing else was available. During the fall, the sky had been a brilliant blue, day after day. There was no rain. But with the coming of winter there were occasional clouds overhead, yielding some rare shower of snow. As the warming April sun rose in the sky, the yellow grass sprang to life and served as a source of food. When they reached a watering place, they washed and drank their fill. They filled their leather water pouches and drank in sips between stops.

When there was food, Frumah recovered quickly and was able to walk when her belly had been filled. But she was the first to weaken when they ran out of solids and water. Her parents and her older siblings took turns carrying her when she was too weak to make her way on her own. In the end, Frumah's body was no longer able to withstand the elements and she died in the arms of her mother. She was buried in a shallow grave in the vast grasslands of the Gobi desert. There was no wood available to mark the spot. The "*El maleh rahamim*," a prayer in memory of the dead, was recited.

Sheva wept and had to be restrained from throwing herself on the grave of her daughter.

A short while later, Shulem urged his wife and three remaining children to resume the trip. "We must continue."

"I haven't seen an *aobao* or even a caravan since we left that town," said Sheva with grave concern one day. (*Aobao* are mounds made of stones set up on high points. They were originally used as directional markers, but later developed into focal points for religious services and festivals.)

"I'm afraid we may have taken a wrong turn back at Sair Usu, but there's no sense in trying to retrace our steps. We couldn't if we wanted to. But I judge, from the position of the sun, that we are still headed south. We can only hope that we will reach some Chinese city."

❖ ❖ ❖

In the summer of 1918, they reached the Inner Mongolian plateau. The landscape was now one of continuous grassland, in contrast to the alternating parched sand and grassland in the Gobi. Within two weeks they approached the first hamlet they had seen in months. By Chinese standards this was a small provincial settlement, but by Mongolian standards it was a major marketing town.

As they walked through the dirt streets of the city, the Ausübels were greeted with curious stares from shopkeepers. Most of the buildings had gently sloped roofs with the higher side facing the street. Puffs of smoke ascended from chimneys, positioned near the front of the houses. Children attired in baggy clothing would come close to the Caucasians, only to be pulled away by concerned adults.

At last, one smiling adult approached. "Are you Russian?" he asked in that language.

"No," replied Shulem.

"From what land?"

"Austria."

The man appeared not to recognize that name.

"We speak some Mongol," interjected Berish.

"Oh," smiled the man in the Mongol dialect. "Welcome to Tukomen. Do you need a place to stay?"

Berish looked to his father. Shulem nodded and Berish replied, "Yes." After a moment he added, "But we have no money."

"Come with me," urged the man.

They followed him down a side street, away from the shops that displayed blankets or saddles. They arrived at their destination. A wall of dull brick surrounded the property, save for a small entryway through which a short path led to the front of the house. As they passed the outer wall they saw mounds of hay, which were positioned near the side of the building and towered higher than the wall. A cow and several pigs were munching at the hay. As they entered the house, Shulem observed the decorative cutouts of birds and other animals positioned about the entryway.

"I have brought home guests from a foreign land," explained the man to his wife.

When the last of the Ausübels had entered the house, their host said, "I am Huhan and this is my wife, Wong Qing. I am a Mongol, although more than half of the inhabitants of this city are Han people. Few of them speak our language. My wife is Han. She speaks both Mongol and Chinese." (The ethnic Chinese, the Han people, make up the vast majority of the population of China. The Chinese government encouraged immigration into Inner Mongolia, and so the Han people became the predominant population group there.)

"I see," said Shulem in Yiddish with Berish translating into the Mongol language.

Huhan then directed his wife to prepare enough food for all of their guests.

"If I may make a request," said Berish. "We do not eat meat. If it is possible, we would appreciate that Qing prepare only grains or vegetables for us. Of course you and your wife will enjoy meat."

"Very well. I did not realize that Europeans do not eat meat."

"Not all Europeans," said Berish. "Like you Mongols here in China, we are but a minority people in our country."

"And what is the name of your minority people?"

"Jews," replied the elder son.

"Jews," mulled the host. "I have not heard of your people until now."

A raised platform towards the rear of the front room served as a table. The Ausübels took pains to eat slowly, so as not to exhibit the hunger they felt.

"Please," urged their host, "take more. My wife will think that you do not like her cooking."

Shulem smiled and Berish made an interpretive statement: "The food is excellent. We all thank your wife for preparing so much. I'm sure that we will slowly consume all of it."

When the food had all been consumed, Huhan offered his guests a drink. "There is no meat in it. It is fermented grain."

"Good," smiled Shulem.

The table was cleared and Wong Qing unrolled a mattress of felt pads on the raised platform.

"It is our bed as well as our table," commented Huhan. "My wife will prepare the back room for you."

The Jewish family remained as guests in the home of their Mongol host. Hunan was a trader who traveled to distant places, from Outer Mongolia in the north to as far as Yan'an in Shaanxi province, hundreds of miles to the south. From Huhan and Qing they acquired a rudimentary knowledge of the Chinese language. The Mongol and his wife, in turn, learned of the reason why the Ausübels were so far from their Galician home, and of the trials they had endured to reach this point. They also gained a basic understanding of the Jewish people.

"To get back to your native land without passing through Russia," ruminated Hunan, "is a trip beyond comprehension. There is much of China to cross. You cannot follow the Silk Road, for it passes through Russian-controlled Samarkand. I believe that Tibet lies to the south of Russian territory, but the mountains there tower to the sky. And to travel still farther to the south through Burma and India on foot would seem impossible. Traders only go so far and then swap their wares for gold or other goods with a second group of traders who will then travel several hundred miles to do the same with a third group of traders, and so forth. And they have horses and a large stock of provisions. So for you to go to India and beyond – I've never heard it done."

He paused and thought for a while. He went on, "But by ship from Shanghai – that's a possibility. I could take you as far as Yan'an on my next trip south. From there you could get to Xi'an; that was the first capital of ancient China. You would be in the heartland of China and might be able to travel to Shanghai, part by river and part by land. There are Europeans in Shanghai who send vessels to distant places. That is your best possibility."

Shulem's eyes lit up. "When might you be traveling to the city you mentioned?"

"In the spring. I do not take the trip alone. There are too many dangers out there. One can encounter bandits and the like. And so we do so as a group of traders – Mongols and Han people as well. With two dozen armed men, we have a better chance to discourage attacks on our caravan and to defend our goods if an attack takes place."

"Do the police or the army afford any protection?" questioned Berish.

"Sometimes it is the army that's the problem," replied Huhan with his face darkening.

"Is it because you are of the Mongol people?" wondered Berish aloud.

"No. You see, China is in a state of turmoil. For thousands of years an emperor ruled the nation. In the days of the Khans, the emperors were Mongols. The Qing dynasty – the last to rule China – was overthrown seven years ago. So China is now a republic. But the central government often has little control. Warlord generals control large regions of the country. And their troops are better armed than the bandits. So when the army intercepts a caravan and demands money, we have no alternative but to pay. Oh, they say that it is a toll or something, but we know better. It's organized banditry.

"But let me not dwell on the problems we face in China. I have seen the heavy sacks which you bore on your arrival. Might they contain the tools you used to build the monastery? If so, you could, if you agreed to it, expand my storage building. In turn, you could stay on in our home and have food abundant to your needs. I could even pay you in currency so that you will have funds to continue on to Xi'an after our caravan reaches its destination in Yan'an."

Shulem and his sons readily agreed to the proposal.

Three months later, the construction was completed. Huhan informed the Ausübels that the traders were going to commence their journey south in five days. "I will supply you and your family with horses, but I'll need the horses to carry back wares from Yan'an. I'll also take along sufficient provisions for you to continue on to Xi'an. That's in addition to the currency I promised you."

The trip was to be a long one. The traders kept close together and gave their pack animals frequent rests. They passed through small villages and larger towns, as well as cities with names like Wuhai and Shizuishan. The road was a dirt road and dust abounded in the air. The buildings were mostly of dried mud in the smaller hamlets and wood in the larger towns and cities. The inhabitants would study the faces and attire of the family of Europeans, and then go about their business. On one occasion, Joseph pointed at some curious items in front of a store as he said something to his older brother. "Don't point," reprimanded his father. "The people might take it as a hostile gesture."

At one juncture, the caravan had to be transported across a river in flat-bottomed boats, a few men and horses at a time. The banks along both sides of the river were elevated more than ten feet above the surrounding land.

"It's the Huang He," Huhan told the Ausübels. "It's the only river we will cross on this journey." The Yellow River, which derives its name from the color of all the silt carried downstream in it, is the muddiest river in the world and has flooded over 1,500 times in the past 4,000 years. Each time it has flooded, it has deposited millions of tons of silt on the riverbanks.

"Why the elevated riverbanks?" inquired Berish.

"Floods. Too many floods."

"Very few boats on the river," commented Berish.

"Very few," Huhan agreed. "The current is too swift after the rains, so the few boats here are kept behind the embankment until needed, such as to take passengers across the river."

On two occasions the traders encountered groups of armed men. The first – a group of seeming bandits on horseback – asked for some food. Huhan handed them several flat breads, but at the same time the traders brandished their weapons. The seeming bandits surveyed the weaponry they were facing and chose to move on.

The second encounter was with a contingent of perhaps a hundred men in army uniform. An officer approached and studied the caravan and its contents, poking at the wares and opening a few sacks. Then he pointed to the Caucasians. Huhan said something to the officer who continued to study the Ausübels curiously. After a long while he turned to Huhan and said something. Huhan signaled to his fellow traders. One by one, the traders handed the officer money and the army contingent withdrew.

"Too many of them," commented Huhan aside to Shulem. "Better to pay their demands than to be slaughtered."

After several weeks, they approached a most amazing structure. A vast wall of stone barred the way before them, as far as the eye could see. It rose and fell in concert with the hills and valleys. Shulem and his sons approached Huhan. "What in the world is it?" asked Berish.

"The Great Wall," replied the Mongol. "It has been there for thousands of years."

"To do what?" asked the elder son.

"To protect against the barbarians," smiled Huhan. "But it never worked."

"And why not?" interjected Joseph.

"Because men are weak. Guards accepted bribes. And so my Mongol ancestors conquered China in spite of the wall."

"How far does this wall stretch?" questioned Berish.

"For thousands of miles. Of course, I've only seen parts of it."

"What a project!" said Joseph.

"It is said that more than a million men toiled to build it. Many of them were prisoners. It is also said that hundreds of thousands of them died during the construction. Their bodies are buried beneath the wall."

"What a tragic loss of life," commented the bearded Jewish father in Yiddish. Berish immediately translated his words into the Mongol language.

"It's the way of the world," continued the bearded father. "Men are but inconsequential creatures in the eyes of the ones in power, to be used as mortar in the construction of a wall or a tomb or whatever."

"Yes," sighed Berish after his father had conveyed his thoughts. Then he added, "Our ancestors were held in bondage in ancient Egypt. They were used in a similar manner to build the cities of the pharaohs of Egypt. The pharaohs were the equivalent of your emperors."

"The world seems the same," said the Mongol. "Everywhere the powerful care little for the well-being of their subjects. Buddhism teaches us that we must endure until the day when we reach enlightenment. When that day comes we shall be released from the sufferings of the world."

Berish sighed, "Our prophets tell us that one day men shall beat their swords into plowshares and turn spears into pruning hooks. When that day comes, nation shall cease to make war against nation and we shall all live in peace. And so perhaps the messages of our faiths agree."

Joseph's mouth hung open as he gazed at the vast expanse of the wall. "All that stone," he commented in the end.

"Not all stone," said Huhan. "Parts are made of earth. There was also brick used in the construction."

"So how do we get through?" asked Berish.

"Oh," smiled Huhan. "There's an arch a few miles to the west. It was made more recently to allow for travel from north to south."

They reached their destination after three months of travel. The structure that aroused the interest of Berish was tall and slender.

"What's that building used for? Does it serve as a watchtower?" asked Berish.

"It's the Yan'an Pagoda. It has religious significance to the Han people."

The traders in the caravan were greeted by fellow traders from Yan'an. Leaving three armed members of the caravan to guard their belongings, the newly arrived traders and their counterparts entered a tavern. An hour later, they emerged with smiles on their faces. The goods from Inner Mongolia were unloaded, to be replaced by other goods, given in exchange.

"Just an exchange of goods?" Berish asked when they were alone.

"And money too. Otherwise we'd never have the funds to pay off the soldiers who may bar our way." He paused, and then went on, "I have spoken to a Han landowner here in Yan'an. He is my wife's uncle, the head of the Wang clan into which she was born. We will stay the night in his home. I have told him of the skills and the tools which you possess. Winter is approaching. Travel may be difficult at this time. He has agreed that you and your family can stay at the family home until spring, or until you decide to travel on to Xi'an. That – in exchange for your services in the construction of an addition to his residence."

He paused, and then added, "One thing more: Do not gamble with Old Wang. His name is Wang Kai Jugang, but everyone addresses him as Old Wang."

The following day the caravan from Tukomen began the return trip north. Shulem and his sons each hugged the Mongol good-bye. Huhan and the Ausübels exchanged blessings. Then the Mongol joined his fellow traders.

Old Wang was a wizened old man with snow-white hair and hunched shoulders. He was dressed in traditional Chinese garb: a brocaded gray satin tunic and trousers above his maroon satin slipper-shoes and white stockings. A maroon-colored squared satin cap with a matching ball of satin atop its center covered the merchant's bald head. He had a sparse snow-white mustache and a thin snow-colored beard.

He ushered them through a high wooden gate into an impressive central courtyard. It was modest in size, but every twist and turn of the stone-covered walk offered a different view. There was a pond covered in part by water lilies and flowers of many varieties. Stelae of white stone, seemingly weathered by age, projected up from the bottom of the pond. Carp of gold and red and black made their way from one end of the pool to another, gliding around the stony obstacles. They darted to the spot where Old Wang tossed a few pieces of grain. The path took Old Wang and the Ausübels over a small bridge that spanned the pond and reached the tile-roofed section of the building directly opposite the gate.

This section of the horseshoe-shaped structure was taller than the rest of the building. As they walked from an entry foyer into a larger room, Shulem looked around. This section alone was considerably larger than Huhan's entire dwelling place. The floors were of polished wood, and they were covered with silk carpets of an intricate design consisting of birds and flowers. Rosewood chairs covered with red satin brocade had been situated on either side of an end table of the same wood in the foyer. A display case of rosewood was positioned against the far wall in the main room. Its shelves, being of different heights and widths, were lined with miniature objects of cloisonné and china.

A long mahogany table stretched the length of the room. Eight straight-backed mahogany chairs with Chinese carvings in their backs were arrayed around the table, and eight more of the same designs were situated at the sidewalls, four against either wall. Fifteen of the chairs were alike, but one, positioned at the head of the table, was taller than the rest and had armrests.

"This is the meeting room of our clan," said Old Wang in Chinese. "I am the head of the clan."

The old man clapped his hands. A servant entered and bowed to Old Wang. After receiving instructions, the servant bowed and backed out of sight. A few minutes later, a tea service was brought into the room. Old Wang assumed his great chair. "You may be seated. Even the women."

"You are Europeans, but you don't resemble the barbarians I have met."

"Barbarians?" repeated the puzzled Shulem.

"We refer to Europeans as barbarians. They are upstarts who have little respect for tradition."

"Oh," nodded Shulem, knowingly. He continued in the imperfect Chinese he had learned in Huhan's household. "But we are not like most Europeans. We are Jews. Unlike Europeans you speak about, we have traditions going back thousands of years."

"Jews," mused the head of the clan. "I have heard of your people before. A missionary once showed me his bible. He told me about your kings, David and Solomon."

He studied his guests, the women as well as the men.

"Are you the head of your clan?" inquired Old Wang of the bearded Jew.

"Clan?"

"Clan. Family. I am the oldest of the sons of my father, who was the head of the House of Wang before me. I became the head of the House when he died. Are you the head of your House?"

"No. Older brother, Judah. I, second son."

"Where is Judah, the head of the House?"

An embarrassed Shulem declared. "Pardon. I not speak Chinese well. Oldest son learned your language. I tell him my language. He speak for me."

Old Wang nodded somewhat unhappily.

Berish then gave a slow translation into Chinese of his father's statements in Yiddish. As names were mentioned, he pointed to the individuals to whom he was referring. He translated Old Wang's words to his father.

"Judah and his wife and children fled our town when the Russians seized it. So did my father's younger brothers and sisters. They said that they were going to Vienna. That is the capital of our country. We have had no communication with them since we were taken to Siberia."

Berish gave Old Wang a brief account of the four years of wandering, up to their arrival in Yan'an.

"These Europeans are truly barbarians," concluded Old Wang. "We do not treat our Mongols and other minorities in such a manner."

"Not all Europeans are the same. Some treat us better than do others."

"Well, let me get back to the present." He turned to Shulem and said, "I was told that the two young men are your sons and that they, like yourself, are skilled in construction."

"Carpenters."

"And the women? Your wives?"

"This is my stepmother, Sheva, and this is my sister, Zivia," said Berish. "With our people, there is only one wife. I mean, my mother was my father's first wife. She was mother to Zivia and me. She died many years ago. My father remarried after her death. Sheva is Joseph's mother."

"You say with your people there is only one wife. But how can that be so? Or are you referring just to common people? Your kings had many wives."

"That was a long time ago. Now, all Jews have one wife at a time," replied Berish.

"As you wish. Our scholars teach us that a man should have many wives. Confucius said so."

"Confucius," interjected Joseph. "Your niece told us he was a great scholar. Did he really say that?"

"I see that among your people, the young ones speak before they are given permission to do so by their elders."

"I beg your pardon," replied the embarrassed younger son.

"But I shall answer you," continued Old Wang. "Look at the tea service. Look at the teapot and its stem. What does it look like? It looks like what a man has as proof of his manhood. Now look at the teacups. They are round like what a woman has so that she can receive her master. Now one teapot can fill many teacups. So it is with a man and his women. One man can fill many women."

Zivia turned away in embarrassment.

"Is polygamy the law in China?" questioned Berish, without having been prompted by his father.

"The law? No, not the law. But practiced, nevertheless. One wife is the law. She is the matriarch of the household. The rest are classified as concubines, but I prefer to call them my wives. A man should have many sons. They are his wealth. My first wife is too old to bear any more children. Why should I stop having sons? I am the head of the House. My seed should continue to multiply. Besides, a young girl is more pleasing to my eye and warmer in my bed."

His eye moved to Zivia. "Do you like to play cards?" he asked the Jewish father without diverting his eyes from Shulem's daughter.

Shulem's face turned red as he remembered Huhan's advice. Berish immediately translated his response. "My father does not play cards and he never gambles."

"We all gamble. You took a gamble in coming to Yan'an. Brigands along the way might have killed you. Perhaps there is something you desire so badly that you will gamble in the hope of getting it."

Berish translated his father's shaking of the head. "No!"

Old Wang's eyes now turned to the Jewish father. "Very well. Let me get back to the task I have for you and your sons. I want an extension built on to my house at the far end, near the gate. My new wife will live there. Wife number five.

"It should follow the shape of the rest of the house and reach the outer wall of the garden. One large room and two smaller rooms – for the children she will bear me. You will make a list of the materials. I will have them sent for. Can you complete the construction in three months? I am growing old and am impatient for her to warm me. If you are finished within three months, you can stay in my servants' quarters for as long as you choose."

Shulem nodded and Berish declared: "We can do it."

There was a knock at the door. A servant entered. He seemed flustered as he bowed and expressed a thousand apologies. A conversation between master and servant ensued, but the words were not audible to the Jewish family. In the end, Old Wang dismissed his servant with a wave of his right hand.

"It was better in the days of the emperor," the head of the clan sighed aloud. "Peasants had respect in those days. Children had respect for their fathers; fathers had respect for the head of their clan, for their masters and for the emperor. If anyone complained, it was off with his head. Confucius taught us that everyone and everything has its place. The loyalty owed to one's master and to the emperor was an extension of the respect due to one's father. Now these republicans seek to destroy the order that has defined the Chinese way of life."

Shulem and sons listened but did not say a word.

"Imagine: peasants breaking the windows of the landlord's house...just because their rents have been raised. The land is all mine; they have no right to plant here unless I grant them that right. And they must pay for that right. Don't they realize that I have expenses! Expanding my house costs money, so it has become necessary for me to raise the rents."

Old Wang walked to the window and peered out through the curtain.

"Well, it is not your problem." he said. He paused for a minute and then added, "I have things to attend to and so we'd best say good night."

Two months later – one month ahead of schedule – the extension to the Wang house was completed. The patriarch of the Wang clan was greatly pleased. A few days later, Old Wang's newest "bride" was moved into the quarters.

The Ausübels remained at the residence in the servants' quarters. Shulem and his sons, when asked to, would do whatever carpentry work was needed. Sheva and Zivia were not required to perform any services. Sheva preferred to keep apart from the members of the household, but Zivia spent some time in the company of Old Wang's wives. She had learned some Chinese, which allowed for conversation. The wives were curious as to the status of women in the West. Zivia told them that she could not speak with knowledge about the status of most women, as she came from a minority, the Jews. Yes, marriages were arranged for Jewish girls, but not always. In recent times, many girls had married the man of their choice. And she had never seen a man living with more than one wife. The wives seemed to approve of those Western customs. In turn, Zivia learned much about life for women in the Wang household. The first wife was the matriarch of the clan. Her eldest son would be the next head of the clan. Although Old Wang no longer slept with her at night, her position was secure. She was the only one of the wives to whom Wang turned for counsel, and the other wives deferred to her in all matters. The patriarch slept most nights with his newest young woman, but at times he spent the night in the bedrooms of three other wives. (They preferred to be called wives, although according to Chinese law they were not.)

From time to time, the Ausübels were invited to join the patriarch for dinner. Old Wang would question them with regard to European customs and tell them a little of life in China. He would sigh, remembering how good it was under the emperor, and he would denounce the upstarts who had brought about a revolution in the recent past.

One evening, Zivia returned to the quarters of the Ausübels after having spent a few hours with Woo Xiuyi, Old Wang's newest bride. "What a terrible thing was done to her," she announced.

"What thing?" inquired Sheva.

"She was gambled away."

Shulem's face turned dark. "I was warned not to gamble with Old Wang. Tell us, how was she gambled away?"

"Her father, Woo Peng, was a small merchant. Sadly, he loved to gamble. One night he was playing cards with Old Wang. That night he lost, hand after hand. The stakes went higher and higher as he tried to recoup his losses. In the end, he had lost not only all his money, but his house and his business as well. He was ruined. Then Old Wang made him an offer: 'If you win the next game I will return your house, your business establishment and all your money. If you lose, I get your daughter.'

"Now Xiuyi was in love with a young man in the city. The young man had spoken to her father of marriage. It was agreed that as soon as the young man had succeeded in his business venture and could pay Woo Peng a given sum, he could marry Xiuyi."

"And the father did not abide by the pledge?" questioned Shulem.

"He did not."

"And he lost," said Berish.

"Yes, he lost. So instead of his daughter being married off to the young man with whom she was in love, she became a concubine of the head of the house of Wang."

"And she had to go through with it?" questioned Joseph.

"She had to and still has to. Old Wang told her that as long as she is good to him, the Woos could stay in their home and run their business. However, the profits, after a small sum to pay for their necessities, would go to the House of Wang. Of course, the house will not belong to the Woos. It will belong to the Wang clan. Now, when Old Wang is gone, his eldest son will head the clan. Perhaps he will let them stay there, perhaps not. Such is life: a gamble."

"Old Wang does not always play cards well," continued Berish. "Huhan once played him a game of cards. At first, Huhan did not want to play, but Old Wang spotted something for which Huhan would be willing to gamble his two finest horses."

"And what was that?" asked Sheva.

"Wang's niece. Huhan won and married her."

"And if Huhan had not agreed to gamble, what would have happened?"

"Old Wang's niece was young and beautiful, a valuable asset. Old Wang could get much for her. But he wanted those two stallions. And so he was willing to gamble his niece for them. Without the possibility of winning two magnificent horses, he would never have given her to a Mongol."

"Would you gamble a son for horses?" asked Sheva.

"A son?" said Zivia. "Of course not. But we were speaking of a woman. Women in this society are possessions. They belong to the clan and Old Wang is its head."

"In all fairness," interjected Berish, "that is not quite so. Old Wang would not gamble his eldest son. The firstborn is destined to be head of the clan. But he did, in a way, gamble his second son of his wife and two sons of his concubines."

"Gamble? How so?" asked Zivia, doubtfully.

"A younger brother of Old Wang had moved to a distant part of the country where he was involved in a new venture. The venture required capital to pay off a general and to acquire items that had been seized by the general's soldiers. It entailed risk, both for the money and for the lives of the individuals involved."

Shulem looked puzzled. "I could understand the risk with regard to the money, but why the risk to life?"

"The younger brother was entering into a financial arrangement with one warlord. But a second warlord had disputed the first general's right to sanction the transport of Ming vases and other goods seized from temples located at the junction of their respective jurisdictions. If the first general won, then there would be great profit for that warlord and Old Wang's younger brother, and a part of it would go to Old Wang and his sons. If the second warlord won, Old Wang's brother and his followers might lose their lives."

"A dangerous business," concluded the Jewish father. "So Old Wang was willing to risk his money in the hopes of making a profit. But why his sons? Couldn't his brother find others to do his bidding?"

"The brother felt that anyone other than a blood relation was not trustworthy. Someone from another clan might betray him to an enemy if offered a large enough sum. And so Old Wang sent three sons, as well as money to fund the enterprise."

"Did the sons go willingly?" asked Shulem.

"They had no choice. The head of the clan is the supreme master of all in the Wang family."

"And what happened to the sons?" inquired Sheva.

"They and Old Wang came out of it with fortunes."

"But Old Wang's sons were not in danger of becoming concubines," insisted Zivia.

Shulem shook his head sadly. "It's true. There's a difference between what Old Wang did with regard to his sons and what was done with regard to Xiuyi.

"Marriages among our people were arranged. But always with the hope of making life better for our children, not as a means of profit for the parents. In any case – to gamble away a child – how terrible!"

"Did we not gamble to get away from the Russians? Did we not lose seven children?" cried Sheva in pain.

"We took risks in the hope of all, or at least, some of us surviving," reminded her husband. "If we had stayed in Tartarsk, none of us would be alive today."

"There should be more to life than simply survival," declared Zivia, her face very sad.

"Of course," said Shulem. "We're trying to get around Russia, back to our home."

"And how long will it take?" pursued Zivia.

"As long as it takes."

"Look, here I have been bemoaning the fate of Xiuyi. But at least she knew love once. And she's three years younger than I am. What chance will I have here? Even if I survive, what will life be for me? An old maid who has never known love? I know that you do not like to talk of such things, but it is the truth!" Zivia hid her head in her hands as she burst into tears.

Sheva drew Zivia to her bosom and held her tight. "Your father is trying to keep us alive. Without life, there is no hope for a future."

"Zivia, I'm the eldest," said Berish. "But I'm willing to wait, like Papa says, for as long as it takes to reach safety in a place where we can go on with our lives."

"You're a man," replied Zivia, half freeing herself from Sheva's grasp. "Look at Old Wang; he must be seventy and he's still speaking about having children. And whom does he choose as the prospective mother? A girl of eighteen! So you've got time."

Shulem studied his daughter. He had not thought about it in the four years since they had fled Tartarsk, but Zivia was indeed a full-grown woman of twenty-two. And she felt as if life were passing her by. The family would have to start moving again, if for no other reason than that Zivia would not give up hope. The World War was over, but Russia, which stood between them and their home in Galicia, was still in the midst of a revolution. They had seen how the White Army behaved towards Jews from their brief stay in Urga. "You're right. We should get started. We must go to Shanghai. From there we can board a ship to some place where we will be with our own people."

One evening, the Ausübels were having dinner with Old Wang. The patriarch was helping himself from a large array of serving dishes in the center of the table. The Jews limited their consumption to noodles and vegetables. Berish inquired of the patriarch as he translated his father's words: "There were many caves in the cliffs outside the city as we approached. Are they used for anything?"

"Shelter from the cold, storage, and I'm told some are even buried there."

Suddenly Zivia began to cough. Sheva felt her head. "She's very hot," trembled her stepmother in Yiddish.

"Please excuse us," said Shulem's elder son in Chinese. "My sister has taken ill."

"Yes," replied Old Wang gravely. "It seems to be going around. Two of my wives are ill, as are many in Hunan. The doctors tell us to keep them cool and urge lots of soup. None of their potions seem to help. You had better attend to her."

Within a week, Zivia was dead. Sheva had taken care of her and now she was ill. Zivia was buried on a patch of ground on the family property given them by Old Wang. A few days later, Sheva died and was buried next to her.

Two of Old Wang's wives – the matriarch of the clan and Xiuyi – and one of Old Wang's sons, as well as scores of others in Hunan, died of the mysterious illness (the Flu Epidemic of 1918-1919) for which none had a remedy. Hundreds more were sickened, but survived.

Weeks went by. Shulem found it difficult to go about the activities of the day. His face was blank much of the time and he stared into the emptiness. It was Berish who now assumed the mantle of responsibility for the future of the family. He spoke of the need to resume their journey to Shanghai and other problems. His father would listen, blankly.

One evening, Old Wang invited the three Ausübel men to dinner.

"It is not good to mourn so long," he said to Shulem. "You have your sons. Besides, you can now take a new wife and have more children. I know of no other barbarians in Yan'an, but you can take some young Han girl. I'm doing so myself. And I'll buy one for you as well."

Shulem spoke for himself in Chinese. "Thank you for kind thoughts. You're right. Must do something. But not marry. My son right. Must travel. Must return to our people."

"Very well," nodded the patriarch of the House of Wang. "A group of traders are starting out for Xi'an. It is a great city, the ancient seat of the

Western Zhou Dynasty that unified China. And from Xi'an you can go anywhere. I will arrange for you to join their party."

❖ ❖ ❖

Xi'an was, indeed, a great city that had expanded beyond a moat, which surrounded its great outer stonewall that towered castle-like above the horizon.

The trip to the city had proved to be therapeutic for Shulem. Unlike their last weeks in Yan'an, he appeared alive to the world around him. He had turned directing the journey over to his elder son.

"Look at that tall building," commented Shulem to his sons as they all looked up from the wagon on which they were seated.

Berish added, "It is a pagoda. One of the traders told me it is called the Big Wild Goose Pagoda, named after a Buddhist shrine in India. The Big Wild Goose Pagoda is seven stories high, in contrast to the Little Wild Goose Pagoda that is also in this city. That building is five stories high."

"The capital of ancient China," commented Joseph.

"Sort of," replied his older brother.

"What do you mean 'sort of?'" inquired his father.

"They say that the capital was Xiangyang, somewhere to the east of present-day Xi'an. Where Xi'an stands was once Chang'an, the sight of the first emperor's palace.

"The Western Zhou Dynasty ruled one of the seven kingdoms of the Han people. I was told that over 2,000 years ago, the ruler of this kingdom defeated the other six kings and unified China under his rule. Qin Shi Huangdi was his name and he was the first emperor of a unified China. His tomb is somewhere to the east of the city – a huge mound that has yet to be excavated. They say that great treasures were buried with the emperor, along with many of his subordinates who were buried alive to serve their emperor in the land of the dead."

"Buried alive," repeated Joseph, shaking his head sadly.

"And where did you learn all this?" questioned his father. "Have you taken to reading as well as speaking Chinese?"

"I'm not good at reading Chinese, although I have been studying their character writing. But one of the traders with whom we are traveling is quite knowledgeable in Chinese history. I've learned much from him. I've been telling him about the barbarians and he's been telling me about his people."

"If you're referring to the Russians, they have, indeed, behaved like barbarians towards our people. But if you're speaking about all Europeans, you shouldn't speak of them all as being barbarians," insisted Shulem.

"I agree. It's just that the Chinese are accustomed to referring to the Europeans as barbarians. They came to exploit China. When the Chinese took up arms against them to end the exploitation, the armies of several European nations plus contingents from Japan and America united to defeat them."

"When did all this take place?" queried Joseph.

"Nearly twenty years ago. It was called the Boxer Rebellion because the revolt was begun by the society of Boxers. Interestingly, the organization had, as its original aim, the overthrow of the Manchu dynasty that had ruled China for centuries, and the establishment of a republic. But the Empress Dowager attempted to use them as a vehicle for driving out the barbarians."

"But China is a republic," reminded Joseph.

"That was the result of a revolt in 1911 to 1912. I am told that it began sort of as a surprise."

"A surprise?" inquired his younger brother.

"Well, there had been many rebellions in the decade preceding 1911. Each was crushed and their leaders, beheaded. Then one day there was an explosion in a city in the south of China – Wuchang, I believe it is called. Some rebels entered the city and the commander of the Imperial troops panicked and fled. Within weeks, most of the garrisons of China defected to the rebels."

"Just an isolated rebellion?" said a surprised Joseph. "No major leader?"

"Sun Yat-sen was the spiritual leader of the revolt that began in the south. His party was the Kuomintang or Nationalist party. When the Emperor Pu Yi – at that time a mere child – abdicated, a General Yuan Shikai took charge in Peking. The general had been a leading advisor to the Dowager Empress who had ruled in the name of her infant grandson, Pu Yi, until her death. When the army in the south went over to Sun Yat-sen, Yuan Shikai declared himself in favor of a republic. Sun Yat-sen resigned his office in favor of Yuan, so as to reunite China. Yuan was a man with imperial desires. He was contemptuous of the newly established parliament. He would have declared himself emperor, had he not died four years ago. Now Sun Yat-sen is president of all of China."

"So what about all the brigands in army uniforms that we encountered on our way to Hunan?" posed Shulem. "Is that what this Sun Yat-sen and his parliament have accomplished?"

"Unfortunately, Sun Yat-sen does not control many of his generals. Some of the military leaders have become local tyrants, ruling areas as large as or larger than Galicia. They are known as warlords and they tax their people mercilessly. They have even taken to growing the opium poppy to line their pockets. In such a state, there is no true justice."

"So much for Chinese history and China present," concluded Shulem. "Now we've got to find a place to stay while we make plans to move on to Shanghai."

"I've spoken to the leader of the caravan," said Berish. "He knows a number of merchants in this city, and even a missionary. He will speak to some of them. Perhaps one of them will be willing to exchange food and lodging for carpentry work. Thank God we brought our tools with us when we left home. They have been the means for our survival until now."

"Why do we need a Christian missionary?" asked Joseph. "We're Jews."

"Of course. But in case none of the merchants will take us in, perhaps the missionary would put us up for a while."

The home of the Lutheran missionary from Germany was Chinese, rather than European in design. The Ausübels were given one bedroom and they were assigned to repairing a part of the mission. Communication between the minister and the Jews was quite easy, since all spoke fluent German.

From time to time, the German minister took the three Jews to see parts of the city and its surroundings. One day they visited a large castle-like, two-story structure that stood more than a hundred feet in height. "This is their city's Bell Tower," announced the minister. "It was built in Tang times. The city was known as Changam in those days and it was a center for trade." They viewed the city with its teeming populace from the upper floor.

On another occasion they toured the countryside on the other side of the Wei River. "Do you see those mounds that rise above the level fields?" began the minister. "It is believed that most of them are tombs of emperors who once ruled China. It is said that one of them holds the tomb of the only woman ever to rule China in her own right."

"Wasn't there a Dowager Empress who ruled China fairly recently?" questioned Berish.

"Yes. But she ruled in the name of her grandson, Pu Yi. The Empress Wu ruled on her own – and for 45 years, it is said."

"Did she inherit the throne?" pursued Berish.

"I don't know that I'd call it 'inherited.' Disposing of every other claimant to the throne is more like it."

"I've heard of her," reflected Berish. "But tell me, was she the daughter of an emperor and did she eliminate all her brothers?"

"No. She was not the descendant of any emperor. She was concubine to Emperor Gao Zong who ruled more than a thousand years ago. First she disposed of the emperor's legitimate wife and assumed that role for herself. Then she murdered or forced into exile all the potential heirs to the throne, as well as any court officials who stood in her way. With the death of the emperor, she seized the throne and ruled for some 45 years. If the Chinese had accepted Christ, such things would never have happened."

Berish turned aside for a moment as he reflected on many similar occurrences in European history, but said nothing.

❖ ❖ ❖

Most evenings, Shulem and his sons joined the minister for dinner. The Chinese cook would serve the Jews vegetables, rice and fish. Their host ate all varieties of meats and pig products, in addition to fish and the vegetarian dishes.

"You told me some time ago that part of your family had fled to Vienna," said the Rev. Dr. Schmidt with a smile. The minister was a tall man with steel blue eyes and thinning blond hair. He reached into his pocket and came up with a sheet of paper, which he pushed forward towards Shulem with a long delicate hand. "I wrote to a colleague in that city and yesterday I received a reply. I have the address of your brother Judah and his family. If you'd like to write to them, I can arrange for it to go via the post. Through my sources, I've also learned that your brother Joseph and his family and those of your other siblings have returned to Rozwadow. Your home town is now under Polish rule."

An excited Shulem expressed his joy and appreciation for the minister's efforts. The German then handed them the paper with the address of Judah Ausübel. Shulem and his sons studied the writing.

"You're Jews. At least, you believe in God...although you have not yet recognized your Savior," commented the minister one evening. "These Chinese are in need of God. I have tried to explain to them that ancestral worship and the like must be abandoned. Some have accepted Christ, but all too many have not yet joined the true church."

Joseph opened his mouth as if prepared to say something. Berish pressed a silencing hand on Joseph's thigh.

After dinner, the Ausübels returned to their room.

"Why did you stop me?" asked Joseph of his older brother.

"Because I thought you were about to say something with regard to the minister's remark about us Jews not accepting his savior."

"So what's wrong with my disagreeing with him?"

"We're here as his guests," replied Berish.

"Guests? We're fixing up his mission."

"But there's no need to antagonize him. He believes that God has given him a mission – to convert the world to his religious faith. Why else would he have chosen to leave his country and live alone in a foreign land? True, we're performing a service for him. But if he senses hostility, we may be forced to leave this place."

"Berish, what I wanted to say is that we Jews are still waiting for the Messiah. When the Messiah comes, the world will be at peace, and brotherhood will be the rule. I don't see any true peace and brotherhood as yet.

"As for the Chinese, I do not agree with everything they do. But I don't know that the seizure of parts of their country by European nations will improve things here. And as for their beliefs, that's up to them, so long as they don't attempt to impose their beliefs on everyone else."

"You say that and he'll feel threatened," replied his brother.

"Do you think he's so blind? What's wrong with people seeking God in their own way as long as they behave well toward others? Dr. Schmidt is a good man. He helps the sick. He feeds the poor here in the city. He even provided us with food and shelter.

"We are taught that the coming of the Messiah rests on three pillars: Torah, Mitzvoth and simple acts of loving kindness. Dr. Schmidt recognizes the Torah: It is part of what he calls the Old Testament. He does not follow all of our 613 Commandments, but in his own way he follows many of them. And he is certainly capable of simple acts of loving-kindness. So he does, in a way, contribute to the coming of the Messiah. And, as a good man, he should accept our right to worship the Almighty in our own way."

"But in his mind, all that Christian charity was not intended simply for the purpose of doing good. It was done to convert others to his religion. If you challenge that, he'll feel that the whole meaning of his life will have vanished. I can picture how he'd respond: 'I had hoped that your stay in the mission and my Christian charity would have convinced you of the need to recognize Christ. It is that Christian charity that compelled me to search for the rest of your family.'

"And this is how I would respond to that: 'My father, my brother and I appreciate your hospitality and the inquiry you made with regard to our uncle and his family. We have tried to reciprocate with our work.'

"And he'd say: 'I know you have suffered at the hands of the Russians and at the hands of the Catholic Church with its Inquisition. But you should not view their actions as an indication of Christian belief. Have you read the writings of Martin Luther? You know he denounced the Catholic Church for its anti-Semitism.'

"'Yes,' I would then feel obliged to reply, 'I studied some of that in the gymnasium. But Martin Luther mistakenly expected the Jews to join his church simply because he had denounced the Catholic Church for its anti-Semitic teachings. And when the German Jews failed to join his church, he denounced our people with as much vehemence as had the Catholic Church.

What he failed to recognize is that we are Jews because this is our faith. We are not against one church or another. We simply wish to remain Jews."

"You say that to him," interrupted Shulem, "and we'd be out in the street. So let's call a halt to this conversation and go to bed."

The Jews sojourned in Xi'an the winter of 1920-21. With the first warmth of spring, the Ausübels boarded a riverboat headed for Kaifeng. They heard that the city had been home to a sizable Jewish population dating back hundreds of years. Shulem and his sons were eager to make contact with co-religionists.

The minister bade them farewell at the riverside. "My colleague in Vienna has informed your brother and his family of your present location and the fact that you hope to make your way to Shanghai. God be with you."

From the boat, the Jews studied the countryside along the Huang River bank. Wheat was the staple in this region of China, and the stalks grew high in the open areas. Towns and cities were interspersed along the river. The buildings along the riverbanks were chiefly business establishments, made of wood with sloped roofs, their wares plainly exhibited. The boat made frequent stops at the larger towns and cities. It took on passengers and freight and let others off with their belongings.

They passed hundreds of junks with their colorful sails, as well as flat-bottomed wooden boats carrying cargo. Each junk had a single rectangular-shaped sail, supported by a vertical wooden pole. A series of narrow horizontal wooden planks held the sail in place. Some had their cargo open to the elements, while others were covered with flat or arched wooden roofs. Small engines powered all the flat boats. Seamen, even small children, would wave to the passengers on the large riverboat. Berish and Joseph would wave back while Shulem stood at the rail, observing the scene in silence.

At night, the Ausübels slept on the boat's benches or against the rail of the vessel, then awoke at dawn. They ate food packed away in their baggage, chiefly noodles and vegetables.

At last they reached their destination. They carried their sacks of carpentry tools and the remaining food off the vessel. The city of Kaifeng was a few miles away. Berish asked instructions and then they headed, on foot, to the city. They reached a large pavilion. Berish stopped to make inquiry. The Chinese man seemed greatly surprised by the Occidental's command of the Chinese language.

"This is called the Dragon Pavilion. It is named for a huge stone at its center that is carved with dragons," said Joseph, his chest puffed out to reflect his command of a fact of Chinese history. "It was used in times past as the place where candidates for the imperial service came to take their examinations. Confucius stressed that those who had proven themselves wisest should conduct the business of the empire. The examinations must have been designed to achieve that goal."

"Correct," added Berish.

"Well, we have no time just now to study the sights. We're loaded with heavy baggage. We had better find a place to stay. There are supposed to be Jews in this city. If there are Jews, there should be a synagogue. That's the place where we can talk to people and find a place to stay."

Berish approached one Chinese man, then another and another. He then returned to his father and brother.

"The third man has heard of the term 'Jew,' but he insists that there is no longer a synagogue in the city. There had been one in the city a long time ago, but it was washed away in the floods years ago and has not been rebuilt. As to the Jews, there are some in the city who claim some Jewish ancestry, but they do not practice the faith. But he did tell me where one man lives. It is not far from here."

They walked down streets lined with homes that were covered with sharply sloping tile roofs. The houses were very close to one another. There were no piles of hay or farm animals here.

Ai Pai Samuel was a robust, middle-aged man with Chinese features and traditional Chinese garb. Yet, he knew a fair number of Hebrew words. He could detail the history of the city and of its Jews. He considered himself to be of Jewish descent; his Jewish ancestors having come to the city more than a thousand years ago.

"My ancestor, a merchant, came here from Hangzhou. Other Jews here at the time were bankers as well as merchants. There are three stelae in the city that commemorate the presence of Jews in Kaifeng. They date back hundreds of years. I will be happy to take you to see them.

"It is said that in times past there were over 1,000 Jews in the city and that they worshipped in a great synagogue. The building was destroyed in one of the floods in the past century. As the Jewish population had fallen off, it was never rebuilt. But there are stones from the building lying here and there.

"There are others, many others besides me who are, in part, of Jewish descent. You know, unlike most cities in China, little pork or shellfish is consumed in Kaifeng. And unlike most of the cities of China, Saturday is our day of rest, not the Christian Sunday. I have two prayer books. They were given to my father, Ai Kai David, years ago. That is much of what remains of our Jewish heritage."

"Prayer books? May my father and I see them?" asked Berish.

"Certainly. When you are in my home."

"And where did your father get them?" pursued Berish. "You said that there has not been a synagogue here for many years."

"They were given to him by a rabbi who stayed in Kaifeng for some time. The rabbi had traveled through much of Africa and Asia before coming to our city. He was searching for the lost tribes of Israel."

"What was his name?" inquired Berish.

"Rabbi Hillel Heilprin."

"Very interesting. I can't say that I ever heard of him," replied Berish.

"Now you say that you are of Jewish descent. But you look Chinese," commented Joseph.

"But I am Chinese. Those Jewish merchants and bankers came to China without wives. There never would have been another generation if they had not taken Chinese wives. I assume the women converted to Judaism before the marriages. And their descendants often married Chinese women. In time, the Jews of the city could not be distinguished from others of the city, except that I have brown hair and my nose is not flattened, whereas pure Han people always have black hair and the bridge of their nose is flattened. You'll find a number of people in the city with brown hair, and others with large noses. And that is not because of some recent Occidental ancestry.

"Now, welcome to my household. You are my guests. Stay as long as you choose. I will show you the city and the site where the synagogue once stood. And if you will teach me some Hebrew and tell me of the Jews elsewhere, I will be ever so grateful."

"Ai Pai Samuel is a most unusual name. Since Ai comes first, I take it to be your family name," observed Berish.

"Correct. I believe it was once Ben Samuel – my Jewish ancestor who came to this city. But in China we use but one family name, so Ai it is. You see, there are but a few surnames among the Jews of Kaifeng. Ai is one of them. There are also Jews with the surnames Chang, Chin, Chou, Huang, Li, Mu, Nieh, Pai, Tso and Yen."

Ai Pai Samuel was a widower who had not remarried. Two of his sons and their wives often came to his house at dinnertime. The Ausübels had little problem with food. At the instructions of the head of the household, the cook prepared dishes of grains and vegetables for every meal. Fish was added at lunch and dinner.

They were taken to see the Iron Pagoda, a thirteen-story building that stood more than 170 feet in height. It was covered entirely in brown glazed tiles and decorated with mythical animals.

"The building is close to 1,000 years old," said Ai.

"Beautiful," added Joseph.

The Dragon Pavilion, which the Ausübels had passed on their way into the city, was a pyramid-shaped building compound containing several massive terraces. As Berish had been told, there was a huge stone in its center on which dragons were carved.

"King Yu's Terrace is a peaceful escape from the cares of the day," said Ai, as they seated themselves in a cafe nestled in a park. "The Old Music Terrace is located in a park in the southeastern section of Kaifeng. It is a place where you can enjoy a glass of wine and listen to the recitation of poetry. Some of the great Tang poets, such as Du Fu and Li Bai, came here. Perhaps you will join me in a glass of wine."

"Prepared from grapes?" asked Berish.

"A rice wine. There is no meat or shellfish or anything unclean used in its preparation. Trust me."

Another time, they traveled to what was one of China's foremost Buddhist monasteries. "The Xianggou Si Monastery was originally founded more than 1,300 years ago. It was repeatedly destroyed by floods and then rebuilt. Floods have been a major problem in our city. Most major structures have had to be rebuilt time and time again over the centuries. As for the synagogue – as I said before, there were too few Jews to rebuild it after it had been washed away."

"I am puzzled," commented Berish to the Chinese host one day. "I know that Kaifeng is a large city, but there are many large cities here in China, many much larger than Kaifeng. Yet, we have not encountered any vestige of Jewish settlement anywhere else in the country, certainly none dating back for centuries. What prompted Jews to settle in this city of all places?"

"But that is quite simple. Yes, it is true that they were the first Occidentals to settle in China. You ask why they chose Kaifeng in which to settle? It was because it was the largest and most important city in China of 1,000 years ago. It was the capital of the Song Empire, situated near the Yellow River for east-west commerce and near the Grand Canal for north-south commerce. It was a center for silks, porcelain, jade and tea. So what better place could Jewish merchants have chosen to settle in?"

The Ausübels stayed in Kaifeng through the winter of 1921-22. They took in most of what there was to see in the city. They helped expand the building in which Ai's business was located, and their host expressed his appreciation for their efforts on his behalf. On Friday nights and Saturday mornings, Shulem and his sons, along with Ai and his sons and several other Chinese men of Jewish ancestry, gathered in the home of Ai Pai Samuel. They had no copy of the Torah from which to read, but Shulem led the service, reciting the prayers from a *siddur* he had brought with him into exile.

Shulem and his sons recited the prayers as if from memory; the other men listened for the most part, joining in when they recognized a word or phrase from the prior weeks' services.

❖ ❖ ❖

When spring came, Berish said they wanted to continue on to Shanghai. It had been more than seven years since they were taken from their home in Galicia.

Ai Pai Samuel arranged for them to go by wagon to Nanjing, and then by riverboat down the Yangtze River to Shanghai.

It was a tearful farewell.

All four men – the driver, Shulem and his sons – sat on the front bench of the wagon. Behind them was a load of hay. The Ausübel luggage brought up the rear.

"It's a long way to Nanjing," commented Berish. "Strange that a wagon would travel several days just to deliver such a load."

"It's taking us to the ferry. I don't want to know about anything else," commented his father.

The following day, two dozen armed men, in the service of the warlord who controlled this area, intercepted the wagon. They eyed the Ausübels curiously and demanded to see their baggage. An officer poked at the load of hay with a stick and then unwrapped the food packages positioned to one side. "They smell," he said, and tossed them back into the wagon. "What are you carrying?"

"Hay," replied the wagon driver.

"And the baggage in the rear?"

"Those are our tools," said Joseph.

"We'll take the bags," announced the Chinese officer.

"We're carpenters and we need them so that we can earn the money to pay for food and lodgings," pleaded Joseph.

"This is a toll road," chided the officer gruffly as he reached for a pistol in his holster. "You Occidentals are rich from all you have stolen from China. What's more, these pieces of wood and metal are not enough to pay the toll. We must have cash money as well."

Shulem reached into his pocket and came up with its contents. He handed the officer the coins and the paper money.

"And what are those pieces of paper still in your hand?" growled the officer.

"Those are tickets for our ship's passage to Shanghai," interjected Berish.

"They cost money, don't they?"

"Of course," replied Berish. "They were a gift from the Chinese gentleman with whom we stayed in Kaifeng."

"Then hand them over!" demanded the officer.

"But what use are they to you?" asked Berish.

"You said that you were carpenters. Not Communists from Russia?"

"Communists?" puzzled Berish.

"Yes, Communists."

"Why should you think us Communists?"

"The Communists have formed a Congress in Shanghai – a source of trouble for China. Russia is to the north. You are coming from the north. And you said that you're going to Shanghai. So there it is."

"Well, we're not Communists. So can we keep our tickets?"

"No. They can be sold for money. Give them to me!"

A dismayed Shulem placed the tickets in the officer's hand.

The officer smiled and then instructed the wagon driver to proceed.

"What are we to do?" asked Joseph, when they were far enough away not to be overheard by the soldiers.

"We'll do what we have to do. If it is the will of the Almighty, we will reach a safe haven," concluded Shulem.

With the Ausübel money gone, the driver and his Jewish passengers slept under the wagon at nights. The soldiers had left them their food and so they did not have to go hungry. Several days later, they reached the shore of the Yangtze River, opposite the city of Nanjing.

"Nanjing played an important role in Chinese history," said Berish, exhibiting the knowledge he had acquired during their years in China. "It was first settled 6,000 years ago and served as the nation's capital during several imperial dynasties. The British bombed the city from ships that had come up the Yangtze during the Opium War. They forced the Chinese to sign a degrading treaty that allowed them to exploit the Chinese. Other Western nations have forced the same concessions from China. The Chinese are a proud people with an ancient civilization. No wonder the Chinese officer exhibited such hostility towards us. In his mind, we represented all those who exploited his country.

"The city was devastated during a rebellion against the emperor that took place in the middle of the last century. The city was also the site where the present Republic of China was founded and where Dr. Sun Yat-sen was elected president. The capital was moved to Peking shortly thereafter, so as to reunite the North with the South."

"Look at the size of the river," said Joseph. "It must be a mile wide. You can barely make out Nanjing from here."

"And when the river floods, there is vast devastation," commented the driver. "Now we go by boat across the river. From there I go on to Wuxi. As you no longer have the tickets for the river trip to Shanghai, please stay with me. Wuxi is much closer to Shanghai."

The Jewish family nodded in agreement.

They passed through Nanjing rapidly, not taking time out to visit the sights. They passed by a lake, surrounded by greenery. Multiple poles were positioned in the water nearby, supporting a series of nets.

"That's Lake Xuanwu. They catch many fish in those nets," the driver informed them. "The tomb of Hung Wu, first emperor of the Ming dynasty, is located in the Jijin Shah Mountains beyond it."

A few days later, they reached the shores of Lake Tai. As with Lake Xuanwu, multiple poles supporting nets were positioned in the water near the shore. Some men and women were harvesting silvery fish from nets that had been removed and spread on the shore.

"The lake seems immense, enormously larger than the one we passed in Nanjing," said Joseph. "Are those islands?"

"The lake is one of the largest in China," replied his older brother. "It is said that it includes more than a hundred islands. It's a popular place for vacation in China."

"Where did you learn all this?" asked an impressed Joseph.

"I read several books on China while we were staying with Dr. Schmidt."

"You can now read Chinese that well?"

"Not really. The books were in German."

"We're not here on vacation, so why the business with this being a resort?" questioned his father.

"I know, Papa. I just said that Wuxi is popular with the Chinese as a resort."

An hour later, they were passing through the city of Wuxi.

"What is the river we are crossing?" questioned Shulem of his eldest son as the wagon traversed a large bridge.

"It is not a river. I believe it is the Grand Canal, the largest in the world. It was built over 2,000 years ago and connects Peking in the north with Hangzhou to the south. While the great rivers of China flow from west to east, the Canal served as the road to connect the north to the south. It was originally designed so that the emperor could send troops rapidly from north to south and vice versa, depending on what force they had to face."

"Look at all those boats," said Joseph. "They have no sails. There seems to be no current; so how do they move along?"

"You see the boatman at the rear of each boat? Each boatman is holding a long pole. The canal is shallow and the boats have a flat bottom so as not to hit bottom. The boatman moves his vessel forward by pressing the long pole against the bottom of the canal. The pole is used to steer the vessel, as well as to push it forward."

The wagon turned right into the first street on the other side of the canal. The driver stopped to deliver a parcel he had kept hidden in a compartment in the floor of the wagon.

"Pity, he hadn't informed us of the hidden compartment," observed Shulem. "We might have been able to hide our money and our tickets in it."

"And those soldiers might have taken out their frustration at not acquiring sufficient loot on our heads."

"It was not intended," Berish concluded sadly.

"Not intended?" queried Joseph.

"Not intended," repeated Berish. "If it were intended, Moses would have passed through the Sinai directly into Canaan, but it was not intended. Instead, he traveled for forty years by a circuitous route before the Hebrews could enter the Promised Land. And as for Moses himself, he was not to enter the Promised Land."

"That always seemed cruel to me. Why should Moses not have a monument to mark his grave?" wondered Joseph aloud.

"Because we do not worship Moses. We worship the Ruler of the Universe and none other."

"And are we going to be wandering through China for forty years?" asked his younger brother with sadness evidenced on his face.

"I know that we are being tried in a crucible. We must prove ourselves worthy. As Papa said when we began our journey, if we have to travel to the end of the earth, we will!"

The driver rejoined them on the front seat of the wagon. "I have one more delivery to make – in Soochow. It is closer to Shanghai. If you like, you can stay with me for the trip to that city."

The wagon returned to the road leading to the east, out of the city.

"If you don't mind my asking," said Berish as he translated his father's Yiddish into Chinese, "why didn't you tell us of the hiding place so that my father could hide our money and tickets in it?"

"Because I promised not to lose the parcels," the driver replied.

"What's in the parcels that is so important?" questioned Joseph.

"I do not know and don't want to know. I have a job and I carry it out."

"And the hay?" asked Berish.

"It shall be there when I return to Kaifeng."

"We wouldn't have said anything about the hiding place," said Joseph.

"Even under torture?" questioned the driver.

"And yourself?" queried Berish.

"Even under torture, I would have remained silent," replied the Chinese driver. "But I could not expect you to do the same."

"You have so little confidence in Europeans?" asked Berish.

"Look at what your father did as soon as the officer asked for money. He immediately reached into his pocket. Once he had done that, his possessions were lost."

"Would he have let us pass if he had not received the money and the tickets?" wondered Joseph, aloud.

"We might have been beaten in an effort to get us to disclose what else we were carrying. But, in the end, we would have been allowed to go on."

"You're sure?" asked Berish.

"One can never be sure of anything," said the driver with finality in his voice.

"And you did not tell us you were going to Wuxi and Soochow," added Joseph.

"What we didn't know we could not reveal even under torture," said Berish. "If anyone had revealed that the wagon was going as far as Wuxi and Soochow, the officer would certainly have been curious as to why a wagon load of hay was being sent so far. Then none of us would have been safe from being beaten, even to death, in an effort to extract information. After that, they would have torn the wagon apart in a search for hidden valuables."

"A wise analysis," smiled the driver.

Soochow was a beautiful city of busy shops and private homes along the narrow streets. "A magnificent place," observed Berish.

The driver smiled. "In the days of Confucius, the Prince of Wu directed his prime minister to build a capital for his kingdom that would mirror the heavens and the earth, where virtuous men and beautiful women would dwell. The prince saw to it that pagodas were constructed on the hillocks, that canals passed through the city, and that gardens of beauty were here in abundance.

"It is situated between lush hills and fertile plains. Flowers bloom here ten months a year. Like heaven, it has eight water gates; like earth, eight foot gates."

"Those canals," commented Berish to the driver. "I saw people washing their food and clothing and dishes in the water, while others were dumping buckets of dark brown material into the same water."

"Night-soil (feces) buckets," said the driver.

"Is that wise?" asked Joseph, disturbed.

"It is not supposed to be done, but some people do it," sighed the Chinese man.

The driver stopped at one private home. He delivered his second parcel and then returned to the wagon. "It is not so far to Shanghai. I believe that my master would not object if I took you as far as that city."

They reached the south bank of the great Yangtze River. The river was far wider than it had been at Nanjing, and wider than any river they had seen back in Europe. Shanghai was a change from all the other cities they had passed through in China. Along the south bank of the Yangtze, it was more Western than Chinese in appearance. The Union Jack of England and Tricolor of France flew from the standards that lined the quay. Tall Sikhs with their red turbans directed traffic in the wide boulevards of the British.

"I must leave you here," said the driver. "The international concessions are not a place where a wagon driver with a load of hay is welcome. One more thing: There is a Jewish community here in Shanghai, with Europeans, rather than Chinese. Unlike Kaifeng, they have a synagogue that still stands. I believe that if you take the street to the right, you will come upon it."

(After the Opium War in 1832, each of a number of foreign powers took control of a section of Shanghai. The city doubled as an enclave for Western commercial interests in China and as a gateway to the interior of China. Residents in these concessions were exempt from the laws of China. Chinese were barred from free access to the concessions.)

"Bless you," said Shulem with tears in his eyes.

"Hurry," said the driver. "Chinese are not welcome in this part of the city unless they can have papers to show that they are servants to Europeans."

"Disgraceful," commented Berish, "that a Chinese should not be able to go anywhere in his own country."

"I agree," replied the driver, "but there it is."

The Jews waved good-bye to the driver. He waved back as he turned his wagon around for the long journey back to Kaifeng.

"What day is it?" asked Shulem in Yiddish. "I have lost track of the days."

"It is Saturday," replied Berish. "There should be a congregation in the synagogue, so let us hurry there."

The Jews in the synagogue were all clean-shaven, in contrast to the bearded Shulem. They eyed the newcomers curiously as the Ausübels seated themselves in the rear. When the service was over, the rabbi approached and inquired in Yiddish as to whom they were.

Berish served as spokesman. He detailed their Galician background and told of the seven years of travel in exile that had brought them to Shanghai. Many of the other congregants had gathered around them to hear the amazing story.

"You'll stay in my house," said the rabbi.

One of the congregants added, "We'll take up a collection after the Sabbath. There's a ship leaving for Melbourne on Monday. We'll use the funds to pay for tickets for the three of them to be on it."

"Where is Melbourne?" questioned Shulem.

"In Australia," said Berish.

"Are there Jews in Australia?" wondered Shulem aloud.

"A fair number," replied the rabbi. "There are two major Jewish communities in Australia. The older one is in Sydney. Many of the Jews there are descendants of the few Jewish convicts who were brought there more than a hundred years ago."

"Convicts? Jewish convicts?" wondered Shulem.

"If the theft involved something worth more than a Pound, the prisoner was executed," said the rabbi. "If less than a Pound, he or she was sent to Australia for seven years of servitude. When the seven years were up, most of them chose to stay in Australia. They bought land for next to nothing and became some of the first families of the colony."

"How much is a Pound?" inquired Joseph.

"Not much."

"So what sort of theft would involve something worth less than a Pound?" he pursued.

"A loaf of bread or a spool of cotton or something of that little value."

"You're speaking of Sydney," interrupted Shulem. "What about the city to which the ship is going?"

"It has a Jewish community almost equal in size to that of Sydney. The Jewish community there is composed mostly of twentieth-century immigrants. And your sons would be quite welcome."

"Any special reason why?" asked Berish.

"Because you're men."

"And is Australia a land of women?"

"Not really. You see, although the Jewish population of Australia is small, a Jew was named commander of the Australian Expeditionary Force that fought in the war. The Jews were so proud that one of them had been named commander of the Australian army division that almost every Jew old enough to fight, enlisted. The Australian army is all volunteer. There is no draft in that country."

"So again, why are two young Jews so welcome?" pursued Berish.

"Because the Australian division was assigned to fight at Gallipoli on the strait that connects the Mediterranean and Black Seas and divides European from Asian Turkey. It lies a few miles below the Turkish capital in Istanbul. The battle proved to be a disaster. You see, the expedition commander had intended to sail up the Dardanelles towards Istanbul. After a mine sank the lead ship, the commander chose to change the landing place to the outer side of the peninsula. The fleet then discharged the invading soldiers into boats that were to take them to the shore. But a change in the winds brought the Australian unit to shore in the wrong place – in a narrow strip of beach with bluffs towering about it. The Turks and their guns were positioned directly above the beach. It was a slaughter. The Australian unit suffered horrendous casualties. In one battle, much of the Jewish male population of Australia was lost.

"So you can see why young male Jews are particularly welcome."

"Where did you learn all this?" questioned Joseph.

"I'm British and I have spent some time with the congregation in Melbourne."

The Ausübels arrived in Melbourne and eventually settled in a suburb called Balaclava. This area was home to many of the Orthodox Jews of the city. They built a home for themselves. They communicated by mail with the families of Shulem's older brother, Judah, as well as with those of his younger siblings. Half a century later, Shulem passed away. Neither Berish nor Joseph married. Perhaps as a result of exposure to the frosts of Siberia and the depravations suffered on the trip across the Gobi desert, neither Berish nor Joseph were able to produce offspring.

❖ ❖ ❖

In 1979, Ian Ausubel, the fifteen-year-old son of Dr. Herbert Ausubel, grandson of Adolph Ausubel and great-grandson of Judah Ausubel, traveled to Australia as a cellist in a youth orchestra. Upon instructions from his father, he sought out and visited his cousins Berish and Joseph.

Ian was the first family member Berish and Joseph had seen since 1915. The elderly brothers were so happy to see him, they didn't want him to leave. Ian had concerts to perform, but he spent every free hour he could with the brothers. They related to him the story of their exile in Siberia and their epic journey that ended in Australia.

"We are a dying twig of a once mighty branch," concluded Berish, sadly. He thought for a moment and then added, "When we began our journey, our father Shulem, rest his soul, was asked how far we would travel. 'To the end of the earth if needs be,' he replied. Well, we did travel, so to speak, to the end of the earth. It is up to you to relate our story that it might not be swept under some carpet.

"It is up to you to keep our tree alive. You should produce a new and vigorous branch that will gather sustenance from the sun...for us, for our family, for our people. So long as you and your descendants carry on our traditions, we live from our homeland in Israel to the end of the earth."

INTO THE VALLEY OF DARKNESS

OUR JOURNEY TO learn of our past has taken Stephanie and me and our children to many countries, especially Israel. One evening, we paid a visit to Avraham Ausubel and his family. They resided in the Geula section of Jerusalem, an ultra-Orthodox Jewish neighborhood.

As I entered their apartment, I introduced my family members and myself and then shook Avraham's hand. Avraham, a lean-bearded man dressed in traditional Hassidic attire, introduced his wife. I reached out to shake her hand. The poor woman back peddled in fright. I suddenly remembered that Orthodox women are forbidden to have physical contact with anyone of the opposite sex. I dropped my hand instantly.

Several of Avraham's children were there, along with a son-in-law who also spoke English. All the males, despite the sandy hair of several of the boys, had the typical yeshiva student appearance. The women all wore long dresses. None wore makeup. Avraham introduced his youngest daughter, a child of perhaps three years of age. I was permitted to touch her blonde hair.

We were then seated, the men around the table, the women on the couches at the periphery of the room.

The conversation was in Yiddish, with Avraham's son-in-law doing some English translation. I asked why they did not speak in Hebrew. Avraham's son-in-law explained that Hebrew was God's language, not to be employed in common conversation.

"But you're living in Israel, and Hebrew is the language of the country."

"Even though they know Hebrew very well, they will not use it in conversation."

"How can they earn a living if they will not speak in Hebrew?"

"Avraham limits his employment to an occupation in which he can follow his beliefs."

"What kind of job is that?"

"The post office. It's alright for him to read envelopes written in Hebrew, just so long as he doesn't have to speak Hebrew when not discussing
religious matters."

"Amazing."

"And that's not all of his religious determination. At the beginning of
the Yom Kippur War he worked on the Sabbath, transmitting military messages. Let me explain: you're a doctor; if you were to refuse to care for a
dangerously ill patient because it was the Sabbath, it would be a violation
of religious law; he worked under the logic he was saving the lives of Israeli
soldiers. But as soon as things turned around and the Israelis were winning,
he refused to work on the Sabbath. When they threatened to put him in jail,
he said he would not violate religious law to save his own life, let alone avoid
going to jail!"

"What happened?"

"They relented."

We were there for many hours, finally taking our leave at about 3 AM.
During that time I learned more about our family's experience at the beginning of World War II.

Over the first four decades of the twentieth century, turbulent events
led to the sons of Moses Ausübel being separated from one another. A World
War had resulted in Judah and his family fleeing for their lives to Vienna,
and then to America. Shulem and his family had exiled to Siberia, from
which the survivors traveled to Australia. The town of Rozwadow was still
home to the family of the third-born, Joseph, in the fall of 1939.

It was a dark, foreboding evening; there was the dream of a bright morn.
It was a day when a people remembered the burning of their synagogue by
the pernicious advanced guard of the New Order; it was the eve of the Festival
of Sukkot, filled with hopeful remembrance of a time past when the Hebrew
people had escaped another terrible oppressor, to journey to a land of freedom.
(During Sukkot or the "Festival of Booths or Tabernacles," Jews live in a temporary shelter, a Sukka, allowing sun and stars to shine through roof covering,
in recollection of wandering through the desert after the Exodus from Egypt.)

Joseph Ausübel stood up, preparing to lead his family into the Sukka.
They were going to enjoy a meal in a house of wood, roofed by reeds that
allowed the stars in, amid the first fruits of the season, to remind them that
even in troubled times, surrounded by enemies who waved their clubs ominously, life could be sweet and good.

He wore a black felt hat, concealing a skullcap and a receding hairline that had almost reached the point of baldness. A long, wavy, gray-brown beard and sidecurls of a pious Jew – whose days were spent in the study of the Scriptures – covered his sage-like face. His dark, thoughtful eyes smiled at the thought of having survived another season to celebrate the Festival of Tabernacles. He was a kindly and unworldly man who felt more at home reading *Ezekiel,* the third of the major prophets of the Bible during the Babylonian exile, than conducting business in Galicia in 1939. A step behind him, in his buoyant departure from the stone and shingle of their permanent dwelling to the wood and reed of the Sukka, was Malka, his wife. The dark *sheitl* that covered her head slipped a bit and she readjusted it with rough, worn hands. They were the hands of a woman accustomed to hard work – managing a dairy and granary, carrying pails of milk, and dragging sacks of flour – in-between making recordings in the ledgers of the family business. She had done all this while she raised a family of nine children and cared for a scholar husband who contemplated the meaning of it all.

One by one, the children followed. At last, they all stood in the Sukka, admiring the corn and the green peppers, the apples and the pears.

There was Moshe, their fourth-born and at present the eldest of their offspring still at home. At 25, he was neither tall nor broad-chested, but he was far from frail. His dark hair was combed straight back from a face that appeared pale and uneasy, as if anticipating the worst.

Chaya – dark-brown hair and downcast, melancholy eyes – seemed unable to summon the right frame of mind for the holiday. *What is there to celebrate?* she wondered. *Germany invaded Poland. So what did the Poles do? Instead of rushing to fight off the Nazis, they looted the homes and shops of Jews. Why should we, of all people, have been the objects of Polish wrath at being invaded by the German army? Sure, there are plenty of anti-Semites among the Poles, but Nazi Germany had made clear that Germany is the enemy of the Hebrew people. So it was a time when Poles and Jews should have been united to fight the common enemy, not a time for Poles to attack their staunchest allies. But bad as the Poles have been, the Germans are far worse. The desecration and destruction they have wreaked! They have no respect for synagogues or cultural centers. And the way they treated us: jostling old bearded men, the jeers, the intimidating insults, the way those black-shirts with their swastika armbands and polished black boots took pleasure in taunting and degrading anything they couldn't understand.* At seventeen, she was all too wise in the ways of the world not to sense the ominous implications of those acts.

Miriam, all pink and healthy, was an adolescent of fourteen, giving promise of blossoming into womanhood. Her fine, flaxen hair rested on slender shoulders. Her rounded face expressed – beneath the smile that covered it – a sense of apprehension and even, dejection.

Finally, there was little Dov, the youngest – dark and mischievous, yet such a source of joy. His cheeks glowed with the gladness that holidays bring.

Joseph was standing at the head of the table. He raised his glass of wine and recited the *Kiddush*. He completed the blessing, but wine never touched his lips.

The door to the Sukka flew open with the resounding crash of rifle butts against it. "Get out! Get out you cursed Jews and don't come back!" shouted a German soldier to the bewildered members of the family as the Aryan and his fellow black-shirted warriors herded the Ausübels out of the house of wood and reeds, using frequent jabs with rifle butts to hasten the steps of their hapless victims.

Terrified, the Jewish family moved as quickly as they could down the street. They were fearful of looking back, lest another blow from a rifle butt or, even worse, the bayonet be received. Joseph rushed ahead breathlessly on nervous energy driven by mortal terror. His face was ashen and his eyes opened wide with dread and confusion.

Malka halted, panting as breath failed her. Her lips turned blue for want of oxygen and her chin sank heavily to her chest, doubling itself. One impatient Nazi raised his rifle menacingly. Moshe grabbed his mother by the arm and urged her forward.

The young ones, unburdened by age or frailty, ran like the wind, far ahead of their parents. At the San River, the children came to a halt, puffing and drenched in sweat. Joseph and Malka, assisted by Moshe, finally joined them. All three were gasping through wide-open mouths and with lungs that pained with every harsh inspiration. For the first time, they looked back at the ghetto of Rozwadow, now enveloped in orange balls of flame and thick gray smoke. Hundreds of others, Jews in a similar state of panic and anguish huddled in groups near the Ausübels. They all watched in horror as the work of a lifetime was burnt to the ground. Many of the older ones could recall a similar event a quarter-century before, when the Tsar's troops arrived in that Galician town. Now, Nazis. Different nations, different uniforms, but for the Jew, the same result.

The Germans, here and there striking an aged straggler with boot or fist or gun or all of them, drove the Jews to the water's edge. The uniformed young Nazi heroes seemed to consider it good sport. They laughed, they mocked, they stamped their feet and they taunted in an ever-increasing roar – calling upon the Followers of Moses to part the waters that blocked their escape. And seemingly enthusiastic German reporters and photographers were documenting all this. Flashbulbs popped. Crews of men with motion picture cameras and bright lights directed at the terrified Jews recorded the event on film, as if this were a Hollywood studio and they were making a Cecil B. DeMille epic.

A ferry arrived – none too soon – and the tremulous Jews crowded on board. The vessel, unaccustomed to so large a number of passengers, dipped low in the water and appeared ready to sink beneath the rushing river water.

"We're going to sink," cried one of the passengers. "There's no more room," shouted another as the last of the terrified Jews on shore pushed to make their way aboard.

Some of the younger boys and girls dove overboard, choosing to swim across the river, thus making room for the last of the frantic mass of bearded men, babushka-covered women and little children.

The flames of burning red, orange and yellow leaped high over the ghetto and the blackened, smoke-filled sky seemed to emphasize the words "and don't come back!"

They arrived on the opposite shore, still dazed, but at least there was now a river separating them from the Germans. The Russians, Germany's partner in the dismemberment of Poland, now occupied the right bank of the San. The survivors – the swimmers and those who had gone by ferry – slowly grouped themselves into families. There were worried queries from dispirited people about the missing. Had the angry, black water swallowed them or could they possibly have escaped by turning back?

Joseph was cheered to see that all of his family had made it – all, that is, who were in Rozwadow. Then darkness covered his face as he thought of his four children, a daughter-in-law and two grandchildren back in Krakow, far inside the German lines. What would be their fate? Would he ever see them again?

Only the vision of Simcha dispelled some of Joseph's gloom. Simcha, with his broad chest and strong, clean-shaven face framed by brown, curly hair, had set off on the road to Palestine a year before. That year now seemed like a millennium. "At least," he sighed, "one is safe."

"Well," said Malka, awakening her family from paralyzing contemplation, "no point in just standing here, waiting for the Messiah. We'd better find a place to stay."

"But where?" wondered her husband, aloud.

"Sieniawa, perhaps?" suggested Malka, in a questioning tone. "Your sister's family are there – at least they were there. What do you think, Joseph?"

"We haven't seen them since Channah died," Joseph reflected. "Still, in all, they should have room for an uncle and aunt and a few cousins driven from their home."

"So come," said Malka with determination. "We've got ten kilometers to cover in this darkness."

There were no relatives to be found in Sieniawa that night. In fact, most of the Jews of the village were gone. And so a barn at the edge of the hamlet served as their lodging in the wilderness on the first night of the Festival of Sukkot.

In the morning, Moshe set out without a coin in his pocket looking for food. An hour later he returned not only empty-handed, but with more distressing news. Russian troops were scouring the villages near the San, looking for Jews who had crossed the river on the preceding day. Moshe, himself, had barely evaded their net. In the Soviet state, there was no room for refugees – people who ate but did not serve the nation. A one-way ticket to a labor camp was the Communist solution.

And so the Ausübels returned to the road – that is, the high grass near the road – and headed for Lemberg, the largest city in what had been south-eastern Poland. The trip was long and it was made even longer to avoid Russian sentries, whose red-starred headdress flashed like a dreaded warning, only second to the swastika. To be caught meant to be shipped to a labor camp somewhere far, far away.

The fleeing Ausübels ate what they could – rotting grain fallen in the field, a few berries growing by the roadside, but most of the time their stomachs growled in discontent. They slept where they could – in a barn or open field – hoping to escape detection. The only conversations were with fellow Jews – bearded men, women with *sheitls* covering their heads, and young lads with the sidelocks of the faithful. Only such folk could be trusted not to betray them; only such folk might transmit a message to loved ones now trapped in Krakow...if, by some stroke of good fortune, they escaped. At the end of a two-week journey, the Ausübels arrived in Lemberg, a city of tall buildings by the standards of Rozwadow.

There were two overriding necessities – food and shelter. The former was scarce and the latter, seemingly non-existent to a family with empty pockets. Their first glimpse of town life was a long line of people, stretching for blocks, yet not moving at all. Seeing a hopefully friendly, gray-bearded face in the line, Moshe inquired as to what they were all waiting for.

"Food," was the answer – simple, yet voiced almost without hope, as if the food they were waiting for were on another planet and there was no inter-planetary vehicle available to transport it. Still, they waited, for there seemed nothing better to do.

Moshe surveyed the gray-bearded man. His face was drawn and pale and his body swayed uneasily on buckling knees in the chilled morning air. "How long have you waited?" questioned Moshe.

"Three days," was the reply. "And I'm still two blocks from the bakery. I don't think I can make it." He coughed – a fitful spasm of coughing – and spit into a rag turned red with congealed blood.

Moshe observed the crimson-colored cloth that served as a handkerchief, but said nothing about it. Instead, he asked, "Why doesn't the line move?"

"Each day they only get a little grain with which to make bread and it quickly sells out. There's not enough for everyone. So we wait day after day, hoping to be alive to get some to survive…to wait again…"

The bearded man coughed again and staggered in a zigzag pattern. Moshe caught him and eased his slide onto the cold pavement. People glanced at the man, but did not move to help. Perhaps it was in fear of losing a place in line; perhaps, because with the grim reaper striking all around them, human beings grow callous to the signs of death.

"Please," pleaded the old man, "keep my place. Here are my food coupons and money. Get some rye bread and you can share it with me."

Moshe beckoned to Miriam and Dov, still lively despite the long journey. He handed them the coupons and the money and instructed them as to the method for obtaining food. Then Moshe, along with his parents and sister, assisted the old man away from the crowd.

"It's better that you rest somewhere where it's warm. My sister and brother will wait for the bread," said Moshe. "Is there a place where you live?"

The old man gave gasping directions as he pointed this way and that.

In accordance with the old man's instructions, they then moved through the narrow streets, to a building some distance away.

"Strange," thought Moshe when they reached the place. It was a large brick building, more governmental than residential in appearance.

"We can't go in now," said the frail old man. "Classes are in session. I sleep in the school at night, when the students are gone."

"And no one stops you?" questioned Malka.

"No. The janitor's my friend. He's a Gentile with a good heart."

Moshe, remembering his little brother and sister standing in line, left his parents and Chaya with the old man. That foursome remained out of sight in an alley near the school, while Moshe retraced his steps to line up in front of the bakery.

But they were not where he had left them. "Perhaps I've forgotten the place," he muttered. Frantically, he searched up and down the line. But they were nowhere to be found. A thousand thoughts rushed through his mind, but one predominated. "They were caught," he reasoned, trembling.

He felt a tap on the shoulder. He turned to see Miriam and Dov, alive and well. They had, between them, four loaves of bread bulging in their arms. Moshe embraced them and asked how they had gotten bread so quickly.

"We crept under everyone's legs," whispered Dov, with a smile. "They were all so tired, no one even noticed."

Moshe blushed with an embarrassment, tempered only by his human hunger for something to bite into. They hastened back to the alley near the school.

The old man shared his unexpected feast with the Ausübels. It was rye bread without butter or cheese. No matter, it was good solid food. The old man ate several mouthfuls, but he was too weak to consume more. Between them, they finished one loaf; they saved the others.

They sought to become better acquainted. Mendel Alter was the name of their newly found friend, a Jew from a village not far away. Now he was separated from his loved ones. They spoke of the villages of Galicia and Lublin, the Germans and the Russians.

"That cough," said Joseph inquiringly of the old man who gasped with each almost convulsive hack, "isn't there anything that can be done about it?"

"Hospitals don't take care of Jews without papers," was the reply.

In the afternoon, school let out. They then carried the sick old man into the building. The janitor greeted them with a look of surprise, but then agreed to allow the new arrivals to sleep in the classroom. The sandy-haired caretaker with pale blue eyes forewarned them not to tell anyone of their good fortune, lest he lose his position and they, a home.

They slept on the hardwood floor and, in the morning, vacated the premises to return to the street. Mendel, too weak to walk, lay in the alley with Malka and Joseph sitting beside him. By nightfall, Mendel was dead, a victim of the times, of disease and malnutrition. A family he had met the day before observed his passing.

"What do we do with the body?" they wondered. "Call an undertaker? Arrange for a burial?"

But they had no papers, no identification for the man or for themselves. And they had no money to pay for a funeral. Furthermore, to call attention to themselves in any way might result in their deportation to a labor camp. And so they adjusted to the times. The old man's mortal remains were left where he lay, to be carried away in one of the carts that circled the city each morning to pick up the dead, like refuse left out to be hauled to the dump.

The Ausübels learned more of the new system, the Russian system, and what was necessary for survival. To communicate with the Russian masters of the system, you had to learn Russian. To get food, one had to get a work-card and to get a work-card you had to have a job, any job. It could be in a factory or a store or pushing a cart in the street – sewing, carrying, anything. Food was scarce, very scarce, and the waiting lines were very long. It was impossible to both work and wait in line for several days, hoping for a new shipment of food. He who could obtain nourishment by day and escape the cold at night might live; those who did not would most assuredly die. It was a world in which only the fittest survived. And the fittest meant those who were able to work and were clever enough to get the food. Crawl under the legs of people who stood numb in the cold, get an extra coupon that was worth a few ounces of bread or a pinch of salt, do anything, but stay alive in a dying world.

And so they survived that winter in Lemberg. They slept in the school-room at night and attended to the other tasks necessary for survival during the day. Malka found a concealed corner of the basement of the schoolhouse where she could wash and mend clothes and prepare simple meals while her family was away. The older children found jobs which entitled them to wages, as well as the work-cards necessary to obtain food. The two youngest, Miriam and Dov, perfected their technique for getting to the head of the food line. Joseph, father and sage, spent his days at the nerve center of the Jewish community, the synagogue.

Jews on the run, exiled from their native villages, lost in the whirling, changing world, would come to the house of worship to maintain that con-tinuity which gave structure and meaning to their existence. In the company of co-religionists, they found comfort in prayers offered up from deep with-in their souls to the amorphous, all-seeing God, who knew the difference between hollow words uttered by men of little faith, and heart-felt supplica-tion from the faithful.

One day, a group of gaunt, elderly, bearded men, Joseph among them, sat around a table in the corner of the synagogue. They were deliberating over a section of the Talmud, while waiting for the evening service. A lad, perhaps nine or ten years old, thin and sallow-faced with large, hollow eyes and closely-cropped, brown hair without sidelocks, entered the synagogue, seemingly lost. The discussion came to an abrupt halt as all eyes focused on the boy, whose head was uncovered in a house of worship where all males wore skullcaps.

"Continue with your discussion," said Joseph, rising. "I'll attend to the child."

He walked over to the youth who stood at the rear of the small syna-gogue. The boy was studying the room and the old, bearded men within it. Bewilderment was written on his face.

"Are you looking for someone?" Joseph asked in a kindly voice.

"Well...just looking around," was the boy's reply. "This is a synagogue, isn't it?"

"Yes, it is. Have you come to pray?" Joseph halted reflectively, then continued, "Perhaps I should first ask whether or not you are a Jew?"

"I...er...am."

"Well then, put on a skullcap and join us. The service will begin soon."

Joseph reached down into a basket near the door. He extracted a skullcap that he placed gently on the lad's head. Then the bearded man handed the boy a prayer book opened to the correct page for the service.

"Bu...but I can't read your language," the child stammered out.

Joseph eyed him for a minute, through eyes suddenly heavier with disappointment. Then a soft smile of sympathetic understanding crossed his bearded face and he placed a soothing hand on the lad's shoulder. "It's your language as well as mine. It's the language of the Torah." Joseph paused for a moment and then went on, "Where do you come from?"

"Berlin – we've been in other places since."

"Did you ever attend *cheder*?"

"That's a Hebrew school. I guess – no. My parents aren't religious."

"And do you want to be religious as you term it? You came here for a reason, is that not so?"

"I came here to see..." said the boy. "We've been running from the Nazis – they call us Jews. I wanted to see some real Jews, to try to understand what they have against Jews. You look different – I mean your clothes and things – but you don't look dangerous."

Joseph smiled dolefully. "No, we're not dangerous."

"You all have beards," observed the lad, aloud. "Are you what they call Hassidim?" (Hassidim maintain a higher standard of observing the religious and moral commandments; it also refers to those who emphasize devotion to God through joyous song, dance and happiness in a mystical ecstasy.)

"You might say that."

"Then why aren't you dancing?"

"We dance when there's cause to dance, not simply for the sake of dancing."

"There's something else I came for..." The boy groped for words. "Tell me, is God here... I mean in this building?"

"The Almighty is everywhere, including and especially in this building."

"But why can't I see Him and why don't you have a statue of Him here?"

"No, you can't see Him. And His law forbids us to have any statues in a synagogue. That would be idolatry. But if you believe in Him – truly believe – you can feel His presence. He is the friend who's always there to share your joy; He is there to comfort you in adversity; He is the parent whose approval we seek; He is the shepherd who watches over His flock; and He's the father who guides your steps when you are lost in the darkness. And for the Jew, there is no intermediary between He who has no name – for that is how we refer to the Almighty – and His children. So we each communicate with Him directly, reason with Him and plead with Him for a redress of grievances. And yes, we even dance and give thanks for His blessings, The Torah, the Law, The Commandments. Come. The service is about to begin. Sit here beside me. Pray in your own words. Later, you can learn Hebrew."

The little boy had been all ears as Joseph spoke. Now he viewed the room with his large, saucer eyes, as if seeing things for the first time. Then he sat and prayed in his new home. After the service, he thanked Joseph and then left the synagogue to pass in the darkness outside – but perhaps, with a new hand to guide him.

And so Joseph spent his days in the synagogue, in prayer, in analysis and discussion of the sacred writings, but also in conversation – conversation with a purpose. Messages were transmitted by sound rather than by the written word, and the voice was to these Jews what the tom-tom is to the African in the jungle. Total strangers would meet in the house of worship, introduce themselves to one another and make inquiries about relatives and friends.

"Have you heard of any Ausübels in your travels?" Joseph would ask. He quickly went through the names of his missing children and grandchildren and the places where they were last heard from.

"Yes, I think so," a stranger replied. "I met Moshe Tendler from Krakow... just last month. We were in Tarnograd at the time. He made mention of an Ausübel...or a name that sounded like it, from Krakow. This Ausübel was headed for Sieniawa. Did you say Itzhak? I believe it was Itzhak Ausübel he referred to."

In this manner, Jews, wandering and searching, left tracks; hopefully to be spotted and followed by loved ones. So it was that Joseph was reunited with Sabina, Itzhak, Chaya and Abraham, the members of his family who had been stranded in Krakow when the Nazis conquered Poland.

The Ausübels worked, they struggled to stay alive; they survived another season. Yet, in the struggle, there were still moments of joy – pleasures that did not require great sums of money, for there were none. One such moment was the marriage of Joseph's daughter, Sabina, to Ernst Leiterdorf, a pallid, gaunt, sensitive Jew who had fled from Vienna. Under a canopy held by four men, in the presence of an overjoyed family and a few friends, they were declared man and wife. The bridegroom raised his foot and crushed a glass wrapped in a napkin as the traditional remembrance of the lost Temple in Jerusalem. A "Mazel Tov" came from the lips of all assembled and they toasted the couple with glasses half-filled with whiskey. There were no hot *hors d'oeuvres* or cold *hors d'oeuvres*, no soup and no meat. Food was scarce and luxuries, non-existent. A few sweets, broken into pieces so that several could share each one, were passed around.

A single, sad-eyed fiddler played light-hearted music to cheer a couple entering bravely, as one, into a somber world. There was a handkerchief dance. (Very Orthodox Jews consider it improper for males and females to touch unless they are married. In the handkerchief dance, the male and female dance with each holding one end of a handkerchief. Thus, the bride can dance with her new husband and then several other men, her father, etc. without violating the injunction.) The dance of the bride and groom was interrupted by a fit of coughing. Ernst buried his face in a handkerchief until the paroxysm ended. Then, displaying a pale, brave smile, he went on as if nothing had happened.

It was summer in Lemberg and the warm rays of the golden sun were comforting, but the heat also brought forth the stench of death – the fetid odor of bodies rotting in alleyways and basements and vacant fields. The men assigned to remove the dead had only to follow their noses until the carts were full. They would dump the bodies in a common grave and then return to the streets to continue their labor.

The Ausübels began to spread out. Itzhak obtained separate quarters – a room for himself, his wife and their children. Sabina and Ernst, likewise, found a small basement shelter in which to begin married life together.

One night in that summer of 1941, the knock which all had dreaded came in the schoolhouse where Joseph's family were lodged. Before they could get to the classroom door, Russian soldiers charged into the room, guns drawn, and ordered the frightened Ausübels out. The Red Army men, however, did allow the Jews to dress and take a few possessions with them.

The Ausübels made two packages of their coats, boots, blankets, an old watch, a few pictures of loved ones and a prayer book, and then carried the bundles out into the near blackness of the street. A pale, sad moon illuminated the shadowy figures that now filled the thoroughfares of the Lemberg ghetto. These were the homeless Jews who had been dragged from their nocturnal hiding places – alleys, basements, warehouses and sewers – like mice called forth by the piper of Hamlin, but with a gun instead of a flute. The hundreds of poor wretches, dark terrified faces surmounting hunched bodies, moved slowly in the same direction. Gun-wielding soldiers urged them on. In ever increasing numbers, they moved towards one central collecting point, the Lemberg Central Railroad Station. There were moans and anxious questions asked by one or the other, but none knew their final destination.

In the station, they joined a sea of refugees huddled in stunned silence. Russian soldiers were guarding them too, keeping sharp watch to see that none escaped.

"Listen," shouted a Russian officer in Polish, seemingly in charge. He was standing on top of a large crate at one end of the platform. "There is no room in Lemberg for so many people, and no jobs for you here. It was Germans who drove you out – not us. But we can't afford to supply idle people with food and shelter. So you're going to be sent to labor camps where you can earn your food and shelter by contributing to the socialist cause. You will be provided with the necessities of life, only on condition that you do a good day's work in the fresh outdoors. There is no place in the Soviet Union for capitalist sponges.

"I want each of you to get on the train when you are told to do so. Be patient. It will take several trains to carry so large a number to Omsk, your intermediate destination. From there, ships will take you to one of several labor camps. If you wish to end up in the same labor camp as others in your family, stay together. Once you reach your final destination, none will be allowed to leave, no matter what the reason."

"Where is Omsk and where are these camps?" inquired a slim, dark young man.

"In Siberia," was the sharp reply.

Piteous cries and subdued moans came from the hopeless. They were the lamentations of the Children of Israel being led into exile. The pious looked in vain for a Jeremiah to comfort them, but there was none. (Jeremiah was the second of the three major prophets in Judaism. He wrote *The Book of Lamentations* to comfort the Jews being taken into captivity by Nebuchadnezzar, king of Babylon.)

"At least Babylon was warm," remarked one unhappy soul, "but Siberia!"

But Joseph had no time for moans. He had work to do. And so he searched through the crowd for Itzhak and his family and for Sabina and Ernst. They were not to be found. "Perhaps," he thought hopefully, "they've escaped the dragnet."

The trains turned out to be boxcars designed for freight, not passengers. Within minutes the cars became hot and stuffy as the mass of Jews, carrying their few possessions, climbed aboard and were packed closer and closer together. The soldiers forced more and more helpless human beings into the limited space, until even a hard push could not crowd another living soul into the cars.

The train began to move and the exhausted and browbeaten people managed to squeeze themselves into a sitting position in anticipation of a long trip. Joseph looked around at the other refugees. They were Jews, like himself, who had been uprooted from a hundred different locales. He spoke to those closest to him about the villages, as if they had existed in another world in the dim, distant past – a world to which they might never return. And, if they returned, would the hamlets be the same? But mostly he sat in benumbed quiet, mesmerized by the chugging of the engine and the turning of the wheels.

Sweat dripped down the faces of the passengers. Within a few hours, the beads of sweat had turned into gushing streams, drenching the clothing of the huddled Jews as the crowded, unventilated cars were turned into Turkish baths with the collective heat of their bodies.

People coughed, spewed phlegm and even droplets of blood into the air. Children, sickened by the continuous bumping and shaking, as well as by the choking closeness of the almost air-tight, windowless car, threw up on their neighbors, for there was no space separating the children from those around them.

The evaporating perspiration, phlegm, blood and vomit gave the car a rancid odor as the suffocating, rising, man-made steam grew so thick you could not see the other side of the car.

The stifling heat gave way to cold – icy cold – as the train ascended the Ural Mountains. Now the refugees huddled together tightly to keep from freezing. Conversation had totally ceased as fright gave way to gloom and gloom to hopeless resignation. Even contemplation ended and the actions of the Jews were governed by trophic responses to heat, cold, water and air, rather than to thoughtful decision.

On the second day of the journey the cars boiled up again as they descended onto the plains of Siberia that sizzled in the scorching heat of the summer sun.

At last, the chugging of the engine and the screeching of the wheels ceased, and the shaking, bouncing cars ground to a halt. The boxcar doors slid open and the first fresh air in two days recalled the refugees from the paralysis of their prolonged confinement without food or water. They reacted slowly to the commands of the Russian soldiers, "Out! Quickly, quickly! Out!" The eyes of the sullen Jews who had been released from the dim grayness of the sealed trains had to adjust to the white light of the sun. The Ausübels grabbed their few belongings and, along with the others, exited onto solid ground. They stumbled uneasily on wobbly legs that seemed to have forgotten their function during the two days of cramped confinement. They assembled alongside the train. Then they trudged in a ragged line through the drab streets of the Siberian city, past one- and two-story houses of unpainted wood. The pointed weapons of the Soviet guards reminded the Jews what to do.

It was a procession of mumbling, weary men, women and children with long, despondent faces. They did not observe the buildings, the shops or the city. The refugees were too numb to do anything but gaze blankly at the road ahead.

The brief trip on foot ended at the river's edge. A steamship, gray against a gray sky, was waiting to take its human cargo for a voyage down bodies of water none of the passengers had ever heard of or wished to hear of. The deck of the ship was quickly packed with its freight – Jews – and the crew cast off the lines that tied them to the dock. Smoke poured out of the stack of the vessel and they were off again.

"At least," mused Joseph when he regained his ability to think, "we have fresh air to breathe. And perhaps, perhaps they'll give us some food and water."

With food and water, sparse though it was, and with the ability to stretch their legs, limited though the deck space was, they began to stir and give signs of life, like patients in a recovery room when the anesthesia of surgery has worn off.

"Where are we?" asked Joseph of a smiling, hearty sailor.

"On the Irtysh River," was the good-natured response.

"Do you know where we're headed?" Joseph pressed further.

"Several places. At each stop, some will get off. In a few days, we'll be on the Ob. That's a river more than three thousand kilometers long. It extends from Mongolia to the Artic Ocean. Our final stop will be near the Altay Mountains. Beyond that, the river is impassible, at least for this ship. It's got rough climate there. Even the summers are cold, and the winters are unbearable. I advise you to get off before that."

"And where are these Altay Mountains you refer to – near the Artic?"

"No," laughed the sailor. "Near China."

A thought crossed Joseph's mind, but he maintained a mask of indifference. "Thank you," was all he said as the seaman moved off toward the rear of the vessel.

Days passed with the ship moving down stream on a widening Irtysh River. It was hot by day and cool at night. From the rail of the vessel, Joseph surveyed lush fields of wheat swaying in the hot summer breeze. The sun revived his spirit and gave color to his face. A week later, the steamship arrived at the junction of the Irtysh and the Ob. Here, the vessel made a sharp turn and entered the Ob, traveling upstream against a swift current that slowed their forward progress.

Several days later, the first contingent of Jews disembarked with somber goodbyes to strangers who had become their friends for the short trip. They were headed for a labor camp in a land about which they had heard nothing but bad things, perhaps never to return. Other groups departed at subsequent stops. But Joseph always kept his family back, so as to remain on the ship.

The number of passengers, unhappy while aboard the ship and unhappy when they left, grew smaller and smaller. The river grew narrower and rougher and the air became colder as the plains turned into hills and the hills into mountains – cold and dark with foreboding cliffs and snow-capped peaks. Still, Joseph directed his wife and children to be the last to leave.

An icy wind descended from the frozen peaks and whistled through the canyon as they sailed toward the headwaters of the river. The vessel was buffeted and tossed. It puffed and coughed and spat dark smoke into the air as it fought its way through churning, slate-gray waters brimmed in white foam, up angry rapids, seemingly against the law of gravity. Chilling mist crept over the face of the water and the ship's horn bellowed mournfully against the dense gray veil that enshrouded them. The sound echoed despairingly through the hills.

Malka and the children approached Joseph who stood at the rail, studying the dark, wrathful clouds that turned noon into dusk. Moshe shuddered, having a premonition of impending calamity.

"Why don't we get off?" asked Moshe with a tremulous hand outstretched in a frenzied, pleading gesture. "The farther we go, the worse the climate becomes; the farther we go, the longer the way back home."

"Into the valley of darkness," replied his father, not turning from the object of his view – dark-gray cliffs merging with a blackening sky. His lips continued to move but the words were inaudible. Then the sound of his voice grew louder and its tone more resolute as if coming from some ancient prophet leading the Children of Israel through their darkest hour. "Yea, though I walk through the valley of the shadow of death, I will fear no evil..." (from Psalm 23, *The Book of Psalms*).

A blast of the ship's horn blotted out Joseph's voice. Malka and the children looked on in panic as Joseph's eyes rose to the heavens. All feared the worst. Could it be that the sage's mind had finally given way under the pressure of repeated misfortune? Had Joseph returned to the Scriptures to escape the decisions of the present world? But who would dare contradict father? Who would be so disrespectful as to countermand the decisions of the bearded Hassid? While Joseph lived, he, and he alone, was the captain of the ship, head of the family.

So they sailed on, against all seeming logic, into the valley of darkness. *But*, they wondered silently and with grave doubt, *will we ever return?*

A HOME IN THE WILDERNESS

THE SKY WAS clear blue. Snow, covering the huge fir trees, glistened in the light of the pale yellow sun like a myriad of sparkling diamonds, turning the forest into an icy wonderland. Miriam dropped the bundle she was carrying and looked up to admire it all. The gentle, warming rays struck her reddened cheeks. She would have longed to bask in the sluggish, wintry sun, were it not for the numbness that quickly stiffened her fingers beneath the torn woolen gloves.

It's forty below, she thought. *You've got to keep moving or be frozen to death.*

A lock of flaxen hair fell forward over her eyes and she quickly replaced it beneath the faded old woolen scarf that covered her hair and crisscrossed over her neck and shoulders. A drab, frayed, brown coat hung loosely over her slender frame. She puffed, producing clouds of vapor that turned into shimmering crystals of ice that fell in the stillness of the Siberian air. Miriam bent forward to retrieve her bundle of twigs and branches and moved on.

"Hurry," cried the impatient Dov. "We're got to hide the wood and get back to work before they miss us."

Eighteen months in a workers' paradise had wreaked havoc on the little boy. His cheeks were glazed and sunken and his dark eyes recessed in their sockets. At an age when he should have been growing, his bulky outer garments, carried all the way from Lemberg, now seemed a few sizes too large. His hands were gloved in odd, frazzled mittens. The mittens had been mended so often, they assumed the appearance of a miniature-patched quilt. Still, they served as a barrier against the frigid air.

Seeing that his sister was following, he trudged on through the snow. He sank into the soft powder to above his knees. Bundled in his arms was a collection of wood scrap that he carried and guarded like precious jewels. Under a tall, stately tree, similar to many other trees in the primitive wilderness, they dropped their load and covered it with snow. Then the children departed in the direction from which they had come.

A few minutes later, they were back at work in another part of the woodland that was a beehive of activity. Chaya was busy assembling pieces of wood, fallen from branches which had been locked in the frozen blanket of snow and ice that covered the wilderness. Her face was drawn, as were all the faces around her. Her dark, melancholy eyes kept searching...for the brown hidden in the white: more wood to fill her quota.

The bigger and stronger workers – men and women, older boys and girls, their brother Avraham among them – were chopping down huge trees. The pines and oaks towered gracefully to the sky, seemingly too strong and majestic to be felled by human efforts. But one by one they came crashing to the ground as someone cried, "Watch out!" A sky full of snow descended from the great limbs of the now-fallen, magnificent works of nature. Flakes and chunks of white were released upward from the earth-covering pale mantle, by the shattering crash of trunk and boughs. Boughs, frozen with cold, snapped, sending showers of branches and twigs flying in all directions.

The adults sawed the fallen giant trunk into sections, each more than a meter in length, while an army of little scavengers – young children and teens – gathered up the lesser pieces. Each placed wood, gleaned from the fallen tree, in a separate pile. Avraham paused for a moment. A sparse beard of golden thread, each hair encased in luminous, reflecting ice, covered his chin, but did not conceal the pallor of his drawn face. His dry, cracked lips moved one against the other, as if they were those of an infant searching for nourishing milk. He returned to his labor, wielding an ax, with the limited power of an emaciated body lacking the nutrition necessary to perform hard labor, no less build muscle. His intelligent, searching gray eyes scanned the scene while he continued to chop wood. Frieda, like Avraham, was busy cutting the tree into sections. Miriam and Dov were collecting scraps. Avraham continued to chop away at a large branch where it met the trunk of the fallen tree. Chips were flying in all directions. At last, the limb was cut clear through. He beckoned to Miriam and Dov, in a matter-of-fact fashion, to join him. Then they all worked busily, pruning the large branch until it had been fashioned into a clean rounded log and divided into sections. The lesser limbs and twigs were collected in a pile.

"Did anyone see you storing the bundle?" Avraham asked Miriam quietly. His hands continued to snap off frozen twigs and his face remained bland, masking his inner concerns.

"Well, one soldier seemed to be glancing our way as we were leaving, but he looked away quickly when I turned towards him. I guess he really didn't see us."

"I wonder," replied Avraham, with concern.

The work went on, hour after hour, under the watchful eye of armed guards, whose red-starred caps were the symbol of Soviet power. An older man, or at least he seemed so – frost covered, gray beard, sunken cheeks and a hunched back – toppled forward like another fallen tree, but with less of a splash. Work stopped. Those around him dropped their axes and saws and rushed to raise his face that lay buried, nose first, in the snow. They lifted the aged bundle, hoping to revive him. But their efforts were in vain. His eyes glassed over and his mouth did not move. He no longer felt pain.

One of the guards joined them, looking over their shoulders. He saw the signs of death.

"You and you," he directed, with his leather-gloved hand pointing to two of the men, "carry the body into the forest and leave it there. It's too cold to dig a hole. The snow will cover him, so he'll stay 'til spring. And come back quickly. I'll be watching the time."

Seeing the others remain motionless, watching their fellow Jew being carried away, the Russian added: "The rest of you get back to work. Haven't you ever seen a dead Jew? Besides, you want to eat, don't you? No quota of wood, less food! So get back to work."

They returned cheerlessly to their labor. A work party, the biggest and the strongest of the sickly occupants of the camp, arrived to haul the finished logs down to the frozen river. There, the logs were to be stacked until the spring thaw floated them to a plant downstream.

Moshe, standing to the rear of the muscle men, blinked a "Hello" to his brothers and sisters. He looked haggard and exhausted from his work. If he possessed the muscles necessary to do the work of a horse, they were well hidden beneath the baggy clothes that hung limply over his spare frame.

Each of the workers in the forest dragged the wood he had harvested to a central collection point. There, Soviet guards, with pencil and paper in hand, assessed the results. The logs were put to one side and the lesser pieces to the other. A sufficient harvest drew a check and a nod of approval. Those short were looked at sternly and an "X" was placed next to their name on the list.

The collecting done, the Russian sergeant blew his whistle and the Jews tied ropes around the massive logs. Then, like pack animals, they dragged the cylinders of dark brown wood down the irregular slope towards the river. The others returned to glean timber from the forest.

The sun was receding in the west. The air was now numbing cold, as an icy evening wind swept down the hillside on which the exhausted band of workers labored. A second whistle recalled them from their toil, barely in time to keep another half dozen from going the way of the gray-bearded man that day. They plodded through the snow, back to the labor camp, carrying branches and twigs bundled in their arms. The anemic rays of light from a descending orange sun filtered through the branches in a myriad of colors – green, yellow, orange, red, purple and blue. But the rainbow of hues did not attract the eyes of the somber workers; only the smoke rising from the chimneys did.

There were guards in front of them and guards behind them, to insure their return to the barbed-wire enclosure that served as home in this wilderness for refugees. The gates opened and they trampled into Vierchne Baraki (Vierchne Barracks). They moved past the rusting, cold, barbed steel wire of the fence. They dropped their loads of wood in front of the sturdy building, near the entrance to the camp that served as home for the Russian soldiers. Then the Jews stood shivering in the cold, waiting for permission to take a few pieces of wood for themselves. Permission granted, they each selected a few branches, under the cold observing eyes of the soldiers whose nod of annoyance indicated that too much had been taken. The Jews now moved in separate directions, each headed for his own quarters.

The Ausübels trudged toward a long wooden building in the rear of the camp. The barracks were drab in the extreme. They were ugly and decaying; varying in shade from drab gray to moldy brown, save for the snow covering their roofs. The door to their barrack, seemingly frozen shut, resisted Miriam's effort to open it. Avraham, applying a shoulder, slammed into it. After momentary opposition, the door screeched open on its rusty hinges. Their footsteps in the narrow hallway attracted attention, and a door in the rear of the corridor opened. Joseph, older and grayer and a good deal thinner than when he left Rozwadow, stood there. A faint smile of greeting appeared on his face. There were no handshakes or hugs or kisses as his children entered the room, only silent nods.

The room was a small one, equal in size to every other room in the camp. It served as kitchen, dining room, living room and sleeping quarters for the eight members of the family. A black, metal stove was positioned against the far wall. Malka, as gaunt as the rest of them, stood next to it, stirring a pot of steaming soup. A slight, quick inclination of her head saluted their arrival, and she went back to her work.

With the exception of Dov, the children were now young adults. Each of them removed his outerwear and then drew as close as possible to the fire, without bumping the others. Each rubbed his hands, attempting to bring life back into frozen fingers and palms.

With a nod from Joseph, all hand rubbing stopped. The men donned skullcaps and the women covered their heads with pieces of cloth. All faced south. With silent, moving lips and undulating movements of their bodies, they recited the evening prayers.

Their stomachs churning, they finished quickly and turned to Malka, who now cautiously lifted a single potato, steaming in its dark skin, from the pot. Using a knife, she sectioned the tuber into equal parts and placed one slice into each of eight rough-hewn wooden bowls. Then she carefully ladled equal portions of hot water from the pot into the eight bowls. Her final project was the sectioning of a fair-sized chunk of graying bread, on a cloth, into eight parts. Frieda assisted her mother, raising the edges of the cloth to catch the crumbs that flew off as the rocky-hard bread opposed the movement of the blade.

Joseph picked up a bowl of potato soup and a section of bread, including a few small, broken fragments. The children followed. Malka was the last to take her portion. Each then sat cross-legged, like Asiatics – men to one side, women to the other – eating the evening meal. Bread was dipped into bowls and savored like herring dipped in wine sauce. Legs were clamped tightly together to serve as tables and to keep so much as a crumb from falling to the floor. Eyes were sharp and allowed nothing to escape. The last piece of stony bread was kept to wipe the inside of the bowl spotlessly clean. The soggy graying piece, like the final delicacy of a sumptuous feast, was swallowed whole. Alas, their stomachs knew better and growled for more. But there was no more. They had finished the last of their allowance of food for the week and there was still one more day to go.

Moshe, having the largest of the wasted bodies in the room, also had the greatest hunger. The little meal slid into his large digestive system like a thimbleful of coal trying to sustain the furnace of an ocean liner. Since he was the eldest of the sons here in Siberia, he felt a need to assert himself, if only to buoy up their sagging spirits. "Mama," he began, attempting to smile some credulity into his words, "I don't know how you do it. The meal was delicious...and filling. A banquet with braised beef and kasha varnishkes couldn't taste better. I've got enough in me 'til after the Sabbath."

"Moshe," she replied, "the delicious – I won't say anything about, but the filling, the braised beef and the kasha varnishkes – your brain is working overtime. Next you'll be chewing wood and calling it roast chicken. You mean well, but from a potato you can only get a potato, with a smile or without it."

"So that's our last potato," said Joseph, looking up from his bowl. "We have nothing left for the Sabbath."

"That's not so," replied Malka, with an embarrassed smile on her face.

"But I'm certain," continued Joseph, "that one potato was all we had in the bin this morning."

Malka's eyes evaded those of her husband. She seemed to have difficulty getting out the words.

"W...we have two potatoes and a carrot that I put aside for tomorrow."

"Two potatoes? A carrot?" puzzled Moshe. "I haven't seen a carrot in months."

Malka squirmed uncomfortably. "I did some wash for the Russians."

"And they gave you a carrot and two potatoes for it?" questioned Chaya.

"Well..." Malka's eyes harbored a look of guilt.

"How'd you swipe them?" asked Dov, his eyes widening joyfully.

Malka blushed with decompTosure.

"Dov," scolded Moshe, "how can you say such a thing to Mama? I have a good mind to –"

"Let him be," interrupted Malka. "It's true. They didn't give me the food. You know how soldiers are. They drop a basket of clothes on the floor and say, 'Hey you, wash these. And make sure the uniforms are pressed. I want them back by this evening.' So I finished the wash and brought the things back to the soldiers' barracks. The kitchen door was open. There were bins filled with food...and we had nothing. I looked around. The room was empty. I thought, 'They have so much. Would they miss a carrot and two potatoes?' What can I say? I did it. May the Almighty forgive me."

"You could have been caught, Mama," shuddered Moshe. "Please be careful."

"I will," replied Malka sadly, her head bent low with shame.

The room was hushed and eyes stared blankly at the emptiness below.

"That's it," said Joseph, breaking the silence. "I must go to work. We can't live like this – the children sharing their rations with us, my wife and children having to steal, and even then not having enough to eat. I must do something or we'll all die."

"But Papa," pleaded Moshe, "you can't. You wouldn't survive a week out in the cold."

"No," insisted Joseph. "We can't go on this way."

There was silence. The father had spoken.

Then Avraham, whose eyes had been focused on an empty bowl, raised his head and addressed his father with calm and dispassion. "Papa, you can't."

They were all stunned. A son – not even the eldest son – had ever disagreed with his father and expressed that disagreement.

While the others remained speechless, Avraham went on. "I mean no disrespect, Papa, but even if you work in the forest in order to obtain a worker's ration, we would all eventually collapse anyway. Besides, no one your age can survive working at forty below. The last older man – and I believe that he was not even fifty – died out there today."

Joseph slowly regained his composure. Avraham's words, even if seemingly contradicting those of his father, made sense. And yet – they did not make sense. "And what do you propose that we do?" inquired the sage. "Starve slowly or lie down and die?"

"Neither," replied Avraham with his eyes growing intent. "I propose that I begin a one-man strike. I will demand a fair ration for those who work out in the cold, and sufficient food for the old and the infirm."

"What are you talking about?" scolded Moshe. "Where do you think you are? Do you believe that the Russians will tolerate a strike? You must be taking that 'land of the proletariat' nonsense seriously. Besides, you're on their troublemakers' list already. You're lucky they didn't shoot you for refusing to work on Yom Kippur. And I wouldn't be surprised if they knew all about our scheme for hiding wood all week and turning it in after sundown on Saturdays so that we can get our rations."

"That's the point," replied Avraham. "Why do you think they let us spend the day in prayer on Yom Kippur? Because everyone followed our lead. When all the people refused to work, they had two choices – punish us or let us pray. Now the Russians need wood. And there's a war on. The soldiers here have safe jobs, while their countrymen are being killed at the battlefront. There are no replacements for us, except the guards themselves, and they're not eager to work like horses in the freezing cold. So they figured that it was better to let us off one day a year and get on with the work.

"As for our not working on the Sabbath, if they knew that we are working extra hard other days and storing wood to hand in after sundown, they won't admit it, for to them, acknowledging that we do no work on the Sabbath is an acceptance of religion by a state that denies the Almighty. So we hide the wood and turn it in later, and they save face. In all this, they have shown that they are practical. That is why I believe they will increase our rations to the point where survival is possible. They will do that if they are convinced that there is no alternative."

"Avraham," interrupted his father, "you speak with the wisdom of a scholar. Your years at the yeshiva in Krakow were not for naught. But where do you expect the Major to get the extra food? There's a war going on back in Europe, a war to the death. Do you think the Russian government will give in to a few hundred Jews in Siberia?"

"Not the Russian government, Papa. They won't know anything about it. The camp commander will furnish the food. As for where he'll get it – they have it already. I've watched the goings on here carefully. The camp is supplied with several times as much food as we receive. They give us crumbs and much of the rest is sold on the black market. That is, after they've taken more than enough for their own consumption."

"Just a minute," interrupted Moshe. "How can you talk of a black market? There isn't a city or even a village within miles of here. Where could the

Major or any of his subordinates sell anything? And what proof do you have for this allegation?"

"Do you remember last summer when Dov tried to escape from the camp by hiding in the ship when it was about to leave?" replied Avraham. They caught him then and brought him back. They locked him up for a day to 'teach him a lesson.' And what did Dov do? Instead of saying he was sorry and promising never to do it again, he told the Major that they might have to lock him up forever because he would try it again, the first chance he got. He told the Major he would never give up trying to run away no matter what the punishment, because it was better to die trying to escape than to slowly starve to death. He said that there was simply not enough to eat and he would not continue to work under those conditions."

"So what has this to do with the black market?" interrupted Moshe.

"I'm trying to make a point," began Avraham, again. "Now you would have expected the Russians to treat him harshly after that, if only to set an example. He was still a boy, but who says that the Russians are so sympathetic to Jewish children? Now what did they do instead? They increased his ration. And since it would not seem right to everyone else that a mere child receive more food than his elders – especially as an apparent reward for an attempt to escape – everyone's ration was increased. How did the Major come up with more food? Do you think that he wrote to Moscow requesting additional supplies for us? Absurd. If a camp commander so much as mentioned to his superiors that he was faced with unrest that could be quelled only by increasing food allotments, he would promptly receive his orders to the battlefront. So the Major would never do something like that... I believe that he chose another approach. In order to increase our rations, he had to have food available – food that was being shipped to the camp, but not previously distributed to us. That's my mental proof number one. Call it logic. Call it intuition. I call it deductive reasoning.

"Now you may say, 'What makes you think he would increase rations again even if he has more food available? And what causes you to conclude that the additional food exists here in Vierchne Baraki?' This is my answer. When the vessel carrying food to the camp arrives, the Major goes down to the ship. We arrive with four wagons. One wagon carries back all the items intended for several hundred Jews, two, for the fifty guards, and one, for the Major. Several soldiers guard a work party of Jews that accompany the Major. Only the Major goes down into the hole of the ship. We remain on deck while the Russian sailors bring sacks of flour and wheat, crates of fruit and vegetables – yes, I said crates of fruit and vegetables – cartons of salt, bags of sugar, and even huge chests of chickens on deck. From there, we carry the load, under the observant eye of the Russian guards, back to camp where the entire amount of food is deposited in the warehouse. We, of course, never see any of the fruit and hardly any of the vegetables. The Russians keep them for themselves, along with the chickens, which we can do without, leaving scraps for us." (Avraham refers to the fact that the chickens shipped to the camp were non-kosher. Hence, their religious laws forbade him and the other Orthodox Jews to eat such poultry.) "And now I come to the wagonload intended for the Major: There are fruits and vegetables in abundance, but there are also sealed boxes. What's in them? Food doesn't come in sealed boxes."

"Really," interrupted Moshe, again. "So you tell us that the fifty Russian guards receive more food than a few hundred Jews. And the Major, one man, takes for himself as much as he allows for several hundred Jews. Are you surprised? Do you think the Russians are going to share anything with us? That generous, they're not! And besides, what has all this to do with a black market?"

"Wait, Moshe," began Avraham, again, "there's more. I agree with you. I believe that it is not simply a matter of the Russian guards eating food intended for us. I am reasonably sure that much, perhaps even most of the food intended for this camp, is never unloaded, and that it remains on the ship, to be sold later on the return trip to Omsk. I believe that the Major knows this and benefits from it. I believe, in fact, that the Major is a key figure in this diversion of our food to the black market."

"Accusations," commented Joseph, shaking his head. "But nothing more than that."

"No, Papa, more than that. Remember I said that the Major goes down into the hole of the ship alone? The guards and we remain behind. Remember I said that the sailors carry everything that is brought from the hole of the ship to the deck? We do not.

"I asked myself, 'Why should this be so? Why should sailors relieve us of the burden of carrying those heavy items up from below deck?' Do they fear we would steal something? But the guards watch our every movement. And we could just as easily, or with just as much difficulty, steal food on our way back to camp or from the warehouse in which it is stored. No. There has to be a better answer. So this is my reasoning. There are things in the hole of the vessel, which they do not want us to see. It could not be weapons, for this is the last stop before turning back. If they had intended to deliver weapons, they would have transferred them to the designated recipients long before the ship arrived at Vierchne Baraki. So it must be food. Yes, food – food intended for us, but not delivered. The Major goes below deck, directs the sailors to bring up certain items and leave the rest behind. The ship's master then negotiates with the Major for the purchase of the remainder and he pays him for it. Then the vessel departs, carrying away our sustenance to be sold downstream, in the cities, on the black market. And so we slave and starve for the profit of others."

"But proof," insisted Joseph.

"Proof! Proof! The proof is in my mind. The Major always tarries when we leave the ship. He arrives back in camp sometime later, with a grin on his face, like a cat that has just swallowed a bird – our nourishment. Now why should he delay his return? He stays to go over the remaining cargo, item by item, and to negotiate the price of the sale."

"Still, that's not proof," insisted Moshe.

"So let me go further," said Avraham. "I have had a conversation with Nashumah, one of Jews in the camp. For five extra potatoes, she cleans the Major's house each week. From time to time she notices something new in his house, like a beautiful lamp. And there are cases of vodka. Do you think that a Russian army officer's pay is sufficient to buy cases of vodka or a fine lamp? But now for the final evidence: The Major has a locked safe in his bedroom. Well, one day the door to it was closed, but not locked. As she was cleaning the handle, the door opened. Inside the safe were bundles of rubles, thousands of rubles. And there was a small wooden box. Curious, she opened the box for an instant. It contained a few diamonds. Quickly, she closed the box and the safe, taking pains to make sure that everything looked the same as when she arrived. So how do you think the Major acquired all that money and jewelry? By selling some of the food intended for us on the black market!"

"And suppose," said Joseph, "you are right in every detail. What can you do about it? Confront him with your accusation? That would hardly seem wise."

"I agree, Papa," replied Avraham. "It would not be wise. I would never mention the word 'black market.' The Soviets treat any theft of government property harshly – as harshly as others treat murder. The Major would then have to deal with what he perceives to be a menace. To the military mind, death to the enemy is the answer to everything."

"So," wondered Joseph aloud, "what have you accomplished in all this? You present us with a very serious problem, but no solution."

"Not so, Papa. Here is my plan –" With an inward wave of his hand, Avraham beckoned his family to draw closer, just in case someone outside was listening. All remained silent, nodding approval at intervals during the next hour. Avraham's golden sidecurls flopped back and forth with the punctuated movements of his head as he went through his scheme. At the end, Avraham halted and looked to his father, awaiting approval.

Joseph sat mute, his face serious and thoughtful. He grasped his bearded chin firmly, twisting it as if to emphasize his inner turmoil. His head turned toward the window and he peered intently at the flickering celestial bodies, as if seeking approval from some unseen power, while his body swayed back and forth in a rhythmic pattern.

At last the twisting and the swaying and the search through the heavens ended. He faced his golden-haired son, the new sage of the family, with a question on his lips.

"Avraham, would it not be better if all of our family joined you in this? Perhaps we could even get everyone in the camp to follow your lead. That would place additional pressure on the Russians."

"No, Papa," he replied firmly, yet with a voice soft enough to convey respect. "If the Major is faced with a seeming revolt, he may react wildly, like a cornered animal. Then he might do something that, while it would prove harmful to him, would be disastrous to us. So it is best that I do it alone. Facing a mildly threatening wind and not a sky-darkening tornado, he might respond with less passion and more caution, taking the measure of the draft before smashing all the windows and doors of his defenses. That is our only chance."

He hesitated for a moment, his eyes darkening, and then went on: "And in the event that my plan fails, it is better that only one of us is destroyed."

The room was deadly still. It was so seemingly obvious, yet the words struck them like a deadly thunderbolt. For even though they tread daily in the shadow of death – lives being snuffed out with fiendish regularity by forces beyond their control – they still clung to the belief that all of the family would survive. The mere mention of "destruction" being visited upon a son and brother sent paralyzing electrical charges through their bodies.

Joseph broke the benumbing spell with a chant. "May the Almighty protect you as he did Daniel in the den of the lions, and look with favor on your undertaking." (The prophet Daniel is in the *Book of Daniel* in the Bible.)

Avraham stood uncomfortably in the cheerless, gray room, shifting his weight from one foot to the other and then back. His keen, searching eyes studied the walls and the furnishings. A large, framed portrait dominated the room. The golden-haired young man recognized the face as belonging to the Soviet dictator, Joseph Stalin. The kindly, fatherly look of the man in the picture, dressed in the dark uniform of a Russian officer, seemed to belie all that Avraham had heard about the "Terror from Georgia" (a republic within the Soviet Union and the birthplace of Joseph Stalin).

His gaze shifted from the portrait to a plain, dark-brown wooden desk that stood before it. Only an ink well and a few sheets of paper rested atop the table, whose surface was scarred and grooved from indifferent use. Avraham had seen it before – never out of desire – and here he was again...waiting, thinking...

The sound of a door opening interrupted his thoughts. He turned to see a Russian guard click his heels together and salute as the commanding officer entered. The soldier, obeying a flip of the wrist that he took to be his major's command, exited.

The officer removed his hat and warm outer coat and hung them on a simple coat stand near the door. Then he strode across the room with paced steps, glancing fleetingly at Avraham, until he reached an old armchair with worn edges that stood behind the desk. The Major sat down and remained uncommunicative, while thumbing through the papers on his desk and signing a few with a quick scrawl. Then he tucked the papers into a small drawer. The officer leaned his chair back on its hind legs, against the wall. He stretched and crossed his legs on the table before him. The heels of his dark brown boots fitted neatly into the worn grooves.

The officer bore little resemblance to any picture of a military hero waiting to receive a medal. His graying sandy hair was long and unkempt. His cheeks were puffed and rounded – the product of time spent at the dinner table rather than in combat. His abdomen was corpulent, too corpulent for crawling under barbed wire or across a battlefield where shells whistled overhead. His boots appeared not to have received a coat of polish since they first clothed his feet.

He appeared satisfied with his job – content to play the role of a self-indulgent slob who avoided anything that hinted of work, filling his stomach over-abundantly while others slaved in bitter cold and withered for lack of food. He seemed happy, sitting back with his boots on the table, interrogating a defenseless Jew, while millions of his countrymen were gripped in a life and death struggle against a real enemy. Yet, not everything in his appearance smelled of evil. There was annoyance in his eyes, but not flamed anger. He was soft and flabby and appeared to lack the killer instinct; so common among those who had become administrators instead of fighters.

Avraham took all this in through perceptive eyes that did not cower before the reflective glare of the red star on the commandant's uniform. Still, there was a hint of irritation in the Jew's face, which, except for his eyes, appeared like a cloak that concealed his inner thoughts.

"Very well," began the Major rhetorically, "what is it now? Can't you keep out of trouble? When your little brother began this kind of nonsense

– well, he's a child – but you're a man, at least you pretend to be by growing a beard and telling us what to do. Where do you think you are? Now get back to work and stop all this foolishness before I really get angry at you."

"Major," replied Avraham in a modulated voice, "I have not gone around stirring up trouble. It simply is this. I have thought over the problem carefully and have come to the conclusion that unless something is done quickly, this camp will be in grave trouble. That difficulty would reflect adversely – unfair as it may seem – on its commandant, with unhappy consequences for a fine officer."

The Major raised his eyebrows with puzzlement and vexation.

"What do you mean – 'trouble for me?'" he sneered. "Do you think that anything you do can harm me? Why, I can snuff you out like a candle. I can extinguish your flame with my two fingers."

"No, Major. I have not made myself clear. I mean you no harm, heaven forbid it. I wish to assist the Russian war effort by providing the brave Red Army with the wood it so desperately needs. I recognize that if things do not change, this camp will fail to meet its quota. It is because of this that I am using this most unseemly vehicle to bring the problem to your attention. I want us to fulfill our task. I want you to get the credit you so richly deserve for that success."

"Hmm…" thought the officer aloud. "You surprise me. I keep thinking there's a trick up your sleeve. You people are a shifty bunch. I warn you, I will not tolerate any of your nonsense. Well, what is it that you think will help me?"

"Major, I have watched our output of tree sections daily for the past eighteen months. During the last two months that output has declined, although no one outside the camp knows this or will know this until spring, when the river thaws and the logs go floating downstream to the mills.

"I asked myself, 'Why?' The answer became all too clear. We started out then with 500 workers   . Now we're down to 210 workers. As men and women fell through cold and hunger, the others had their workload increased, so as to keep total production the same. They can no longer continue to make up for the lost workers. And if something is not done quickly, the output will further decline 'til we reach a point where, even with the assistance of all the heroic Russian soldiers here in camp with us, our efforts will fall short.

"What a tragedy that would be. High-ranking officers, who spend the winter in well-heated offices somewhere in the brightly lit, big city, will then be coming here to demand an explanation. I hear that fine, brave officers have been transferred to the front or, even worse, shot as an example to their brother officers that orders must be carried out. How unjust! Now I have some suggestions to make that would save this camp to the credit of our illustrious leader." Avraham halted to allow his words to sink in.

During the Jew's discourse, the Major had sat up, removing his legs from atop the desk. His elbows now rested on the desk, below hands cupped to support his jaw. He was all ears, waiting for Avraham to continue.

"Well," he said impatiently, "go on."

"This is what I have in mind," began Avraham again. The officer slid back on his seat and resumed an attentive posture. "Our workers are dying off from the cold, but mostly for lack of food. They need more food – much more food than they are getting now – if they are to continue to harvest trees or even survive long enough to finish the job. So we must double their food allowance."

"What!" interrupted the captain, angrily. "Can't be done!"

"Please, hear me out – I said that we must double the food allowance. And now as to the old and sick here at Vierchne Baraki – they must have more food too, thrice the few scraps they're getting now. A cat couldn't survive on their present allowance."

"Avraham," shouted the Major, "you're mad! Give more food to parasites? Never! Let them get out and do some work, or else let them die."

"Please, Major, I had work in mind for them. We need at least 200 able-bodied men and women out there to do the work required of this camp. We have, at most, 180 such people in the camp, plus thirty older men and women who would collapse before the week is out if they tried to work out there at forty below. But we have fifty Russian soldiers – big, powerful men in perfect shape for cutting down trees and dragging them to the river.

"Now, we're out here in Siberia, 2,000 miles from the German front and near the Chinese on the other side of impassible mountains. They have no desire or even the ability to attack the Soviet Union. So why do we need fifty soldiers standing around, doing nothing but waiting for an enemy that does not exist? The people in this camp are not violent criminals or captured German soldiers. They are Jews who want to see the Nazis defeated. And they have as much or even more reason than you do to see the German army crushed. They don't need guards to motivate them. So let our Russian comrades join us in the work. As for what the soldiers are doing now – keeping an eye on the warehouse, waiting for the phone to ring at headquarters, tidying up the barracks and doing the laundry – let the old and infirm attend to those duties.

"With our workers well fed, and with the emotional and physical support of our Russian brothers – no disrespect intended – we will make up the deficit and have our quota ready by spring."

"Have you finished?" asked the officer, acidly. "Do you expect me to have my soldiers working like common laborers? And do you expect me to leave the warehouse unguarded? Besides, where do you expect me to get all this food from – or are you a magician too?"

"Major, the food presents no problem. Really. We had, including the elderly, 500 people in camp when I came here. Since your superiors expect us to meet the same production goal, they must assume that we have the same population and hence the same food needs. But there are only 210 laborers, as you call them, here now. Logically it would be quite simple to increase the rations by at least as much as I have suggested, and even more, from what is being shipped in now.

"As for the soldiers working – this is a Communist state, as I'm sure you recognize. The Soviet people take pride in performing labor. Soldiers should not separate themselves from the masses. Isn't that what Lenin taught? It is good for your men to feel part of the proletariat. Besides, it will keep their bodies in shape, just in case they ever get into battle.

"Last, we get to the guarding of the warehouse. I agree that it is dangerous to trust anyone, unchecked, with all that food. I recommend that an inventory be kept of everything in the warehouse. It should be checked at each change in shift to see to it that none is stolen. I know how serious a crime theft of government property is in the Soviet Union. Let us also record all distributions in a log to see to it that everyone in the camp gets his or her fair share.

"I realize that your soldiers may not be happy with the still modest rations I propose we all receive. I have an idea that might just solve that problem. I have come to know you as a clever leader and marveled at how you get men to follow your lead through your powers of persuasion. You are friendly with the master of the supply ship. Now, if you could use your brilliant mind to induce him to give us more food, there would be more for everyone. And, in such an instance, I would feel it only fair that you receive at least a token of appreciation for your efforts, say an extra chicken or two, some fruit for your table, some meat – if you could obtain it – and even a bottle of vodka. After all, a leader who sees to it that all those under his command are adequately clothed and fed has earned the respect of his followers and should, to please them, accept the humble gift they offer him as a mark of their esteem."

He paused and then added, "One more thought. Think of the alternative. Unless we meet the quota that was set for this camp, your superiors will be down on your neck and there's no point in getting unpleasant. Why, when I think of all those purges, I shudder."

The Major sat back, thinking hard of many things – rubles, a nest egg for the future and, finally, his neck. He quivered. "Is there anything else you have to suggest?" he asked sarcastically.

"Well, it's bitter cold out there. Numb hands are slower to work. A pair of gloves for each of the men and women harvesting trees would improve production considerably."

"What! And where do you think I'm going to get all those gloves?"

"Major, I can see that you and the ship's master get along well together. A nice word from you and, perhaps, a bottle or two of vodka could work wonders. And remember, when we exceed quota, you may be in line for a promotion to colonel."

"Gloves! Vodka! What else have you dreamed up?"

"Well, I hadn't planned to mention it, but as long as you are asking – yes, one more thing. People work better if they have a day of rest, a formal day of rest. In fact, they can do much more work in six days than they can in seven, provided that they get a day off. Let us each choose one day of rest – we Jews, on Saturday, you Russians, whichever day you prefer."

"Very well, get on with it before you come up with any more suggestions. But I'd better see results."

"You will," nodded Avraham, smiling within.

RETURN TO THE LAND

"Well, what is it now?" demanded the captain. "Do you people love Siberia so much that you want to stay here permanently?" His question was aimed at Avraham Ausübel, but his eyes were directed towards the river.

Before them lay a steamer. It was docked at the river's edge, waiting for the human cargo to board. The vessel's master tooted the ship's whistle impatiently. Some of the sailors stood at the rail, gazing in half-amusement at the mass of bearded men in their tattered garments, haggard-looking women whose gaunt faces were partially hidden beneath patched and frayed kerchiefs, and children with sullen, anxious faces atop dwarfed bodies. There stood this band of Jews after two years of forced labor in the icy north, holding tightly to one another and resisting all efforts to get them onto the ship.

Avraham's face was serious.

"They want to go all right," he responded, "but they do not want to be separated from their loved ones. If you do not have enough room for all, then take them according to family."

"Well, if that's all they want..." laughed the Russian officer.

An hour later, the Ausübels were aboard the vessel, sailing down the Ob. Joseph and Avraham stood at the rail, taking one last look at Vierchne Baraki. Ahead of them, the sun was retreating in the west leaving a darkening sky behind. Illuminated by the fading rays of sunlight, their faces were somber, devoid of any hint of cheer. They looked back at the snow-covered mountainside stripped of its trees. It looked like a massive unshaven chin with its rows of stumps projecting like stubble above the powdery surface. The mountain that had stood so green two years before, with its majestic fir trees towering upward, was now despoiled of its beauty and left without a shield against the elements.

As they looked back, they remembered. There was the cold that never left their bones, day and night. They remembered the dead lying out there all winter, against all Jewish tradition, to be uncovered by the melting warmth of the spring sun and found – unchanged. (By Jewish tradition, the dead must be buried within twenty-four hours of their death or one day later if it falls on the Sabbath.) There was the look of the faces of the dead – the glassy eyes that would not be shut even by death, and the silent, rigid lips that seemed to cry out to an unanswering sky. How could they ever forget that? And they remembered burying the dead when spades could at last break the ground. They had hoped to finally put the dead to rest, but could rest ever really come to the living who remembered such events?

"Papa," asked Avraham with a puzzled, sad look, "why did we come here? I mean here rather than some place downstream?"

The old man's face tilted downward toward the water that now was black as night, except for a streak of reflective moonlight. "I thought...it was closer."

"Closer to where? China?" Avraham had difficulty understanding his father's words.

"Closer for the return...to Palestine. There's only one place for us. We can never return to Lacejsk or anywhere else in Galicia, or anywhere in Europe. It is a graveyard, all of it, Lacejsk, Lemberg, and Vierchne Baraki. Simcha is safe in Palestine. Dov is safe in Teheran and will join his brother as soon as he can. So it took Anders to get one of us to safety. And we – I had hoped that if we were closer to the border, we might somehow get across it and down to Palestine. But the mountains were too tall and forbidding. But we didn't lose everything. We're still alive and somehow, I pray, we'll find Itzhak and Sabina and their families. But I no longer have the strength. You and your brother will have to lead us. Look to the south, to warmth, to Palestine." (General Wladyslaw Anders was a Polish officer who organized a Polish brigade in Russia. Many Polish children, mostly Jewish children, were sent to safety in Iran.)

The steamer reached its final destination and the passengers alighted. They were mostly Jews from camps in Siberia, but there were also a few young Russian soldiers heading to the front. There were no guards to keep the Jews in line. The Soviet Union was now too busy fighting for its survival to pay much attention to the millions of refugees who roamed across its land. A few, like those leaving the vessel that day, were headed westward. But most of the wanderers, dazed and exhausted, were running towards the east. They were trying to put as much distance as possible between themselves and the horrors of a war in which no quarter was given. Having fled a land of exploding shells and scorched earth, even the ice of Siberia appeared inviting to them.

Omsk was the city they had tramped through just two years before, on their way from the choking, sealed boxcars to the ship that took them into the valley of darkness. And yet, the city was changed. No longer was it a quiet river port on the way to nowhere. It was now a bustling communication center, a connecting link between the east and the west. Thousands were crowding its streets. Some marched assertively. Others were just standing or waiting for something: for news, for food or for the unknown to happen.

The Ausübels did not have a *kopeck* between them and it became rapidly apparent that in Communist Siberia no one gave you anything for nothing. They had to plan their next move. Since Palestine was their goal, south was their only direction. Tashkent, in the land of the Uzbeks, looked appealing on the map.

"Now what do we trade for tickets?" wondered Joseph, aloud. The answer came out of his pocket – a dark metal case which, when rubbed turned like a Persian lamp into shining silver. He looked fondly at the magnificent workmanship, the intricately carved figures of blossoms that stood out in relief on the watchcase he held caressingly in his hand. "My grandfather's great-grandfather's watch: 200 years of memories and now to be converted into railroad tickets." He looked up to Moshe and extended his arm. The watch was there in the open palm. "Here, take it to the station. Find out the cost of eight tickets to Tashkent and then trade the watch for at least enough rubles to pay for them. We'll wait here."

An hour later, Moshe returned, smiling, and handed the heirloom back to his father.

"What's there to laugh about? Wasn't the watch case valuable enough to cover the cost of eight tickets?"

"Better than that," replied Moshe. "I got eight tickets to Bukhara which is closer to Palestine."

"But how?" asked Malka, unable to believe what she had heard.

"The ticket-seller looked at the silver watch case and said that he wouldn't give me five rubles 'for that piece of tin.' But he spied that huge, ugly monster of a watch that I have. You know – the one that has that mouse from America on it. For that piece of junk, he offered me eight tickets to Bukhara and twenty rubles more. I'm certain there's no silversmith in his family."

They all laughed a hearty laugh. The laughter would have continued, were it not for their fear of attracting attention.

"We're leaving in an hour," announced Moshe. "Quick, let's get our belongings down to the station."

Compared with the bustling Omsk, Bukhara was quite small. Still, it was larger than any city in Galicia with the exception of Krakow. But its streets were mostly unpaved and the houses, for the most part, were one- and two-story drab wooden dwellings that had never seen paint. Almost all the inhabitants were Mongol in appearance. They had beardless faces that needed no razors, almond eyes that scrutinized foreigners carefully, and sturdy bodies that mirrored ancestors who had galloped, in hordes, across two continents.

There were no welcome signs out anywhere. It seemed that no one in Bukhara had ever thought of renting rooms to travelers. The streets and the alleys were the only lodging places for wayfarers. Fortunately, it was summer and an occasional evening breeze made sleep possible. They had to pay inflated prices for the little food available for sale, and so, in a few days their pockets were nearly empty.

A notice was posted in the city square. "All Jews who wish to go to Palestine, register at City Hall." Joseph could not believe his eyes. How simple! How miraculous! In the middle of a frightful war, someone was looking after the scattered Hebrew people and endeavoring to return them to their ancient homeland.

By afternoon, all the Ausübels were waiting in line, along with more than a hundred fellow Jews. Like ants attracted by the scent of a piece of cake, these Jews had emerged from their hiding places. The Russian bureaucrats at the city hall all seemed polite and concerned. They asked questions such as "What is your name? Where are you from? Where are you staying? Show me your papers."

The Jews had been conditioned by adverse experiences in the past. And so they were ordinarily wary of any stranger. This was especially true of Soviet officials. But the questions, now posed by the Soviet officials, were being asked so naturally and with such seeming compassion that the Hebrews responded readily and held nothing back. "Just wait in this room," said the official, reassuringly, "together with the rest of your family. I would not want you separated from the others."

"I wouldn't have believed it if I hadn't seen it with my own eyes," said the smiling Joseph to his family, after the door was shut.

"I'll believe it when I see Palestine," muttered Avraham.

The smile vanished from the sage's face and his cheeks paled with apprehension. "Nothing we can do now," the father added. "What will be, will be."

A few hours later they were led to the railroad station, along with some of the other Jews. There they boarded a train. The interior of the car was spartan, but at least there were some seats. The women sat; the men stood.

Two hours later, the engine whooshed to a halt. The Ausübels emerged, not in the Promised Land, not at some port with a ship waiting dockside, but in a sea of green plants stretching as far as the eye could see.

The purpose of those notices in Bukhara Central Square became apparent to them in the next few weeks. It had been used as a device to round up "parasites" and put them to work where the state had use for their services.

The Ausübels were now cotton-pickers in Telma, situated somewhere in the Uzbek Soviet Socialist Republic. When the cotton crop did not require all their attention, they picked peanuts. By day, the sun beat down on their sweat-soaked bodies as they labored in the fields. Still, it was better than the icy, numbing cold of the Altay Mountains. They now had a home of their own; a three-room house made of earth and wood and covered with a roof of straw.

"We did not come all this way to become Russian farmers," said Joseph, firmly, one day. "We must keep moving south."

At last, the harvest was over. There was now no need for all the man-power and so they were permitted to leave.

Leninabad, in Tadzhkstan, was a modest-sized city. It was drab, like every other city they had seen in Siberia, but magnificent, snow-covered mountains surrounded this one. They walked through the dirt-covered street in front of the station and studied the shops and the faces.

"Avraham! Avraham Ausübel!" came out of nowhere.

They all looked around, apprehensively.

"Leibel Wexler," shouted Avraham, dropping his bag as a smiling, robust man with open arms rushed towards him. "How did you get to this place from Krakow?"

"I could ask the same of you," was the glad reply.

Excited greetings were exchanged. This was followed by introductions to the other members of the Ausübel family. Leibel led them to his quarters, and he promptly insisted on sharing them with his guests. It was a two-room apartment with a kitchen in one of the rooms. Leibel introduced the newcomers to his brothers, Lazar and David, and to Chaim, the husband of his late sister.

Twelve shared a meal, intended for four. Still, it was more than Joseph and his family had eaten in months. Their stomachs puffed with delight at being filled as they had not been filled in so long.

"Excuse me if I seem too inquisitive," began Joseph, "but all this... I mean where did you get such food here in Russia? What kind of work do you do?

"A little of this, a little of that," replied Leibel. "We're in the leather business. But, if a Russian major has some extra food – say fifty bags of potatoes – I find customers. He gives me a few potatoes as a sort of finder's fee. People need papers – they want to go somewhere. The governor can supply papers for a price, but he does not like to have personal contact with these people. I arrange the transaction and the governor gives me a few rubles. With a little of this and a little of that, we get along."

"I wonder," began Joseph, again. "Is it possible to ship a package through your contacts? We don't have much money; in fact, hardly any. But Itzhak, my oldest son, is in European Russia. I have gotten word of his location. He has a wife and two small children. They are worse off than we are. Would it be possible to send them a package? It might help keep them alive."

"Consider it your first commission," laughed Leibel.

"Commission?" puzzled Joseph.

"Certainly," said the jovial Leibel. "We're all partners. We work together, we share together. We'll sleep in the kitchen and you all can have the bedroom. After all, the women need their privacy. Besides, I'm sure that your wife is a better cook than David. He knows how to boil potatoes and carrots, but not much more."

Miriam sat on a worn, old chair, facing a mirror that had lost much of its reflective surface to cracks. There were silvery condensations on its surface that looked like giant immobile tears. They distorted her image, reduced its clarity and removed the lines of deprivation and anxiety from her face. Miriam imagined that she saw the face of her youth, the little girl in Lacejsk, there in the shattered glass.

Hearing footsteps, she turned. Her mother had just returned from the kitchen after completing preparations for what seemed an unusually large evening meal. Miriam said softly, "Mama, would you comb my hair...like you did when I was a little girl?"

Astonishment was the mother's initial reaction, but it gave way to a sweet, reflective smile, to memories long suppressed in a turbulent world that knew only survival or death, food and warmth or starvation and numbing cold, a universe from which even the thought of beauty had vanished.

"Sure," replied Malka. "Dinner's ready...and I have a comb, perhaps a few teeth missing, but still a comb."

She hunted through a bag of odd objects – a few buttons, a scissor with the points broken off, several spools of thread and a comb, broken, distorted, but a comb nevertheless.

Malka stroked her daughter's long, fine hair that had for so long been hidden beneath a drab cap to avoid attracting attention from those who might do her harm. Alas, the gold had faded into a dull brown; the treasure of Miriam's youth had sunk beneath the sands of time and had been washed away by the relentless waves of adversity. But for the moment, Malka, too, was caught up in that vision of the past that was just a few years, and yet, a millennium ago.

Miriam studied her past self in a broken mirror and Malka imagined it in the strands of hair that now shimmered in the candlelight. Malka sang a tune from the past, of a rabbi teaching little children in the village.

"Mama," asked Miriam when the lyric ended, "will you miss Lacejsk...? I mean not going back to it?"

Malka paused for a minute, holding the comb aloft. The question had taken her by surprise. Then she replied, "No."

"But, Mama, didn't you like it there?"

"Like it? What does it matter? I liked Rozwadow well enough too, I guess. When I married your father, we were living there. We scrimped and we saved and we built a house in that town. But it all went up in smoke in the first war, not because of the shells and the bullets, but because of the hate. So the Russians drove us out of Rozwadow and burnt our homes to the ground. Papa was away in the army and I had to flee with Itzhak and Simcha and Sabina, all the way to Vienna. When the war ended, Papa and I returned to Rozwadow to start all over again. Some said Lacejsk might be a better place in which to do business. They, too, were rebuilding from the ashes of their ruins. So we moved to Lacejsk.

"And we struggled, and we built a house and a store. And we had, thanks to the Almighty, a family – nine beautiful children. Lacejsk was a nice enough place all right...in the good days. But you would never know when it wouldn't be such a good day. You could never tell when the bad day was coming, when someone suddenly might take a disliking to us, to the Jews, and then puff – beards cut off, men beaten, women... It's too horrible to mention. It could be anything – an Easter sermon, a missing pail of milk, or a missing child.

"When troubles arose in Lacejsk and the Jews were blamed for it, we returned to Papa's hometown, Rozwadow. Then the animals came back – this time the Germans – to drive us out and to demolish our homes. 'And don't come back!' they shouted as they chased us into the river. If that ferry had not come, who knows how many more would have perished. So they beat us and they drove us because of their hate. So what do we have to go back to in Lacejsk or Rozwadow – the hate?"

The comb was still. Her hand clenched it so that the teeth were digging into her palm. It was as if the torment of recollection had numbed her body to the perception of pains of the flesh. Her body shook with the anguish of her thoughts. She would have continued, but the words died, stillborn, on her lips.

She sought to calm her racing heart.

"Papa's right," she began again. "We'll go to Palestine – if the Almighty wills it – and start anew in our own land."

The words acted as a tonic to the sickness of her spirit and she began to comb and smooth her daughter's hair again. She started to hum once more a village tune from the past, as she returned, for the moment, to the pleasures of the past, combing the fine locks that covered little Miriam's head.

"Mama," interrupted Miriam, softly, "how old were you when you married Papa?"

"As old as you are now," the mother smiled.

"What's going to happen to me?" wondered the daughter, aloud. "I'm eighteen years old and we've been running from place to place. My hair is turning brown and my cheeks are sinking in and losing their color. I mean, who's going to want to marry me? I might be too old by the time all this ends."

"Miriam, Miriam, do you think I was born an old woman with a *sheitl*? Do you think I have forgotten what it is to be young with the worries of the young? You've got plenty of time to get married. And don't worry. A little nourishment and you'll fill out just fine. With the world being the way it is, we're all lucky to still be alive. When we get to Palestine, there'll be lots of Jewish boys standing in line, trying to make a match with Papa. In the meantime, keep your head covered and your face plain. We don't want to attract – perish the thought – any hooligans who might do you harm.

"But enough of this. There's good news. I want you to help me set the table. There'll be one more for dinner. Your brother, Itzhak, will be here. Papa is meeting him at the synagogue and they'll come home together."

Miriam's face bubbled with excitement.

"You see," said Malka, "you've got to have faith. We were separated twice and yet we all survived. And now, miraculously, we'll all be together again, except for Dov who's safe in Teheran, and Simcha who's safe in Palestine. Who could have imagined, when we fled Rozwadow in the night, that we'd find your brothers and sisters in Lemberg? And then a second miracle happened. We survived the two years in Vierchne Baraki while so many were dying all around us. And now, after being transplanted from one end of the globe to another, a third miracle. The merciful One, blessed be His name, brought your brother Itzhak to us.

"Your father has that faith. He prays every day – morning, afternoon and evening – and his prayers have been answered. If the Almighty saw fit to bring us through all that has happened to us, do you think He would have trouble finding you a husband?"

Joseph sat alone in the little synagogue of Leninabad. The room was simple and spartan, with several rows of backless, wooden benches facing a Holy Ark of olive wood. The poverty of the Jewish community, along with the restrictions placed by the Soviet authorities, would not allow for more elaborate furnishings.

His days at the synagogue had enabled Joseph to learn much about the Jewish community here. There had been Jews in these mountains for as far back as any recorded settlement at all, from the days of the Khazars and even before. (The Khazars were a Turkish people from Asia who migrated across Siberia to Russia. Their rulers converted to Judaism in the eighth century.) These Jews did not speak Yiddish or Ladino. They were not Ashkenazim (Yiddish-speaking Jews of Northern Europe) or Sephardim (descendants of the survivors of the expulsion from Spain in 1492 who spoke Ladino). They were Jews who had been isolated from the rest of world Jewry, save for the turmoil of a world at war, which brought co-religionists from the west flee-ing to their city. The Jews here were so poor and the curbs placed on them by the authorities so great, that there was but one prayer book for the whole congregation. These Jews committed the *siddur* to memory, but they would all look to the sole prayer book held up high by one of the congregants dur-ing the service.

The door opened and Joseph's eyes lit up as he viewed the raw-boned face of his eldest son. Itzhak was but a shadow of the young man he last saw in Lemberg. Deep, dark sockets ringed with lines of misery were recessed behind a taut, shiny nose. Hollow cheeks merged with a dark beard. His clothes were old and threadbare, intended for a man of larger dimensions than those of its wasted occupant. Still in all, it was his son, alive and able to make the trip all the way to Tadzhikstan.

They embraced one another and exchanged a hundred excited ques-tions about the trip and loved ones, long separated. After half-an-hour or so, they sat down on a bench, exhausted from the excitement of a joyous reunion.

"When the evening service is over," instructed Joseph, "you'll come home with me for dinner. You'll stay with us, of course. Mama can't wait to see you. Two years here can seem forever. As for quarters, our room can fit nine as well as eight.

"Did you get the packages we sent you – three in all? I was so ex-cited when I heard where you were. You know, it was quite by accident that we learned where you were. I was just exchanging questions and answers with people in the synagogue, always hoping, but never knowing. Then, one day, a man said he had seen you during his travels. It was in the syna-gogue in Bukhara that we had that exchange. Bukhara is in another province altogether. Strange are the ways of the Lord. So we wrote and you replied. Then Leibel Wexler – he and his family took us in here in Leninabad – showed us how to get a package to you."

"Yes, we got all three packages and they really were like manna from heaven. The children were starving and Batia was so skinny and weak; it was terrible." He paused for a moment and then asked, "So what do you do here to stay alive?"

"We manage. What can I say? We do things we would never have dreamed of – sell on the black market, take a commission from Russian officials for bringing in Jews who are prepared to pay heavily for papers to get from one place to another. There's no dignity to it, but that's how we were able to get money to buy things. That's how we got the packages to you. It goes against my grain, but we do it to survive."

"I know what you mean, Papa... Say, have you tried writing to your brothers? Maybe they could send help. They're rich and could certainly spare it."

"Judah in America, Shulum in Australia. I don't think I could get any mail through to them. The boys have already asked their Russian contacts and were told it is impossible now. But why do you say they're rich?"

"I mean...well, Judah must be rich. Remember, he sent you money to build a house when his wife died and you said *Kaddish* for her. And he has lots of property."

Joseph eyed his son with surprise. "How do you know he has lots of property? I never mentioned such a thing."

Itzhak blushed. "Wh...when I was passing through Rozwadow on the way to Lemberg," he stammered, "he has several parcels of land there; some of the peasants told me so."

"You're lucky they didn't turn you over to the Germans. But how did they happen to tell you about his property? Did someone recognize a family resemblance in your face? Judah hasn't been in Rozwadow for over twenty-five years."

"I asked around," replied Itzhak, defensively. "You know – Rozwadow is the town you were born in, so I asked around."

"No matter. Not much good would property in Rozwadow be to a Jew now, or property in Lacejsk for that matter."

"But it did some good," Itzhak blurted out.

"But how?"

Itzhak's cheek twitched nervously. "Well... I sold one parcel. I didn't get much for it, but it was enough for us to survive until we reached Lemberg."

"Sold one parcel? What parcel? You mean our home in Lacejsk...or the land on which it stood?"

"No, Papa, one of Uncle Judah's lots in Rozwadow."

The old man's mouth fell open in disbelief. He twisted his gray beard in agonizing thought. Joseph had seen the hollow sockets of his son's eyes and, at first, had taken them for the manifestations of hunger. But now he saw more in them – anguish, haunting guilt, a hollowness of spirit.

"But how?" the father demanded. "Judah's alive...and he has sons. How could you...?"

"You, yourself, said so. He hasn't been there for a quarter of a century, so I told them he had died and that I was his son."

Joseph shook in inner torment. The words had seared his flesh and he was convulsed with pain. "How could you do such a thing? To say he was dead – heaven forbid it. He's your uncle..." Joseph could not go on. He clutched his chest and pressed hard in an effort to relieve the burning sensation he felt.

"I only sold one lot," Itzhak pleaded. "He still has the others. We needed the money to survive. If he were there, I'm sure he would have said, 'Take it. Sell it all. Save yourselves with the money.' But I only sold one lot. Just enough to get to Lemberg. We have all had to do such things to stay alive. You, yourself, said you were forced to..."

"Stop!" demanded Joseph. "It's true. We've all done things we would never have dreamed of. Still, I thought..." He smoothed the back of his head, contemplating the situation for a moment. "When this is all over," he began again, "there will have to be an accounting. If I am alive, I will write and beg his pardon. If I am not, you will have to do so. It's true, I'm sure, that he would have told you to take it all, if he were there. But he wasn't there. You know... I can't repeat it."

He paused for a moment and then went on. "Do you know what kind of man your uncle is? Then again, how could you? You were only six when the first war began. Perhaps you saw him in Vienna after that. Well, let me tell you a little about him. Maybe then you'll understand how terrible I feel that you wished him dead. You known that to say a man is dead, is in a sense, to wish him dead."

"You know I didn't mean that at all. It's just that we were desperate."

"I understand that, too. But let me continue. Judah was the eldest of us five children. Our mother died when we were all very young. And my Papa took a new wife, who later had children of her own. My father was a poor man – learned and proud, but poor. And our new mother, she didn't think of us as her children, but as extra mouths to feed. So Judah, the eldest, was sent to work. Well, he worked hard and finally became a master craftsman. But bitterness was not part of his nature. He would always see a positive excuse for the actions of others, even when those actions proved detrimental

299

to him. So the first thing he did when he earned some money of his own was to buy a piece of property and build a house on it. The house was not for himself; it was for our father and his second wife and for his sisters and brothers. Only after he had provided for his father did he begin to save for himself. After more years of work and self-deprivation, he had the money to buy property for a home for himself. But even after Judah married and had a family of his own, he still worried about his younger brothers and sisters.

"He always had respect for learning even though he, himself, never had the opportunity to go to school. And so when the Baron de Hirsch School opened its doors, he wanted me to get an education there. He knew that our father was going to send me off to work so that I could contribute towards our household expenses. Well, Judah said he'd give our father money each week – more money than I would have been able to earn at that time – on the condition that I go to school instead of being hired out. And mind you, Judah already had children of his own – a son old enough to go to school and two others as well. And he was barely earning enough to support them. So you see what kind of man he is.

"Now for you to say that he was... It's a sin for which we must beg the Almighty's forgiveness and Judah's pardon as well."

The synagogue was still for what seemed an eternity as they each reflected and pleaded with the unseen power that filled the room. At last, Itzhak lifted his bent head from prayer and asked: "Papa, I know you may not care for my question, but why did Judah ask you to say Kaddish for his wife? Don't they observe the faith in America?"

"I wouldn't say that. It was rather that he considered me the *hassid* of the family – one who would never miss a *minyon*... Besides, he was her husband. Fearing that his sons might miss saying the Kaddish one day, Judah had me say the Kaddish for his wife for the entire eleven months."

(A *minyon*, a minimum quorum of ten men, thirteen years old and over, is required for public worship. According to Jewish tradition, a widower recites the Kaddish for one month; the sons of the deceased, for eleven months. Therefore, the husband of the deceased could not say the Kaddish in place of his children.)

"You look surprised, Itzhak. Well don't be. Judah was always that way. It goes back to his childhood. While I was living at home in my youth, I could go to the synagogue for Shaharit, Minchah, and Maariv (morning, afternoon and evening services). But Judah was an apprentice to a master who wanted him at his workbench on weekdays and not in the synagogue. So Judah would pray at his workbench every morning, every afternoon and every evening amid the half-finished chairs and sawdust. Still, he always felt ashamed that he was there in the workshop and not in the synagogue. He had great respect for those who did attend services, as if their prayers were more meaningful than his.

"My little older brother always thought himself the smallest of men, an unschooled worker amidst the great scholars in the synagogue. But if he could not debate the points in the Talmud, he wanted to make sure that all those for whom he felt responsible had the schooling that would enable them to do so. And so he sent his children to school, and he sent me money to build a home for my family and myself after I was married. He reasoned that I was too busy with the business of the Almighty to attend to the world of making a living.

"But let us say no more. People are coming to the service now." He paused and then added, "And say nothing of this to Mama or your brothers or sisters, at least not tonight. It should appear as a happy family reunion, even in my sorrow."

"So tell us, Itzhak, how did you and Batia and the children get out of Lemberg?" questioned Frieda, eagerly.

"We wanted to stay, so we hid when the Russian soldiers were turning the city upside down looking for Jewish refugees. But a few weeks later they caught up with us in another of their searches. We were very unhappy at the time – like you were, I'm sure, when they broke into the schoolhouse – but in the last analysis, it was all for the best. The Almighty works in mysterious ways. Had we evaded the grasp of the Russians, where would we be now? In the hands of the Nazis. I shudder to think of it. And I shudder to think of what must have happened to those who hid in Lacejsk, when they drove you out.

"Well, anyway, we moved eastward, farther and farther into the heart of Russia, farther and farther from Galicia. We were like fish in the river, being driven by the current to some unknown waters, unable to swim against the force of the rushing swells."

"You're so skinny," observed Chaya. "I can imagine how Batia and the children must look. We'll have to fill a large package for you to take back to them. Perhaps you can get them to Leninabad. Then we'll all be together."

"That will take a lot of money," replied Itzhak. "We can use as much as you can spare. I mean... I know how hard it is for you all here. But for us, it's worse." Itzhak turned to his mother and evaded his father's eyes. To his dismay, her eyes were filled with alarm.

"Joseph," she cried, "what's the matter. You look ill."

They all turned towards Joseph, whose face now had an ashen hue. The father's arms were clutching his abdomen. "It's all right," responded Joseph. "It's just some gas. Let me lie down for a while. It will pass."

Conversation ended and all watched anxiously as Joseph lay there, in silence. He was swaying back and forth, while his hands remained glued to his mid-section. The sage called for a pan and returned his undigested dinner into it.

"Papa," said Avraham, "let me call a doctor."

"Wait a little," replied his father. "I've had such pains before and they passed. It was a fine dinner. I must have eaten too much. My stomach's not used to a full meal."

"But, Papa," pleaded Miriam, "you once needed an operation for just such a pain...in Galicia. Let the doctor decide."

"And where would you get a doctor? We're still not here legally. It's too late now to bother some official to get papers for us all. I couldn't take that chance – endangering you all. Wait 'til morning. If the pain is still there, we'll ask Leibel to get us some help."

The sage had spoken. They were all deeply troubled, but they obeyed.

The morning came, but Joseph did not see the first light of dawn. He was dead.

"What shall we do now?" asked Miriam the following day, after the funeral.

"Do what Papa instructed," replied her mother. "He told us to return to the land – to Eretz Yisrael.".

"He went ahead," added Avraham, "to intercede for us with the Almighty. For who could better render our pleas than a tzadik? With such a supplicant, we are bound to receive a favorable response. In the meantime, we must survive." (Avraham alludes here to the biblical Joseph, son of Jacob. In Jewish tradition, Joseph is known as Joseph HaTzadik – Joseph the righteous.)

WE WANT OUR OWN HOMELAND

"Every man and woman who survived those years of horror has a story to tell – nay, a host of stories that would fill a book and bring tears to the eyes and tear at the heart of any human being who possesses eyes to see and a heart to feel.

"The time will come when I can speak of it, but for now, let me just see Palestine. Let me touch the soil of the land of David and Solomon and taste its sweetness; let me be bathed in the fruit-scented air and the warm sunshine that graced the brows of Ruth and Boaz. For 2,000 years we have wandered in exile and suffered – oh, how we have suffered! We've had our fill as strangers in the lands of others. We have been laughed at and derided, beaten and spat upon. Our women have been violated, our children, murdered in the sight of their parents, our men and women, butchered by knife, slain by gun, killed by fire and gas, buried dead and buried alive. Enough! We want our own homeland, our only homeland, Eretz Yisrael."

The words, coming from a gaunt figure, shrunken and scarred, with waxen, sunken cheeks and eyes that burned like glowing coals, rang in the mind of Miriam Ausübel. She recalled his skeletal hand pointing eastward – toward Palestine – as their ship, *President Warfield*, set sail from the port of Sète in France in the dead of night on its appointed mission. And now he was there – somewhere – in the teaming masses of afflicted humanity that crowded the decks of the ship like tiny sardines squeezed into a tin whose top had been stripped off. They were packed so tightly together that none of the rusting steel or rotted wood of the surface of this ancient, gray relic was visible.

Miriam stood there, leaning against the rail on the shell of this turtle-shaped vessel. She was looking off into the distance, beyond the shadows of the past, in the twilight of a sun that had turned from bright gold to orange, to dull red, and that now was gone, leaving clouds of crimson and purple fading into a dull gray. She inhaled the cool air. The spray of the sea seemed to revitalize her body, which was stiff and sluggish after days of concealment in a crowded room. Then she turned to look back at the ocean of suffering souls: Men, women and children dressed in rags and huddled together – sickly bodies with heavy hearts.

Yes, she thought, *they each have a story to tell, as I do. But how and when? To recall, and by recalling to relive those days, those years of terror – what was done to us and what we had to do to survive – to be forced to sink to such depths to live! And after all that, the guilt of having survived when all around us perished! How strange it would sound to the ears of normal people, people who did not have to face the horrors that almost all on this ship had faced – to feel guilty for having survived.*

Miriam remembered the anguished cry in the night, "Mother! Mother!" coming from the mouth of a poor wretch shaking, whose face was drained of blood, whose eyes were filled with dread and despair, as they stared into the blackness of a German sky devoid of moon and stars. He rose, as if from the dead, to relive that moment when he had to extract the gold teeth from the pained, dead mouth of a victim of the gas chamber – his own mother!

Could a world of people who sat back in armchairs and read of the events of the day – people who had not lived through it and experienced it – understand that a human being could be so debased by the Nazis that he would do this to live another day, perhaps to survive, so that those faces be remembered? Those distorted faces with pleading open eyes that death would not shut; those rigid bodies with reaching, grasping, climbing hands covered with freshly-dried blood – hands that had tried to climb stone walls or batter down steel doors in vain as the burning, choking gas enveloped them and snuffed out their lives: It all had to be remembered, lest their very existence be made meaningless.

Miriam recalled that ghost-like form standing in the darkness, hands cupped as if to receive cleansing water. The hands twisted and rubbed and tore at one another as if trying to remove some unseen blemish, 'til palms and fingers were raw and bleeding.

And Miriam was called back to the past, to a day nearly eight years before she boarded the *President Warfield*; to that day when her journey began. She recalled how her family had been driven from the *shtetl*. She reflected on the wanderings across two continents, from city to city, through planted fields and over barren, wind-swept, desolate lands, through the gray-green of giant forests that blotted out the sun, and across frozen rivers. For a time, those wanderings may have seemed to be going nowhere, and yet, they were going somewhere – to Palestine.

The scenes of her youth appeared before Miriam's eyes and she became part of them. It was the eve of the Festival of Sukkot when her sad wanderings had begun. The glass of wine fell to the ground, shattering into a thousand reflective pieces that mirrored the gray and black that was to be her lot. She had become wedded to a nomadic existence from which no divorce was possible. The wails and shrieks of women and children, the anguished, pleading cries of bearded men sinking in the rushing river waters, and the sadistic, booming laughter of the black-shirted Nazis all echoed in her ears, reverberating in the canyons of her mind, until they fused into one unbearable roar.

She cupped her hands to her ears to silence the voices. Finally, the last echo floated off, above the caverns of her past. She was left with a whistling wind, which descended from an icy mountain onto a twisting ribbon of water. In her mind's eye, she could see a little vessel on that ribbon of water. Like a child's toy, it puffed and chugged, coughed and spat, as it seemingly climbed a mountain of water. At last it came to a halt. The small vessel discharged its strange cargo of unhappy little puppets with their dark outer garments. Bent by the weight of their affliction and the dirt-covered sacks slung across their backs, this depressing rag army trampled into the blackness of exile.

In the blur of the images of her past, spring thaw dissolved the snows of winter. The ice was now turned into glimmering, bubbling streams of cold refreshing water that gushed down from heights, renewing life, as tiny green shoots pushed up through the white mantle. But the warming rays of spring sun also uncovered the remains of more than a hundred souls who had long slept beneath the blanket of snow.

The horror of all those bodies! Those despairing faces with vacant eyes stared up at a bright blue sky that ought to have revived them. She thought of the judgment day when the dead would rise and accusingly confront an indifferent world, whose desire for untroubled rest had caused it to give Cain's answer to the Lord's question, "Am I my brother's keeper?"

Miriam peered through the mist at a cemetery gate creaking back and forth in the wind. Black clouds hovered low and a cold, dismal rain beat down relentlessly on a family of mourners who stood there in the gloomy gray mist of early morning. A sage had returned to the earth, yet Miriam's brother was telling them that their father had risen to the heavens to clear a path for his children to the Promised Land.

The joy of war's end, the triumph of the forces of good over the arch demons of evil, and the words "You're free to leave the Soviet Union" lit up her eyes, reflectively. But the gladness was tempered by the sadness of the prior five years of suffering: what she had been forced to do to survive and what she had left behind – her father, her friends and the innocence of youth.

Bielsko was but a stopping point – a splintered remnant of a world now ended. It was a place where some of her fellow survivors had chosen to start again. (Bielsko was a town in southern Poland, home to 5,000 Jews before World War II. After the war, a group of Jews resettled in the town, but they were not well received.)

But to Miriam, it was a dead town – at least for Jews. The roofless, charred wood and the graying, cracked mud shells of what had been a *shtetl* were the ashes of the past, the debris of lives permanently uprooted from this land. The doors to emptiness slapped back and forth in the breeze. To Miriam, they were the cemetery gates to the graves of a people and a civilization that had vanished in the flames of hatred, the final product of those years of anti-Semitism. Bielsko was no home for her; it was a graveyard for shattered dreams. There was no monument to recall millions who had lived in these villages and cities; the Nazis had removed even the tombstones, to be used as paving stones. A single crimson rose, withering on a thorny bush, gave mute testimony to the love a former inhabitant bore for this land, from which he or she had been so violently uprooted.

Of the flesh of those who had perished in the Holocaust, there was nothing left now but bits of gold torn from their dental fillings, the bars of soap produced from the molten tissues of their bodies, and the lampshades made from skin stripped from their flesh. A way of life and a people had vanished from the land, leaving it barren and desolate.

Miriam stared at a flapping curtain, lacerated by the sharp edges of glass of the broken window. Its simple pattern was reminiscent of her own bedroom. It brought back memories of her rising early in the morning and looking past the window at the snowy beauty of a winter's day.

A gust of wind drew the curtain out through the window frame. The teeth of glass bit through the material, transecting it, and the drapery flew up into the grayness of the sky and disappeared.

She left on the first train to Krakow, along with hundreds of other wanderers.

A displaced persons (DP) camp with its barbed wire surroundings had been her next stopping point. Another followed this in Ulm and a third in Frankfort. In the camp near Frankfort, Frieda married another homeless Jew – a moment of happiness. But Miriam's thoughts were focused on getting to Palestine. She had no desire to remain in Germany, of all places!

And now she was standing on the deck of an aged and decrepit vestige of a former era, with 4,500 other stateless Jews, including her brother, Avraham, and sister, Chaya. She was staring toward the east in the darkness of the night, yearning to reach Eretz Yisrael. Somewhere, back in Europe, were her mother, four of her siblings and their families; ahead were Simcha and Dov and home.

The decks and giant lounges of the ship contained a veritable "United Nations" of European Jewry. There were Jews from every corner of the continent, as well as from North Africa. They had come from the far north of Scandinavia to the Mediterranean shore of Italy, from the cities of France to the villages of Poland and Russia, and so many places in between. There were fair-haired, blue-eyed Jews from Denmark and swarthy men and women from Morocco. Physicians, scientists and teachers were crowded together with laborers and artisans. Many spoke Yiddish; some were fluent in Ladino, and still others understood neither one nor the other.

Hassidim, with beards and sidecurls, stood alongside adults and children who pictured the word "Jew" as some sort of curse word employed by their enemies against them. There were those who knew the prayer book by heart, and others who had never been inside a synagogue. Yet, here they were alongside Miriam and Chaya and Avraham; a sickly, unhappy, bedraggled army of wanderers, driven out of the bowels of hell that Europe had become for the Hebrew people.

At the same time, they were being pulled by some unseen magnetic force, back to the land from which their ancestors had been driven so long, long ago. An odyssey had begun; the sons and daughters of Jacob were returning to the home of the Patriarchs.

But the morning light brought lines of distress to Miriam's face. A large gray vessel steamed into view. It bore the flag she had learned to associate with England – the Union Jack. Her chest pounded with fear as the *President Warfield* slowed to a halt and then bobbed up and down with each rise and fall of the sea. Pushed up by the swells, her heart rose and became lodged close to her throat. It pulsated violently and cut off her breath.

Miriam turned to Chaya who stood beside her at the rail. An old threadbare brown scarf covered her sister's brown hair, but it could not conceal the look of terror in her eyes. "Is this it?" Miriam asked worriedly, with eyes that pleaded for a denial of her question. Suddenly, the last drop of blood appeared to have been drained from Chaya's pallid face, producing the ghostly look that comes from hope being dashed. Seeing that her question had mirrored her sister's apprehensions, Miriam went on in a lowered voice, with her head shaking back and forth: "Have we come all this way only to have our journey ended a few hours after we set sail?"

"Not just yet," spoken in imperfect Yiddish, surprised them. It was a strong, cheerful man's voice coming from behind them.

They turned to see a round-faced young man with curly blond hair pulled in every which way by a strong sea breeze. His pale eyes – cheerful, yet hinting of some inner sadness – smiled at them. It was not a handsome face, but a good face, a kind face, the gentle face of which a mother might say, "This is my son. Isn't he a fine young man?" He was stocky, with strong shoulders sloping down to sturdy arms. Still, there was a softness about him. He was youthful in appearance, yet he seemed experienced far beyond his tender years.

The girls smiled back, uneasily. "You're one of the sailors," Miriam said, observing his garb. "Do you know what's happening?"

"Not much," replied the young man, reassuringly. "They've spotted us – the *Mermaid*'s her name – so our captain slowed to let them give us a good look. Now it's a war of nerves. Don't worry; they won't touch us at this time. We're not in British waters and we're flying a Uruguayan flag, so they stare at us and we stare back."

A buzzing sound came to their ears from above. They looked up in the direction of the noise.

"One of their planes, no doubt," added the young man. He studied the aircraft with intent eyes, which his hand shielded from the bright sun. "Giving us another look-over. Well...let them look. They knew we were coming and we knew they knew. Just give them a smile and a wave. They'll hate that. The mouse is not supposed to smile at the cat."

Avraham, upon hearing the commotion outside, stepped on deck. He observed his sisters in conversation with one of the crew and then made his way through the crowd to them. "I'm Avraham Ausübel," he interrupted, like a father interjecting himself between his daughters and a stranger. "I'm their brother. And you...?"

"William Bernstein's the name, Bill for short."

"You speak Yiddish," remarked the bearded Avraham to the clean-shaven young man. "Where are you from?"

"San Francisco...in America." Seeing the look of surprise in the bearded man's eyes, he went on: "Most of the crew is from America, except for a few from the Haganah." (The Haganah was an underground Jewish defense force in Palestine, formed during the British Mandate. At first, they defended Jewish settlements against Arab attacks. Later, they helped illegal immigrants trying to enter Palestine after the British reversed the earlier free immigration and forbade Jewish entry into Palestine during the Holocaust. After Israel's independence was declared, the Haganah became the IDF, the army of the State of Israel.)

"So our deliverers are from two ends of the earth – Jews coming to rescue the remnants of their people from the slow death of the DP camps," said Avraham.

"Not all..." replied William.

Seeing the raised eyebrows of the three Ausübels, he added, "There's one gentile in the crew – the lofty man there near the bridge of the ship."

William's finger was pointing to a tall, intent-looking man with shoulder-length, fine blond hair that was blowing in the wind like the mane of a proud stallion. His face was, to say the least, striking. It was elongated and lean, with firm cheekbones showing through the pox-marked, tightly drawn, tanned skin. The jaw was small and receding. The eyes, steel blue and unblinking, studied the lines of the British vessel with a penetrating, icy stare. A small gold cross was lifted from his chest by a gust of hot Mediterranean air as he leaned forward. The cross glimmered in the sun and then fell back on the long chest of its owner. He moistened his lips with a slow, curling movement of his tongue and then, pursing his lips, turned to enter the wheelhouse.

"That's Grauel," said William. "Reverend John Stanley Grauel...a Methodist minister. He has made our cause his cause."

Avraham nodded and said nothing. But his mind was busy thinking.

What a strange lot they are, he thought. *Not a beard or sidecurls among them... Jews...and even a Christian who, between them, have probably not spent a week in a ghetto – drawn from the distant corners of the world to this vessel to save the homeless and the friendless. The ways of the Lord are truly mysterious.*

The ship's engines started up again and the *President Warfield* began to move once more. The hundreds of refugees on deck uttered a collected sigh of relief.

"Gotta get back to work," said William, with a wave of his hand.

He halted for a moment and added, "By the way, what are your names... if I may ask?"

"I'm Miriam and this is my sister, Chaya. My brother Avraham has told you our family name, Ausübel."

"See you all in Palestine," William said hopefully with a broad grin. "We can have a drink together...on me."

The young man disappeared into the interior of the vessel. Miriam stared at the gray steel door through which he had vanished.

"You see," said Chaya, nudging Miriam to gain her attention, "the British ship is leaving us."

Miriam watched the warship as it fell behind. Then she hugged her sister with joy.

"I don't know about leaving," corrected Avraham. "Just dropping back. You heard what the sailor said. They've looked us over and now they're just watching and waiting."

"Waiting for what?" asked Chaya.

"For us to try to enter Palestine," he replied firmly, yet ominously.

❖ ❖ ❖

The decks were the only escape from the intense heat of the ship's interior that served as home for the thousands of homeless Jews. They spent as much time as they could on decks, which were so crowded that there was standing room only. When exhausted, the refugees returned to their quarters for rest. There was a great high-ceilinged room on each floor. These had served as the lounges of a pleasure craft designed for midnight cruises in Chesapeake Bay. Where bands had played and audiences danced, hammocks had been positioned. There they were strung, one above the other, from floor to ceiling.

At night, the occupied hammocks creaked and rocked slowly, back and forth, with the rolls of the moving vessel. In the faint, pale light that entered through the portholes, the hundreds of slumbering refugees looked like a school of sleeping fish, suspended in the shifting water of the vessel's interior.

Razil, a short, bony orphan girl, probably in her teens, occupied the hammock to Miriam's right. The scraggly child awoke in terror one night, in the encircling heavy darkness of the night. She remained hidden beneath her blanket with only her upper face showing, seemingly chilled in the stifling heat of the huge room. Razil's body shook violently as she looked around with wide, nervous eyes, waiting for enemies to close in.

A horrid, muffled cry wakened Miriam. She looked around, quickly. Her eyes came to rest on the terrified face of Razil, which was projecting forward beneath closely cropped auburn hair. It was a young face, but with a bizarre, unworldly look. It was devoid of color; the face of the dead. The shadowed, deep lines surrounding the dark, staring eyes suggested dread of unseen monsters.

Miriam slipped down from her hammock and approached the child. She raised her hand slowly so as not to cause alarm. She touched Razil's head, soothing back the child's auburn hair, reassuringly. Miriam began to sing, almost in a hum.

"Sleep, Razileh, (little Razil) sleep Razileh, sleep, sleep. Mother's here, sleep, sleep..."

The lines on Razil's face softened and finally were smoothed away. Pink returned to her cheeks. Her eyes grew calm and her lids, heavy. At last, she passed back into slumber.

Dawn brought the sleeping fish back to life. The passengers lined up for food from the huge galley that was now feeding far more people than it ever was intended to nourish. But the refugees were happy to be alive and to be eating at all. Wrapped in their dream of returning to their ancient homeland, they gladly waited their turn in the long lines that circled the vessel.

The Orthodox began the day with prayer. The decks of the ship were crowded with men continuing the tradition of an ancient people. Heads were covered with skullcaps, atop which rested little black boxes of *tefillin*, which, in many instances, were frayed at the edges. Heads bobbed up and down with each mention of the Holy Name. Lips buzzed with remembered prayers, while eyes focused on prayer books. Upper bodies were covered with tattered prayer shawls – some with shreds of beautifully embroidered silk brocade to recall the love and respect with which these coverings were worn. Shoulders, bent from years of suffering, swayed slowly to and fro with the fervor of the words being recited. Veins bulged beneath seven windings of the black leather band of the *tefillin* on their left arms, in addition to the bands around the hand and third finger. It was as if the turtle-backed vessel were one gigantic synagogue, with the open sky for its roof.

Not all those on deck were there to pray. Some watched with curiosity during the supplications of the righteous. These were the survivors of assimilated European Jewry: Men and women who had sought to enter the mainstream and become part of the European world that, in truth, had never accepted them. The lesson of history had been made all too clear to them: a Jew is still a Jew in the eyes of his neighbors, and a clean-shaven face and a fashionable suit change nothing. Almost against their will, they, too, were drawn into the spirituality of the chanting and they became participants in the ritual. They had returned to a world which they could never tear out of the fabric of their souls.

To Avraham, prayer was an essential part of his being. The Almighty was everywhere – over land and sea, in the tiniest house in the *shtetl*, and even hovering over a refugee ship. Avraham communicated fervently with his Maker. Nothing was concealed; all cards were on the table.

"Master of the Universe," he pleaded, as tears rolled down his closed eyes, "is it not time for us to return? We have obeyed Your commandments, as best we could, even in the frozen wastes of Siberia. And if our yearning for survival prompted us to bend a little, it was not through lack of piety, it was from starvation: the gurgling of empty stomachs until the mind could no longer resist; the craving of human beings for a bit of food to revive their enfeebled bodies. Did we not observe the Sabbath and the Day of Atonement, even when enemies threatened to destroy us for doing so?

"Lord, look around this ship. What do You see? The pitiful, wretched handful of survivors from thousands of places, of a thousand unspeakable horrors; the remnants of European Jewry. Were all those centuries of pious devotion and study of the Scriptures for naught? Did our ancestors cling to Your commandments for 2,000 years in exile, only to see the last of their descendants perish at the hands of our enemies?

"Please.., open the gates of the Promised Land to us. You can do it. A thick fog in the middle of the night as our ship dashes those last miles to the shore. It's not so difficult a thing for the Ruler of the Universe. A little mix up among the English soldiers, so that they are not waiting on the beach to seize us: Is that too much to ask? And with Your great compassion, couldn't You instill some of it into the hearts of the British leaders and weaken their stubborn resolve to keep us from our land? Have mercy on us, forgive us and grant us atonement. And please,… Help us. Amen."

He wiped his eyes and then took his place in line, waiting for the morning meal. Chaya and Miriam stood beside him.

❖ ❖ ❖

The next few days were filled with anxious preparations, as well as grave uneasiness. Warship after warship was spotted, all flying the British flag. The largest was a cruiser with huge, bristling guns mounted on its deck. Two minesweepers, a frigate and several destroyers were also pointed out by those more knowledgeable of naval ships. It was a frightening royal escort for the little ship with its cargo of survivors of the Holocaust.

Bill Bernstein, displaying the expertise he gained at the United States Merchant Marine Academy and from service at sea, pointed to the subtleties of the various ships: the length, the design and the guns that differentiated one ship from the other.

"That's the *Ajax*. It fought against the *Graf Spee*,…the German battleship," he said, pointing to the largest of the British vessels. To Miriam, one armed enemy ship was too many and eight great Men of War, an insurmountable foe. The very thought of battle sent her heart racing.

The following day, the passengers received instructions in the methods of repelling a British boarding party. They were also told what to do when they landed in Palestine. But there were to be limits to their resistance. Yossi Harel, their slender, golden-haired young Haganah leader, insisted that no guns be used. The refugees were ordered to turn in any concealed weapons, immediately. Yossi did not wish to give the British army any additional excuse to slaughter thousands of Jews.

"Why don't they leave us alone? Haven't we suffered enough?" shouted Hirsch Yakubovich, as he stared angrily at the British vessels. The gaunt, dark-haired, dark-eyed lad seemed to be expressing the sentiments of all on board.

"Philosophers may suggest answers," replied Avraham, looking with understanding at the teenager, "but what does it matter? We intend to enter Eretz Yisrael and they appear determined to stop us. They don't care much about our suffering, so we might as well go on with our business…"

Tears fell from the boy's eyes and rolled down his sunken cheeks. He turned away to hide them.

"All alone," observed Avraham, tenderly. "Don't turn away. There's no disgrace in crying, only in indifference."

The boy wiped his eyes and turned back to the bearded Hassid.

"You all alone, too?" he inquired.

"No. I have two sisters on this ship, brothers in Palestine, as well as family back in Europe.

"And you...? Any family?"

"All dead," the boy replied, lowering his eyes. "All I have is myself and a number tattooed on my arm." His eyes rose and he looked Avraham in the eye. "I'm not going back there, no matter what happens."

Day after day, Avraham observed his shipmates as they journeyed eastward toward the rising sun. The hot July sun warmed their faces, restoring vitality to their features. Life returned to their skeletal frames, not from food – for there was little enough for so large a mass of humanity – but through the cleansing hope for a new beginning in their old land. It was the hope of a dying man from Minsk, for a breath of invigorating mountain air from the Galilee of his dreams; it was the prayer of a bearded man in his foxtail hat, to see Jerusalem before shedding off this mortal coil; it was the anticipation of a groom, after centuries of separation, of beholding his promised bride.

That hope had sustained them and kept them from giving in to the release of death. That hope had restored them and given them purpose.

And now, the tattered remnants of a people, having been molded into an army of determined Jews, scanned the horizon. They looked at the birds and the waves and waited to catch sight of the beautiful white sand of Eretz Yisrael.

Life went on amidst the waiting and the wondering, the dread fear and the bright anticipation. A baby was born – new life breathing its first breath on a sea of hope – and a woman died in childbirth and was buried at sea. Life vanished beneath the waves and life began anew, and they waited.

A column of British warships, crews of white-clad sailors and officers lining their decks, moved, with enviable precision, past the *President Warfield* in the bright light of a summer sun, under a clear, blue sky.

A loudspeaker on the last destroyer blared a message to the refugees:

"You are suspected of going to Palestine with illegal immigrants. This is forbidden. If you enter Palestine waters, we will board you and seize you, using force if necessary."

The next day, the performance was repeated. This time, some of the crew of the refugee vessel, standing on the bridge of their ship, saluted the passing British Men of War and the *Warfield's* loudspeaker greeted the British with a recording of Sir Edward Elgar's "Pomp and Circumstance."

❖ ❖ ❖

A week had passed since they left on their fateful voyage, surreptitiously, in the dead of night. An angry wind was now gusting overhead and the sea had become choppy as the sky darkened ominously.

"Will we make it?" asked Miriam of her brother. As they studied the blackness of the sky from the rail of the ship, she waited, hoping for a reassuring reply.

"I don't know...for who can know the plan of our Maker? Who can tell whether the storm is intended to hide us from the warships out there, or is meant to symbolize the hopelessness of our present position? I believe that the Jewish people are destined to return to Eretz Yisrael. It's the how and when of which I am uncertain."

Miriam gave him an inquiring stare. "'How and when' you say. How are we to return, if not on this ship? As to 'when,' if not now, then when, if ever?"

"I see that my words are confusing to you. I do not mean to suggest that we stand idly by, waiting for the Messiah to rescue us. No, we must act as planned. We must try to run the blockade and we must resist, with our bare hands if necessary, as long as we have any strength to oppose those who bar the way. Our wanderings must come to an end, one way or the other. We must not accept another camp, no matter where it is, unless it is in Palestine.

"I've been speaking to many of the others: the survivors of Auschwitz and Buchenwald and Dachau. I've spoken to Jews who spent the last five years hiding in holes in the ground or in the forest, running from the enemy when he approached, and living like wild animals. I've conversed with men who have lost their entire families to the gas chambers and the ovens. These people need a reason for living. That reason is Eretz Yisrael. Accepting another camp would, to them, be surrendering their souls. So we must go on. As to whether we get through: That is up to the Almighty."

"Avraham, you speak in riddles. You say that we should struggle, yet you have doubt that the struggle will be successful. What can we do against warships and armed men?"

"These are not the Nazis, thirsting to kill. They're not even the Russians imbued, for centuries, with a loathing and deep hatred for Jews. Theirs is a nation with democratic traditions, a nation in which Jews have lived peacefully for centuries. But they are concerned for the splotches of red on the map of the world, their empire on which the sun never sets. They have long held it together, ruling this vast mass of land and hundreds of millions of people. They have done so by playing one group against the other. Diplomacy is what they call this. And now, to please some Arabs (while the British flag flies over much of the Arab world), they would like us to disappear, or at least be silent. But if prodded or embarrassed, they will be forced to wrestle with the question they have long sought to avoid answering. A major goal of this voyage is to challenge their conscience and, indeed, the conscience of the world. They must not be allowed to sweep our problem under the rug. The British are now compelled to answer our cries – no, our demands – in the glaring light of day, under the watchful eyes of a world aroused from its slumber of indifference. How can a government that only three decades ago proclaimed its acceptance of a Jewish homeland in Palestine, deny us entrance now?

(The Balfour Declaration of 1917 stated: "His Majesty's Government view with favor the establishment in Palestine of a national home for the Jewish people, and will use its best endeavors to facilitate the achievement of this object." Arthur James Balfour was the British foreign secretary at the time.)

"The answer must be theirs. Will they let these poor wretches into Palestine or will the slaughter of these martyrs be necessary to awaken the conscience of their nation and the world?"

Miriam might have replied, but the sky suddenly turned brilliant blue as flares and searchlights coming from all sides illuminated the *President Warfield*. The refugee ship's whistle sounded the alarm and people, half dressed, poured out of the interior of the vessel to see what was going on. A terrifying great shadow emerged from the gray mist. Miriam's heart was racing.

There was a sudden, jarring crash: the rasping, screeching sound of steel grinding against steel, wooden planks loosened and flying about, and the cries of frightened human beings, as ships collided in the night. Men, armed with clubs and pistols, swung from the attacking ship onto the deck of the *Warfield*. Stunned by the commotion, Miriam remained glued to the rail. She stared ahead toward the bridge of the ship. There, two members of the crew were flipping over the board that carried the ship's name. She could make out the new name painted on the opposite side. *Exodus 1947* was their new designation. It would serve as the symbol of the determination of these Jews to return to the Promised Land, just as their ancestors had done in the days of Moses. The Star of David, white and blue, had been raised and now it flew proudly above their vessel.

Refugees and crewmembers threw boxes and cans and parts of the ship's gear at the attackers, in an effort to hold off the invading force. The sound of gunfire was heard. Someone, dressed in a T-shirt, staggered across the bridge of the ship, holding his jaw.

"Quick," Avraham nudged his sister. "Get off the deck before they get here. Go back to Chaya. I'm going forward."

"Be careful," she pleaded. Then she left and entered the great, dark lounge. In the midst of the panic and confusion that prevailed, she found and embraced her sister. Excitedly, she passed on the news of what was happening outside.

People were scurrying to and fro. Some were running to join the fray; others sought a safe place in which to hide; and some, bloodied from the battle on deck, were being carried away for medical attention. Again there was a mighty crashing sound. People were tossed about the great lounge like matchsticks. Some shrieked in pain as heads, arms and legs struck bulkheads and floors.

"Must be another British ship ramming us," Miriam concluded breathlessly.

The door burst open. It was Grauel, the Christian minister with his cross of gold that glimmered in the dim reflective light of the battle outside.

"Come on," he shouted in Yiddish. "Follow me. Get out there and fight!"

A dozen teenagers, momentarily forgetting their fears, came out of hiding under bunks. They followed him onto the deck.

For what seemed an eternity, the sounds of warfare continued. From time to time there were more crashing noises and the vessel shook violently with each of the blows. Women and children huddled together, tremulously, to keep from flying in all directions.

By dawn, it was all over. The *Exodus 1947*, battered and leaking, had surrendered.

The huddled masses slowly rose from their crouched positions and emerged from the interior of the ship to gaze at the devastation. The sides of the vessel had large gashes. The deck, itself, looked like a giant junkyard in which packs of wild dogs had fought. There were warped and distorted metal, splintered wood covered with dried blood, broken bottles and bent cans, chunks of beef and crushed fruit. They also saw two British destroyers, one on either side of their ship. These vessels, too, bore the scars of battle: the twisted steel planking and fragmented lifeboats, the result of the repeated collisions. But the Star of David still flew proudly above *Exodus 1947*.

After the long night of terror, Miriam and Chaya were relieved to find their brother alive and unmarked, although his face was blackened with soot.

The decks grew more and more crowded as human beings, like ants crawling out of the hole of the vessel, kept filling every inch of available space in the sun. Skeletons with hollow cheeks, the survivors of every cruelty that man could impose on fellow human beings, pushed toward the rail and stared eastward.

By afternoon, land was sighted. The imposing hills of Carmel came into view as they sailed northward. The ship turned in the direction of Haifa harbor and a strange, golden-domed, marble building was seen towering above the vessels in the port.

The refugees spontaneously broke into prayer. It was Friday afternoon and this was to have been their first Sabbath in the Holy Land. But much of the joy they felt was smothered by the realization that they were in the hands of an enemy who probably had no intention of allowing them to set foot in Palestine. Still, this was the sacred soil of Abraham, Isaac and Jacob. They stood erect with grim determination and sang the "*Hatikvah*." ("The Hope"was the anthem of the Zionist movement, the movement to return to Palestine. It has since become the national anthem of Israel.)

The *Exodus 1947*docked alongside a long pier.

There was a sudden series of underwater explosions, as if to emphasize the words: "Don't anyone try to escape."

The dockside looked like a war zone. Soldiers, lined up in columns two deep, surrounded the entire area. Their rifles were held at the ready. Civilians had been kept far off to the rear, with the exception of two men standing near the dock. One of these men was dressed in an all-white suit; the other, in light summer attire and a straw hat.

"Must be some big shots," commented Avraham to his sisters as they stared at the scene.

A ramp was connected to the ship. Two members of the *Exodus* crew were led down the gangway, under guard, and hustled into a dark motor vehicle. Ambulances pulled up to the dock and British servicemen proceeded to carry off the casualties. Some of the wounded, wrapped in bandages, waved sadly to their fellow refugees.

"That's Bill Bernstein, the American sailor," Miriam gasped. "He is not moving."

"William was defending the bridge of the ship," Avraham replied. "They crushed his skull with clubs."

"Look," Miriam shuddered. "They're carrying off two covered bodies."

"Hirsch Yakubovich, the fifteen-year-old who was the only surviving member of his family, and Mordechi Baumstein, who lived through years in the concentration camps, only to die within sight of Eretz Yisrael."

"But how?"

"Hirsch was hiding under a lifeboat. At the sight of those poor, frightened, sunken eyes, a British marine became alarmed and shot the lad. Baumstein was hit in the stomach by a bullet."

"And what will they do with us now?"

"Look there," said her brother, directing his eyes to the tall, golden-maned John Grauel who was striding down the gangway. "Did you know we had a member of the press on board?"

"I thought he was a minister."

"A minister he is, but for now he will be an American reporter, telling the world our story. A cross goes a long way with the British. They could not believe that anyone wearing one could be with us for any reason other than to write a few lines for publication."

To the surprise of the refugees, a British officer gave the order to disembark. Others repeated the command in a dozen tongues. Dazed Jews moved slowly down the ramp to land, at first by ones and twos, and then in groups.

Even in the presence of a double file of soldiers, they wept and kissed the ground. If there were to be no tomorrow for them, at least they had touched the soil of Palestine today.

"Keep moving," shouted a stern-faced sergeant in halting German. "We've got to get you all cleaned up and deloused. All baggage will be inspected and marked for shipment to Cyprus. Come on there, keep moving. We don't have all day."

An emaciated young man, his eyes widening with alarm and his face turning gray with terror, coughed violently and refused to budge.

"Come along," said Avraham, reassuringly, as he grasped the young fellow gently, but firmly, by the hand. "This is not Auschwitz and these are not Nazis. They're spraying us with something to kill bugs, not people. And we're going to Cyprus, not back to Europe. In a few weeks (the Lord willing) we'll be back in Palestine."

As they moved forward, hand in hand, Avraham looked up at one of the British ships resting alongside the dock. The cages he spied on the deck made him wonder as to the truth of his own words.

Slowly, the Jews made their way down the narrow path between the columns of British soldiers who tried to maintain a professional appearance – eyes erect, chins in and chests out. Here and there, a look of sadness or dismay or pity crossed a British face, only to be wiped clean at the sight of a superior.

At the end of the line stood a desk where each refugee, in his turn, was interrogated. They were then searched from head to toe by armed guards, following which they were sprayed with DDT and then directed to one of the three awaiting vessels for deportation. Their torn baggage contained a few tattered garments and perhaps a picture of some loved ones who had been exterminated by the Nazis. The British soldiers went through these bags with a disdain, usually reserved for going through a trash pile in a search for a missing jewel. A hand was frequently raised to the nostrils by the examiner to suggest a putrid odor rising from the contents of the torn luggage. Anything conceivably resembling a weapon was removed. The baggage was put outside, tagged "For shipment to Cyprus."

"So that's where they're taking us," sighed Miriam, with resignation in her voice.

"Have courage," whispered Avraham. "Something will yet come of all this. Surely the Almighty did not intend for all this dying and all the struggling to come to naught. We'll go to Cyprus for now..."

An English soldier approached. Avraham became silent. "You there," the Englishman said in an awkward German, "go that way...to the ship. Quickly."

Avraham and his sisters moved slowly. With leaded feet and heavy hearts, they left Palestinian soil and climbed the gangplank to the *Ocean Vigour*, a British transport. The ship filled slowly. The British pushed and shoved the refugees forward whenever resistance was shown. Finally, the animal cargo – some 1,500 Jews from *Exodus 1947* – had been crammed aboard and the cage doors were slammed shut. Frantic refugees clung to the mesh screens that covered the ship's deck, trying to get a last glimpse of Eretz Yisrael as the vessel steamed out of Haifa harbor.

The next few days were amongst the unhappiest of Avraham's young, yet trauma-filled life. To have come so close – in fact, to have been there – and then to be separated from his homeland; to have seen his fellow Jews violently dragged aboard what they considered a prison ship; to be sailing westward, away from the Holy Land and caged aboard a ship somewhere in the Mediterranean. Such misery seemed to parallel the painful test of Job's faith in the Almighty. (Job's faith was tested in the *Book of Job* in the Bible. He was subjected to many forms of suffering to test his faith in the Lord, and he endured them all without losing that faith.) But it was a challenge he had been well trained to meet. It was an ordeal he was determined to endure unflinchingly, for he was his father's son, a sage descended from sages, and nothing would shake his fidelity to the Lord. As long as he had that, no bars could hold his soul and no mesh screen could block communication with his Maker.

Avraham scanned the horizon through the confining wire that separated the British crew from the involuntary passengers. Dutifully, he attended to all the daily prayers, following which he meditated and kept up his mental dialogue with He who has no name.

By the third day, he was grim-faced.

"Chaya," he said with a calm that masked his bitterness, "do you remember that British officer telling us that we're going to Cyprus for awhile? A smirk crossed his face as soon as the words left his mouth. If he found the word 'Cyprus' amusing, their intent must be far worse. We put them to the test with our arrival in so large a number. And our stubborn resistance, when they demanded that we turn back, challenged them. So now they have taken up that seemed challenge. I believe that they consider it a matter of British honor. In their eyes, the preservation of that honor requires that they crush us and silence us forever. But they can never succeed as long as we keep our faith and do not lose our determination."

"Avraham," replied his twin sister, "where are they taking us?"

"Nowhere," he replied, his eyes narrowing a bit.

"What kind of answer is that? 'Nowhere.' What does that mean? Have you lost your senses to the heat?"

"Look, they can try to take us somewhere. But if we resist, if we refuse to leave this ship unless we are returned to the Holy Land, then we will finally succeed in achieving our goal. Despite all their bluster and determination to have their own way, deep down inside, they probably don't care that much one way or the other. Eventually, they'll have to throw up their hands and say, 'Do what you will.'"

"Are you sure?" wondered Chaya, aloud.

"What's sure in life?" Avraham smiled, for the first time in days. "But it sounds good to me."

"You Jews up to what?" conveyed ungrammatically in German, interrupted the conversation.

Avraham and Chaya turned in the direction of the growling voice. It was an English sailor dressed in a sweaty T-shirt, atop grimy white bell-bottoms. He stood on the other side of the wire fence. The seaman was pushing a large wagon that smelled of lunch. The refugees poured out on to the deck, attracted by the scents emanating from the carts.

"Grateful you should be," continued the sailor. "Your chow on that pigsty *Exodus* good like this?"

"Does the lion, caged in a zoo, feel happy about his confinement?" replied Avraham in a biting tone. "Would he not rather hunt for his own food and, in so doing, be free? Would you be grateful to be restrained by prison bars as long as they filled your belly with beef and a pint of ale? Answer me that and then ask yourself why all this is done to us. Ask your officers, 'Who gave them such wisdom and such a sense of justice that they turn men into animals and think themselves humane?'" The Jew's body shook with indignation and his eyes flared red for a moment.

"What you want from me?" replied the flustered seaman, having difficulty finding the words in a foreign tongue. "I sailor, not the first minister. They say; I do."

❖ ❖ ❖

They ate and they slept and they studied the sea, looking for something. The sun rose early in the eastern sky and set late in the day. The heat was intense, as it usually is in the summer on the Mediterranean. But the refugees had other reasons to boil. Every day brought them seemingly farther from their goal. The world had tilted sideward and they were being swept off the end.

At last they saw land. At first, it was a speck of brown and white off in the distance. Then it was a harbor, plainly in view. There was something strangely familiar about it. They groaned in anger upon realizing that it was Port-de-Bouc, close to the site from which they had embarked on their journey only two weeks earlier, but which seemed an eternity.

The ship docked and a gangway was attached. The command was given in every imaginable language for the refugees to disembark.

The faces of the refugees blackened with anger and they resisted in the extreme. Even Avraham, a man given to contemplation and prayer rather than to violence, would not accede to the British order.

"Better that you kill us now," shouted one rag-clad skeleton as he ripped open his shirt to expose a chest full of ribs beneath a layer of flesh no thicker than tissue paper. "I'll not go back to Auschwitz, alive. It's Palestine or nothing."

The deck was in an uproar and the Jews, like caged animals, shook their bars violently. The look on the faces of the British officers betrayed their sense of uneasiness.

"See," said Avraham to his sisters, "this is a French city and those are newspapermen with cameras at dockside. The Gendarmes will never stand for Englishmen assaulting us on French soil. Too many witnesses."

Before the sun set that day, two other ships anchored in the harbor. They were the *Runnymede Park* and the *Empire Rival*. Aboard them were the other 3,000 refugees from *Exodus 1947*, all caged like beasts of the wild.

The refugees on all three vessels were offered the option of returning to the barbed-wire enclosures of the DP camps on the continent where six million of their brethren had perished, or remaining where they were, baking in the steaming decks of the ships, behind steel wire, the symbol of their confinement. The Jews howled and wailed and they shouted their determination to return to their ancient homeland. They refused to return to the graveyard of their people – Europe.

"See how the reporters take down notes," Avraham said to his sisters. "The newspapers of a hundred nations will be filled with the story, "'4,500 Jewish refugees demand to go to Palestine! British lock them in cages!' The ghost-like survivors of a thousand horrors will become the symbol of Jewish determination to return to their homeland!"

That night, the refugees gathered below deck in each of the three prison ships. They were there to decide their future course of action. There were many things to be considered.

The old and the frail were too weak to survive the challenge of steaming-hot quarters, no less a possible hunger strike and the ever-present threat of British brute force. Therefore, they were instructed to go ashore. The rest of the refugees would remain on board, come what may.

A pledge was made by crewmembers who represented the Haganah. There would be no rest by their brethren on the outside until the last Jew who set sail on *Exodus 1947* had been repatriated to his ancient homeland, Eretz Yisrael. Each of the refugees agreed to the compact that was signed and then stamped with the seal of the Palmach (the Haganah's mobilized striking force) – the olive branch and the sword.

As the Ausübels were leaving the hole of the vessel, the dark-eyed Chaya halted for a moment and looked intently at her flaxen-bearded brother.

"The pledge was made with every good intention, but do intentions alone bring results?"

Avraham stared back at her with a special glow in his eyes.

"Each day I become more convinced that our course of action will lead us back to Israel... I said to Israel, the nation of the Jews. The Almighty works in mysterious ways. And yet, when you look back at it, there is a logic and purpose to it all.

"They named our ship *Exodus 1947*. This, too, had a purpose and a meaning. Think back to that first Exodus in the days of Moses, our teacher. Our people were in exile, sojourning in the land of strangers. Their oppression became unbearable and efforts were made to annihilate them. (The *Book of Exodus*, 1:16- describes the command of Pharaoh to kill all newborn Hebrew males.) It was time to return to the land of the Patriarchs.

"But was leaving simple? No. Pharaoh's heart had hardened against us and he sent powerful military forces to bar the way. In a like manner, the hearts of those who rule the British Empire have hardened against us now, and they have sent an awesome navy to keep us from our land.

"In the days of Moses, there were the doubters – those whose belief was not strong enough – and there were those who had given in to the weakness of the flesh. So it is today. In the ancient Exodus, they did not travel across the Sinai straight to the Promised Land. Instead, they wandered across the desert for forty years. It was a time for cleansing away the sins of the past. The doubts, the omissions and the surrender to immorality – whether for survival or otherwise – had to be ended. And the ancient Hebrews were tested in the scorching, hot sands and in the crucible of misfortune, again and again. And the road was made long and arduous, for the prize was great.

It was a prize reserved for those whose faith and determination were worthy of so great a reward.

"So has our journey in this day and age been made long and seemingly impossible to complete. We take two steps forward and then are driven three steps back. We touch the soil of Palestine and then are forcibly dragged back to nowhere. Only a people who remain firm in their belief and unwavering in their actions will earn the prize, the new State of Israel."

Miriam had listened to the exchange in silence. She thought for a while after Avraham was done. Then she smiled. "Just like Papa. For everything in life, there's a scripture that explains it."

Her brother grinned. "That's what makes us what we are. After all, we're the Children of the Book, and as long as we hold firmly to what it says, we'll be traveling in the right direction."

The three of them started up again. They climbed to the deck. Outside, they stood next to the wire mesh of their cage, studying the murky water. Miriam arched her slender neck towards her brother.

"Just one more thing," she began. "I never asked you what you were doing that night..., the night the British attacked our ship. The next morning, when we found you, your face was blackened with soot. Chaya and I were so relieved...but we wondered... You're not usually given to violence. What made you change?"

"I didn't... I mean I'm not given to violence. I would fight...if I had to..., if there were no other way..., but I didn't that night."

"Then what in the world were you doing out there?"

"I remembered... We had a Torah on board. I had to make sure it was safe."

"But your face," interrupted Chaya. "It was blackened with soot."

"From the smoke," he replied. "They were tossing oil and things all over the deck. The flames would have destroyed the scrolls."

Miriam's mouth hung open with amazement. "You ran out in the middle of a battle to rescue a —"

"Now remember," he interrupted, "we're the Children of the Book."

The next morning, sixty of the oldest and weakest went ashore. Then the battle of the spirit was continued in earnest. The refugees ran up a flag over each of the prison ships. The Star of David fluttered in the hot breeze. The one over *Ocean Vigour* was stained red with the blood of Hirsch Yakubovich, having previously been used to cover the body of the orphan murdered by the British. Banners, made from bed sheets, were hung from the portholes. These proclaimed the determination of the Jews to go to Palestine, and denounced the British for having seized them on the high seas, sending them back to Europe.

Members of UNSCOP (the United Nations Special Committee of Inquiry on Palestine) came on board the vessels to interview the refugees. Secretaries took reams of notes – the testimony of the victims of Nazi persecution and the demands of the homeless. Then they left.

Three weeks went by in this war of nerves. Nothing changed. The ships were just as hot in the intense August sun. Finally, the refugees received a warning: "This is your last chance," barked a British officer over a loudspeaker. "I have received word from London. Disembark in this harbor within forty-eight hours or be taken, in these ships, to Germany, to the British Zone of Occupation. There you will be on British-ruled territory and any and all necessary force will be employed to get you off the ships."

The faces of the Jews blackened with anger as the translation was read. That look was slowly replaced by the gritted teeth and pursed lips of their grim determination. Jew looked at Jew – searching for any hint of weakness in the other's eyes, a sign that resolve had faltered in the blackness of their plight. They saw only piercing, steady eyes.

"Germany," shuddered Chaya. "They plan to send us back to an existence among the ovens of Auschwitz."

"We'll do what we set out to do," replied Avraham. "What pleasure can the British lion have in being forced to beat the ailing survivors of gas chambers, frail widows and little, homeless children? How will the British government look in the eyes of its people, let alone to the body of world opinion? So we stay. It won't be easy, but when was it so for a Jew? It won't be caviar, but I've never tasted any and so I won't miss it."

He looked up to the heavens. The sun hid behind a dark cloud and then peeked out again at the three prison ships resting in the murky water.

"Truly," the bearded sage continued, "the hand of the Maker must be in it. For what greater outrage could the rulers of the empire commit than this? They have done their worst and it shall fail. And with that failure shall their resolve crumble. It is the beginning of their end in Palestine. When the smoke clears, we shall again be a nation with the City of David as our capital."

Not a single Jew bowed to the British demand to disembark that day.

Within twenty minutes of the expiration of the ultimatum, the first of the prison ships set sail westward in the Mediterranean. The three ships headed through the Strait of Gibraltar, north in the Atlantic and then into the North Sea. In Hamburg, a British army awaited them. Standing on the dock were 2,500 soldiers, waiting to drag the survivors of the Holocaust back into the barbed wire camps in Germany. Paratroops and military police used fire-hoses and clubs to force the Jews on to trains, taking them to the camps.

The Jews were forcibly hauled to the new prison camps. The British interrogated them and each of them was asked to give his name and country of origin. Each gave a biblical name. They all had one country of origin: Israel.

A few months later, the resolve of the British Empire melted in the face of an outraged world. Backed into a position they no longer could account for, either to themselves or to anyone else, they threw up their hands and evacuated their military forces from Palestine. A Jewish state was established.

On September 7, 1948, a telegram sent by the Jewish Immigration Bureau in Europe arrived in Israel. "We have sent off the last of the *Exodus* passengers from Germany... We have kept our promise."

The last of the refugees on that ship arrived in the Holy Land. All the able-bodied, including Avraham Ausübel, promptly took up arms in defense of their beleaguered state. The survivors of the Holocaust joined the fight against the combined armies of seven Arab nations.

They wanted their own homeland: They fought for their own homeland, and the Star of David again flew over Eretz Yisrael!

Avraham Ausübel went to Jerusalem, the City of David. He married and raised a family in the traditions of the sages of old. Miriam and Chaya each married survivors of the Holocaust and began life anew. All nine children of Joseph Ausübel lived to return to Eretz Yisrael, along with Malka, their mother. And the seed was replanted in an ancient land.

ESCAPE

On Rosh Hashanah (the beginning of the year, a day of judgment), the Book of Life is opened. For eight days, the Lord of Hosts holds it in His hands while He considers the fate of all who inhabit the world. It is a time for reflection; it is the period of the year when the Jew takes stock of what has been done and what should be done to make it better.

The last jasmine rays of sun filter into the synagogue on Yom Kippur. The prayers of the faithful are being recited with growing fervor while He who has no name is determining who shall wax rich and who shall know only poverty, who shall live and who shall die. The shadows of dusk grow long; the *shofar* (a ram's horn sounded in the synagogue during the High Holidays) blows; the Book is sealed shut; our destiny during the next year has been inscribed in it.

This is the belief of the observant Jew. Yet, this belief does not turn the Followers of Moses into a group of sheep standing idly in the meadow, waiting for manna to drop from the heavens. On the contrary, the Jew toils and struggles; he works all the harder to achieve...a loaf of bread, a place to sleep, and perhaps, a bit of security for himself and his family.

Yet, if the Jew has learned anything from history during the 2,000 years in exile, it is that he should have no faith in the idols of wealth and position; his material possessions have so often been confiscated. And it has been violently called to his attention, over and over again, that no matter where he dwells in the Diaspora, it may not long be home. Today's hospitable nation may become tomorrow's Third Reich. The Jew has traversed every inch of the globe; he has saluted a hundred flags; he has donned the uniforms of countless nations and shed his blood in their service, only to be forcibly reminded that he is an outsider, hated and despised, a creature to be beaten and slaughtered in 1,000 horrible ways. Still hoping for a better day and a better world, he prays and carries on. The wise will also keep scenting the winds and studying the clouds for storm warnings, while making contingency plans to escape.

During the closing two decades of the nineteenth century, violent Pogroms in Russia sent two million Jews fleeing for their lives. They swarmed westward through Germany and Austria, most pausing only to catch their breath before continuing on to the United States or other places across the sea. But some, including members of my family, chose to remain in Western Europe, hoping they might live in peace, and perhaps, even prosper in these civilized nations. As thousands of refugees from the land of the Tsar trekked through the provincial villages of Galicia, their brethren in these hamlets suddenly became aware of the danger. Before long, Jews from Galicia, frightened by tales of horror in the East (only a few miles away), and lured by stories of greater prosperity in the West, joined the migration towards the setting sun.

In 1905, Kalman Ausübel left Galicia. He found the city of Stuttgart in Germany appealing and decided to take up residence there. His wife, Hannah, and their five children joined him.

The children grew to adulthood, now perceiving themselves as Germans (although they carried Austrian passports, and later Polish passports, after the collapse of the Austro-Hungarian Empire). As loyal Germans, the men of the family served in the Kaiser's army. (Isadore, the eldest of the sons, died in battle during World War I.) Like many of the Jews of Germany, they became small businessmen.

Sigfried, one of an Ausübel set of twins, founded a wholesale and retail men's underwear business and took in two of his younger brothers as partners. During a business trip to Switzerland, Sigfried met and married Bertha Schmidt, a young Jewish girl recently arrived from Krakow. He escorted his bride back to Stuttgart, returning to the tranquil middle-class life in the outskirts of a busy city. He wished nothing more than to raise a family in quiet German dignity. His orthodoxy was beardless in a land where most Jews prided themselves on their assimilation. Bertha gave birth to a son whom they named Herbert. Business was going well, and a reason to give thanks for living in the Weimar Republic (the German republic set up after World War I).

But storm clouds were blowing over Germany, concealing the light that had once shone on German civilization. Adolph Hitler had come to power. He told his countrymen that Germany had not lost the war for lack of strength; rather, it was because of the Jews who were traitors to the nation, boring from within to destroy the German will. The Führer demanded racial purification of his nation: A goal he intended to achieve by driving every last Jew out of the land.

Some German Jews refused to believe their ears. Hitler, they reasoned, was just using this ridiculous theme to whip up support among fools and malcontents. Once secure in power, according to this logic, Hitler would return to a more sane policy. Then the Jews could resume their former tranquil lives.

The Ausübels of Stuttgart were not of that opinion. Henry, Sigfried's twin brother, was the first of the children to leave. In 1937, he obtained visas for himself, his wife and their children. They promptly boarded a ship sailing for New York. A few months later, Bertha, Sigfried and their son received affidavits of sponsorship from Ausübels in the United States, but by now America had shut its gates. The cries of Jews trapped in Nazi Germany fell on deaf ears in Washington. Sigfried found it impossible to obtain American visas.

The following year, the Jews of Germany were forbidden to work. The Ausübels, like all of their co-religionists, would have to survive by drawing on their savings and by selling off their possessions. Failing that, they would starve.

Shortly thereafter, the German government ordered the deportation of all Polish Jews. The persecution had begun with organized demonstrations by black-shirted youths. Boycotts of Jewish-owned shops and Jewish professionals reached heightened fury in the Kristallnacht – night of the crystal or glass. (The assassination of a member of the German Embassy in Paris by a Jew was used as an excuse by the Nazis to destroy the businesses and synagogues of the Jews. The shattering of glass of shops and synagogues gave the night its name.) Forbidden to work, beaten and spat upon when they ventured forth with the obligatory yellow Star of David on their garments, the Jews were now obliged to pay a collective fine of one billion marks.

One day, two German soldiers stopped Sigfried on the street. In the search that followed, he was found to have a Polish passport. This resulted in his arrest and deportation on the first train to Poland. His wife and son were still in Stuttgart. A few months later, he managed to get back into Germany on the pretext of disposing of his business. His actual purpose was to get his family out of the country.

On a steamy day early in July in the year 1939, Sigfried sat on a kitchen chair trying to teach German grammar to his eleven-year-old son. Beads of perspiration formed, rolled down the father's rounded, clean-shaven face, and formed again as he reviewed the conjugation of a verb. The sides of his full head of brown hair were soaked to a reflective gloss. Small slits called eyes were barely able to force their way open between the heavy, exhausted lids. It appeared difficult for Sigfried to continue. Still, he went on with the instruction.

"Papa," said his son, interrupting the lesson, "when am I going back to school?"

"They don't allow Jews in the schools here any more," was the sad reply. Then, trying to feign enthusiasm, he added, "When we get out of Germany, you'll be able to go to school again."

The lad looked puzzled and annoyed. "But you and Mama go out every day. Mama told me that you've gone to all sorts of places. Why can't you get us the tickets to leave?"

"I guess," replied his father, heavily, "because we're Jews. No one wants us. There was a shipload of Jews: They went to Cuba, then America, only to be turned away. They had to come back to Europe. So you see it's not easy."

"What do they have against us? Are we hurting anyone?" The boy rubbed his forearm with his opposite hand as if suddenly feeling unclean. "Did you see that book *The Poisoned Mushroom*? Why do they say that we are poison?" (*The Poisoned Mushroom* was published in Nazi Germany. A picture book for children, it depicted Jews as a poisoned mushroom intended to poison the Aryan people.)

"It's not you." Sigfried patted his son on the back, reassuringly. "It's not any of us. It's them – the Germans...and the others who stand by and watch it all but say nothing and do nothing to help us."

"Why?" Tears glistened in the child's eyes. He suddenly remembered a little stray dog being chased down the street. Oh, how he wished he could have taken in the pup. (The German government considered owning pets to be a means for enjoyment. Jews were forbidden to keep them. All pets were removed from Jewish households and killed.)

The boy's hurt aroused pain and anger in his father. "Do you think they need reasons? They can sit up all night and conjure up reasons faster than I can stitch underwear."

The tears came tumbling down Herbert's face profusely.

Sigfried drew the boy into his arms and held him for a long time.

"But why?" asked the boy again in a cracking voice.

Sigfried released his son and then looked him in the eye. He began to speak in gentle, reassuring tones. "Do you remember the story from the Torah that is read in the synagogue on Yom Kippur, the one about the goats? In ancient times, the people would take a goat and heap all their sins upon it by laying hands on the goat. Then they would kick the goat out into the wilderness, thinking that they had ridden themselves of all sin by so doing. So it is with the Germans. We have been made the scapegoat for all their sins. And when they beat us with sticks and rocks, they really believe they've gotten rid of their sins."

At that moment, they heard a key turning in the door. It was Bertha with a broad smile on her elongated face. Her green eyes were shining. She took three steps into the room and then whirled about in a circle of joy, with her dark-brown hair flying as she turned. Giddy, she stopped and announced:

"Sigfried, Herbert – in our own apartment I can call you Sigfried and Herbert – I have good news." (According to a German law enacted in 1938, Israel was to be the first name of every Jewish male except for those already named Moses. All Jewish women and girls were to be named Sarah. This would enable Germans to identify Jews and thereby avoid contact with them.)

"What is it? Are we going to leave Germany?" Herbert asked excitedly as he ran to embrace his mother.

She threw her arms tightly around him and bent her face to his head. "I've got visas – visas for all of us. We're going to leave."

Sigfried rose from his chair and hastily joined in the hugging and kissing. After a time, excitement gave way to more practical considerations.

"Where are we going?" wondered Sigfried, aloud, as he smiled with anticipation.

"To Siam."

"To where?" Sigfried looked perplexed. He withdrew his arms from his wife and now held them in front of him, palms up, in a half-questioning position.

"Siam," she replied. "It's near China. I got visas to Siam from the French Counsel."

Sigfried, his face expressing confusion tinged with gloom, returned to his chair near the table and sat down. He thought briefly and then spoke. "How are we going to get to Siam? And what will we do there?"

"We'll get there somehow," was her answer. "The main thing is that it gives us a way of getting out of Germany. We'll stuff our bags with everything we can carry. When we arrive at our destination, even along the way, we can sell some of the things to pay for our food and lodgings. We'll have to hide what money we have in our clothes. They only allow emigrants to take ten marks with them."

"Hide money? But how? They'll search us." His face darkened as he added, "They send people to concentration camps for concealing money."

"I'll sew money in the hems and belts, in trouser cuffs and in the shoulder pads of our clothing: places in which they would expect some thickness.

Now I'd better get to work. It's not wise to keep the lights on all night. Someone might get suspicious."

"You seem to have figured it all out, Bertha. But tell me, how do we get to Siam? By ship?"

"I don't know. We go to Switzerland first. Then we'll see."

Two days later, on July 15, they were on a train going to Switzerland. The train came to a halt on the German side of the frontier. Border guards, in their dark uniforms, went through the train questioning all the passengers and examining their papers. A soldier surveyed Sigfried, Bertha and Herbert carefully from head to toe. He studied the Polish passports of the parents and the birth certificate of the child, as well as three visas to Siam. "Empty your pockets," he said acidly. "And you, father, take off your jacket. I want to inspect it more carefully."

All they had was ten marks per person.

The tall, blond German twisted a shiny button on his snappy black jacket. The swastika band around his arm seemed to pulsate with anger and he stamped his right foot with such force that the floor shook. "Where are your bags, Jews! I want to examine them."

Sigfried motioned to his wife and son. They all rose from their bench-like seat. Sigfried began pulling down valises from the overhead rack, while his wife and son tugged at bulging suitcases wedged beneath their bench. They placed the cases, one at a time, on the seat so that the soldier could check the contents. Methodically, Prussian hands sifted through the articles of clothing. The soldier felt each item, and then tossed it to the floor like discarded rubbish. By the time he had emptied the last case, there was a large mound of clothing on the floor. He shook the empty cases and pierced each one with an ice pick, searching for a hiding place. Bertha and Sigfried displayed stoic composure through all this, but the boy appeared frightened.

"Where is it?" the German asked with frustration written across his face.

"Where is what?" replied Sigfried, innocently, question for question.

"The money – the gold, the silver, the jewels!"

"But the law only allows us to take –" began Sigfried.

"I know what the law allows!" the guard broke in. He reflected for a minute, and then added, "So you turned it into clothing. What for? It's supposed to be hot in Siam, yet you're carrying enough winter wear to supply an army in Siberia."

"We took what we have," replied Bertha, as Sigfried hesitated for a moment. "That's all right, isn't it? Perhaps you would like some of our underwear? It's freshly laundered."

"What? And be contaminated!" he snarled at Bertha. He turned to Sig-fried and looked him in the eye with a frosty stare. "Where is your beard and where are those funny curls? You Jews think you're smart. You think you can fool a German by cutting them off. Well, you're not! Get out of Germany and don't come back! We've had enough of your pollution!"

Sigfried did not answer. With a blank expression masking his inner thoughts, he waited for the guard to return the travel documents as well as his jacket. The German thrust the papers into Sigfried's open hand with a blow that carried through to the Jew's abdomen. As Sigfried doubled over with pain, the soldier turned to leave. Despite the sharp hurt he felt, the Jew looked up at the German and asked whimsically, "The jacket – did you want to keep it as a remembrance?"

"What?" replied the German, turning around. He looked down at his hand and saw the jacket in it. "Ach!" he shouted disdainfully as he tossed it at the Jew's face. "More of your contamination."

The German left, slamming the compartment door so hard their ears pained from the crash of metal against metal. Bertha hugged her trembling son to still his fears. Sigfried began repacking the cases. After a while, his wife and son joined him in the effort.

The train started up again. They could feel a freshness in the air.

"Let's hope we've seen the last of those Germans," said Sigfried, softly.

"Let's hope so," Bertha replied, exhaustedly.

A hundred yards later, the train came to a halt. Their hearts began to race anxiously. Then they saw a Swiss flag through the window. Their spirits soared.

Swiss border guards in their pine-green uniforms came through the train. "Welcome to Switzerland," said one in German as he examined their papers. He completed his task and handed the papers back to Sigfried. "But you don't have visas to stay in Switzerland," he began again. "Better finish your business here within a week or get papers to stay longer. Otherwise you'll have to leave."

Even those words did not seem to frighten them, for they were here and the German side of the frontier was over there.

They were alone with their thoughts while the train started up again. It chugged its way through the tall trees of Swiss forests and past the tumbling mountain waters that seemed to wash away some of the terror of that all too recent experience.

"What if he had taken you up on it?" wondered Bertha aloud, when she was sure they were not being overheard.

"Take me up on it? He was already leaving with the jacket in his hand. It was our only chance. If I had simply requested my jacket, he might have grown curious and inspected the linings. The word 'remembrance' was what did it. He couldn't wait to get rid of the 'pollution.' You recall his reaction to your offer of some underwear."

"Yes," laughed Bertha, reflectively. "That's the way a Junker would react. And these days every young German bully thinks himself one." (A Junker is a younger member of the Prussian aristocracy, generally narrow-minded, haute and overbearing in personality.)

"You really fooled him," said Herbert, joining in the laughter.

"Let's not get so giddy we forget that we're not out of the woods yet," cautioned Sigfried. "Remember what the Swiss guard said: We've got one week."

A few hours later, they were in Zurich. They lugged their bags down the narrow, winding streets, in search of a place to stay. Herbert looked up with strange fascination at a few oriel windows adorning the intricately designed wrought iron sculpture. Bertha tugged at the boy's hand to remind him that they had more important things to do. At last, they spotted a hotel sign and went in.

Half an hour later, they were making the rounds of consulates and Swiss immigration authorities. A temporary extension of their stay was refused. They kept trying. Their luck improved minutes before closing time. They obtained visitors' permits at the Italian Consulate.

A few days later they were aboard a train again, traveling across the lush green countryside, through long, dark tunnels, and beneath mountains whose towering peaks were covered with snow, even in the heart of summer. The lakes along the way assumed the colors of the sky and the landscape, changing from gray to green to blue, as dark clouds swooped in over the valleys, only to be replaced with an azure sky. After several hours of travel, they reached their destination.

Milan was a huge city with bustling streets and exuberant people. Bertha and Herbert waited outside the railroad station, watching the bags, while Sigfried went looking for a place to stay. Several times they had to wave off porters anxious to lend a hand.

Sigfried returned. They dragged the heavy suitcases to a dingy building a few blocks a way. Sigfried had rented a small apartment.

Again they began their rounds of consulates and immigration offices, this time without success. The French official informed them, almost apologetically, that the visas to Siam were no longer valid.

"Maybe we'll have better luck tomorrow," sighed Bertha.

There was no verbal reply, only a sad nod from her husband.

Each morning they would start on their rounds, going from consulate to consulate, hoping to obtain visas to anywhere, as long as it was farther away from Nazi Germany. Each day they encountered the same people during their travels, the dispirited refugees and the harried officials. The look on the faces never seemed to change, unless, by some stroke of fortune, one received a visa. Then the refugee's eyes lit up and even the official seemed pleased to have been part of it.

In the afternoons Bertha and Sigfried would take a few articles of clothing to the flea market, where they attempted to exchange the things for money or food. If they were successful, they ate; if not, they went hungry. As for the money brought with them from Stuttgart, it was kept hidden away for the day, God willing, when they would get visas allowing them to leave. They would need every *pfennig* (penny) for the passage.

The days grew into weeks and the weeks into months. Germany invaded Poland. France and England joined the conflict. The world was at war. The Italian borders were now closed. And to make matters worse, Italy and Germany were now allies. Dr. Goebels had arrived in Italy to instruct the Italians on how to treat the Jews in the New Order.

Sigfried continued to make his rounds to the decreasing number of foreign consulates. He seemed to do it out of habit, almost without hope that he would ever get visas to leave. One day he was resting on a park bench after completing his fruitless tour. He sat dejected, his head buried in his hands. He did not take notice of an approaching officer.

"Let me see your papers," said the officer, officiously.

"Oh," responded Sigfried as he raised his head. He reached into his inside jacket pocket and then placed his passport, his Italian visitor's permit and visa to Siam in the official's outstretched hand.

"You're Polish," said the Italian as he studied the papers. "Polish what?"

"I don't understand your question."

"Are you a Jew? That's what I mean." There was a sense of irritation in his tone of voice.

"I am a Jew," said Sigfried, softly.

"You don't have to mutter it. All I wanted was a straight answer... Now your visa to Siam is outdated. And your visitor's permit has expired. So I have to take you in."

"But where will you take me?"

"To police headquarters. From there to a camp for Jews. That's the regulation. Foreign Jews without proper papers are not permitted to remain at large."

"Please, I'm not a burden to anyone. I'll get off the street right away."

"You don't understand. You're under arrest!"

"Just give me a day, a few hours... I'll go to the immigration office for an extension... Please," he implored with moistened eyes.

"Sorry," replied the Italian, evading the Jew's eyes. "You'll have to come with me. I'm just a simple policeman with a family to support, and orders are orders."

Sigfried was taken to the police station. A small, olive-skinned man in a black uniform questioned him. "And how did you get into Italy?"

"I entered by train from Switzerland, sir."

"And who came with you?"

"I...eh...came alone."

"I see... And where are you staying?"

"Staying?"

"What's the matter with you? Don't you understand Italian?" The official rubbed his hands impatiently while his eyes bore in on Sigfried with growing annoyance.

"I have some difficulty with the words." His voice trailed off.

"See here: I will not wait all day for an answer. Now where are you staying?"

"No place."

"What sort of nonsense is that? Do you vanish at dusk?"

"No, your Excellency. I mean that I sleep in the park."

"Do you expect me to believe that? Where are you hiding? Now don't lie to me. That could get you into serious trouble."

"You see, your Excellency, my luggage was stolen. I have no money. So I sleep in the park."

"Well then, you'll be much better off in the camp to which I'm sending you," declared the official, smugly.

"Where is that?" inquired Sigfried, hesitantly.

"Calabria...in the south. There you'll have a nice bunk all to yourself. Now isn't that better than sleeping on a park bench all winter?"

"Do I have a choice?"

The official snapped his fingers. Moments later, two guards appeared and led Sigfried to a cell which he was to share with three other men.

The others in the cell were Italians. They said but a few words to Sigfried and he made little effort to engage them in conversation.

The following day, Sigfried was told that he had a visitor. The man presented himself as a representative of a Jewish organization that sought to help co-religionists ensnared in the police net that grew tighter every day. Sigfried was suspicious at first. Above all, he did not want to put his wife and son in further danger. The problem, to Sigfried, was how could he be sure the man was whom he claimed to be? Fortunately for Sigfried, the man spoke Yiddish. Still, reasoned Sigfried, he could be a German. Sigfried twisted the conversation towards a discussion of synagogues. The other man understood both the direction and the purpose of the questions, and so he not only replied but also expanded his answers. He was most convincing.

Sigfried, speaking in Yiddish in a hushed voice, revealed the existence of his wife and son. He asked the man to inform Bertha and Herbert of what had happened to him and to tell them the name of the camp to which he was being sent. In his message, Sigfried urged them not to contact him in the concentration camp. That might result in their arrest.

"Let them keep their Jewish identity to themselves," he said in conclusion. "To reveal that you're a Jew is a one-way ticket to a concentration camp."

The man nodded in agreement and also promised to do his utmost to assist them. "Maybe the concentration camp won't be so bad," he said, trying to buoy up Sigfried's spirits.

"How good can a concentration camp be? Last September they started rounding up the Jews of Stuttgart and sending them to concentration camps. Several of my relatives were among them. I've not heard a word from any of them since the day they were dragged off the street. God knows what has happened to them! And now Italy's doing the same thing to us."

A few days later, Sigfried was placed under guard aboard a train. Several other Jews similarly escorted and under restraint, boarded the same car. Under other circumstances he would have found the trip exhilarating. There was the gleaming gold of ripened hay wafting in the breeze, and the shimmering green of the olive leaves spread amidst the ancient twisted wood of the branches. He gazed at walled villages of white, brilliantly outlined against the turquoise sky, and great monasteries standing in cold stony solemnity, atop high cliffs. From his train window he watched the people going about their business – singing an aria to an open sky while harvesting the crops, encouraging a donkey forward, or resting in the shade of a two-hundred-year-old tree. But as a prisoner being torn from his family, with each chug of the engine taking him farther and farther from those he loved, it was a journey to despair.

At the end of the long trip, Sigfried found himself in the concentration camp in Calabria, a region in the boot of the Italian peninsula. The presence of thousands of other Jews in the camp, similarly caught in the roundup of displaced persons, did nothing to lighten his sorrow. True to the police officer's words, Sigfried was given a bunk all to himself. It was the third one up, in a room containing more than a hundred other men. His only comfort was that Bertha and Herbert were still free. He hoped against hope that they would somehow get out of Italy.

One day, several months later, Sigfried was summoned to the office of the camp's commanding officer. In his state of dejection, he expected to be informed that he was being shipped back to Germany. Instead, the officer announced, smiling, that Sigfried would be placed on the first train back to Milan and there he would be released. Sigfried was elated, but still too fearful to ask why this was being done.

That afternoon he was led aboard a train, with an officer wearing a black trench coat and narrow-brimmed black felt hat accompanying him. Hours went by. The railroad cars were ferried individually around a break in the rail line, and then reassembled into a lumbering giant that began to puff its way northward through the countryside. As they made their way in a polar direction, the dried fields of southern winter gave way to snow-covered terrain. From time to time the train stopped at one of the cities along the route. Sigfried studied the names of the places, trying to calculate how long it would be before they reached Milan. The officer sat beside him, his dark eyes buried in a newspaper. He paid no heed to all of this.

The farther north they went, the more excited Sigfried became. His heart began to pound, as the names of the cities grew more familiar.

The train came to a halt past a series of winding valleys and dark tunnels. Someone was signaling up ahead. What it was, Sigfried could not make out. The engine started up again, belching violently as it ascended an incline. Without any warning, it lurched to the right. Sigfried's heart skipped a beat. Suddenly he understood the meaning of it all – the stopping and the signaling. The train had shifted onto an adjoining track. They were now headed northeast rather than northwest. He raced through the map in his mind's eye. Where were they going? Milan, he thought, was to the left. What if the commander had been lying when he assured Sigfried of his release? Had he been saying it only to keep a Jew content during the long journey? Was he, in reality, being sent back to Nazi Germany?

The guard sitting beside him appeared indifferent to it all.

The snow grew deeper. The wind howled against the window of his car. The sun dipped low in the west, then faded from view. Darkness now covered the land. Still they moved on, hour after hour.

The guard snored in spurts, his black woolly mustache vibrating with each sonorous breath. From time to time he opened an eye, just a crack, to check on his charge.

Snow came down in sheets, and black clouds obliterated the moon and the stars. It was impossible to see anything.

Thoughts crossed Sigfried's mind. Should he attempt to escape? How? His heart raced with dread and his hand throbbed with intense pain.

The lumbering giant coughed and spat again. Its wheels screeched as it came to a halt. Through the grayness, Sigfried could see the lights of the station.

It was Milan: A sign told him that. As if by a miracle, he spotted his wife and son standing on the platform. Forgetting six months of cautious silence, he blurted out their names. He rushed to the door of the train, which had now come to a halt. He had closed his eyes to the fact that there was an Italian officer with him. The door opened and he rushed out to embrace his wife and child. The man in the black trench coat came up behind him and tapped Sigfried on the shoulder. Suddenly remembering, Sigfried felt a sharp pain. He had revealed what he had tried so long to conceal.

"All right," said the Italian, matter-of-factly. "I'll leave you now. My job is done... Just see to it that you're out of Italy within forty-eight hours." With a tip of his hat and a "Good evening, Signora," he vanished into the grayness.

Sigfried walked back to their old apartment, with his arms around his wife and son. It was good to be out on a street again, even in a storm. His snow-covered head turned first to one, then the other, smiling broadly at each of them. Finally, they were in their apartment. He stamped his feet dry while Bertha toweled his head. At last he could sit in his chair.

"Bertha," he began, "how did all this happen? My release, you being at the station. And what did the officer mean when he said we should be out of this country in forty-eight hours?"

"The officer meant that we must leave almost immediately."

"But how and where?"

"Sigfried, you know that I've been trying to get visas for us every day that you've been away. I've tried and tried. I was told where you were and I obeyed your instructions not to write. We've kept our Jewish identity a secret. Well, finally I got tickets to Lisbon. You know, the capital of Portugal. I gave someone a thousand lira to get them for us. It was from the money we took with us from Germany."

"That's wonderful. Visas too?"

"Transit permits...good for forty-eight hours," she smiled with pride.

"So it starts all over again. We'll have our work cut out for us when we get there. Now when do we leave?"

"Tonight."

They packed their bags quickly.

"And now we must wait 'til 2 AM," said Bertha. "That will give us just enough time to meet the train. We don't want to be standing in the station too long. Someone might stop us for questioning and ruin our escape."

The hour arrived. Sigfried, Bertha and Herbert went to the station, dragging their baggage along. They tried to be as quiet as possible. The three reached the station with just two minutes to spare.

Although Sigfried had not slept in more than twenty-four hours, he was wide-awake. The whistle of the train moving along through the night was music to his ears. They passed through France and Spain; darkness turned to day and day to night. Cities became alive with vibrant music; the countryside glowed in the noonday sun; the sea turned a brilliant orange as the sun set in the west. It was good to be alive and free, and to have his family beside him.

At journey's end, they were in Lisbon, dragging their bags down streets covered with mosaics of black and white tiles. Laughing men and women were clinking glasses together at a sidewalk cafe. From a side street came the haunting refrain of a Fada (a lover's lament, a type of music sung by women dressed in black, traditional style in Portugal). It was well past midnight when they found a cheap room in a ramshackled old lodging house. Then they rested until dawn. In the morning they reported to the immigration office, hoping to extend their stay. This was refused.

"You cannot remain in Portugal," they were told. "The pass is a temporary one. It allows just enough time to board a ship or whatever to a final destination. Those arrangements should have been made in advance. You must leave within the forty-eight hours or risk being deported to the country of your origin."

The Ausübels, long faces sinking to their chests, dragged their bags back to the station. They used some of their depleted financial resources to pay for tickets to Madrid. Perhaps they would be given permission to stay there.

The train came to a halt on the Spanish side of the border. Sigfried's heart began to pound when he saw a Spanish border guard accompanied by a man wearing a German uniform approaching them. Sigfried pictured that their end had come as the two men in uniform examined the Ausübel papers.

"What's your religion?" asked the German in his native tongue. "Your passport does not contain the information."

"Protestant," answered Sigfried as he put his arm across Herbert's chest to hold the boy back.

"Protestant!" said the German, scowling. "Who do you think you're fooling? A Protestant in Poland: I don't believe it."

Up to now, the Spaniard had stood to one side, closely studying the faces of the three passengers. At this point he interjected, "Let them go. You've gotten enough Jews today." The two uniformed men left and the train started up again. The three Ausübels breathed a collective sigh of relief.

At Madrid, they got off the train and soon found a place to stay in a nearby rooming house. Again they began their rounds of consulates and embassies, hoping to obtain visas. They showed their affidavits from relatives in the United States to American Embassy officials. There was no positive response that day. "You'll have to wait your turn under the Polish quota," was what they were told dryly by an American secretary.

"But how long will it take?" Sigfried asked, concerned.

"Maybe two to three years, maybe more. It's hard to say," was the answer. (Under a directive issued by Assistant Secretary of State Breckenridge Long, American consulates throughout Europe were instructed to "postpone, postpone and postpone" the issuance of visas to Jews who wanted to emigrate to the United States in order to escape Nazi persecution in Europe. As a result, thousands of Jews who might have been able to enter the United States, even under the limited quotas, were kept from receiving visas to the United States. Most of the Jews deprived of American entry visas ended up in the death camps run by Nazi Germany.)

The Spaniard officials were more helpful. The Ausübels were given time to make arrangements to leave.

Sigfried and Bertha decided that their son's education must be resumed. They might be staying in Spain for some time. And the boy's studies had been neglected for so long. They enrolled him in a French school for poor French children stranded in Spain by the war. Priests ran it.

The Ausübels had their routine. Each day, Herbert went to school. At the same time, Sigfried was making the circuit of embassies and Bertha was trading the decreasing number of items of clothing they still possessed for a loaf of bread or piece of cheese.

One day Bertha returned home to find Sigfried and Herbert waiting for her. She held out her accomplishments for the day – a little fish and a packet of rice. "Today, we feast," she said, smiling broadly. Then she headed for the washbasin and began cleaning the fish. "And how was your day, Sigfried?" she inquired without turning from her task.

"The same," he replied half resignedly. "Maybe tomorrow, maybe next year."

"And you, Herbert, how was your day?" she asked.

"We learned about Saint Joan." There was enthusiasm in his voice.

"Hmm... Did you learn your lesson well?" she probed further.

"Yes, Mama. The priest asked the class questions when he was done telling us about her. I was the only one who knew the answers." His eyes shone brightly. Abruptly, they turned dull as he reflected aloud, "One of the boys said that I had no business answering because I am a Jew."

"And what did the priest say to that?" asked his mother.

"He told the boy to worry more about learning his lessons and less about my religion."

A few weeks later, Herbert brought some guests home with him on his return from school. Bertha, caught by surprise, dried her hands hastily with a towel while apologizing for their simple room and drab furnishings. She begged them to be seated while she prepared some tea. Bertha put up water to boil, then stepped out of the room. Her hair now swept in a tight bun, she returned to serve her guests some tea. She added a measured quantity of tea leaves to the boiling water and poured the brew into tall glasses. "Sugar?" she questioned sweetly, as she handed each of them a glass.

Both nodded affirmatively. One was a tall, lean young man with a dark blue suit and striped tie. The other was a shorter man with cheerful eyes.

Bertha considered this a hopeful sign, but still she was concerned. "Herbert," she began, looking to her son, "you're forgetting your manners. Please introduce me to these gentlemen."

"They came home with me...from school... I'm sorry. I don't remember their names."

She turned to the two men, now seated, sipping hot tea. "Has Herbert done something wrong? He's really a good boy."

"No. Nothing wrong. And we're not really from the school," rejoined the taller man. "We're here to take your son to the United States."

"What?" said Bertha, appearing stunned by the words. "I don't understand. Who are you and why do you want to take Herbert to America?"

"Don't worry," replied the man with the cheerful eyes. "We'll only take him if that is your wish. We're Quakers, you see – part of an organization that is trying to save some of the Jewish children in Europe. A priest at the school told us of your son. We will be taking several hundred Jewish children to the United States by ship. When the ship gets there, the children will be placed in foster homes. Even if there is no way of getting you into the United States, I'm sure you would want your child saved."

Tears came to the mother's eyes. She threw her arms around Herbert and wept over him. Turning her face to her guests, she cried, "Of course I want him to go. I thank you both from the bottom of my heart... Only one favor..."

"Yes," said the shorter guest.

"We have relatives in the United States – my husband's brother, Henry, and his wife. Could Herbert go to live with them, rather than in a foster home?"

"Of course. That would be fine... Where do they live?"

"In New York City," said Bertha.

Bertha wrote down Henry's full name and address on a slip of paper and handed it to the taller man. The two men said good-bye after reviewing the arrangements.

❖ ❖ ❖

At three o'clock in the morning, on a cold March day of the year 1943, Sigfried and Bertha stood on a platform in the Madrid Central Railroad Station. Beside them was Herbert, dressed in his best suit. It was two sizes too small, giving the boy the appearance of a growing lad wearing his younger sibling's garments.

The station was alive with activity despite the hour. Men in uniform shouted directions; porters pushed huge carts or huffed as they carried heavy luggage. There were smiles and laughter, although not much of that, but mostly there were tears amid muffled expressions of hope.

Bertha and Sigfried both knelt facing their son. They hugged and kissed his face. They admonished him to be good. They reminded him that he must insist on living with his Uncle Henry and Aunt Rose. They reviewed, in rapid order, all the things he was to do upon arrival in America.

"I know. I know," pleaded Herbert. "You've told me all these things a hundred times already. What I want to know is when you're coming to America."

A tinge of sadness crossed their faces. Sigfried caught himself quickly and forced a smile to his lips. "Soon," he replied.

They kissed the boy again with increasing fervor, and then carried his suitcase onto the train. There were scores of other children jamming the car. The Ausübels noted many other tearful farewells between parents and children.

"Last call. All visitors off," cried the conductor.

Bertha and Sigfried left the train. They waved good-bye to their son, his nose now pressed against the window of his car until long after the train disappeared from view. Then they looked at one another and held hands.

"Do you think we will ever see him again?" asked Sigfried, longingly.

"The Almighty did not preserve us this long to die in a strange place. We will see him again. You'll see," was her answer.

Months went by. Life continued in a mechanical fashion. There were morning rounds at the embassies and afternoon efforts to sell some of their few remaining possessions. They were down to their last suitcase.

One bright day in September 1943, they received glorious news at the American Embassy. Their quota numbers had been reached. (This was because everyone ahead of them was dead.) They were told to leave immediately for Lisbon and there board a ship bound for New York.

They rushed home to pack their one case. Bag in hand, they headed for the railroad station.

The following day they were in Lisbon. At the shipping office they showed the officials their papers, including the precious visas entitling them to purchase two tickets. As they left the building, Bertha looked at her husband. Her green eyes looked bright as they had not looked for years.

"In six days," she sighed, "we'll be on a ship. Then New York. We're going to see Herbert!"

Time now passed all too slowly. Their bag was packed and repacked. There was not much to pack – just bits of clothing and a few treasured remembrances. They would study the pictures, then put them carefully in a wool sweater to protect them against bruising during the voyage.

On the day before their scheduled departure, they brought their one remaining piece of luggage down to the dock and had it placed aboard the ship on which they were to sail. This accomplished, they returned to the bareness of their room in town.

They both stood at the window, studying the narrow street and taking in its vibrance. They listened to the hawkers of food in the market, singing out the wonders of their produce; they watched women, their heads covered with dark shawls, testing the meat and the fruit; they smiled at the children who were laughing and running without care. Tomorrow, this would be just another remembrance of the old world; tomorrow it would be as if in the distant past; tomorrow they would be off to a new world where a Jew could join in the singing and the laughter.

There was a knock on the door. Sigfried opened it. It was a woman. Her face conveyed distress.

"Please," implored the stranger. "You must help me."

"Come in," said Sigfried, solicitously. "How can we be of help?"

The woman stared at Sigfried, and then her eyes darted to Bertha. There was a sense of urgency in her watery-blue eyes. She was dressed in a neat mauve suit with matching purse. The garments were well tailored, but appeared to have seen better days. Her shoes were of good quality, though worn to the point where most of the heels were gone.

"I must be quick about it," she said. "There is hardly any time left. Please. You must help me."

"Surely," replied Bertha, comfortingly. "What can we do to help you?"

"Switch tickets with me: that's what you can do," responded the stranger.

"Switch tickets?" puzzled Bertha, aloud. "You mean switch tickets on the ship? But what difference can that make? We'll all get there at the same time."

"You don't understand. I have two tickets on another ship – one scheduled to leave in an hour – and you have two tickets to sail tomorrow. Exchange tickets with me. I implore you."

"But why?" queried Sigfried. "Aren't both ships going to the same place?"

"They are. Of course they are." She paused for a moment, and then explained.

"We are five in our family. My husband is a physician and we have three little children. We have been running from the Nazis, always together. Then came the waiting for the visas to enter the United States. Three years, we waited. Now finally we have them. But they assigned us two tickets on the ship leaving today and three on the one leaving tomorrow. We have come all this way together as a family. We don't want to be separated on the final leg of our journey. Will you help me? Will you help us?"

"But our bag has already been stored away on the ship that leaves tomorrow. It contains all our possessions. Not that the clothes are worth much, but our keepsakes, our family pictures..." Her voice trailed off questioningly.

"I'll guard your package as if it were a child," responded the woman, folding her arms on her chest as if holding a baby. "I'll bring it to you as soon as we reach New York. Just tell me where you will be staying."

Bertha looked at her husband. "Sigfried, let us help this woman. Forget about the clothes. We'll wash as best we can. Now quickly write down Henry's address for the lady. Then let's take a taxi to the dock. For such a mitzvah, we can spend the money."

"Please," insisted the woman, reaching for her purse.

Bertha extended her hand to block the woman's effort. "Oh, no. It's our mitzvah."

In the meantime, Sigfried had printed the address on a slip of paper. They exchanged tickets. Half an hour later, Bertha and Sigfried were at harbor side, boarding a ship.

Several days later, they arrived in New York, without luggage and without any relatives waiting at the dock. However, Hebrew Immigration Aid Society representatives were there. They telephoned Sigfried's brother to come for the couple. A few hours later, Bertha and Sigfried were reunited with their son, as well as with Henry and his family.

Days went by and they did not hear from the woman with whom they had made the exchange. The absence of news was troubling.

Sometime later, they learned of what had happened. The other ship had never arrived because it had been sunk... All on board had been lost at sea.

Behind Bertha and Sigfried were the ashes of the past. They would never again see Sigfried's brother, Solly, or his sister, Martha, or Martha's husband and son, or Sigfried's uncles, aunts and cousins by the score, or Bertha's father and three sisters and their husbands and children. The death camps of Nazi Germany consumed them. Ahead lay a new life in a new country.

On Rosh Hashanah, Sigfried stood in the rear of a small synagogue in Brooklyn. He chanted the *Kaddish*. As he remembered the dead – his own and all the others – he wondered, for a moment, at the meaning of it all. He and his wife and son had escaped on that yesterday. Now the Book of Life was again open and judgments were being made. This year, who shall live and who shall die? And *why*?

He sighed and went on with his prayers.

SAVE THE CHILDREN

As a child, I had been made well aware of the disaster facing the Jewish people. Current events were but an extension of the history of the Jews to me.

Following the Final Revolt in Judea in the second century, the Romans had depopulated Judea, shipping the Hebrew people into slave exile in Europe. For the next 2,000 years, Europe was home to the bulk of world Jewry.

The Holocaust became a defining time in Jewish history. Could the Jews stay alive as a people? If they were to survive, the next generation would have to be saved.

In the years since the end of World War II, stories have come to light about some heroes who made efforts to save Jewish children who would have otherwise ended up in the gas chambers. These included a number of gentiles whose deeds should never be forgotten. They are remembered by plaques in the Memorial for Righteous Gentiles in Yad Vashem in Israel. (Yad Vashem is the Holocaust Martyrs' and Heroes' Remembrance Authority.) There were, of course, Jews who partook in this effort to save the children. Among them, as I later learned, was a member of my family.

In the shadows of the night, two figures sat in a room which was illuminated only by the shimmering light of the moon and the stars which came through an attic skylight.

"When do you leave?" inquired Willy Ausübel-Mohar with a look of concern tinged with the sadness of parting. Hidden beneath horn-rimmed glasses were dark, thoughtful eyes that looked at a world turned upside down and tried to make sense of it. It was the youthful face of a man in his twenties, yet its first lines of anguish were already visible in the dim moonlight.

Willy leaned forward in his chair. Slowly he smoothed back his straight, brown hair that was parted at the side. He tilted his head forward with strained emphasis, to view his sister, Rosa. His neck was taut, as if his body were being pulled backward by powerful arms determined to remove him from the scene, while his head yearned to remain in the room a while longer. His full nose sniffed the air to capture scents that would soon be gone. A small jaw pushed forward, trying to convey a sense of confidence in the future, in a situation that had all the earmarks of impending disaster.

"As soon as it is dawn," was the reply. "That will give us 'til sunset to reach our destination...before curfew."

Rosa's smile, a facade of buoyant optimism, could not hide her frightful doubts. She was small and slender, a dark-eyed, delicate girl with moonbeams dancing reflectively in her hair. Rosa looked up at the skylight, wishing to fly through it to a land free from care and worry. But alas, she had no wings and the world she hoped for did not yet exist.

"Don't give me your location. Just in case..." Willy broke off, his face turning sad.

There was no need for him to say more. The meaning was all too clearly understood. The less he knew, the less they could torture out of him.

"We'll be in Walloon country," she replied, grasping his hand, "on a farm. No danger in your knowing that much. Dov has the blond-haired, blue-eyed look of the peasants. We'll pass for Belgium farmers until... Don't worry. We'll make it."

Her eyes flew up again through the skylight, to the stars, and then back again to her brother.

"Willy, do you remember when we were children and you spoke about a perfect world: Each man and woman free to work and contribute to society, each secure, assured of food and clothing and shelter, free from fear and free from want. You spoke of a civilization in which people labor together as brothers and sisters to better their lives, a world in which people would decide their future in a democratic fashion. Do you think we'll ever have such a world?"

Willie looked at her intently. "Yes, I believe it down to the very fabric of my soul, even now."

"I wonder," she smiled sadly. "When we were children and would sit in the parlor on Shabbos (the Sabbath, in Yiddish) singing and telling funny stories and... Well, at such times, I wished that the day would never end – that it would be Shabbos forever, that we would remain free from the cares of the week... But it always ended. Everything ends."

"Who knows? Antwerp may have ended for us, but Shabbos, never! Wherever we are – in Antwerp or Brussels or God knows where – there will always be Shabbos when we can lean back and remember... Papa and Mama and happy friends, Dusseldorf and Antwerp. Come to think of it, you're too young to remember Dusseldorf."

"Not really," she objected. "I was four when Papa died and I can still remember scenes, like Renoir paintings – blurred images of busy streets, people rushing to and fro, going somewhere. I can visualize those beautiful shop windows filled with mannequins dressed in the latest fashions of that day – slim flapper dresses, form-fitting chic coats, hats and jewelry. Even through the mist of the past, I remember those mounds of toys of every description – sad-eyed dolls, brightly-colored tin soldiers, tiny chairs and tiny tables, tiny tea sets and a big doll house, trains and planes and cars. And those lollypops and chocolate treats! I can remember it all! And I remember Papa in his black suit and dark tie. Do you remember those steadfast gray-green eyes? They could see right through me, every mischievous thing I had done. Yet, they expressed the love he bore me. I can see him in my mind's eye: his short, reddish-brown beard – always so impeccably combed – projecting forward dramatically to the world as if to declare for all to hear that 'This is a rabbi.'"

"I'm surprised. You were so small, Rosa."

"Not as small as Ari, but small enough. And you were nine – not as big as Raphi or Yeshi or Baruch, but big enough. And after Papa died and we moved to Antwerp, I remember you in your uniform."

"Uniform? Do you mean the Belgian army uniform?"

"No. Long before that, when you joined the HaShomer HaTzair." (A Zionist-socialist pioneering youth movement whose aim it is to educate Jewish youth for kibbutz life in Palestine.)

"Oh, that uniform. Well, the organization is still active, trying to build that bright new world. That's what I'll be doing after you leave."

"What do you mean?" Rosa inquired, puzzled. "What do they hope to do here in Belgium?"

"Save the children. We've got to get our young people out of here before it's too late and send them to Palestine."

"But how? The Germans are everywhere."

"We've got members of the movement in different places. A picture here, a stamp there, and we hope it will pass inspection by the Germans. We're planning to slip groups of three – one adult and two children – down through France, to Switzerland. There, they'll be safe 'til it's all over. If possible, we'll fly them out to Palestine."

"And you, Willy? When will you get out?"

"At the end."

"Will you know when the end has come?" she murmured in a throaty voice, feeling a lump swell up in her neck.

"If I'm caught, I'll know it's the end for me. Otherwise, when the last child is out or when they're closing in on me." His face was very serious.

There was a long pause as they visualized the hazards of the future.

The first pale rays of dawn filtered through the skylight. They knew that the hour had come. Embracing, perhaps for the last time, they remained silent, holding on to what would soon be but a memory.

Rosa broke the silence. "Dov is waiting." She turned to leave, but lingered to ask a final question. "What chance do we have?" Gloom spread over her face and darkened her eyes. Tears rolled down her soft, reddened cheeks, against her desire to leave with at least the appearance of optimism.

"In Palestine," he replied with hope in his voice. "In Ein HaHoresh. It's a kibbutz founded by our movement. I'll look for you there. Remember. Ein HaHoresh." (A kibbutz is a communal farm settlement run by its members on the basis of democratic principles and sharing the fruits of their labor.)

It was a trying year, to say the least, from August of 1941 to the following summer. The German overlords imposed anti-Jewish rules in Antwerp. These became more and more restrictive. The Star of David, sewn on the outer garment, was required wearing for all the Hebrew people. Failure to do so was a criminal offense and would result in imprisonment. Curfew time was 8 PM. Any Jew found on the street after that hour would be arrested and sent to one of the concentration camps from which none returned. Jews were barred from almost all occupations.

Willy was a skilled diamond-cutter, but now he could rarely find work splitting gems, and only in secret. He worked in his attic room, splitting diamonds for owners who wished smaller stones capable of being concealed in their garments during hoped-for escapes from German-ruled Belgium. The meager earnings were insufficient for Willy to survive on, and so he sold his few family heirlooms of silver and gold to help pay for food.

What kept Willy most occupied was his work forging documents, which would enable his organization to smuggle children abroad. Group by group set out on the journey through France, to Switzerland. How they fared was an unknown quantity. Slowly, the Jewish population of the city diminished – some via escape, but most disappeared after a sudden knock on the door by the Germans. Those taken this way were never seen again.

In August 1942 Willy sat at a table in his attic room. He was reviewing a collection of papers and booklets. One at a time, he went through several documents, holding each paper up to the light to check the quality. He studied the pictures and the signatures and finally the emblems of their Nazi overlords. Satisfied with what he saw, he turned next to a booklet containing time schedules of buses and trains. His eyes were tired from long hours of painstaking mental labor.

He removed his glasses and wiped his eyes. A fleeting shadow crossed the table on which he was working. He raised his glasses at an angle before him and began to clean the sweat from their surface. In the process, he studied an image reflected in the lens. Calmly and quietly he slipped the documents into his inside jacket pocket. He rose from his seat and walked to a closet across the room. Opening the door, he stepped into the chamber and quickly closed the door behind him. The room remained still and empty for several minutes. Then there was a sudden crash of glass from above and two Gestapo officers landed on the floor, pistols drawn.

"Where did he go?" shouted one to the other.

"Through that door."

"But the others, downstairs, didn't see him come out."

They yanked open the closet door. There was nothing within, save for a few items of clothing resting on hangers. They tore through the clothing and hammered at the walls. Finally, they located two boards that gave way to a secret passage. They followed it in the darkness, down hidden stairs, to a cellar and then to a grating to the street above.

He's gone," said one.

"Too bad," replied the other.

The train to Nancy, France, was delayed. Willy sat in a train compartment between two young men. A sandy-haired, blue-eyed slim lad of perhaps seventeen was seated to his left. A still younger, dark-haired, chubby youth occupied the portion of the seat to his right. Opposite them were two women and a boy. A plump, tight-lipped, middle-aged woman, her eyes and nose turned up in indifference, sat next to the door. At the window, a young lad, wide-eyed, watched the landscape that didn't move. Between them, a slender girl of twenty or so held a book before her. Her eyes moved surreptitiously above the printed page and she studied the three men with her cat-like green eyes.

The caps, the jackets, the trousers and the boots were those of farmers, yet she sensed that there were things that didn't fit. The faces were too pale and the hands appeared too smooth. She lowered the book and smiled a coy, inviting smile. Willy wondered, but pretended not to notice.

There was a stir in the corridor – the sound of excitement, the sound of trouble. The compartment door flew open and two men in uniform entered. One was a French Gendarme, the other, a German Gestapo officer.

"Your papers," said the German in a harsh, commanding tone of voice. He studied the documents and compared pictures with faces. Looking at Willy and his two companions, he added, "So you're going all the way to Pontarlier, near the Swiss border."

"Yes. We work on a farm near the town," Willy volunteered.

"Very good. I'll hold your papers until you three get off," said the Gestapo officer. "It's routine." If there were something wrong, the German gave no hint of it.

The Gendarme stood back in silence. He eyed the passengers and his German counterpart in a casual manner. Then the two uniformed men turned to leave, the Gestapo officer exiting first. "They'll be removing Jews in Ribbeauville," said the Gendarme in a loud voice, to no one in particular. "That's in two stops."

The door slammed shut and the train began to move again. A few minutes later it came to a halt in Nancy for a brief stop.

As the train left Nancy, the girl looked up from her book. The seats opposite her were empty.

Willy and his two younger companions approached a farmhouse nestled in fields of golden hay. The sky was threatening ominously: Dark gray puffs merged into an angry purple, bolts of lightning streaked in a jagged pattern across the heavens, claps of thunder rumbled, echoing through the hills. A torrential downpour inundated the hillside, turning the ground they walked on into soft mud. Their shoes sank deeper and deeper as they pressed forward.

Soaked to the skin, they arrived at the house and knocked loudly at the door. There was no answer. They knocked again and again. Still no answer. Willy looked through a window, into the darkened house.

"I guess he's gone." Willy's face darkened as he spoke.

"What could have happened to our contact? Do you think the Germans got him?" asked the sandy-haired boy.

"God knows." Willy's brows wrinkled with the effort of thought. "Look," he continued, "we're almost there. By my reckoning, Switzerland should be on the other side of that mountain. If they took him away, they'll be looking for us. So we can't stay here. Our only hope is the weather. The Germans couldn't possibly know we would arrive today – a week late. And

I doubt that they would willingly wait out in the field in a pouring rain on the off chance that they might catch a few Jews.

"The crest is too difficult to approach. I suggest that we split up. You two try the path on the left and I, the one on the right. If one way is blocked, double back and try the opposite route. If both are blocked and we all return, at least we'll know that we can't make it here. Which ever of us gets over the hill first should not wait for the other. It's too dangerous to loiter near the frontier with no legal papers. We're out of money so we'll have to make our way, as best we can, to the Jewish Agency office in Zurich. With our French contact gone, I can give you no better instructions."

They all joined hands. "Comrades," continued Willy, "we'll meet at the Jewish Agency in Zurich, but regardless, in Israel. God bless you and keep you both safe."

The dark-golden fields churned like angry waves driven by stormy winds. The ground resisted his steps as Willy plodded steadily upward, breathless from the effort. His face was a dusky red and a hissing sound emerged from his mouth with each struggling expiration. His chest felt encased in rough concrete, limiting his ability to breathe and making each inspired breath as painful as having his raw flesh grated over jagged stones. He paused, exhausted, and lifted his rain-streaked glasses to examine the landscape.

Just a few hundred meters and he would be in Switzerland! There was no one to be seen. Still there was anxiety, the feeling that things were too good to be true: There was no German barring the way. He resumed his upward movement to the ridge that marked the dividing line according to his calculations.

At last, he reached it. Suddenly, as if Moses had parted the sea, leaving the Children of Israel on dry land, the rain stopped. Dark clouds gave way to a bright-blue sky. Behind was Nazi-occupied France; ahead was Switzerland. He ran excitedly down the slope. Waist-deep hay, soggy earth, nothing seemed to matter. His heart raced with exhilaration.

"Halt," spoken in French, suddenly echoed through the hills. Those words cut off his breath like a hand placed against his throat. "Hands up!"

His hands rose as his heart sank.

Could it be? thought Willy. *The ridge should be the frontier and I'm at least a hundred meters past it. To have come so far and yet...gone nowhere.*

A form emerged in the waving field of hay and grew larger as it approached. Willy studied the man, obliquely. The figure now appeared to be that of a farmer. He was of medium height, with broad shoulders and muscular arms bulging under the sleeves of his gray shirt. In Willy's mind, those were the arms of a man accustomed to pushing a plow over irregular terrain and lifting and tossing bale after bale of hay. Unkempt, fine, sandy hair flopped over the farmer's lined forehead. His cheeks were a weather-beaten red. His lips were thin and tightly pursed together. His eyes narrowed with suspicion as he approached, and he gripped a pitchfork before him like a spear pointed at an enemy.

Willy was uneasy at the menacing sight, but at least it was not the real enemy. His heart revived and he could breathe again, though with difficulty. "Is this Switzerland?" he wondered aloud, in French.

"This is Switzerland," was the sharp reply. "But who are you?"

"A Jew. I have come to Switzerland for refuge," pleaded Willy.

"This is not an official border-crossing. If you have the proper papers, go to the frontier post. How do I know you're not a spy? Better that I chase you back over the hill."

"Please," Willy trembled. "Back there, I'm a dead man. I have family here in Switzerland, cousins, Joseph and Ida Liebovitz in Zurich. They'll vouch for me. For the love of God, don't send me back!"

"I don't know," puzzled the farmer. "I'll take you to the priest. He'll know what to do."

At the direction of the farmer, pitchfork projecting dangerously near Willy's back, the refugee moved across the field and then down a paved road to the village. They stopped in front of a church. The muscular farmer, with a sharp twist of his head, beckoned Willy to enter. The Jew obeyed.

They walked down a central aisle, past simple wooden pews with cushioned kneeling-benches illuminated by the weak rays of light that filtered through stained-glass windows.

In the nave, a priest, on bended knee, faced the alter. Brown hair stood out like a dark crown surrounding the central bright reflecting spot of his bald head. A floor-length, dark-brown robe of coarse wool, tied at the waist with a belt of twisted, brown cloth, encased the body of this silent, seemingly unworldly man. The priest, completing his mute prayer, crossed himself. Then he rose and turned to greet the new arrivals.

"What is this, Claude?" the priest inquired with concern. "Do you enter a church, armed? Who is this man?"

"Father, he's a Jew. At least that's what he told me. I caught him coming over the hill...from France. For all we know, he could be a spy. He has no papers allowing him into Switzerland. Besides, who needs him here – Jew or otherwise?"

"Where is your Christian charity?" said the priest in an admonishing tone. Now put down your pitchfork and let me question him."

Reluctantly, the farmer obeyed. He sat down in the front pew, but he kept his hand on his weapon. The priest, a small, gaunt figure of light surrounded by darkness, turned towards Wilhelm and studied him carefully through gentle, gray eyes.

"Who are you?" he asked without a hint of harshness in his voice. "And how did you happen to come to our country?"

Willy hoped he had found a sympathetic soul. He proceeded to describe the misfortunes of the Jews trapped in the Nazi web in Antwerp. He told the priest that the merciless Gestapo appeared to perceive their every move, as if possessed with the tactile sense of a spider. One by one, Jews were seized by unfeeling jaws and vanished into concentration camps – the intestines of the monster – to be converted into juices to satisfy the demon's hunger for human blood and for a new world devoid of everything but spiders. He told of his efforts to save the children of families who were waiting their turn for extinction. Willy depicted the net that had closed in on him and his race to escape. That race had ended with his arrival in Switzerland, exhausted and penniless. He pointedly avoided mention of his two companions, just in case the priest turned out to have less than the Christian charity he spoke of. Finally, the Jew pleaded to be allowed to join his cousins in Zurich.

The priest listened with a solemn, thoughtful face. His lips compressed and his head shook with pain as he heard Willy's description of the tragedy that had befallen his people. Bearded men had been beaten senseless by the black-shirted representatives of The New Order; women and children had been seized on the streets; knocks on the door in the middle of the night were followed by Jews being dragged away. And all led to the same end – concentrations camps from which none returned.

The story ended and was followed by silence. What more could be said? The priest sat for a long while, engrossed in thought. Finally, his eyes softened and he bid Willy wait while he went to a room in the rear of the building. A long minute later, he returned.

"Here," said the priest as he handed Willy several Swiss francs in paper currency. "This will buy you a ticket to Zurich."

"How can I thank you?" asked Willy, overwhelmed.

"Live," replied the priest in a dramatic tone. "Now hurry...before the police come and arrest you as an illegal alien."

The farmer had observed the proceedings. He now rose to object. "Father, how can you? He's not one of us."

The priest's face turned red with anger. "Claude," he said warningly. "Not another word!" Then turning back to the Jew, he added, "Well, what are you waiting for?"

"Father," said Willy, "there were two boys with me. They're Jews, also penniless. They took the other trail over the hill. If they…"

"Do they know where to go?" the priest cut in.

"Yes, Father. To the Jewish Agency in Zurich."

"I'll send someone to look for them, someone I can trust. If your friends are found, I'll give them money to get to Zurich. Now please hurry. The station is down the road to the left as you leave."

With the shrill sound of a train whistle, Willy found himself seated in a packed compartment of a train, with strangers surrounding him on all sides. Eventually, the door slid open.

"Zurich. We are in Zurich," said the conductor in German.

Willy and the other passengers made preparations to leave. Some reached for baggage. Willy, having arrived empty-handed, was the first to get to the door. Quickly, he passed out of the railroad car and headed across the terminal, towards the nearest exit.

"Just a minute," said someone with a deep bass voice, in German, as Willy neared the exit.

The command came from behind him and so Willy turned his head in that direction. It was a police officer – sturdy and unsmiling.

"Your papers," demanded the officer, officiously.

Half an hour later, Willy was seated in the cellar of police headquarters. He was being questioned. The interrogator glared at Willy through cold blue eyes, apparently indifferent to the plight of the Jew.

"I see it this way," concluded the interrogator. "No visa, no papers. You're here illegally. One solution. We push you back across the border and pretend you never arrived. Tonight you'll sleep here under lock and key. Tomorrow, you'll be back under German rule."

"Please," implored Willy. "Let me speak to someone from the Jewish Agency. I have cousins here in Zurich – Joseph and Ida Liebovitz. They'll vouch for me and provide for me. I won't be a burden to the state. You can't send me back to the Nazis!"

"Can't I?" replied the Swiss officer with a mocking smile on his face. "It may interest you to know that my government does not consider Jews to be political refugees. It's simply a racial problem, none of our concern. Good day."

The door slammed shut with a resounding thud that shook the room. The interrogator was gone. Willy slumped onto a cot, moaning softly.

The heavy steel door creaked on rusty hinges and then flew open. Willy, despair written on his face, looked up at the guard.

"You're in luck," said the guard. "They're not sending you back. So cheer up."

"Thank God," said Willy in a whisper, his throat choked with emotion.

"And thank the demonstrators," added the guard with a short laugh.

"Demonstrators? They demonstrated for me?"

"For all of you." He paused for a moment and then went on: "I heard about it on the radio. The Jewish Socialist Youth Movement is what they call themselves. They organized the whole thing and yesterday they took to the streets. There were demonstrations all over the country. Others, even non-Jews, joined them. Demonstrations can be embarrassing to a government. Makes them look like a bunch of ghouls. So our government decided to stop pushing illegals back across the frontier...at least for now. You're going to Belechasse instead."

"Belechasse," repeated Willy, savoring the sound of the word with the verve of a lover of wine picturing the bouquet of a bottle of Chateau de Rothschild. "I've never heard of that city."

"And you never will. It's not a city; it's a prison. You'll be taken there this morning."

Willy looked across the dank, squalid cell. A fellow prisoner sat there, hunched over, leaning against the vertical bars at the foot of his drab, prison-gray iron bed. Dr. Horodisch was a delicate, thin man of about fifty. He had somber, brown eyes and receding dark-brown hair that was graying at the temple. A sensitive face and a high-domed, intelligent forehead gave but a hint of the real self of this man who was now dressed in dark prison garb.

The diamond-cutter from Antwerp might have wondered how a man who had risen so high could fall so low. Horodisch had been a prominent physicist at the prestigious Prussian Academy of Science in Berlin, a man who had been Einstein's co-worker. And now all this potential for a contribution to the advancement of scientific knowledge was being wasted as the physicist languished in prison.

Willy might have asked, *How could they take such a mind – the mind of one of a handful of men who could comprehend the nature of the universe – and place it in limbo while his frail body is being destroyed by slow starvation and overwork?*

He could have cried out. *How could you treat a man like this – or, for that matter, any man who had done no wrong – as you would treat a murderer or rapist, confined in a maximum-security prison? You force such a man to smash stones and drag boulders by day under the watchful eye of armed guards, and then have him sleep on a cot infested with bedbugs at night? How can you call yourselves civilized when you do such things to this man?* But hunger and exhaustion took precedence over logic and wisdom. Aloud, he inquired plaintively, "How can they expect us to survive on so little food? Working in the fields, dragging heavy stones: That's hard work and we need something in our bellies to do it."

The professor looked up, recalled from his daydreams, and said simply, "It's not the intent of the Swiss government to kill us. What's happening to us here is Rotmund's fault."

"Who's Rotmund?"

"The police minister. He doesn't care for Jews, to say the least. Sent 25,000 back to France. I hear that he telephoned the Nazis, with the time and place, when each group was to be pushed back across the border. Too many Jews in Switzerland as far as he is concerned! As for the food, I wouldn't be surprised to hear that someone is selling the food intended for the prisoners. The Swiss are not known to starve people to death."

It was dark, as only the countryside could be dark, on a night when thick clouds had blocked all light from moon and stars. The two men sat there, wondering. Their lips were silent, but their stomachs churned hungrily, unsatisfied by the evening meal that had consisted of soup containing nothing but water and a few tomato seeds, a sliver of onion and half a potato.

Trying to keep his mind off his stomach, Willy gathered the courage to ask, "Why would they send a man with your background to prison? I mean...a physicist from one of the most important scientific institutions..."

"For the same reason they sent you here. Being a scientist from a prestigious institute doesn't carry much weight when you're a Jew without a passport." The professor paused. "And what were you doing, Willy, when the Germans invaded Belgium?"

"I was in the army. My brother Ari and I had been called up. I was caught at Dunkirk. That was a real horror."

"How so? Wasn't that the place from which the British were evacuated?"

"Yes. But the real horror began after the evacuation. Belgium had already capitulated to the Germans, and so Belgian soldiers were not taken on the vessels. The British ships bombarded the city to keep the Germans from the beaches. The Nazis thought that the British were still in Dunkirk and so they, too, blasted the city. Between them, not a house was left standing and the civilian casualties were staggering."

"That's war," said the professor, sadly. "But what did you do before the war?"

"I was a diamond-cutter...working on big stones. It paid better. But my first love was art. I had a degree from the Academy of Art in Antwerp and was into painting and graphics in my free time."

"And when it's all over, what will you do?"

"Farming," smiled Willy.

"Farming?"

"Yes. I belong to HaShomer HaTzair, the Young Guardians. It's a pioneering organization with the aim of settling Jewish youth in Palestine. They've founded several *kibbutzim*. I spent the first two years under Nazi occupation working secretly in the movement. We've been trying, along with others, to smuggle young Jews out of Belgium to join the pioneers."

"But why farming?" wondered the professor, aloud. "You're a city dweller with city skills and interests."

"We have to return to the soil in a land of our own if we are to survive as a people."

"Who knows?" reflected the professor. "It's a crazy world. That makes more sense than anything else I've heard."

"Enough with the talking," shouted the guard from without. "Be quiet. You'll need your sleep if you're going to be working in the fields at the crack of dawn."

The days of drudgery merged into weeks and the weeks into months. Summer departed and leaves fell from the trees. Snow fell, covering the fields that rose to high ridges. After several months of frost, the warming rays of spring sun dissolved the ice and sent fresh, cold water tumbling down the mountainside. A year was like a millennium. The prisoners in Belechasse, their bodies engaged in never-ending toil, ceased to count the days or weeks or even months. But the seasons... Well, they still meant something. Winter symbolized the passing of old life and spring was the new beginning, a source of hope, faint as it was, that something would change for the better.

On a particularly dark, stormy day early in the spring, Dr. Horodisch sat, in shadowy gloom, on his bed. He hadn't opened a book or tried to solve an equation in a long time. *Nothing*, he thought, *makes a difference. What's the use?* His cellmate had returned, but the scientist did not look up.

"Professor," said Willy in an excited whisper as he seized the older man by the shoulder, "we're getting out of here soon."

The physicist looked up in disbelief. "How do you know, Willy? Did the guards tell you? I do not go in for their black humor."

"No. My fiancée."

"Your what? You never mentioned one before. Besides, you were arrested the day you arrived in Switzerland. Where did she come from?" His voice rose with annoyance.

"Sh-h-h. She's not really my fiancée. She's my contact. Smuggles letters out in her bra and brings news. She can do the same for you. Anyway, things are changing."

"How so?" whispered the professor, catching on.

"The Germans were pushed back at Stalingrad, and the Americans and the British are pursuing the Nazis up through Italy. The Swiss are getting the idea that the Germans will lose the war, so they want to improve their image. That means that we will be moved from a prison with walls to a camp surrounded by barbed wire. And those Russian soldiers here – the ones who escaped from German prison camps – well, they'll be moved to camps as well."

In September 1943, Willy was released from Belechasse and went to work in an internment camp. He trained Jewish youth to be future pioneers in Israel.

In May 1945, the war in Europe ended. Willy was transferred to Barcelona, Spain. There he joined a shipload of Jewish survivors of the Holocaust, mostly children, on the ship *Plus Ultra* that was going to Palestine. He became a member of the Kibbutz Ein HaHoresh, a farmer in a new ancient land.

On a hot summer day several months later, he was returning from a day's work in the fields under a scorching sun. The sweat ran down his now fuller, bronzed face. The ache in his back was a good ache –the ache of muscles that were building the world he had dreamed of, a land of free men and women, a homeland for the Jews.

In the distance, he saw two blurred forms, images from the past. He walked faster and faster. It was... He started to run, arms outstretched.

"Rosa, Dov!" he shouted. "You made it."

Tears flowed from Willy's eyes and fused with the tears on his sister's cheeks as they embraced. Dov joined in and pressed Willy and Rosa to his chest. They couldn't speak, although there was so much to be said. Arm in arm, they walked back to Willy's room.

"The others?" asked Rosa when she at last found words. "Have you seen any of the others?"

"Baruch is here. Wait 'til he sees you at dinner. And Raphi – he's in Haifa. From Mother, Yeshi and Ari, I haven't gotten any word."

"They're dead," replied Rosa, her face sinking. "Auschwitz... The gas chambers... I made inquiries before we left Belgium."

Again there was silence.

"We can't bring them back," said Willy. His face grew tense with resolution. "But we can see to it that no Jew is ever again shipped like a cow to be slaughtered."

"How?" wondered Rosa, aloud.

"By having our own land – here in Israel. From Israel we were driven. To Israel we have returned. And in Israel we will stay. No more will we be a nation of wanderers driven from place to place. We will sink our roots deep into the soil. We were a nation of farmers and shepherds two thousand years ago and we can be farmers and shepherds again. We must be self-sufficient. Sure we will have cities and they will grow with the industries of the modern world. But these will be built on top of the sturdy base of a people who inhabit all the land. No more shall we be only the Ghetto inhabitants of cities surrounded by hostile strangers.

"And we will fight for this land. We may even have to die for this land. But at least, we will die a free people – die for a purpose – so that our children will live in a nation they can call their own. You'll see. The Star of David will fly again!"

I WANT TO LEAVE

IN THE SEVENTEENTH century, some of the descendants of David ben Yosef Azubel, having sifted the turbulent winds of impending disaster, fled Budapest shortly before Christian armies seized the city from the Turks. Thus, they averted being liquidated when those armies proceeded to slaughter the Jews, whom they viewed as being too loyal to the Ottomans.

The surviving Azubels made the gigantic Kingdom of Poland their next home. When Poland's three neighbors, Russia, Prussia and Austria, proceeded to dismember Poland a century later, my direct ancestors ended up under Austrian rule, while a second branch of the family, living just miles to the east, ended up under the rule of the Tsars of Russia. While my forebears were renamed Ausübel in Galicia, the branch of the family living under the Tsar's rule were called Azbel in Russian Cyrillic. After the Russian Revolution, the Azbels were living under Communist rule.

In May 1972, a heavy-set, middle-aged Russian colonel sat at his desk. His head was tilted downward as he studied the writing on a series of cards. His face was grim, with massive brows accentuating the darkness of his eyes. One hand moved from the papers to his forehead, smoothing back a few strands of thinning black hair that had fallen forward to obscure his vision. Without looking up even for a moment, he thumbed through the cards, rattling off names and places. He paused after each one, while peering intently at the cards, as if he were searching for information hidden somewhere between the lines. There was a feeling of uneasiness in his voice as he spoke, a concern that something important had been overlooked – some clue, some hint of what was to come – which could portend disaster. He tried hard to picture the face, to pick out the name of the one who had the ability, the determination and the opportunity to do it, the one who might bring down the house of cards above his head. He shuddered for a moment, thinking that his years of work might come to naught if anything went wrong. *Men have been sent to labor camps for less – even colonels*, he reflected silently, as an icy chill froze his hands to the paper, burning his fingertips.

A young lieutenant stood at attention on the other side of the desk. His trim, youthful body was that of a man perpetually taking in deep breaths – shoulders back, chest out and stomach in. He listened carefully with exuded respect as his senior officer went through the checklist.

The colonel was done. The cards were neatly packed into a box which he slid into a drawer. He rose and went to the window. He looked out at the bustling street: People, like hundreds of elongated ants, moved quickly to and fro, never stopping to talk and never smiling. *This is Moscow*, he mused, tight-lipped. *It is good to see such industry – not like the jovial, slovenly attitude displayed in the capitalist world*. At last, he cleared the cobwebs from his mind and smiled the smile of confidence.

"We're ready," he announced with certainty in his voice. "The Jewish activists are all in custody. We've got the bus terminals, train stations and airports under constant surveillance. Every passenger entering the capital is being screened against our list of potential agitators. And our KGB men are keeping an eye on all suspected dissidents. We're ready for the American president. There will be no demonstrations."

The door opened and a young soldier entered. He was dressed in a snappy gray uniform with polished black boots. The soldier clicked his heels together, saluted and handed the colonel an envelope.

The colonel paled as he read its contents. Then a flush spread across his face, rapidly turning reddish purple as if his breath had been cut off. His eyes widened, giving him the appearance of a man possessed by a demonic power. His teeth flashed in a snarl and he hissed a strange whistling noise. "What! Who is he? He's not on my list. Is he a CIA plant, here to embarrass us? Or is he some crackpot professor in need of shock treatment?" He handed the note to his junior officer and added, "Lieutenant, get up a dossier on him immediately. And have your men *protect* the doctor from himself. Make it look good. You know –have men, dressed as civilians, rough up any visitors to his apartment. Make sure he's dismissed from his position at the Institute... But don't arrest him now. We'll *fix him* after the Americans are gone."

Later that day, newspapers in the Western world reported that a prominent Russian scientist, Dr. David Simon Azbel, was demanding the right to leave the Soviet Union. He had walked in front of the Kremlin, just as President Nixon arrived there, carrying a placard that stated that he wanted to leave the Soviet Union. Many in the West wondered why a man, who had reached the top in his field, lived in a large apartment and seemingly enjoyed all the comforts of life, would renounce it all. Who was this man who threw caution to the winds and cried out for freedom, and why did he do it?

In the eye of the storm of controversy, David Azbel, a twentieth century descendant of the Azuvels of ancient Israel, sat quietly on a sofa in the living room of an apartment in Moscow. He was reviewing his notes. There were additional sheets of paper, tucked in neat piles, lying on a wide coffee table in front of him. If there were any anxiety within, it was not visible on his face. His eyes, crowned by bushy brows, were intent, yet occasionally smiled knowingly as he studied a page, abstracted it for storage in his mental cabinet and then went on to the next. Messages were moving through his remarkable circuitry, being lifted from page to eye and then, with lightning speed, fed to the appropriate compartment in his brain – enclosed behind his broad forehead. Sparse, billowing hair, lifted by a gentle breeze coming through a crack in the window to his left, crowned his head like a gray halo and accentuated his huge cerebral container. His eyes circled the room, appraising it. The two cushioned chairs were in their places, one chair on either side of the coffee table. The desk with its matching dark-wooded chair was in the corner to the left, positioned beside the window. Bookcases, lined with volumes of scientific books and stacks of journals, rested in their customary location against the far wall. They stood like sentries on either side of the securely locked door.

The aroma of cinnamon and honey attracted him and he turned to the archway at his right, beyond which lay the kitchen. A Russian ballad, hummed sweetly in lyric tones, came from its interior and fell, with winsome ways, on his ears. His broad shoulders moved forward, reaching out to the melody. He raised a wide, spade-like hand to his chin, reflectively.

The clutter of dishes pulled him to an upright position and he waited expectantly as steaming vapors came closer. It was Rachael. He looked at her, wide-eyed, as if seeing her in a way he had not for an age. The time machine in his huge bundle of gray matter zoomed in reverse, washing away years and the lines of tension that clawed at her eyes. She was again the beautiful young woman he first beheld so many years before, standing on the stage in Irkutsk, Siberia, singing in a lovely soprano voice. *What is she doing now*, he wondered absently, *in a plain housedress, serving tea*? He smiled a gentle, inviting smile and patted the sofa, encouraging her to sit down.

"Oh," he said, suddenly realizing that there was no place on which she could rest the tray. Hastily, he gathered all the sheets of paper on the coffee table and placed them in a single pile to one side.

Rachael set the tray, with its sturdy stoneware tea service, on the space made vacant. She then slid onto the sofa next to her husband.

"I was thinking," he began, "of Irkutsk. You, in that colorful peasant costume, those soft reddish curls outlining your delicate, pale face. You sang with such enthusiasm. How exciting it was...especially for me. It was like being re-born that day, experiencing the beauty of life after years among the dead."

"It was so long ago," she laughed. "David," she added, turning serious, "at a time like this, you think of such strange things."

"Is there something better to think about?"

"What's 'better' to do with it? You could be in jail by morning... You could be back in Siberia..." Her voice trailed off in distress.

"I could," he considered.

"Aren't you worried about what they'll do to you?" she asked anxiously. "I'm frightened, frightened to death."

He put his hand on her shoulder. "Don't trouble yourself so. I considered it calmly and carefully before I made my move: What would be their reaction if I pushed a pawn forward, if I challenged with a knight or if I castled. I weighed the stakes and I computed the odds. Then I cast it all aside and studied my face in the mirror, looking myself in the eye. Did I have what it took to do what must be done? I knew, that very moment, that this is what I had to do."

"You talk of it as if it were a chess game, but it's our lives that are hanging in the balance – yours, mine and Vladimir's. Have you taken that into account?"

"Of course I have. After all, I'm no youngster. Most of my life is behind me. But you're much younger, and Vladimir – his whole life is ahead of him. As for chess, I've had lots of practice."

She smiled a sad, reflective smile. "Yes," she said, nodding her head. "You've had lots of practice..." She halted, wincing a bit, then suddenly went on with a look of curiosity on her pallid face. "But you know, even though you've told me so a hundred times, I still have trouble understanding it. I mean...how could you keep all those pieces in your mind, the positions on the black and the white... And even if you could do all that, what was the challenge of making the moves for each side when you knew the strategy of the opponent – since you were playing both sides?"

"Let's say that I viewed the board from each side, one move at a time, and tried to make the best move, the one most favorable to that side. It's marvelous training – trying to analyze positions and possible moves from opposing points of view. It enables you to understand the potential of your foe, clearly and dispassionately."

"But didn't it drive you mad – trying to remember everything?"

"Just the opposite. I did it to stave off the process of mental wasting so common in those living tombs. I had to constantly prod my brain into action, to keep its circuits busy and functioning. Above all, I did not want to go the way of my Uncle Aaron."

"Uncle Aaron... I never met him. Tell me, what was he really like? I mean, I know who he was, but why? That's what's so puzzling."

"Why puzzling? Wasn't your family exiled to Siberia? You don't even know why. For a Jew it was no novelty, so you all accepted it, helplessly. But should it be so surprising that a Jew decided to fight back, to change it all?"

"I can understand that easily enough. It's just the part about him and the Communists that I find hard to fathom. Why did they turn on him after he had cooperated with them?"

"Because he was *with* them but never *one of them*. Sooner or later it comes down to that. They'll use you as long as they have need of you. When they feel strong enough to run things on their own, watch out! Then again, there was the added madness – Stalin. To him, every person who thought or even looked as if he could think on his own was an enemy."

"So why did Aaron support them?"

"Because he was not all-powerful or all-wise; because he was a human being with the hopes and aspirations of human beings. He saw the Communists as a new force with new ideas, not all to his liking to be sure, but he thought they were free from the prejudices of the old regime. His idea was to join forces with them and then try to steer them in a more desirable direction. He was, of course, sadly mistaken. The Communists had overthrown the Tsar, but they were still Russians. To them, Jews were outsiders – a people with beliefs and loyalties beyond Russia and beyond Communism."

"And Aaron, with all his study of Russian history and Russian-Jewish history, couldn't foresee that?"

"Put it this way: He tried."

Loud noises coming from the hall outside the apartment interrupted the conversation. David rose and moved quickly to the door. He opened it cautiously, to find two men in street clothing, scuffling. One of the two, a red-faced, slender young man in a business suit, rushed to the opened door. "Let me in!" he pleaded in English.

David obliged and then slammed the door shut behind him.

"Who are you?" questioned David, in English, as the young man was brushing off his clothing.

He was an American correspondent covering President Nixon's visit to Moscow.

"You're Dr. Azbel?" the young man inquired.

"Yes."

"I had a lot of trouble finding out where you lived. I wanted to get your story after I saw you marching in front of the Kremlin today. And what sort of people do you have here," the correspondent asked with annoyance, "who rough up foreign reporters? Don't the police put a stop to that sort of thing here in Russia?"

"That was the police," laughed David, bitterly, "or rather the KGB..." Seeing the young man's dismay, he added, "I'm sorry. I didn't mean to suggest that it was funny – your being assaulted. That's just their way, you see. They don't want people from the West to see me. I'm a troublemaker and what I have may be catching. So they beat you a little, to keep you away. But don't worry. I won't give you a rash. Now perhaps you'd like to wash up. We have a sink – all the modern things. Then we can sit and talk."

The young man appeared uneasy.

David caught the direction of his eye.

"Oh, I'm sorry," said David, "This is my wife, Rachael."

"How do you do?" said the reporter with a slight bow of his head.

Rachael blushed, then turned to her husband and blurted out a few words in Russian.

David replied in the same language, ending with a directive nod. He turned to his visitor again, smiling. "I'll have to teach her English. Now please, Rachael will show you the way. Wash up, you'll feel better."

The young man followed Rachael. He returned a little later, appearing more composed. Following David's inviting wave of his outstretched arm, they all sat down – David, with Rachael beside him on the sofa, and the reporter in the cushioned chair closest to the scientist.

"You speak English quite well," began the young man. "Have you been to England or The States?"

"The States?"

"The United States."

"Oh, no... But I'd like to."

"Where did you learn the language – English I mean?"

"In Siberia."

"Hmm," replied the reporter with raised eyebrows.

"I had an English-Russian dictionary once," explained David, eagerly. "I was able to keep it for a few days. I taught myself English... But I need improvement. I must study. In your country, I will study. Then you'll see: I'll speak better."

"Are you serious? I mean about having learned English in just a few days...all by yourself?"

"I did not intend to suggest that I spoke English this well after a few days of study. That took practice. I did so almost every day. I went over the pronunciation; I began to set words together; I constructed sentences. I even tried to think in English. That was hardest of all."

"With whom did you practice?"

"With myself. There was no one to talk to...and certainly not in English... Later, my knowledge of English was put to use. I was assigned the task of translating scientific articles into Russian."

"You *are* serious."

"Of course."

The reporter reached into his inside jacket pocket and came up with a small black notebook. "May I ask a few questions? And would you mind if I took notes? That's what I came for – to interview you. I'd like to do a story on you. But first I need an angle."

"An angle? You must be referring to another meaning, something other than a mathematical angle."

"Mathematics? Oh, not that kind of angle. I mean a catchy title, something of human interest that would capture the attention of my readers."

"Of course. I understand. You want to write about me – an article. You want it to be good. You want people to read it. That's fine. I'm happy that you're writing such a story. I don't mean that I walked in front of the Kremlin to ask for an exit permit because I like being written about in the newspapers, but you see, it is necessary to have Western newspapers publish such articles. It's the only way I can get my family out of Russia.

"Don't be surprised. Do you think the Russian government likes to receive petitions, let alone someone requesting permission to leave the Soviet Union? Why do you think that man in the hall attacked you? I'll tell you what they would like to do – send me to a labor camp."

"If you knew what their response would be," wondered the reporter, aloud, "why did you demonstrate in front of the Kremlin? Do you have some sort of martyr complex? Do you want to be shipped to a labor camp in order to call attention to the evils of the system?"

"Certainly not. I like to think that I have courage, but I'm not a fool. If I believed that there was no chance to get out, I would not have done it just to make noise. You see, I did not ask to leave just anytime; I asked now when your President Nixon was here in Moscow. At this time the Soviet government is going to a lot of trouble to make friends with your leaders. They have their reasons. So they smile and try to look civilized and friendly. They don't want your president to see people dragged off to jail for saying they want to be free. They don't want newspapers in your country writing bad things about the Russian leaders. Not now when they want something from your country! And so the more you write and the more newspapers write about me in the West, the harder it will be for them to arrest me. I will be like – how do you call it – a sharp nail, a thorn sticking them. After a while, if I keep sticking them and if they can't get rid of me by sending me to a labor camp or some place like that, they may get tired of it all. Then they may give us exit permits. So you see, you came here to get a story that will sell newspapers, and I need your help to get out of Russia. We will work together: I will help you and you will help me."

"I'll scratch your back and you'll scratch mine," smiled the reporter.

"Another American expression... I must remember it."

"You seem awfully calm about it, awfully sure you've made the right move."

"If I seem so, it is because I have already made the decision. I have already asked myself a thousand times, 'Should I or shouldn't I?' I have done what I must do. There is no turning back. Now I have to keep my eyes and ears open. I must be alert to what they are doing so I can calculate my next move. Getting excited does no good. You can't think clearly. So you see, I must stay calm.

"My friend,"David's voice rose questioningly. "I hope you don't mind if I call you my friend?" He smiled. "After all, you did take a risk coming to see me. You might have been hurt."

"I don't mind your calling me your friend at all. As for the risk: I hadn't planned on being mugged – that's an American expression for being attacked in the hall the way the KGB man attacked me, but a reporter has to be willing to take risks. Otherwise, he won't get his story."

"Ah, you see," said David, beaming, "we're alike. We both take chances. Now I'll be glad to answer your questions as well as I can. But you spoke of taking notes. Please, my friend, be careful. There's no point in taking unnecessary risks. The KGB will still be waiting outside; you can be sure of that. They will take the notebook from you. What you write down, they will read. And you can be certain they will not return your notes. They may then use your notebook to do you harm. After all, I'm a scientist. I have done much here in Russia and I know many things they do not want people in the West to know. Someday I will put all this down on paper when I am in the United States. I intend to write two books, one on scientific matters and one about my experiences here in Russia. But all that must wait."

The reporter, reflecting on David's words, slid the little black notebook back into his inside jacket pocket. "I won't ask you about any secret matters. As for the rest, I'll have to rely on my memory," he concluded aloud.

"Now please have some tea. When you talk a lot, you get thirsty." Looking towards Rachael, David added, in Russian, "Pour our guest a cup... And bring in some of those cakes. He must be hungry after using all that energy wrestling in the hall."

Rachael filled three cups – one for each of them. Then she exited, to return a minute later with a dish of small brown cakes that smelled of cinnamon and honey. The reporter rose as if by reflex. Rachael resumed her place on the sofa, after which the young man sat down again.

"Please," said David, "don't stand on ceremony. My wife and I have lots of time, but you may not. Ask me what you wish. You can enjoy the tea and the cakes while listening to my replies."

The reporter cleared his throat and then began: "Why does a man like you...or rather, why do you want to leave Russia?"

"To be free. So that my family can be free. Is that hard to understand?"

The reporter blinked, as if making mental note of what was said. He continued: "You say you want to leave the Soviet Union to be free, and yet you've never visited the United States or England. Have you been to any of the other democracies?"

"No. I've never been outside Russia."

"Then how can you be sure? How can you take such a risk for something you've never seen?"

"I've never been to America, yet I think I know what it would be like there. Despite all the efforts of the Russian government to block it, we do hear about your country. I don't mean what they write in *Pravda*, but the truth. I hear it on the radio, from stations in Western Europe. It is forbidden, but we listen anyway. The news then spreads from person to person. We look around, making sure that no stranger is within earshot. Then we repeat, in a whisper, what we've heard."

"So the Voice of America and the Voice of Free Europe are the cause of your desire to leave. You have been spurred on by glowing descriptions of life in the Free World."

"That's part of it."

"Only part... And you mentioned wanting your family to be granted permission to leave. I see you and your wife. Is there anyone else?"

"Yes, a son. Vladimir is his name. He is a student in college."

The reporter paused, shaking his head in thought. His face appeared vexed again. "And you're convinced that it is possible to get out of the Soviet Union by making a pest of yourself?"

"That seems to trouble you."

"Doesn't it trouble you?"

"I can see from your face that what I'm doing doesn't make sense to you. You ask if the possibility of failure doesn't trouble me, but you think much more. Your eyes wonder whether I've lost my mind. You think, 'He's a scientist. He's doing work in his field, important work – or so he says. He has, or at least he had until now, a good position. The apartment is nicely furnished; they don't appear to be short of food; so he must be well paid. And he has a son in college. So what more does he want?'

"If I were a poor man, a hungry man, you would not wonder why I wanted to leave. But a successful man, an important man – that makes no sense to you.

"I said I wanted freedom. You are an American. You were born in a land where people can say and do as they choose. Yet you find my wanting those same privileges for myself and for my family, surprising?

"Perhaps it is because I said that I know things the Russian government would not want people in America to know. You say to yourself, 'How can he think they will ever let him out? He must be crazy.'

"But you see, I am not. I don't scream or knock my head against the wall. I will explain it. Then you will understand why I want to leave.

"Listening to radio broadcasts from the West is only a small part of it. To want to move to another country, you must first desire to leave your native land. That kind of desire you don't get from Radio Free Europe. You get it here – every day of your life: what you see going on; what you live through. And I want very much to leave so I must have lived through a lot. You most likely don't know it, but I was a prisoner here in Russia and I spent much of my life in Siberian labor camps. Even after I was released from the labor camp, I was forced to remain in Siberia. They call that 'Internal Exile.' So you see: I know what it's like to be in a Russian hell."

The young man's eyes widened with growing interest as David spoke. "Go on," he urged. "This could be my angle."

"In 1956, Khrushchev denounced the Stalin years as the work of a demented man. He tried to wash the slate clean, so to speak, and so the government allowed a few survivors like me to return to European Russia. It was a sort of pardon after all those years in labor camps and Siberian exile. Once back in Moscow, I returned to school to broaden my knowledge and to bring it up to date. I worked hard and, after a time, got a good position. I wrote papers. I gave lectures. I became a respected scientist. But they continued to observe my every action. They were using me because they needed my brain, but they never really trusted me 100 percent.

"So I had a nice apartment and good pay. But that is not enough. I want something more. I want to be able to say and do what I like; I want my wife to have the same freedom; and I want Vladimir not to have to live his whole life in fear. Is that really so much to ask for?"

"First rate! I can see it now – the headline: 'Scientist Returns from Communist Hell and Demands Freedom.' I'll need more information, of course; information regarding your experiences in prisons and labor camps, things my readers haven't heard before, things I can expand upon in the article." He reflected for a moment and then added with concern, "And you're willing to risk a return to that hell on the slim chance that they will let you leave the Soviet Union?"

"Correct. In life, you must make decisions. You have to decide what you want in life. If what you want is important to you, very important, then you should be prepared to take risks to get it – even big risks."

"But why was it so important? You said that they pardoned you. You said they let you work your way up to an important position. Even if they never really trusted you, is it likely that they would ever have troubled you again?"

"Look, my friend. Things may seem good for me today, so you think I have no problem. But the system has not really changed; only a few faces. They still drag people away in the middle of the night –perhaps not as many as under Stalin, not with the same violence as in those days, but still horrible enough. You can never be sure you'll not be next. I know of good people, innocent of anything you would term criminal in the West, being sent back to labor camps. Someone may overhear you speak of listening to broadcasts from the West; someone might report that you expressed views the government disapproves of; or someone in authority may simply take a dislike to you. The next thing you know, you're in Siberia. I don't want to live under such a system anymore. I don't want to live in fear, in distrust, always looking over my shoulder. So there it is."

"Tell me about your imprisonment. That seems worth pursuing. Why were you sent to jail?"

"I was arrested in 1935. They said that I was one of a group of conspirators in a plot to kill Stalin. That was their usual nonsense at the time."

"A plot to kill Stalin," repeated the reporter, reflectively. "I remember reading about a 'Doctors' Plot.' Which one were you involved in?"

"I wasn't involved in any plot. I was *accused* of taking part in a conspiracy – the 'Doctors' Plot,' as you call it."

"I thought they were all executed."

"Most of them, not all. Some were sent to Siberia; I among them."

"What was the length of your sentence?"

"Five years in a labor camp."

"1935," considered the reporter. "That was thirty-seven years ago. How old were you then? And what were you doing at the time that got you into such trouble? You're a doctor, but I thought it was a Ph.D., not an M.D."

"I'm not a medical doctor, if that's what you're asking. I was twenty-four years old when they arrested me. I was an assistant professor at the Moscow Institute of Chemical Engineering. I knew a few of the doctors they accused – not so well, but that did not matter. I had been seen with them and so I was arrested."

"Was there a real plot?"

"No. I said I knew some of the doctors. They were all fine men, dedicated to their profession. They had as much to do with any plot to kill Stalin as you have in a plot to kill your president. The plot existed only in Stalin's mind."

"I'm interested in learning more about the preparation for trials here in the Soviet Union. I've heard and read a great deal about how they brainwash the accused so that he will confess to everything and anything. Is that true? Were you brainwashed? And what was your trial like?"

"What you've heard about trials in the Soviet Union is only part of the truth. The reality is much worse. Trials are for show, if they are held at all, not to find out who is guilty and who is innocent. Everything is decided before the state prosecutor says a word, and everyone is expected to play his part. There is a lot of practice before the trial to make sure everything goes according to the script. The one who needs special attention is the man they are going to punish. That is tradition here in Russia: Every accused confesses. That is what we have always been told. Every time another prisoner confesses to a crime you are sure he has not committed, it adds to the feeling that the state is all-powerful and that it is useless to oppose it.

"But there are some with great emotional strength, with the will to resist. The prosecutors try to find this out before any trial takes place.

"It is not really interrogation: They don't shower you with questions. Rather, they are interested in learning of your state of readiness, whether you will play your predetermined role in the proceedings to come. It is a rehearsal. The interrogator sets forth what the state has determined the world will hear and what evil the prisoner has done. If the prisoner does not agree, the interrogators will repeat what they have said, this time in stronger language and with a more threatening look. If the accused still refuses to cooperate, to practice saying his lines, then the real torment begins. There are the ordinary methods – fists and other things.

"But there is more – what you call 'Brainwashing.' The prisoner is made to feel alone. They point out to him, coldly, that his position is hopeless, he is powerless, and so he might as well cooperate with those who have the power. His tormentors are the only ones in position to change his fate. And the more he resists, the more they are angered by his stubbornness, the worse his fate will be.

"But there is more. The prisoner has family and friends still living in Russia, under the thumb of the police. Their fate also rests on his performance in the courtroom. This is made abundantly clear to him."

David paused to sip some tea.

"Go on," said the reporter, encouragingly. "This is fascinating stuff."

"Yes," replied David, sadly, "terror can hold such strange fascination to people. Well...the interrogators go at it even more strongly. I say interrogators because there are several of them. They work in shifts. There is no rest for the prisoner now. For hours and hours at a time they hammer at him, repeating the story they want him to repeat like a parrot. Then suddenly, the interrogation stops. He is permitted to go to sleep. But a few minutes later they drag him from his cell and begin again. There seems, to the prisoner, to be no pattern to the interrogation. It may go on for days or be stopped abruptly after a few minutes. Day becomes night and night, day; flashing lights follow questioning or no questioning in the night and during the day with windows sealed and shuttered to keep out the sun. During all this time the interrogators repeat again and again: The only thing that will end the physical and mental torture is a confession. More and more, the prisoner begins to feel that resistance is hopeless. He asks himself, 'Why have all those others confessed?' He concludes that they must have some special tortures at their command that no one can resist. In the meantime, his mind has been dulled from lack of sleep. He can't fall asleep, even when they allow him to rest, because he has so often been awakened just as he dozes off. In that fog he begins to feel a sense of guilt. 'What have I done to deserve this?' he asks himself. He is promptly told the answer. He begins to believe the answer. The outrageous falsehoods he has been told become truth to him. Like a penitent sinner, he is eager to confess. There is something strangely Christian in his feelings (which, of course, no Communist would agree to): Confession will cleanse the soul. The prisoner is now in their power."

"But they look so well at the trial – at least, they looked so in some of the pictures I've seen. They must have been rested to look that well."

"They're allowed to rest before the trial, and they're fed better. But you still look troubled."

"Yes, I'm troubled. Look, many of the accused face certain execution. Wouldn't at least some of them – even *one* of them – have recovered enough to cry out at the trial, to renounce the false confessions?"

"Renounce?" repeated David with perplexity mixed with a bit of annoyance.

"Renounce, deny, you know what I mean, take back his confession. It's hard to understand why not one had the guts to speak out if those confessions were all false."

"Please, my friend, forgive me for saying so, but you think and talk like a Westerner who has not lived in Russia and suffered under a system that deprives people ever of hope. You picture the hero making one final, glorious gesture – crying out for truth and justice in the courtroom when everything seems hopeless, and in so doing, winning the hearts of the judge and the jurors. Who says it doesn't happen here in Russia? I mean, the man renouncing a confession or refusing to confess, just because you have never heard of it. Remember, Western reporters are not allowed into Russian courtrooms unless the prosecutor wants them there, unless the interrogators are absolutely certain of what the accused will say. Certainly that was the case in the Stalin years.

"And suppose the accused does what you just asked. His words will fall on deaf ears. A Russian judge is not there to listen to or weigh evidence, but to do what he is told. That is the system. The prisoner's gesture will go unheard by the outside world. It will remain sealed in the cold stone of the courtroom. Finally, and most important of all to a decent human being, his family will suffer the consequences for his 'glorious gesture.' So don't look down on the poor, miserable man who confesses to crimes he never committed and does not stand up and denounce the lies."

"I see," said the American, nodding sadly. "Is that how it was in your case?"

"No. I was not brainwashed. Then again, I was not tried, only sentenced. So you see, there was no courtroom in which I could have acted out the part of the hero."

"No brainwashing? No confession? No trial? None?"

"No trial and no confession," repeated David with finality in his voice.

The reporter scowled like a schoolboy who had listened with rapt attention to a story of real life, only to discover that he had been told a fable. "But if you weren't brainwashed," he inquired with pique, "how do you know they employ it? And where did you get all the graphic detail?"

"My friend, I am a survivor of the system, here to tell the story not only for myself, but for others who suffered at its hand but did not survive, and those too fearful to speak for themselves. I have spent enough time in Soviet prisons and labor camps to have witnessed much of what I just told you, and to have learned the rest from those who went through it."

"It's hard to believe," said the American, again shaking his head.

"I know," replied David, heavy-hearted. "Until it is you who is the victim of the system."

The young man was lost in thought for a few minutes and then concluded aloud, "We can't use it. It's not *your* story and hearsay does not have as much punch. We'll have to think of something else." Again he was silent as his eyes studied the lengthening shadows on the wall. Suddenly his eyes brightened and he began again, "So your association with a few physicians led to your arrest and imprisonment. Was there anything else? Any political activity?"

"The doctors in question were all Jews, as I am, too," said David. "That, I believe, has something to do with it. As for your question about politics, I had an uncle who was involved in politics, but I personally had nothing to do with any political movement. I was just a chemist, working in a laboratory and teaching students."

"Who is or was your uncle?" questioned the reporter with interest.

"Aaron Weinstein. He was my mother's brother. Uncle Aaron was a leader of the Jewish Socialist Bund (Alliance) before the First World War. And he was involved in the publication of *Di Velt* (The World), a radical newspaper. He also organized underground Socialist cells and spent time in jail, as well as in Siberian exile under the Tsar."

"Was he involved in any plot to kill Stalin?"

"I'm sure he wasn't. In fact, after the Revolution, he urged his fellow Socialists to cooperate with the Communists to improve Russia."

"What happened to him?"

"Uncle Aaron was arrested in the 1930s on the charge of 'Bundist nationalism.' He committed suicide in prison. The authorities also arrested his wife, my Aunt Elana. She spent eight years in prison. We were told that she was killed in an automobile accident immediately after her release from prison. We never had a chance to speak to her." His voice trailed off.

"So they were both killed by the Communists," thought the American aloud, picturing the new composition of his story.

"I didn't say that. I said that my uncle committed suicide. That's what we were told."

"Was he so afraid...of what they were going to do to him?"

"Fear is a terrible thing... Perhaps he just didn't want to be part of a show. Perhaps he hoped they would spare his wife if he were dead."

"I know you'll say I shouldn't judge what I haven't lived through, but I can't help thinking it would have been better to speak out. After all, his wife never really got out of prison –" He paused again, looking for a new approach.

"What of your parents?" he began again. "Were they involved in politics?"

"No. My mother was killed during the Revolution. But it was the White Russians who killed her, not the Communists. That was not because of her political beliefs. It was because she was a Jewess. My father, who never engaged in any political activity, died a natural death."

"It's a dead end," said the reporter, shaking his head in dismay. "Socialists joining Communists, Socialists committing suicide out of fear; too muddy for public consumption. And I don't want to get involved in a story involving religious oppression, not that kind anyway. Too controversial. Might offend lots of Russian-Americans." He frowned as he searched for a new beginning.

Rachael had slipped quietly from the room and now reentered with a fresh batch of cakes.

"Have some more," David urged the young man. "They're homemade. Take your time. Ideas will come to you while you're eating."

"They're good," replied the reporter, gulping down another cake. "Let's try Siberia. That may be a better way of handling it. Tell me, where were you imprisoned and what was it like?"

"In the Gulag Archipelago. It's a sort of network of Siberian prisons." David smiled a melancholy, reflective smile. "Shall I describe to you what it was like, living in solitary confinement?"

"Sure. Tell me what it was like – what was happening and how you reacted to it."

"Very well..." David's eyes peered through the window as if trying to catch a last glimpse of the setting sun. It was gone, leaving only angry, gray clouds moving swiftly across a blackening sky. His mind pressed forward through the blackness, against all logic, despite the warning puffs of jet smoke that seemed to cry out, *land of the dead. Do not go further.* He disregarded the ominous markers and pushed onward through billowing, dark clouds that roared in his brain like a mountain of water. He splashed his way upstream through rapids, struggling, feeling the sharpness of the rocks, the painful force of rushing water, the numbing cold of a mountain stream, and finally the frigid blackness of Siberia. He closed his eyes to the blackness, trying to shut it out. Then reopened them. His eyes stared straight ahead as if he were trying to discern images, a vision of a world that had vanished in some past cosmic explosion, leaving only light waves spreading through the emptiness as a memory of that existence. He began to speak and words came forth profusely, describing what he saw.

"It was the clanging of metal against metal, the gray ladle against the opening in the gray steel door of my cell. It was morning, time for breakfast. What time was it? Who knows? The window at the upper limits of my underground room was so tightly sealed and well covered, I had never seen or felt a ray of sun coming through it. I had often wondered, 'Is it a window or is it just make-believe?'

"But the clanging was real. It was time to take my food. There was no point in waiting too long. Ivan would become restless. He would withdraw the food. Not that it was so good. It was terrible, in fact. But it was food. Besides, my failure to take it would be interpreted as a challenge and result in further punishment.

"My back ached. Oh, how it ached. It had been almost one with the pine of my coffin bed, my tomb-like shelter in the night. I lifted my head and peered beyond the gray pewter candlesticks on either side of the coffin at the thin ray of light coming through the slot in the door. I had grown accustomed to it. I could tell. It was the pale incandescence coming from an electric bulb. Besides, it was winter. They would never have let me rest 'til sunrise.

"I stretched, loosening the knots in my back, then rose quickly. There was no time to waste. I had to get the food and the water. I stepped out of my coffin. The tar on the cellar floor stuck to my feet like icy glue. I moved across the five feet of black ice and picked up my gray pan. Without delay, I pushed it into the slot, taking pains not to appear threatening. There was a loud clanging sound, the handle vibrating in my grasp. This was followed by a softer clink. I waited for more. There was silence. I withdrew the pan to find a chunk of rock-like, mold-covered bread, but there was also a small piece of sugar with some minute fragments of the white crystal around it. I had been lucky that morning: Sugar was a delicacy here. Swiftly, I put down the pan and pushed my small pail into the opening. I could hear the splash of water being ladled into my container. Then all was still again. I drew the pail back and inhaled the distinctive vapors of hot water.

"There were no sounds coming from outside my cell door, yet I could tell Ivan was smiling. I could not see his face. If I had been able to do so, he would never have smiled. He had not suddenly flipped my pail over, scalding me. And he had given me a lump of sugar.

"I waited and listened, listening for the grating of leather against the concrete of the floor, listening to ascertain whether he was leaving, listening to know that there was someone – a human being – on the other side of that door. Ivan knew that I listened: I'm sure of that. Sometimes he would withdraw with loud, thumping steps. Other times, as if to test my senses, he would tiptoe away. But I always listened and I always heard. And I knew he was there.

"He never spoke to me... At least, he hadn't done so for two years. He was, in fact, many men. I was never told their names. But to me they were all one man – Ivan, Ivan the Terrible, as unpredictable and as cruel as a Tsar who would smile sweetly one moment and then, without any warning, gash you with his knife while he laughed a coarse, victorious laugh.

"Today, Ivan tiptoed away.

"I went back to the coffin which served as my bed, my chair and my table and squatted in it. Again I savored the rising steam, contemplating the pleasure with which I would sip it. It was life giving, liquid nourishment that would enable the fluids of my body to flow; it was lubricant for my joints; it was warmth in a land of seemingly perpetual winter cold. But I did not drink it just yet. I only savored its vapors.

"I picked up the dark brown stone bread with its green and orange patina of algae and fungus. My hand pressed against it; it was too rocky to break, let alone to chew. I dropped it carefully into the steaming water, making sure that not a drop of the precious fluid escaped the pail. It was to be a soup – a meal of stale bread and hot water flavored with lichen. When the bread was sufficiently softened, I dissected it with a spoon. Some of the lichen separated from the bread and floated in the broth, giving it orange and green tints that I could imagine being vegetables and chicken fat. I drank it slowly, carefully, delighting in having eaten, in having survived another day. I licked the pail dry, like some thirsty desert animal savoring the sands of a depleted water hole. At the end, I had my dessert – a piece of sugar that was my babka.

"The meal was over. A few scratching sounds on the concrete floor outside told me that Ivan was back. He was never gone too long – returning to watch me, determined to keep me from resting. And so it was necessary that I display a level of responsiveness at all times. I had to simulate the response of Pavlov's dogs in order to keep Ivan contented, to reassure him that I was the prisoner and he, my jailor.

"I would lie in the coffin as if in a stupor, glazed eyes directed at the nothingness above, but my mind, separated from the body, soared high above, above the blackness of my confinement, above the cruelties of my oppressors. There, my brain was free to play mental games, to study languages, to inquire into physical and chemical relationships and to contemplate the meaning of it all.

"It was time for my English lesson. Today I would review the tenses of 'begin.' 'How does it go?' I asked myself. I strained to picture the page in the book, the book I had read so long ago. 'Begin, began, had begun, I am beginning: That's the way it goes.' I smiled within, though my face remained expressionless. I had to go on. Next, I wanted to use the word in sentences. Finally, I tried to use it in my thoughts. That was always hardest of all – thinking in English.

"Heavy steps which slowly faded in the distance told me that Ivan had left. He was satisfied.

"Now I could resume where I had left off the previous day. I tapped on the wall nearest the coffin. I used combinations of long and short taps. Then I waited for a response with my ear pressed against the cold stone. It was not long in coming. The next few hours were spent in this manner – series of taps on the wall by me, followed, after pauses, by taps coming from the other side. It was a code that dated back to the Decembrist uprisings of 1825, and I was using it to communicate with another prisoner. We were playing a chess game with pieces on a board that existed only in our minds. I had never met the man with whom I was playing. Perhaps, if we both miraculously survived the years of solitary confinement, I might see his face, the face of a fellow sufferer determined to keep from going mad in his isolation cell. I hoped so. A brief flurry of taps from the other side told me that the game had come to a halt. My fellow prisoner was being watched.

"I sat there in the darkness, in the silence, moving my hand along the icy, bare wall. My fingers made out rough etchings, crosses and Stars of David – symbols reflecting the beliefs of the carvers that the power of the Almighty could penetrate this creation of the devil. There were also names and dates and even brief messages scratched out by bare hands on the cold stone, chiseled by prisoners hoping to be remembered. They had left word of their existence on the walls of their tomb for some future generation to find. They expressed hopes as well as the feelings of despair. Who knows how many, if any, of these poor souls survived imprisonment in this cell? For the moment, I sensed their despair, the overwhelming hopelessness they must have felt as scratches on the wall informed them that all this had been going on, essentially unchanged, for generations, and that all that was left of their predecessors in this hellhole were a few scratches on a darkened wall.

"I could feel areas worn smooth, thinking that it must have taken tens of thousands of collisions of flesh against unfeeling stone to wear it so smooth. I wondered how many human beings had used these self-same taps to communicate with others of God's creatures locked in this underworld, how many poor wretches had delivered their last words with hands swollen from striking stone in this black emptiness, yet feeling it better to suffer raw, bleeding flesh than to be cut off from human contact.

"The walls have no ideology: They are the product of a sickness of the human soul. It matters not to the wall who is master – Tsar or Commissar. I wondered how it was that this same code had been handed down after the change in command that took place with the success of the Communist Revolution. You would think that the prisons, containing the enemies of the old order, would have been emptied, and that there would be no inhabitant left in them to transmit the tragic story and the language of the past to a new generation of prisoners. Yet that was not so. The code of 1825 was still being used.

"I conjured up an image of that sad event – in one cell, a prisoner of the Tsar, and separated from him by the stone wall, the first of the prisoners of the new order. There stood the prisoner of the Tsar, perhaps a radical who had written pamphlets calling for freedom, now caged in eternal darkness, but hoping against hope for deliverance. Taps on the wall now told him that the old order had been crushed, that the Tsar was dead, that the Communists now ruled. This was followed by an excited exchange of questions and answers drummed out on the stone. The prisoner of the Tsar, with restless impatience, now awaited his release... It did not come. Slowly but surely he came to the realization that the change in rule would not result in a change in his fortune. Cries for freedom were as unwelcome in the new order as in the old. The faces of the guards were different; their methods, the same. And the walls...were indifferent.

"I slid back in my coffin, now fingering the candlesticks, symbols of my entombment, and I listened for a sound behind the door. There was none; Ivan was gone. I closed my eyes and fell asleep."

David reached for a cup, filled it with tea and then sipped its warmth slowly.

"But you see," he added, smiling at his guest, "they did not succeed. I am here."

The young man had listened attentively to the story. Now he looked at David with bewilderment. "I didn't want to interrupt you – the story was so fascinating – but it differs from what I've heard about the labor camps. It's more like the story of Edmund Dante in *The Count of Monte Cristo*. I've read *A Day in the Life of Ivan Denisovich* by Solzhenitsyn and its description of the Gulag Archipelago. I guess Solzhenitsyn is a hero of yours. Anyway, I don't recall his describing isolated cells. The prisoners in his book were packed together in a single room, like sardines in a can."

"That's true. Solitary confinement was not the rule. I described life in solitary confinement because I thought you wanted 'an angle' as you call it. I thought you wanted something different from what you already learned from other sources. However, I was kept in solitary confinement for five years and so I can give testimony as to what life was like in those hell-holes." He paused for a moment, and then added, "As for Solzhenitsyn – he may be a staunch anti-Communist, but he's not my hero."

"No?" said the reporter, frowning. He shrugged his shoulders and went on, "Let's not pursue that... Now why were you kept in solitary? Was it because you possessed secrets they didn't want passed around?"

"Not for secrets, but for resisting. I started my term of confinement as an ordinary prisoner packed, as you call it, like a sardine pressed between other sardines in a can."

"What sort of resistance are you speaking of?"

"Not violent resistance, if that is what you're thinking. With all the weapons in their hands, it would have been madness for a prisoner to attempt the use of force against them. I resisted with words, with complaints. And I went on a hunger strike to protest conditions – the lack of warm clothing when we worked in forty-below-zero cold, the inadequate and rotten food and the miserable, vermin-infested beds. When they saw that I was not taking food or water, they put a tube down my throat and force-fed me. Then they added ten years to my sentence, one year for every day of my hunger strike."

"Why the tube and the force-feeding? Were they concerned with your survival?"

"Yes and no. You see, thousands died in that prison and in the other prisons of the Gulag Archipelago. But that was different. The authorities had made the decision to starve the prisoners and to let the poor wretches freeze to death. Here, I had decided to go on a hunger strike and to, perhaps, end my life...and I was doing so without permission. To the monsters who ran the labor camp, that was counter-revolutionary. To think is to be an enemy of the state. And for a prisoner to act on such thoughts... Well,...something had to be done to crush my will to resist. I had to be made to suffer; there would be no quick end for me. I had to be made to curse the day I violated the system. I had to become the one to denounce my conduct, the one who confessed his sin and begged for forgiveness. In short, I had to be turned into the automaton they sought to create.

"To this end, they punished me with confinement to the blackness of hell, to a living tomb containing a coffin and candles. And this was also to serve as a warning to all the other prisoners. Each time one of them looked at the building in whose underground I was confined, each time some one glanced at the sealed window of my cell, he would remember the pronouncement: In Russia, the rulers make all the decisions – life, death or suspension somewhere in between – not the prisoner in a labor camp and not the worker or the peasant."

"And did you? Did you become the automaton they desired?"

"They may have thought so for a while. But no, I did not. However, I was determined not to invite further punishment, so I pretended. I sat in my cell as if in a trance – never smiling or laughing, never crying, in fact, never displaying any emotion, just existing – eating and sleeping and attending to necessities. But my mind, my mind was always working. I was thinking; I was learning; and when they were not looking, I was communicating with others. Yes, even a game of chess is important if it keeps you from decaying. And so you see, I never gave in."

"So you spent ten years in solitary confinement?"

"No. I said five. After that, they returned me to above-ground confinement with the other prisoners.

"Now listen, my friend, you'll be wanting to ask lots more questions. We would be delighted to have you return as often as you wish, but I must caution you that each visit entails risk. What you experienced earlier is only a sample of what they can and will do to anyone coming here. So as long as you're here, it would be better if you stayed and asked everything now. Join us for dinner. You can continue questioning me as you fill your stomach."

After receiving an affirmative "thank you" from the reporter, David turned to Rachael and said a few words in Russian. Obediently, Rachael withdrew to the kitchen and the correspondent returned to his questioning.

"You said that they added ten years to your sentence for going on a hunger strike, but you spent five years in solitary. Why did they let you out?"

"I can't say with absolute certainty. They wanted to put my scientific knowledge to use. That may be it. After all, a lot of things were happening outside – a war, for one."

"What sort of work did you do for them?"

"They wanted me to work on atomic experiments. This, I refused."

"But why?"

"Because I observed that many of the men doing nuclear experiments were dying. They were working without any shielding. It was obvious to me that they were being heavily exposed to radiation. My doing nuclear work might have resulted in a weapons gain for Russia, but it also would have killed me."

"What happened when you refused?"

"They were very angry, as you might expect. I was uncertain as to what they would do, whether I would be sent back into solitary confinement. But then they decided to have me translate a description of nuclear explosions from English into Russian. I had succeeded in escaping certain death."

"The part about the English interests me greatly. You described your study of English while you were in solitary. How did you get started on the language?"

"It began when I got hold of a Russian-English dictionary. Since I had a photographic memory, I proceeded to commit it to memory, page by page. A few days later, I was discovered reading it. They immediately confiscated the book. During the succeeding years I reviewed what I had learned. I chewed and digested the words. I practiced speaking English and even thinking in that language."

"Had you already been planning to leave Russia?"

"No. I had no formed idea of that. I was merely using the study of English as a device – a way of keeping my mind active; that and the games of chess and the delving into mathematics and physics."

Rachael appeared at the archway and smiled invitingly.

"Please, my friend," said David with an encouraging wave of his hand, "come into the kitchen. Seat yourself at the table. Rachael makes the best *piroge*, a Russian dish of meat wrapped in dough."

They all went into the kitchen and began to eat.

"Have a KGB cocktail," said David, as he mixed several liquors together.

"It's good," smiled the reporter. Running his tongue over his upper lip, he tried to analyze the contents of the brew. He gave up with a shrug of his shoulders and asked, "What's in it?"

"Vodka, for the most part. We call it a KGB cocktail because of its knockout punch."

During the meal the correspondent continued his questioning. "When were you finally released from the labor camp?"

"After sixteen years. It was in 1951. There was still one more year to go in the sentences they had added during my confinement in the camp, so by their standards they were being generous to me."

"Where did you go from there?"

"To work in Siberia...on coal gasification and other projects. They called it 'rehabilitation' – working in Siberia. I was not permitted to return to Moscow."

"But you did eventually get back to Moscow."

"As you see, I am here."

"How long was it before you were given permission to return? To Moscow, I mean."

"Five years.

"You know, it was a blessing in disguise – my being forced to remain in Siberia. Otherwise, I would never have met Rachael... She was in the opera in Irkutsk and I was a lonely scientist just out of a labor camp."

The reporter inclined his head towards Rachael. "What brought you to Irkutsk? Were you on tour?"

She looked anxiously towards David.

"She has not had much practice with English," interceded David. "I will explain for her. Her family was exiled to Siberia several generations ago. We don't even know why. Rachael was born and raised in Siberia. A red-headed Jewish girl born in Siberia, and I found her. When you think of the law of probabilities – our finding each other in such a place, well, it staggers the imagination. But we did. Perhaps some higher power guided our steps."

"I see," replied the reporter. "But we're getting off the track. How did you both finally get to Moscow?"

"We got our chance in 1956. As you may remember, there was an upheaval in the Communist Party after the death of Stalin. The new leadership now conceded that most of the charges and convictions under the Stalin regime were the products of his paranoia. Unfortunately, many of those falsely accused and convicted had been shot or had died in prison before 1956. Exoneration was of no help to them. But I was still alive, so they allowed me to begin all over again. Rachael and I went *back* to Moscow. I should say that I went back to Moscow; for Rachael, she was seeing Moscow for the first time."

"And what did you do when you got back to Moscow?"

"I went back to school."

"After sixteen years in Siberian prisons?"

"Yes, after sixteen years in labor camps and five more in Siberian exile, I went back to school."

"Weren't you sapped of energy after all that? I mean, you were no youngster. And after all you'd been through, how could you cope with it, with the pressure of competing with people half your age?"

"I was 45, but I still felt young. I told you I kept my mind constantly active in Siberia. I never stopped thinking and analyzing, I never stopped the process of learning. So I was as ready and eager to apply my mind as an 18-year-old student."

"What sort of school did you enroll in...after your return to Moscow?"

"Well, I wanted to catch up with the newer advances. I had learned much of what had happened and was being done in the sciences when they had me do translations in the labor camp, and later, when I was working in Siberia. I now wanted to broaden my basic knowledge in the allied sciences, so I studied for a doctorate in chemical engineering. Following this, I studied mechanical engineering and received a doctorate in that field as well."

"My god! And what did you do after all that?"

"Research...in energy and other areas. I wrote scientific papers. About sixty of them were published during the next several years. There was other... secret work. But it's best that you not know the details, just in case they try to force information from you...about our conversation. I was appointed to a professorship at Moscow's Polytechnic Institute. I was well compensated. I was given this apartment plus a thousand rubles a month. That's about $1,200 in your money."

"That, I take it, is quite successful by Russian standards," concluded the reporter.

"Yes, very successful. But you know, they never really trusted me. They used me, but I was always suspect. That is why they would not let my son Vladimir go to a major university in Moscow, only to a provincial college in Siberia. He wants to become a doctor. They will never allow him to go to a leading medical school. At best, if I am still of use to them, they would allow him to go to some third-rate school. They do not want a new intelligentsia, especially not a Jewish intelligentsia. Their aim is a continuous cycle of new blood from the peasantry, preferably a Russian peasantry, the clay of the Soviet Union. There are to be no continuous attachments, no links to the past, and no transmission of ideas, philosophies or concepts that might cause one to doubt the system. The peasant will presumably be grateful for his promotion and be convinced that he owes it all to the Party. The rulers of the Soviet Union hope to mold this clay into unquestioning followers of the Party line. The son of a professor might have gotten some ideas on free thought from his father. So Rachael and Vladimir and I must leave Russia if Vladimir is to be able to develop his abilities. Otherwise, we will be part of the cycle – on top of the intellectual world today – ready to be ground down into the floor, tomorrow."

"But what if you don't get out?"

"In all those years in a dark, damp cell by myself, with no sunshine, no beauty, breathing in the soot and the stench, roasting in summer and freezing in winter, in the endless hunger of the calculated starvation they forced on me, in the confined space in the cellar where tar stuck to my feet like icy glue, while sleeping in the coffin with the two candles standing beside me as if to remind me of what they planned for me, with taps on the wall, like cries from hell, telling me that men were dying all around me every day, I studied English, I played chess with myself, and I pictured chemical reactions in my mind. And I never asked myself, 'What if you don't survive?' And I *did*... I *survived*."

"Doctor," said the journalist, rising, "you're a remarkable man. I hope you do make it. You know, I came here looking for a story. I leave here with a cause. Your story will not be buried."

The colonel sat at his desk, reading a report in a manila folder, page by page. Deep gullies formed on his forehead as he strained to picture the man behind the words.

There was a knock on the door. It opened.

The colonel shut the folder and looked up. The young lieutenant strode into the room and came to a halt immediately in front of the desk. The junior officer stood silent at attention, as if waiting for permission to speak.

"Well," questioned the colonel, impatiently, "what have you come up with?"

"He had a visitor today, an American journalist." His face remained blank. "Here are some pictures of the journalist," he added, extending a hand holding a small packet.

The colonel reached for the envelope, opened it and studied the photos. "I see," he mused. "Is he a real journalist? Have you checked him out?"

"He has the credentials..." The junior officer's voice trailed off. "He's a known reporter, not well known, but he has been photographed elsewhere."

"How long were they together?"

"Four hours and ten minutes."

"Four hours and ten minutes! That's a *long* time."

The colonel studied the expressionless face of his junior officer. The lieutenant remained silent.

"I'm waiting," said the senior officer, bristling with growing impatience. "What did you learn about their meeting?"

"Sir," replied the lieutenant, uneasily, "I said he had the credentials of a reporter. He must have been conducting an interview."

"Lieutenant, in four hours and ten minutes he could have learned the history of the Soviet Union. He took notes. Where are they?"

"There were none," replied the lieutenant, shifting his weight nervously from one leg to the other.

"I thought you said he was a journalist. Journalists take notes. Spies carry away messages hidden on microfilm beneath a dental cap. Did your men search him when he left? Do I have to teach you all how to pick a man's pockets? How can I run a department with incompetents?"

"Sir, he was picked clean..." began the junior officer, defensively, "in a scuffle... he had nothing but a blank notebook and his credentials, plus some money, of course."

"And you kept all of it, his credentials included?"

"Certainly."

"Fool! Now we'll have some sort of international incident on our hands. He'll complain of being assaulted and robbed at a time we want things to appear peaceful. Well, they can't be returned now. He just lost them. That's what we'll say."

The colonel paused and then went on: "You said the notebook was blank. Didn't you find that suspicious?"

"Did I say blank? I meant blank with regard to his visit to Dr. Azbel's apartment. Actually, there was a description of the flight to Moscow, something about the reception at the airport, and a summary of the comments of the American president. It all checks out with what we have learned from other sources. He was one of the journalists who accompanied the American president."

"And not a word about Azbel?"

"We even analyzed the paper. There was nothing found." The lieutenant looked troubled. "Sir," he began again, "does that mean that he wasn't really a reporter?"

"No, he was a journalist. Otherwise he would not have gone to the Azbel apartment. An American agent would have known it was being watched. And he certainly would not have stayed that long. It takes only a few seconds to slip someone some microfilm. The answer is simple: He was cautioned not to take notes."

"By whom? The CIA?"

"What CIA?" The colonel tilted up his nose scornfully. "I told you – if it were one of their operations, they would have employed a more clandestine means for transmitting messages. Azbel warned him. Yes, that Azbel is a shrewd one. They always are."

"Scientists?"

"Jews!" shouted the colonel, seemingly tried beyond all endurance, like a parent who had been continually asked to explain the obvious by a small child. Then he added, "You just can't trust them... They have *never* learned their place. Observe any of our scientific institutions. Look for the Jew: He's easy to spot. He's the one still working long after the others are asleep or are enjoying their third glass of vodka. They don't simply do their job, they *excel*. If we did not put great obstacles in their way, they'd be running everything in our motherland. And what do they do when we permit them to attend our schools, when we allow them to obtain an education, and when they rise to positions of importance despite all the restrictions we place upon them? They request permission to emigrate! Look at this one, the doctor, the only one to survive in the whole bunch arrested in that plot; you'd think he'd be so happy to come out alive, he'd shut his mouth forever. But no, not him! He plots. He conspires. With whom, I don't know yet. He even goes back to school. Can you believe it? A 44-year-old man, after sixteen years in labor camps, five of them in solitary, and after exile in Siberia, goes back to the university as a student! For what purpose? So he can worm his way into an important position, to get at our secrets and then, when the moment is right, he strikes...like a snake."

"Pardon my asking," began the junior officer, eyes brightening, "but why don't we arrest him? He spent sixteen years in labor camps even though he was innocent of any crime; why not send him back for another sixteen years? At least this time it would be for something – for asking to leave the Soviet Union. And if you don't like the idea of prison, we could commit him to a sanitarium, or even arrange a suicide."

"Idiot! Don't teach me my business. I've been in the KGB too long. I know all the tricks... And since when was anyone sent to Siberia without cause?"

The colonel's eyes were like burning coals and the lieutenant stepped back, away from the searing heat.

"But Khrushchev said –" began the junior officer.

"Never mind what he said. Instead, look at the results of such talk. When you allow doubt to arise with regard to what was done in the past, then people begin to question what we do today. It's like the position of a building when it is settling. If a crack develops, it may enlarge and spread. There is no telling how far it will go. It may even weaken the foundation, causing the entire building to collapse. So the KGB *never* admits mistakes or even concedes that such a thing is possible. Don't you *ever* forget that." He stopped for a minute while his fiery eyes were simmering down to a dull gray. "It's the times," he added, sighing.

The lieutenant stood there, red-faced, afraid to speak.

"Oh, calm down," said the colonel, condescendingly. "I won't strip you of your rank."

The junior officer struggled to regain his composure, but his hands were still trembling.

"You've got to understand," began the colonel again, more sympathetically. "We're in a new phase...for a while, anyway. They call it 'Détente.' Our chairman and their president shake hands and then sit down to tea. We've got to put on a show, pretend we like to drink tea with decadent Westerners, making believe that we abhor all that went on in the Stalin years. So we don't arrest Azbel and we don't shoot him – not just yet. We wait. When things quiet down, when he is isolated and forgotten by the West, then we'll fix him. Or else, when the game of Détente is over, he'll get his desserts. Either way, he's finished. In the meantime, we'll keep up our guard. We'll harass his family, we'll squeeze him slowly but steadily and see if he cracks."

"Will it work? Will he crack?"

"Perhaps... Probably not."

"Why not?"

"Sixteen years in prison, lieutenant. He's a survivor. That's why. You don't last sixteen years in Siberian labor camps unless you're made of something special. Study his record. Someone should have. They should never have let him out alive. The man was resistive. He had the audacity to go on a hunger strike. And he refused to cooperate even after five years in solitary. The man's got endurance...and he has a brain. You've got to admire..." The colonel flared with anger again. "Why did you smirk just then? A brain is a brain, Jew or otherwise. If you go on the presumption that all our enemies are stupid, you'll be worthless to the KGB." He paused, and then added in disgust, "All right, get back to work. Keep him under surveillance with his apartment observed at all times. Disconnect his phone. Rough up anyone who comes near him. But don't kill Azbel."

"Yes, sir," snapped the lieutenant. He clicked his heels together, saluted and then left.

The colonel reopened the folder. He flipped through the pages until he came to a photo of David Azbel. "Yes, he's an anomaly," mused the officer, nodding. "The head of a scientist grafted on to the body of a wrestler. Look at those shoulders, those arms, that chest. The head's Jewish, but the body – ? There must be some Russian blood in him. If he were only a Russian; if he were only one of *us*. We could use people like him." He closed the folder and sighed. "What's the use! They'll never change."

Two years later, after his demonstration in front of the Kremlin, joint protests with Andre Sakharov, many clandestine meetings with foreign journalists, unauthorized telephone calls to England and the United States, a seventeen-day hunger strike by David, petitions by groups of scientists and others in the West, and articles and editorials in newspapers throughout the Free World, David Simon Azbel and his wife and son were allowed to leave the Soviet Union. Dr. Azbel later became a senior consultant to the American government on nuclear reactors.

SIGN HERE AND YOU'RE FREE

THE *REFUSENIK* movement, which included members of my family, gathered world attention during the 1970s. But why, reasoned the Communist rulers of the Soviet Union, would anyone want to leave this "worker's paradise?" And so it served as an embarrassment to the Soviet government. The authorities were determined to stamp it out.

"Sign here and you're free," directed the heavy-set Soviet interrogator.

The heat of several spotlights, although not directed at him, had turned the dark-haired official's pudgy face into a series of rivers of sweat, which ran down his forehead and tumbled from his bushy eyebrows like waterfalls, converging into lakes around his thin lips and filling the crevice in his dimpled chin. A day's growth of his beard had shaded his face blue-black, with stubble appearing on the face like a freshly planted rice field. His double-breasted gray suit was soaked through in the armpits and across the back, with creases at the elbows and lapels having assumed permanent form. A tightly-knotted drab blue tie hung loosely around his neck, with little of it concealed by the collar of his wrinkled white shirt, now a shade of gray and unbuttoned at the neck.

Impatiently, he stared at the gaunt, balding Mark Azbel, who sat on a stool on the opposite side of the table. The little remaining hair on Mark's crown was nearly pure white. His eyebrows and several days' growth of hair on his unshaven face were fast approaching that color. There was but the vaguest hint, at the fringes of the snowy halo, of the reddish-gold of his youth. His broad forehead was deeply furrowed. Beads of perspiration would appear on the ridges, swell into shimmering balls of pungent water and then run off into the deep horizontal channels. The pale skin below, sucked dry by the leaching springs, was now waxy and sunken. The dazzling spotlights were reflected from his steel-rimmed glasses. A slight movement of his head changed the direction of the mirrored beam of light, revealing his tired eyes, recessed between full, graying brows and the puffed and wrinkled lower lids. Those eyes had once shone, but now a deep sadness was in them. A full nose, accentuated by sunken cheeks, dominated the central portion of his face. It shaded his dried and cracked lips. Mark attempted to moisten the membranes with his parched tongue to no avail. A deeply cleft chin that gave the appearance of the letter "w" rose and then sank back, glumly. Mark's head moved again, ever so slightly, giving a different cast to his eyes. They were still sad, but they seemed to suggest to the observer that this wasted, white-haired man, looking decades older than his 45 years, was fixed and firm in purpose.

Mark arched and stretched his shoulders back, and then hunched forward again. He was weary from the long hours of continuous interrogation: from sitting on a backless stool and from the booming voice of his inquisitor. His shirt, once white, had now assumed a grayish-brown hue. It was frayed at the elbows and around the collar, with the ripped and creased look of a garment that had been worn so long; it almost had become part of his body. His trousers were made of quality material, but they, too, had seen better days.

Despite the brightness and the heat of the lights and the interrogator's repeated demand for a quick decision, the balding, white-haired man sat there in silence. His heavy-lidded eyes studied the typewritten sheet of paper, word by word. The interrogator wondered what was keeping the sickly-looking Jew from accepting an offer that the heavy-set man felt could not be refused.

"See here," said the pudgy-faced official, warningly, "we've got enough on you to send you to Siberia for the rest of your life, and a short life that would be! You'll never see your family again and they'll be in our clutches. Stop studying every word, and sign."

He paused and then went on: "As soon as your signature is on the document, you can leave on the next plane with your wife and children. You can join your Zionist friends or do whatever you damn please. That's a lot more than you deserve. So sign already!"

But Mark persisted. The words on the paper reverberated through his mind:

"I, Mark Azbel, hereby confess that Anatoly Borisovich Sharansky approached me and asked me to join in a conspiracy, the Jewish emigration movement, designed to defame the Union of Soviet Socialist Republics. He told me that he was an agent of the CIA and that their purpose was to discredit the Soviet government in the eyes of the world by acts of hooliganism and the dissemination of Zionist, anti-Soviet propaganda. He persuaded me to pilfer secret documents and smuggle them abroad through foreign contacts, including Prof. Eric Fawcett; join in illegal meetings with other disloyal Jewish scientists; and attempt to embarrass the Soviet government by demanding an exit visa, knowing full well that the authorities could never allow me, as one who had access to secret military information, to leave the country. Anatoly Sharansky told me that he, himself, had stolen many secret documents in his computer work, and was passing them to his CIA contacts through Robert Tuch, who was posing as a newspaper correspondent. I declare all this willingly and without any inducement."

Below this, there was a line with a space above it awaiting his signature.

"All right," barked the interrogator, angrily. "You must have read it a hundred times by now. My patience is worn thin. Sign!"

The gaunt, balding Jew looked up from the paper, studied his restless inquisitor, and calmly replied: "I need a few minutes to formulate my reply."

"What for?" growled the heavy-set official, clenching his huge fist. "You have no choice..."

He paused for a moment, wiping his brow. Then he added thoughtfully: "But I'll give you fifteen minutes. I want to wash up anyway."

With this, the interrogator motioned to two armed guards standing near the door and to a lieutenant seated on a straight-backed chair near them. One of the soldiers unlocked the door and the pudgy-faced official exited.

Mark Azbel remained in his seat, with his eyes seemingly focused on an object beyond the confines of the room. Visions of the past appeared in the distant shadows beyond the glare of the lamps. For an instant, he was a youth again. He was back in Novograd Seversky, in the ghetto of a small city nestled amidst the waving golden wheat fields of the Ukraine. There was the wrinkled face of his grandfather, Aaron, and the weathered face of his father, Jacob; faces that expressed silence. It was the suffering silence of a people weighed down by centuries of persecution. And yet, there was much more in those weathered visages. Every line reflected unyielding determination: They would never give up their identity. No matter what the external threat might be on one hand, or what carrot might be offered as inducement to renounce their heritage of four millennia on the other, they would remain Jews. And hidden deep in their eyes was a glint of joy – the quiet, happy times reserved for those moments when the glare of oppression was not on them. Mark shuddered as he remembered something of the anxiety of being known as a Jew in the Stalin era. Those were the days when imaginary plots of Jewish physicians planning to kill the Georgian-born tyrant, products of the warped mind of the Soviet dictator, had become the latest excuse for the persecution of the Hebrew people.

Time advanced. He smiled softly, thinking of the more peaceful post-Stalin years. He reflected on his days at the university – Mark Azbel, a Jew, bathing himself in the luxury of the finest education available in the Soviet Union. His eyes lit up as he recalled the excitement of his post-student days. He had been working on the frontiers of science, of genetics and physics. There were meetings with leading intellectuals in Russia. Mark had been recognized for his work and had advanced to the rank of professor at the university. He sighed, picturing his beloved Lydia, their son Vandim, now getting close to college age, and their little Julia. Oh, how he wished he could draw them closer. He reached out with inner yearning.

The images were gone. He was back beneath the oppressive glare of the spotlights. He now recalled the crucial decision that had brought him to this place, and the act that had sent the weighty stones of an angry Russia tumbling around his body. The step he took ended that promising career in Russia. He lost his job. And he and his family became subject to constant harassment, both mental and physical. That day in December 1972 was recalled from the mist of memory. It was the fateful day on which he applied for a visa to leave the Soviet Union for Israel. His internal passport, a document carried by all Soviet citizens over the age of sixteen, had always been stamped "Jew." Now Mark had requested repatriation to the land of the Jews – Israel.

Mark thought hard about his reasons for giving up everything he had acquired through such painstaking effort. He considered the idea; he had thought of the principle; but in the end, it was the steadfast determination of a people to hold on to their identity and their belief in the Almighty. Employing this celestial logic, he had come to the realization that, in truth, he was giving up nothing. For what are position, comfort and security, if attaining them requires the surrender of one's soul? How could he continue to live in a land where the teaching of Hebrew is a crime, where a well-dressed member of the KGB sits at the entrance to every synagogue and records the names of all those who dare attend a service, and where an expressed belief in God is a guarantee against future advancement?

He was painfully aware of what happens to those in the Soviet Union who seek to retain a Jewish identity, an identity other than that of the majority. He had learned of Lev Genden's suffering. "Persons unknown" had beaten Lev senseless on the streets of Moscow. Then he was arrested and beaten again by the KGB. All this was brought about by Lev's request to emigrate to Israel. Mark had also been witness to the misfortunes of Vladimir Slepak when he applied for a visa. And he knew how they had treated a Sharansky or a Levitch or a Lunts when a Jew asserted his identity. (Prof. Benjamin Levitch was a physicist, expelled from the USSR Academy of Science when he applied for an exit visa to Israel. Prof. Alexander Lunts was a mathematician, arrested for "violation of foreign currency regulations" and "anti-Soviet activities" when he applied for an exit visa to Israel.)

He had developed an understanding of the power structure in the Soviet Union. A ruler who obtained and maintained his rule by force made all major decisions at the top. Power at the top changed only by death or backstage intrigue and not by popular will.

In Russia, a Jew might be granted permission to attend a university one day, only to be arrested on the very next day as a result of a sudden whim or a festering sickness in the mind of someone in power. In a land where all this was reality, security was transient at best.

The price for his safety and prosperity today was the surrender of his identity as a human being. Mark would be obliged to become an automaton in the Soviet system. He would be free to do his work, only when that work suited the purposes of the state. But such surrender would not allow him the freedom to practice his religion or to search for answers to the grave moral questions that confronted Russia. To Mark, this was too high a price to pay.

And so he was now paying the other price, the price of dissent. He had been dismissed from his position at the university. This meant no income to support his family. Both he and his wife had been threatened and assaulted. His children had been derided and beaten by their classmates. And yet, there were also moments in this period of trial which Mark found rewarding. There were the meetings with other dissident scientists in clandestine symposia. For Mark, the meetings were part of an effort to keep his mind alive while his body was in limbo, as he waited for the hoped-for visas to leave the Soviet Union.

Mark's daydreams ended abruptly with the return of the interrogator. Gone was the stubble from the official's face, and gone were the sweat-drenched garments that clung, like glue, to the layers of fat. But a shave only removes hair; it does not change the character of the face. The clean blue suit and a fresh shirt and tie did not disguise the purpose of the man. The beefy, black-haired hulk of a man growled at the pallid scientist: "Well, what is your decision? Is it life outside Russia for you and your family, or a slow death in Siberia for you and slower starvation for your wife and children?"

"Let me review the options as I see them," replied Mark, seriously, his eyes fixed firmly on the bloated face of his adversary. "You ask me to sign a fiction –"

"What fiction?" interrupted the interrogator, annoyed.

"Please, hear me out."

The interrogator slid back in his chair. "All right. If you must... Continue. But I must warn you: Grief will be your only reward for challenging the actions of the State."

Mark cleared his throat, then continued: "Anatoly Sharansky is not an American agent. He is a Jew who wishes to remain a Jew. He wants to join his people in Israel. He never told me, nor do I believe that he ever held a meeting with any member of the CIA. You know perfectly well of his desire to leave the Soviet Union: Anatoly never made a secret of it. On the contrary, he publicly announced his wish to emigrate to Israel. Apparently, what galls you all the more is that he cried out for the right of all Jews – their religious practices and the teachings of their traditions having been pared down and steadily constricted by the glare and the fist of the State – to leave for Israel. But Sharansky's efforts are no violation of law. It is precisely what the USSR agreed to in the Helsinki Accords."

The interrogator flared impatiently: "Where *is* all this leading? You're not here to discuss Helsinki. You're here to sign this paper. You're guilty and he's guilty."

"So it comes down to that," nodded the Jew, sadly. "Asking the Soviet Union to carry out its solemn international obligations is not permitted. Calling attention to such violations of international law by the Soviet government is a crime."

"Stop your speeches!" demanded the official, eyes glaring. His burly frame was thrust forward and his clenched fists vibrated against the table. "You deceitful worm...questioning the actions of our government. Let us get to the real truth. We know that your relative, David Azbel, was the chief CIA operative in Russia before we deported him. And didn't you pass secret military information to Prof. Eric Fawcett of Canada?"

"I handed my scientific notes to Prof. Fawcett, but there was nothing of direct military significance in them. To verify this you have only to buy a copy of my book when it is published in the West. Review all the scientific information contained in it. Then tell me how any of it relates to Soviet weaponry."

"But you *did* smuggle it abroad," smiled the interrogator, sarcastically.

"I did. It was the Soviet government that forced me into a position where I would have to employ circuitous measures if I wished to have my work published. You know perfectly well – it was done at your behest – that I was dismissed from my position at the university and that publication of my writings in Russia was forbidden. All this for submitting my application to leave the Soviet Union for Israel. Is it a crime to want to be a Jew?" There was a mournful appeal in the Jew's last words.

The interrogator's fists opened and closed again into weapons of fury. "Listen here! Sending documents abroad is against Soviet law. On that account alone you could spend years in Siberia. Besides, you *must* be a traitor. Who, but a traitor in the pay of our enemies, would give up a blossoming career in a fine university? Who, but a traitor, would give up good pay and good quarters to leave the Soviet Union? Who, but an enemy agent, would denounce the very government that permitted him to get his education in the finest universities for free, and even allowed a *Jew* to advance to so high a position? It enrages me to think of your ingratitude!"

The interrogator paused, straightened his tie and smoothed back his full head of black hair. Having calmed himself, he continued: "Nevertheless, you have my word for it – despite what is written on the paper – as soon as you sign, you and your family can leave Russia."

Mark, his face drawn and his eyes resolute, looked his adversary straight in the eye. "Your word," he repeated with disdain. "And what of Sharansky? Does he get to go to Israel? Are you giving him *your word too*?"

"Never mind Sharansky. We'll deal with him in due time."

"Then 'no' is my answer," Mark said with emphasis.

The interrogator flushed angrily.

"Do you realize the consequences of that decision?" he cried. His eyes bore down on the Jew. "You're a dead man," he spewed with smoke in his voice.

Mark remained calm. There were no tears and not even the hint of a whimper. Instead, he replied in a soft, yet resolute tone. "I cannot sign a statement false in every detail. I cannot denounce an innocent man. Do what you will with me."

The official looked puzzled.

"Is Sharansky more important to you than your own family?"

Mark fixed his eyes on the perplexed face of the interrogator. He now responded with rising passion in his voice. "I love my family deeply. But there are some actions that are not acceptable, even if they are taken to save your own life or the lives of your loved ones. In the eyes of the Almighty, we are all brothers. I cannot denounce Anatoly or contribute in any way to his destruction, even to save my own family.

"What is more, my request for visas for myself and my family was, in itself, an expression of my love for them. I love my children enough to think more of their future than of my own. I had a career here in the Soviet Union. I had a comfortable home and good wages. I have lived long enough as a Jew, the son of silent Jews who witnessed the pogroms under the Tsars and the terrors of the Stalin era, to have learned the art of silence. But what of my children? Are they to live out their lives in a country where the whim of a new ruler, a new Stalin, could terminate even the limited opportunity a Jewish child now might have to acquire an advanced education? Are they to spend the rest of their lives in a land where you may consider yourself 'secure' today and yet find yourself in jail tomorrow?

"Already we can feel the wind of change. We see bright young Jews, the children of accomplished scientists and scholars, being denied admission to universities. They are considered untrustworthy because they are Jews and because they are the children of scholars – leaders in the intellectual community. A fear seems to have gripped those in authority, a fear of truth and the spread of truth, a fear of knowledge and the dissemination of knowledge, paranoia towards new ideas and the transmission of such ideas. (As if you could stop the spread of ideas by only selecting the children of peasants for the next generation of university students.) I love my children too much to have them remain in a land where thinking is considered dangerous; where expressing new ideas can lead to imprisonment; where objecting to the evil around you is treated as insanity; with the individual subjected to barbaric, experimental 'therapy' to break his will to resist the State.

"I love my son and daughter too much to keep them shackled to a land where they would be restrained from learning of their Jewish heritage and be forced to conceal that which had been transmitted to them in hushed tones, behind closed doors and dark curtains. My feelings for them are too deep and all encompassing to allow 'Jew' to be stamped on their internal passports in a nation where the Jew is considered an internal enemy unless he or she ceases to be a Jew. Yes, I love my family too much to allow all this to happen to them without at least trying to bring them to a place where this would not be their future. For us that place is Israel.

"But of all this I have said nothing all these years. I have only asked for our visas, as Jews, to emigrate to Israel."

The look on the interrogator's face changed for a moment, from a constant scowl to one of sadness. He seemed, for an instant, to be ready to join in a heart-to-heart talk with his prisoner. The Jew perceived that look, whether sympathy or pity, and for that melancholy eye blink there was an unspoken bond between them that time could not erase. The interrogator spotted the look of surprise on the face of the lieutenant across the room and he quickly resumed his former expression. Finally, he felt able to speak.

"Professor," he began in softer tones, trying to convey his message with a sense of logic, "applying for permission to leave the Soviet Union, such as you did, is bad enough. Publicly denouncing the Soviet government and accusing us of violating human rights before the foreign press the way Sharansky did – well, that simply cannot be tolerated. Even so, we might be disposed to let him off lightly if he cooperates in ending this emigration nonsense once and for all. As for you – you're a fool. Whatever we want to do with Sharansky will be done with or without your signature. Don't you realize that?"

Mark sat silent, clenching his fists tightly, out of sight, beneath the table. At last, he replied: "I have not lived my 45 years under Soviet rule without learning something about the system. You will do what you wish with Sharansky...and with me as well, regardless of my signature and regardless of 'your word' as you call it. I did not apply for a visa five years ago without anticipating that it might end this way. But some must show the way for others too timid, too fearful, to cry out what they feel within. You may imprison or even kill two of us, ten of us, a hundred of us, even thousands. How will the Soviet Union then look in the glare of world opinion? Are your masters prepared to announce to the world that the dreaded days of Stalin have returned?"

The interrogator's eyes flared red. A flaming agony had enveloped his body; the burning coals of truth to which there was no reply had scalded the flesh. He pounded the table with his heavy hand, trying to stamp out the pain. "Get him out of here!" he screamed to the guards.

The two guards led Mark out of the room into the corridor. Shortly thereafter the lieutenant joined them. The guards, following the officer, escorted Mark to a truck parked just outside the rear of the building. The back of the vehicle was opened and he was hustled into the windowless interior of the truck. He sat on a cold wooden bench in the darkened rear of the vehicle. The lieutenant sat alongside him and the vehicle moved off to a destination unknown to the Jew. There were the starts and stops of traffic, and the sounds and smells of the city. Then for a long stretch, there was silence, except for the hum of the engine. The air grew cold and damp. Time ticked on in the clock within Mark's brain. He felt that every second was bringing him closer to a dark end. He reflected on what he had said and done. There was nothing he would have changed. He had done what he had to do; they had done what they felt must be done.

The vehicle came to a halt. The lieutenant pointed to the door that was being opened from the outside. Mark stepped out.

To his amazement, he was standing alongside an airport runway. His wife and children were running towards him. Mark grasped them in his arms. Tears fell from all eyes.

"Get on the plane, over there," directed the Russian officer who had come up behind him. "Do so immediately – all of you."

Mark looked back, open-mouthed, at the lieutenant.

"And keep your mouth shut in the future," continued the officer, warningly. "That's the least you can do in gratitude for your release. Remember, you still have family here in Russia to pay the piper for anything you do against us abroad."

In July 1978, Anatoly Sharansky was brought to trial in Russia. Mark Azbel sent a signed and notarized document to the court. In it, he detailed the attempt of the interrogator to get him to sign a false confession implicating Anatoly. At the time, Mark was a professor of physics at Tel Aviv University. He offered to leave that position and return to the Soviet Union to testify for the defense. The Russian government denied him permission to enter the country and the court refused to hear or even read his deposition.

As the interrogator had foretold, Anatoly was tried and convicted. The trial was a mockery of justice by any standards.

Before being sentenced, Anatoly addressed these words to his wife, Avital, in Israel and to his fellow Jews who, with the exception of his brother Leonid, were not permitted into the courtroom: "In March and April during interrogation, the chief investigators warned me that in the position I had taken during the investigation and held in the court, I would be threatened with execution by firing squad or imprisoned for at least fifteen years. If I would agree to cooperate with the investigation for the purpose of destroying the Jewish emigration movement, they promised me early freedom and a quick reunion with my wife.

"Five years ago I submitted my application for exit to Israel. Now I'm further than ever from my dream. It would seem a cause for regret. But it is absolutely otherwise. I am happy. I am happy that I have lived honestly, even under the threat of death.

"I am happy that I helped people. I am proud that I knew and worked with such honest, brave and courageous people as Sakharov, Orlov and Ginzberg who are carrying on the tradition of the Russian intelligentsia. I am fortunate to have been witness to the process of liberation of the Jews of the USSR.

"I hope that the absurd accusation against me and the entire Jewish emigration movement will not hinder the liberation of my people. My near ones and friends know how I wanted to exchange activity in the emigration movement for life with my wife, Avital, in Israel.

"For more than 2,000 years, the Jewish people, my people, have been dispersed. But wherever they are, wherever Jews are found, each year they have repeated, 'Next year in Jerusalem.' Now, when I am farther than ever from my people, my Avital – 'Next year in Jerusalem.'"

Then Anatoly turned to the judges and continued: "Now, I turn to you, the court, who are required to confirm a predetermined sentence: To you, I have nothing to say."

A crowd of somber people waited outside the courthouse. They included Anatoly's mother and reporters from the West who were forbidden to witness the proceedings inside. Anatoly's brother, Leonid Sharansky, emerged from the courtroom after the sentence was pronounced. Trembling, he told the crowd that Anatoly was being sent to Siberia for fourteen years. Then he read, from scrawled notes, Anatoly's declaration to the court. When he was finished, the ragged band of persecuted people threw off their looks of fear. They each stood erect and joined in the singing of the "*Hatikvah*."

THE CALL

In 1964, Stephanie gave birth to our son, Ian. The infant added a new dimension to our lives. I was determined to work all the harder to provide a future for our offspring. And so any thought of travel and my quest to follow the track taken by my ancestors was put off.

One day early in 1965, I was obtaining a history from a new patient. He was a burly man who pumped gas at a Mobil station. In the course of the questioning, I learned that he had come to the United States from Turkey.

"It's a wonderful country," he insisted.

"I agree,"

"Have you been to Turkey?"

"Why, yes. My wife and I were in Istanbul two years ago. Fascinating city."

"Fascinating, of course. But you should see the rest of country. Istanbul, Ankara and Izmir are fine to see, but you have not really experienced the country until you've seen the underground cities that hardly any westerners have visited, and the cities carved out of the limestone cliffs at Cappadocia. You have to have yogurt and raki in an outdoor café deep in the interior!"

"Raki? That's alcohol! Turkey is a Muslim country."

"Well, we're Muslim, but our kind of Muslim. We're not Saudi Arabia."

"I assume traveling in the interior would be expensive. I mean, renting a car with a driver, hiring a guide and so forth."

"What are you talking about? You take a bus like the rest of us. And you don't need a guard. Turkey is a safe place. In fact, my new son-in-law is going to Turkey. Like you, he's an American. Of course my daughter is going with him, so it will be cheap."

"What do you call cheap?"

"My daughter is a member of the Turkish Club of America, so her husband goes for the same price: 250 dollars round trip on a chartered plane. They even throw in a week in an Istanbul hotel. But, of course, one of the couple has to be Turkish to join the Turkish Club of America. If you travel by bus, you can go 100 miles for an American dollar. And an American dollar will get you food for two in the interior."

"I never heard of a round trip flight to Istanbul for only 250 dollars, let alone a hotel for a week."

"The flight is a charter flight. As for the hotel, almost none of the people on the plane ever stay there for more than one night. They're anxious to visit their families who live far from Istanbul."

"I guess I should join the Turkish Club of America."

"You're Turkish?"

"Well, my ancestors came from Turkey. One served as a physician to a sultan."

"Really!"

That evening, I posed a question to Stephanie: "How about a three-week trip to Turkey?"

"We've got a son."

"I know. That's why I'm working seven days a week, to make sure the two of you are provided for."

"So what happens to Ian? You're not planning to take a one-year-old to Turkey?"

"Of course not. Look, I've spoken to your mother. She'd be happy to stay here with him."

"You've discussed it with my mother without telling me?"

"Don't be angry. I just spoke to her about a trip in general."

"What kind of trip do you have in mind? What about the expense?"

"That's just it. It will be our *own* tour. We'll travel across the country by bus and eat in local restaurants. It will be fun. And we can get to visit the places where my ancestors lived, study the landscape, picture their lives. It will be an adventure."

"An adventure with diarrhea! And not having a protective guide, we'd be lucky to get back alive."

"You've got it wrong. The Turks are a tough people, but they have great respect for the law. The authorities don't take crime lightly. Steal a pocketbook and you'll be smashing rocks in the equivalent of a chain gang for ten years, if you live that long. That certainly discourages crime."

"What about the cost?"

"That's the best news of all. Only 250 dollars each for the airfare and hotel in Istanbul. It's a special. All I have to do is join the Turkish Club of America. That costs five dollars. And the bus trips and the hotels are very cheap."

"It sounds crazy. You don't even speak the language, and you know nothing about the country."

"I've read books on Turkey since my childhood, and I have a map of the country in my mind. You know I've always sought to understand the past and where I came from as a vehicle for understanding who I am. It may sound crazy, but it is reality to me. Why did my direct ancestor leave Turkey and what happened to those who remained in that land?

Stephanie found it hard to refuse.

A few weeks later we went to JFK to board our chartered plane. One by one, the passengers approached the counter, carrying their baggage.

"You can't be serious about going on that plane," Stephanie whispered in my ear. "Look at all the baggage they're bringing to the counter. Two strong men can barely lift one of those trunks. And there must be a hundred trunks! They're carrying the United States back with them. The plane will never get off the ground!"

"This is not the first charter flight to Turkey. This is a multi-million dollar jet. I'm sure the crew will weigh the luggage."

"Weigh those trunks? It would take a crane to lift one of them."

"It's an adventure."

"So you said."

Two hours later we were on a plane packed to the rafters. The woman seated next to me had a young man seated on her lap. At Stephanie's urging, I approached a stewardess. "How can the plane take off with a passenger seated on another passenger's lap?"

"The woman has one ticket. That's a child on her lap."

"A child! He must weigh 150 pounds and he needs a shave!"

"What do you want me to do? Throw her off the plane? She's a poor woman and probably cannot afford a second seat. We're all Turks."

I returned to my seat.

"What happened?"

"I can't have her thrown off the plane. We'll survive."

Several times during the night I felt a sharp pain as the young man rolled onto my leg, but I did survive. I was going to uncover another piece of the puzzle, and that was all that mattered.

As advised by my Turkish patient, Stephanie and I traveled eastward to Ankara, the capital of Turkey, then southward through towns and villages to the southern coast of the country, then westward along the Mediterranean Sea, and finally northward, reaching Izmir before returning to Istanbul to board a jet for our return trip to the United States, We traveled by local busses, stayed in local hotels, and ate in local restaurants to experience the Turkish life. It was an adventure to remember.

Travel by local bus in the hinterlands of Turkey in summer is something few Americans would volunteer to endure. And yet, it gave us insight into the lives of the inhabitants of that country. The temperature in the bus felt as if it were 120 degrees. With no air-conditioning, we were drenched in sweat. Stephanie opened a window. A woman, her head covered with a shawl, rushed over and closed the window, pointing to her baby clothed in woolens!

When we came to the next stop, a woman was waiting there with baggage and two live chickens in hand. The driver immediately tied the baggage and the chickens to the top of the bus. The woman took a seat on the bus.

Five miles later, when we arrived at the next town, the woman departed, taking her baggage and chickens with her.

In many places we visited, they had never before seen an American. In one town, the mayor, learning of our arrival, came out to greet us as if we were American ambassadors. We were introduced to all the town dignitaries, following which we were taken to a local restaurant. Musicians were summoned to entertain us while we ate yogurt and local delicacies, washed down with raki.

In another town when we were walking through a park, a group of about ten Turkish men who were seated at a long table beckoned us to join them. We sat down at the end of the table. There was a very large bowl of yogurt and cucumbers on the table. Each of us was handed a large glass, which one of the men filled with raki. The man at the head of the table took a spoonful of yogurt and cucumbers in his mouth, downed it with his full glass of raki, and then handed the bowl to the man next to him. He, in turn, did the same thing, and passed the bowl to the man sitting next to him. My wife looked at me, askance. There was only one spoon in the bowl of yogurt.

"What are we gonna do?" she whispered to me.

"Don't worry. The alcohol'll kill anything!"

In another town we were invited to a local wedding. They seated us on the dais, next to the bride and groom! We were introduced to all the important people there. Waiters brought all sorts of treats for us. Entertainers performed directly in front of us: singers who employed special vibrating use of the tongue, and dancers who executed wild eastern dances that took my breath away. Each would bow to us in appreciation when we applauded.

At one point, one of the men came over to my wife and asked, "Do you play?" He obviously meant, "Do you dance?" He then proceeded to escort her to the middle of the dance floor. She was the only woman who was dancing, since the native women did not partake in such activities, and she did a great job! It wasn't easy trying to follow the energetic steps of the Turkish fellow.

Another time, after being driven over a dried out riverbed for about thirty miles by an adventurous taxi driver, we came to a stony area impossible to cross. Several farmers nearby waved to us to join them. They placed several blankets on the ground and proceeded to bring out food and drink for us. Later, when we had finished eating, they offered to show us through an underground city hidden beneath a great hill on their property. It seemed that the last foreigner to see the place was the archeologist who described it in a book I had read in my childhood.

In each instance they refused payment for any of their services. Fortunately, I had brought a number of Kennedy silver half-dollars with me. I would hand one to the person or family that had treated us so royally, as if it were a medal being presented by the President of the United States!

It was as a result of what I learned on that trip and subsequent trips to Turkey and Israel that I was able to piece together some missing parts of my heritage.

When migrations occur, not all take part in it. Some remain behind, feeling more comfortable in their accustomed surroundings. Dr. David ben Yosef Azubel accompanied Suleiman the Magnificent when that Ottoman ruler conquered much of southeastern Europe, but much of the family remained in Smyrna, which had been renamed Izmir by the Turks. Thus, there were still Azubels residing in Izmir when the nation of Israel came into being again, 2,000 years after the Jews had been forced into exile.

"*Allah akbar, Allah akbar, Allah akbar. La ilaha Illa Hallah, Mouhammed rasool Allah. La ilaha Illa Hallah, Mouhammed rasool Allah...*" (Arabic for "God is great. There is no God but He and Mouhammed is His messenger.")

The shrill cry came from a thousand minarets and echoed through the streets of Izmir, summoning forth the faithful for the evening prayers. In the shadows of approaching darkness, Yaakov Azubel, a slender lad of 18, quickened his step. His eyes were bright with excitement and impatience as his forward progress was hindered by the teeming masses of humanity that filled the street. His face was pale – almost out of place amidst the olive-skinned Turks around him. A black cap covered his head, but the careful observer would have spotted the black sidecurls tucked up neatly under the sides of his headwear.

He made his way through the narrow, winding streets of irregular stone, amid the busy shops whose windows were packed with all the exotic wares of the East: trays, cups, lamps and samovars of beaten brass that glowed like a treasure of Spanish gold; pipes of moon-white meerschaum, dark wood and shiny metal carved in the shapes of heads – pasha, sultan, sheik or sailor-pipes more than two feet in length, as well as little ones which could easily be concealed in a shirt pocket; giant water-bottle pipes with a yard of coil from brass stem to exotic bottle to flowering brass ball with lit tobacco in its center, and beautiful silver pipes with magnificently ornamented stems, and elongated tobacco cases that appeared to be designed for use in an opium den; glistening lacquered woods inlaid with mother of pearl in the shapes of animals, warriors on a chess board, jewel boxes, backgammon sets and objects of furniture of every size and description; and woven carpets of wool and silk, large and small, burning red, warm orange, golden yellow, pea green and sapphire blue – trees of life and patterned shapes.

A shopkeeper halted from fingering his worry beads and bowed invitingly to a foreign-looking lady, but Yaakov was not distracted. He had seen all this countless times before. His mind was elsewhere. Seeing an opening, he quickened his step. He passed young hawkers carrying trays of steaming, golden-colored tea and thick, dark Turkish coffee whose aroma wetted his mouth. The hawkers poked their trays past open shop doors or into the faces of pedestrians, announcing the items they were selling. One bumped into Yaakov, fortunately not hard enough to cause the loss of tea or coffee.

Apologies were exchanged. Yaakov then continued on his way past a café, outside of which sat a long row of elderly men dressed in the seedy jackets and baggy trousers of men not born to wealth or position. Yaakov glanced in their direction as he passed. It was as if they were glued to their chairs. Each of them had the vacant gaze characteristic of smokers of water-bottle pipes – the gaze induced by the hashish or Persian tobacco that glowed like burning charcoal above the balls of the pipes, filling the air like incense.

Yaakov turned down a wider street, past the bus stop where vendors sold cold buttermilk and hot charred corns, giant cucumbers split down the middle and cups of yogurt to the disembarking passengers. A woman descended from the bus, dressed in a long, black coat. She was holding together the sides of the lengthy black scarf that covered her head, so that only her nose was visible. She led a scrawny, black-spotted gray goat down the bus steps and then waited until the driver unloaded her belongings from atop the bus – a bundle wrapped in a blanket and tied with a rope, an oil lamp and two live, frightened chickens that had been tied to the rack atop the vehicle on its journey into the city. She reached for her possessions with both hands. A gust of wind blew her scarf open. She dropped her belongings, freeing her hands to pull her scarf shut quickly in order to conceal her face from the view of passing men.

At the next corner, most of the men turned to the right, under the arch into the courtyard, in the center of which stood the great mosque. But Yaakov turned to the left, into a narrow yard-like street. He moved past houses shaded in darkness, through an open gate, to the door of a seemingly insignificant, shuttered building marked only by a small Star of David barely visible above the door. He opened the door and entered hastily.

Some 40 men were busily engaged in the evening prayers, each murmuring softly, so that the sum of their voices was a humming sound that floated through the room – a small synagogue in Izmir in twentieth-century Turkey. Their lips moved in rapid, bird-like cadence. Their bodies swayed back and forth and they turned from side to side with the fervor of their inaudible prayers as they faced southeast towards Jerusalem, towards the land from the past that none could ever forget. They held their prayer books before them, but their eyes moved so rapidly across the pages that it was evident that the words had been fixed in their minds and came forth from their lips, as the response of men who had ingested the books whole and made them part of their being. They were as if in a trance, separated from the troubles of the outside world, yet remembering all of it, communicating directly with their Maker and entreating Him to help them, to redeem His people from poverty, misery and exile.

Yaakov moved quickly down the aisle. Nodding glances of men busy at prayer greeted his arrival. He reached the row of seats he was looking for and slid alongside two young men who were occupied reciting the *Amidah* with now silent, moving lips. (*Amidah* means "standing." It is the core and main element of the daily services and is recited silently in the standing position, facing Jerusalem, and then repeated aloud by the reader leading the prayers.)

Immediately to Yaakov's right stood his brother, Benjamin, dressed in a threadbare gray jacket and seedy dark trousers, with a graying shirt, unbuttoned at the top. He was only a year older than Yaakov, but his broad shoulders and full face dwarfed the dimensions of his younger brother. A head of darkening-blond, curly hair was visible below his skullcap, with sidecurls dangling freely from the corners. His nose was full-sized and the faintest suggestion of a moustache separated it from lips that seemed in perpetual motion, despite the absence of sound. Benjamin turned the page in his prayer book and bowed his head as he repeated the name of the Lord in silence. Then he handed the book to Yaakov, pointing to the place they were up to. Benjamin picked up another prayer book and turned to the correct page, all without interrupting his prayers for a moment.

To Benjamin's right stood Shmuel, a fair-haired man of 28 and the eldest of the brothers. His clothes, like those of Benjamin and most of the other members of the congregation, were old and drab, as if they had been purchased for economy and durability, rather than for style. He noted Yaakov's late arrival with a stern nod, but continued in his prayers. His dark eyes slid back and forth down the page until the *Amidah* had been completed. Then he looked up towards the raised platform in the center of the synagogue.

Swaying back and forth behind the lectern atop the platform was the imposing figure of Isaac Ibn (son of) Eliezer haKohen. Manicured fingers moved across the page of the prayer book on the lectern as the wealthiest member of the congregation – a man of medium height and large girth – led them in silent devotion. He wore a fashionable, dark blue suit, matching tie and clean white shirt, with a *tallit* (fringed prayer shawl) covering his head and body like a large, fringed shawl that emphasized his respect for the Almighty. He paused, looked around, and seeing that all lips had ceased to move (indicating that they had finished the silent *Amidah*), began to read aloud.

Yaakov's mouth opened as if he were about to speak, but a sharp glance from Shmuel sealed the young man's lips. Yaakov read the message in his brother's eyes. "Not now. Not during prayers."

A few minutes later, the evening prayers were completed and Shmuel turned to the youngest of the family. "Well, what was it that delayed your arrival and almost interrupted the service?" he asked, somewhat annoyed.

"The call."

Shmuel and Benjamin looked at him, perplexed.

"What call?" asked Shmuel. "Are you referring to the Muezzin's call from the minaret for evening prayers? You should have taken that into account. Knowing that the Muslims would be heading for evening prayers, you should have started out earlier."

"Not that call," replied Yaakov. "I meant Ben Gurion's call. I heard him on the radio...from Israel."

The members of the congregation had been packing their belongings in preparation to leave. Upon overhearing the brothers' conversation, several of them stopped what they were doing and moved closer.

"Listen everybody," continued Yaakov in a loud voice. "I heard David Ben Gurion on the radio. A Jewish state has been declared. He's calling on all of us to return to Israel as quickly as possible."

"A Jewish state!" repeated an older man in near disbelief. Tears of joy welled up in his heavy-lidded brown eyes and ran down through the stubble on his face, disappearing into the small gray beard on his chin. "That I should have lived to see this day..." He halted, choking on his tears. Through the tears, a smile appeared on his face. He dried his eyes with his jacket sleeve and then blew his nose into a faded handkerchief. "I must rush home and tell my wife and children. We must pack immediately."

"Yes," agreed a middle-aged man in the rear of the synagogue. "We must pack."

"Wait a minute," interrupted Isaac Ibn Eliezer. "What are you all packing for? I'm as happy as any of you to hear of the proclamation of a Jewish state, and I'll send a substantial contribution to help them out, but packing up – that's another matter.

"Our families have lived here for centuries, side by side with the Turks, and some were here even before the Turks arrived. When the Spaniards drove many of our ancestors out of their country, the Ottoman Empire was the only nation to welcome Jews to their shores. We have homes here, property here, and *roots* here. We speak the language and get along well with the Turks...perhaps not the best, but far from the worst. They let us have our synagogues and keep our property. It's not the most marvelous of all possible worlds, but it's a world that we're used to, a world in which we can get along. The Turks have not shipped us off in boxcars to death camps the way the Germans did. So why should we leave?

"And how do you all plan to get to Israel? By waving a wand? There's no Moses here to part the waters, and there are several hundred miles of open sea between Izmir and Israel.

"My advice to you all is 'Wait.' Wait and see what happens. Wait until the State of Israel stands on solid ground. Wait until it's safe. Then, if you still want to go, pack up all your belongings, sell that which you do not wish to take with you (cautiously, so as not to lose almost everything you have in a forced sale), buy a ticket (or tickets for your entire family) for safe passage on a plane or ship, and set out sensibly for the Promised Land."

A murmur went through the room. Here and there, men were heard to comment softly; words such as "He makes sense" or "He's got a point."

In the rear of the synagogue stood Haim Russo, an olive-skinned lad of 17 who was the youngest of the men attending the evening's service. Below a skullcap-covered head of closely twisted, jet-black hair, his forehead was now lined with concern. His searching brown eyes studied the faces of those around him. His ears, like antennae, took in the softly spoken words with dismay. His short, wiry body was tense, seemingly ready to vibrate if touched. His hands tightened into fists with the fingers digging into the palms, turning the flesh beneath them pale white and the rest of the palms an angry reddish-purple. Then he spoke with rising anger in his voice.

"Can I believe what I hear? Is that all we have learned in nearly 2,000 years of exile – to let someone else, a fellow Jew – fight our battles for us? To let others make the sacrifices? To sit back while others shed their blood for us, and then if they succeed, if they survive, join them like gentlemen invited to a banquet? Is that how the Hebrew people under Joshua redeemed the Holy Land? God forbid that we should stoop so low!

"Our people are at a great moment in their history – the rebirth of the State of Israel – but they are also at a moment of crisis. It does not require a genius to recognize what is going to happen in a few days, or what may be happening right now. All the Arab countries have declared that they will never accept a Jewish state. They have stated that they intend to drive the Hebrew people into the sea. Seven Arab armies, maybe even more, stand poised to annihilate the 600,000 Jews of Palestine. Our brethren in Israel have called upon us to join them in their hour of need, in *our* hour of need. It is the duty of every Jew, no matter where he finds himself, to come back to Israel, for we are sojourners here, as we were in Egypt in the days of Moses. We are duty bound to take up arms to defend the land the Lord promised to the descendants of Abraham, Isaac and Jacob, the land of David and Solomon. For it is the only land the Hebrew people ever called their own and the only land our nation will ever call its own.

"For 2,000 years the Hebrew people in Exile have prayed for this day, and for many years we, their living representatives, have waited eagerly for this announcement. Many of you here have seen relatives and friends set out in small boats in the middle of the night (to avoid detection by the Turks), to sail to Israel. Some of them were intercepted by the British and sent back to Turkey. Some were drowned when their boats went down in rough seas. But some succeeded in getting to Palestine to take part in the rebirth of *our* nation. Did they risk their lives then, and do they continue to risk their lives now, so that we can sit back on soft chairs and watch the show? Is our flesh more valuable than their flesh? Is our blood more sacred than their blood? Am I to tell my brother, Aaron, who shoulders arms in Israel, or am I to explain to the soul of my brother, Mordechai, of blessed memory (who was swallowed up by the sea en route to Palestine) if we meet in the hereafter, that I was too important or too delicate to fight for our nation?

"You heard Yaakov bring news that David Ben Gurion has called on us to return to our native land. Yaakov did not term it a 'plea,' he said it was a 'call.' The *shofar* does not beg you to observe the faith: It commands you to follow the beliefs of our people. As Israel is the nation of every Jew and his safe haven in our hour of danger, so is the battle to preserve the state, the battle of every Jew. Let each of us, like soldiers, pack a few necessities for the trip and leave, by whatever means available and as quickly as possible. Yaakov, Benjamin, will you join me?"

"Of cou –" began Yaakov, eagerly.

"We must discuss the matter with the rest of our family," interrupted Shmuel.

"Then there's no point in my staying here." Haim bit his lower lip in pain. "I must be off. There must be some *men* in Izmir."

The door closed with a heavy thud after Haim departed hastily from the synagogue. There was a stunned silence in the room as men wrestled with their consciences, weighing security for themselves and their families against oaths they had uttered in prayer countless times before. They remembered the words "If I forget thee, O Jerusalem, let my right hand lose its cunning," and they knew where their duty lay. (These words were recited by every Jew for the past 2,000 years expressing the fact that Jerusalem is central to the Jewish faith.)

"Those were fine words," said Isaac Ibn Eliezer, "but those were the words of youth, of boiling blood not tempered by caution – the wisdom of age. He has no mother or father who will worry over his health; he has no wife or children who require his sheltering arms; he has no sisters here in Izmir, whose virtue he must protect. He is a good lad. He is the stuff that heroes are made of. But are not the rest of us, who worry about our parents in their old age, our wives and children and their need for safety and security, worthy too?

"I urge you all to go home and consider what has been said here to-night, and much more that has not been spoken of, such as how the Turks take to the idea of a large number of Jews leaving this country for Israel. After all, the Turks are Muslims. And with the Arab states opposed to and attacking the State of Israel, the Turks may feel impelled to stop any Jews who attempt to leave for Israel. Let us wait until after the Sabbath to discuss our future plans.

"In the meantime, we can watch events and hear more from Israel. Let none close his mind until we meet on Saturday night. After the service, let us remain in the synagogue. Then, in the presence of the guiding wisdom of Rabbi Siegora, let us discuss Ben Gurion's call for Jews to come to Israel. Until then, a good Sabbath and a good night."

Slowly, one by one, the congregants left the House of the Lord, with a softly spoken "*Shalom*." (Peace be unto you. It also means "Hello" and "Good-bye.") They made their way through darkened streets, back to their homes. The Azubel brothers did not speak to one another until they were at the doorstep of their house.

"Shmuel," wondered Yaakov aloud as they waited for someone to come to the door, "why did you stop me from joining Haim?"

"Papa," replied his eldest brother.

Yaakov and Benjamin were puzzled by Shmuel's remark, but they chose to defer a reply.

Victoria Azubel, their mother, opened the door. She was a thin, but not frail woman in her fifties. She looked like many a poor Jewish mother in Izmir: a wig covering her head; a brow furrowed beyond her age by toil and tribulation; sunken eyes that had seen much and had learned to bear much in silence; a simple black dress hanging down formlessly over her body; and bony hands with palms roughened from years of scrubbing floors, washing and mending clothes, and handling pots of boiling water and trays of hot fresh bread just out of the oven without the benefit of gloves. She considered the faces of her three sons and sensed that something was troubling them. But she did not make any inquiries, other than the customary "How are you?" and "Who led the evening services?"

Dorah Azubel, a pale, slender girl of twenty-four, already was seated at the table. Honey-colored hair, in large, flowing curls, fell softly on her shoulders. Her eyes were dark brown and radiant, and her face, bright and unpainted. She greeted her brothers with a smile and a nod. (To have kissed or even shaken hands would be unthinkable in an Orthodox home, where no man touched any woman but his wife, even though she be his mother or sister.)

An eerie stillness hung over the dinner meal. It was like the uneasy quiet of a village situated near a volcano after the ground had been felt to vibrate; it was the anxious silence of people waiting, waiting for something, but exactly what, they were not sure. The food, sparse as it was, was quickly consumed. Dorah rose to pour the thick, dark-brown Turkish coffee from the brass pot into demitasse cups which were passed to all those seated at the table. At last Victoria broke the silence.

"Well, what's going on?"

"It's the call," bubbled Yaakov. "I heard it on the radio while I was rolling cigarettes. There's a Jewish state now, and Ben Gurion is the prime minister. He is calling on all Jews to return to Israel. I want to go but –"

"Mama," interrupted Shmuel, "this is a serious undertaking. There'll be war over in Israel, with Arab armies attacking from all sides. I've read what the Arabs said in the United Nations. They will never allow a Jewish state to be established. So for those Jews who go there now, there will be great danger. But there'll also be opportunity – opportunity to build a land of our own. We need your guidance in this matter."

Victoria considered this briefly. "We'll go," she said assertively, "as soon as possible."

"But Mama," said Dorah, "you came to a decision so quickly. Didn't you find that hard to do?"

"Not really. We're leaving nothing and going to something. Something, even with all the danger, is better than nothing."

"How can you say that?" asked Dorah, upset. "Our family has lived here as far back as anyone can recall, and we've lived in peace. The Turks have never attacked us. So why are we rushing to leave?"

"Most of our ancestors were born in Izmir and lived out their lives here," her mother answered. "A few were born in Russia and came to Turkey to escape the Pogroms. There are Azubel tombstones in the cemetery here from even before the Spanish Inquisition, back to the beginnings of the Jewish community in Izmir. So we've managed to live alongside the Turks for a long, long time. In fact, we know from the dates on some of the tombstones that there were Azubels here even before the Turks conquered Anatolia. Our people have not been massacred. And they have not been persecuted, the way the Jews were in Russia and other places. True, Jews have been mistreated here on occasion, but no worse than many others. 'So why leave?' you ask.

"To be in a land of our own is the answer. Only in a land we can call ours can we really be secure. Have you forgotten your history? There was once a large Greek community that flourished here in Izmir. Where are they now? Dead or in Greece. There were once millions of Armenians here in Turkey. Where are they now? In unmarked graves or scattered like sand across the face of the earth. The Turkish leaders heard their cry for independence, and so the existence of Greeks and Armenians in Turkey was viewed as a threat.

"We Jews are small in number compared to the Turks, and so we are not thought of as a danger to the territorial integrity of the state. But what of tomorrow and after tomorrow? What if our numbers should increase, or the prosperity of a few Jews arouses their envy? Will the Turks of tomorrow, like the Egyptians of old, consider us a danger to their nation? The Hebrews were enslaved in the days of Moses. Jewish mothers were ordered to cast their newborn sons into the river. In the modern world, nations are more civilized. They just exterminate a whole minority as the solution to their perceived problem!

"As for our great stake in Turkey, we have none. We struggle just to survive. Jews are the last to get a job and the first to lose it when times are hardest. I have scrubbed floors and washed clothes. I have cared for the homes of others while trying to maintain our own for 18 years, and where am I now? Still poor, still scrubbing floors for the Keti Sabans and the Rabenu Cohens! And if I live to 120 years, I'll be no further along. The day that I'm no longer able to work, my wages will end. Shmuel, you served in the Turkish army for five years. How long did it take you to find a job when you got out? And you, Benjamin, and you, Yaakov: How long did it take you to find employment? And what kind of jobs did you get? Rolling cigarettes! Putting filling in boxes! You started that way and, if we stay here, you'll end up in the same jobs – if your fingers hold out. The Jews born to poverty remain in poverty. Nothing changes.

"But that's not the worst. To be poor and to live in the land of others, to know that your children will be just as poor and just as insecure as you are, that is far worse.

"At least in Israel there's a chance. I don't expect the streets to be paved in gold the way some speak of America, but in a country of our own there is a chance. That's all I ask for. And even if we end up just as poor as we are now, to be free in a land of our own – that is a form of wealth that cannot be measured in gold. Only one of my children now enjoys the wealth of freedom, and that is your sister, Eliza. When she sailed to Palestine three years ago, in the quiet of the night, she sailed to freedom. She became a free woman and will give hope to the children she will someday, God willing, bear in our land.

"Have you forgotten so soon how we yearned to get to Palestine when the way there was so difficult? How we pooled our meager savings to buy small, rickety boats and bribe the Turkish guards to look aside while our young men and women sailed away in the darkness, to brave the dangers of the open sea and warships of the British navy, just a few short years ago? Did they expect an easy time of it? No. They knew that they were voyaging to a life of hardship. But they were buoyed by the fact that they were journeying to a land of hope.

"We, at least, do not have the British navy blocking our way. We will face Arab armies most likely, but does not Eliza, and do not all our brethren in Israel, face the same now? The more of us who go to Israel, the greater the numbers to swell the ranks of the defenders of the Jewish state, the better the chances for our people. So let's get packing. With the little we have, that can't take long."

"But –" began Shmuel, hesitatingly.

"But what?" interrupted his mother impatiently?

"But what about Papa?" he continued, uneasily, before coming to a halt.

"Papa?" Victoria's eyes widened with amazement. Somehow that question had never entered her mind during the excitement of the news of Israel's independence and the call to return to the Holy Land. It was something she had thought much about in the past, but had never spoken of. But now that the question was asked, it had to be answered, not with the calming reassurance of a pat on a child's head, but with candor. She cast her eyes on the faces of her children, one by one, and studied their troubled expressions.

413

"Is that what troubles you? You're all worried that your father might return and find no one here? I've seen that anxious look in the eyes of each of you when you heard of an Azubel in another country or even a name that sounded like it. It was the look of a child who felt abandoned, and yet it was the look of a child who was hoping against hope that his father is alive, that the father has not forgotten his children, and that the father will someday return. Well, forget it. As far as we are concerned, he's gone forever and must be presumed dead.

"Shmuel, you were nine years old when he set off for Buenos Aires in 1929. Dorah was five and Eliza, four. Benjamin, you were just a year old and I was pregnant with Yaakov. We were poor, very poor, with no hope of doing any better. Your father could not get work and it hurt him terribly to see your scrawny bodies, sunken faces and hungry, pleading eyes, day after day, with him unable to provide for you.

"A sailor, from a ship scheduled to carry cargo to Argentina, became ill while drinking in a nearby tavern, and died just as suddenly. Your father was there in the tavern when all of this happened. He tried to help the man, but it was to no avail. The man was a stranger, and so the tavern-owner and he went through the man's papers to see who he was. They found no information about him, save for his ship's papers. Your father saw it as a message from a higher authority that he must leave. He saw it as a chance to break out of the trap of poverty and get a fresh start in the New World. He came home and told me about it. He was going to Argentina. Moshe promised to send word of how he was doing, as well as money as soon as he got a job in Buenos Aires. He pledged to send for us all just as soon as he could. Then he took the place of the seaman and boarded the ship. I watched and waved until not even smoke was visible on the horizon."

"So what happened?" inquired Yaakov.

"What happened? I don't know. I never heard from him again. Maybe he died. God knows, there are enough cut-throats on ships who will do someone in, hoping to steal the contents of his pockets. Maybe he's still alive. I will not speak ill of him because he is your father. I do not wish to remember him as anything but a good and loving husband and father, so I assume he is dead. Besides, if such a person were alive and had left a pregnant wife and four small children to starve to death, can you imagine him returning 19 years later to see how they were doing? No man could face such guilt."

The room returned to a state of silence as each member of the family pondered over what had just been said.

"Dorah, help me clean the table and wash the dishes," instructed Victoria. "Shmuel, Benjamin, Yaakov, as soon as the Sabbath is over, we will start packing."

The boys headed in the direction of their bedroom while Dorah collected the dishes.

"One moment," said their mother as an afterthought. "Don't say anything to strangers about our leaving. We don't want the whole Turkish army waiting at the dock."

❖ ❖ ❖

It was a long, hot, humid night, with the air thick as smoke of a fire. None of the family could sleep. At the first light of dawn, Yaakov arose from the bed that he shared with Benjamin. He washed, ate, and then went to the synagogue.

On his way there, he chanced to meet Mustapha Okyar, a short, wiry, olive-skinned youth with kinky hair and dark eyes.

"So you're here," said Mustapha. "I thought you were on…"

"On what?" asked Yaacov, unable to restrain his curiosity.

"On the boat that left last night. My brother told me about it. A bunch of young Jews were on it. Haim Russo was one of them. You're his friend, so I thought you'd be with him."

"What are you talking about?"

"You know what I mean. Yesterday, when we heard the news about Palestine… You were so excited, I thought you'd jump out of your skin when you heard what that fellow said about Jews rushing to Palestine."

Yaakov thought for a moment. "Well, I guess you were mistaken, thinking that I was going any place." He paused and then added, "By the way, was your brother there when they left? You know, the boat you were speaking about."

"Well, he was on duty at the dock… Say, keep quiet about what I told you. I don't want my brother getting into trouble over a few liras. You know what I mean."

"Don't worry. I won't say anything."

"But they won't be leaving anymore," muttered Mustapha, with emphasis.

"What do you mean?"

"It's the colonel. He heard about the Arab armies entering Palestine to liberate it. So he thought it wouldn't look good if he let all you people go there to oppose them. After all, they're Muslims like us… I mean like the colonel…and me." Mustapha's face reddened with embarrassment.

"No offense, Yaakov. You're not a bad sort, so I wouldn't want you getting shot trying to sail away. With the colonel down on the backs of his men, they can't accept money to look away."

"Thanks for the tip."

It was a grim-faced group that sat around the table mulling over the news that Yaakov had brought home. None had an appetite for food, and they sipped their coffee mechanically, as if the flavor of the dark brew had vanished.

Just 24 hours earlier, the decision had been made to leave. That previous night, despite their concerns about the dangers they might face, they were determined to go. Time could not pass quickly enough for them, for they had planned to make their escape as quickly as possible after the Sabbath. They had been restless to get on with it, to leave for Israel. Now, one day later, the rush to the dock seemed pointless. It was as if the last train out of Izmir had left and the gates to the station were now slammed shut. And someone out there was attaching explosives to the track as a further reminder that escape was impossible.

"If no one is going to eat, we might as well put the food and the dishes away," concluded Victoria. "Dorah, give me a hand."

The women rose and set about their task.

"Is there a way out?" wondered Shmuel, aloud.

"Overland is out of the question," said Victoria, grimly, as she continued to wash the dishes. "For a Jew to journey to Israel through Arab lands would be suicide."

The three brothers leaned forward in their chairs, each with a sullen face supported by the palms of his hands, elbows resting on the table. They were trying to picture a way out of the dilemma. Benjamin's face lit up for a moment. "They're meeting at the synagogue tonight," he burst out with hope in his voice. "Perhaps someone will have an idea."

"Perhaps," replied Shmuel. "In any case, we'll be there."

In an observant Jewish community such as the one in Izmir, Saturday morning services were well attended. On Saturday evening there was generally a smaller crowd assembled. But on this Saturday evening, the house of prayer was filled beyond capacity. The benches were completely occupied, and chairs had been placed in the rear of the sanctuary and even in the aisles in order to accommodate the overflow, much as on the High Holidays. At the completion of the service, the room was buzzing with excitement.

It seemed as if the whole of the Jewish community of Izmir were there. Many, who only rarely frequented services, and some who had not been seen in the synagogue for a year or more, were in the room. They were busily engaged in conversation. Among them was every Azubel over the age of 13 – Albert, Haim, Mordechai, Yehuda, Aaron, David, Isaac, Amos and their sons. Most were close relations of Shmuel Azubel, but some were so distantly related that the family connection had been forgotten.

Shmuel Azubel and his two younger brothers were seated to the right of the central raised platform. They spoke to one another in muffled voices. From time to time they would nod or extend a vocal greeting to friends or relations.

Rabbi Moreno Siegora was on the platform in the center of the synagogue. During the service, he stood facing the Holy Ark (an ark in the synagogue that houses the Torah scrolls). When the service ended, he turned around. His long, flowing beard of graying brown and his piercing dark eyes brought the room to silence. His face was serious and thoughtful as he began: "We have gathered here for prayer and now we remain to discuss our future: Izmir or Israel, now or in the future; who shall go and who shall remain behind; and if to leave, how to leave. For those who wish to go, there is good news. The government in Ankara has let it be known that anyone wishing to depart will not be stopped. For those of substance, there is a hitch. You can take with you the clothes on your backs and a single bag not containing gold, silver, jewelry or more than a few hundred liras. In brief, you may leave Turkey as a penniless wanderer. All valuables are to be left behind.

"Since this is a decision which will affect every one of you, I suggest that the judgment be made by each for himself and his family. That judgment should not be binding on the rest of the community. We can exchange ideas so that everyone can employ the best knowledge before coming to a decision. Well, does anyone wish to begin the discussion?"

Yaakov Azubel rose to his feet. "Rabbi," he inquired, "does that mean that the colonel's men will not shoot at any of us leaving by boat?"

"That is my understanding," replied the bearded man. "Any officer who violates orders from above would probably be sentenced to death."

Yaakov's face brightened. "Then we're free to leave as quickly as we acquire boats."

"Why leave in rotting boats?" asked Ezra Hazzan, a swarthy, middle-aged man with stooped shoulders, a rounded face and large, melancholy eyes. He was standing in the rear of the synagogue, but now moved forward. "If no one is going to stop us, we might as well make it a safer voyage. Let us negotiate with the ship-owners to transport to Israel all who want to make *Aliyah* (a Jew's immigration). The cost of the passage for a single trip could hardly be more than the expense of buying a boat that no one wants. What is more important, we're more likely to arrive at our destination if we engage a large vessel with a skilled captain and crew. After all, we're not sailors and we don't have the expensive instruments necessary for making judgments at sea.

Moreover, we can't predict the weather. In little boats, we're as likely to be tossed into the sea or onto an unfriendly shore as we are to get to Israel alive."

A murmur of approval went though the room.

Isaac Ibn Eliezer rose. Again the room quieted down as the eyes of the portly man of wealth swept the room and then came to rest on the face of the rabbi.

"Rabbi, it is all well to allow Jews to leave, but to leave penniless would be a most unhappy turn of events for some of us. Many here are poor and may conclude that they have nothing to lose by leaving. But those of us, whose families have acquired property through decades of toil and sacrifice, might find such an alternative unacceptable.

"Yet, even for the poor, a flight to Israel, at this juncture, is filled with hazard. We hear on the radio and read in the newspapers that Egyptian, Syrian, Jordanian and Lebanese armies, joined by forces from Iraq and other Arab states are marching into Palestine. These forces are equipped with planes, tanks and artillery. And British officers lead the Jordanians. What chance do a handful of Jews have against such an array of armies? The Haganah defense force was systematically stripped of its weapons by the British during the colonial regime. Can will alone withstand tanks, brave cannon fire, and blunt a bayonet charge? Can boys and girls and old men and women, using ancient muskets and heaving seltzer bottles at the enemy, drive back thousands of well-trained soldiers? Can prayer defeat an enemy who is far better equipped? Does right make might? We all hope so, but I have grave doubts.

"It would seem to me that the Turkish offer is not altogether altruistic. I hear that the Iraqis and the Yemenites, who are Arabs and certainly no friends of Israel, are letting their Jews leave for Israel. This would make sense only if they felt certain that their armies would be victorious and that they would thereby be permanently eliminating the Jewish minority in their lands. What if Israel loses with the resultant slaughter of all its inhabitants? Are we to become extinct as a people? Would it not be better to have some remain outside Israel to keep Judaism alive if such a catastrophic event takes place?"

Isaac paused for effect. It was soon obvious that his words had achieved their intent. Men, previously fixed in their determination to leave, began to waiver and rethink their positions. But not all were so easily swayed by cries of danger.

Nissim Nunez, an intense, pale young man with fire in his eyes, jumped up. "We have always had our doubters," he cried out. "There were always those who would turn back in fear, even when the goal was in sight. Even when Moshe *Rabenu* ("Moses our teacher") was climbing Mount Sinai to receive the Ten Commandments, there were some who gave up hope and sought to return to Egypt. They even gained majority support and forced Aaron (older brother of Moses, the first priest of Israel) to fashion a pagan idol. But they did not win in the end. The Children of Israel regained their faith and went on. And the walls of Jericho were awesome – seemingly impregnable until the blast of horns sent them tumbling down. Do not be swayed by prophecies of doom. Join hands and join hearts. Come, let us return to the land of the patriarchs."

Like the outlook of a scoreless soccer match in its closing minutes, in which one team was locked in what looked like an untenable position with its goal open to the deciding score, Nissim had rallied his forces with a dramatic save. He had sent the opposition into retreat in disarray, guaranteeing a victory for his side. The congregants had regained heart. One by one, they declared their intent to leave for Israel.

Isaac Ibn Eliezer accepted the will of the majority with grace. For all his wealth, he had never been aloof from his people. When money was needed to sustain his impoverished brethren, he had always been the first to dig into his pocket – not with a loud "I gave you this money" but with a silent and generous hand that would have pleased even Maimonides, who specified various degrees of giving charity.

"I can see," he began, "that most of you are determined to leave. Since that is the case, I agree with Ezra Hazzan that the wiser course would be to sail in a large seaworthy vessel, not in rotting boats that the Turks would be happy to unload on us at inflated prices. I shall be glad to use my skills to negotiate with some of the ship-owners. This could keep the cost of passage down. The ship-owners realize that I have considerable knowledge with regard to shipping costs. And so they would be less likely to cheat me."

"I intended no disrespect to your person," said Nissim, moving towards Isaac and extending a hand as he would to a comrade in the struggle. "You know that I regard you as a good Jew and much more, though we may differ on the time to leave."

The eager youth and the cautious man of middle-age embraced as brothers.

"God be with you," whispered Isaac. "God be with you all."

After a long minute they released one another. Nissim turned to the rabbi and asked, "Will you go with us, Rabbi?"

The bearded man pondered for a moment and then replied: "My heart goes with you, and my body will as well, if all choose to leave. But if some remain here in Izmir, I must stay. For there are many rabbis – fine rabbis – in Israel, but if I depart from Izmir, who will guide this flock and teach their children? Who will keep Judaism alive here on the shore of the Aegean, where our people have lived for 2,000 years? May the Almighty bring you safely to Eretz Yisrael and preserve you and all Israel. And we say 'Amen.'"

The crowd, anxious to get home with the news, dispersed, leaving only Isaac Ibn Eliezer, like a humble congregant, helping the rabbi put away prayer books left on the benches and chairs in a moment of haste.

"Isaac," observed the rabbi, "some of our people may not be able to afford the passage to Israel."

"Have no fear, Rabbi. It was my intent to see to it that every Jew who wishes will be able to go. That's the least I can do for our nation."

The sage-like, bearded man nodded with his now-moistened lids.

"Please, Rabbi," continued Isaac. "A favor. Do not repeat anything of what I have just spoken. Let it remain between us."

"And the Almighty," added the rabbi.

Twelve thousand Jews of Izmir heeded the call and traveled to the Promised Land, fought in its War of Independence and in subsequent conflicts to preserve the state. And they contributed to the development of the Land of Israel. Among them was every one of the 40 Azubel families of Izmir. Like their fellow Jews of Izmir, the Azubels are now spread throughout the length and breadth of the land the Almighty had promised to their patriarchs. They are to be found in cities and towns, in the *moshavim* (farm settlements based on individual enterprise), and in the *kibbutzim*.

Two thousand Jews remained in Izmir. The Jewish community, with the help of its philanthropic members, maintained a Jewish hospital. There was even a rabbinical court, which Chief Rabbi Moreno Siegora led until his death in 1968.

HOME

THE ASSYRIANS conquered the northern Jewish kingdom 2,700 years ago. The Jews of Israel were then deported to distant areas of the kingdom. Their descendants became the Jews of Samarkand and Bukhara in current Uzbekistan, the Bene Israel of Bombay, the Cochin Jews of the Malabar Coast of India, the Manas people of eastern India, and the Jews of Afghanistan and China and other Asian countries.

Two hundred years later, the Babylonians sent the Hebrew people of Judea into exile after conquest. They were subsequently allowed to return to Judea when King Cyrus conquered Babylon. However, Jews remained in what later was to become Iraq and Iran.

Half a millennium later, the Romans made Judea part of their empire. Initially, it was a subservient state in which Herod the Idumean reigned as a vassal of Rome. (Idumeans were a non-Semitic people from the desert.) After the death of Herod, Judea became a province in the empire. But the Hebrews proved to be a stiff-necked people, who resisted the Romans who suppressed aspects of Jewish religious practice. After two major revolts, which forced the Romans to send a major portion of their army to crush the insurrection, the Romans imposed their "final solution." The surviving Jews were deported to Rome as slaves.

The descendants of the Jews exiled from their native land moved from country to country, mostly to escape persecution. There was virtually no place on the European continent in which the Jews were not ill-treated or massacred or from which they were not expelled at one time or another.

"If you will it, then it is not a dream," said Theodor Herzl, (the father of political Zionism and the founder of the World Zionist Organization) when he concluded that a Jewish nation in the Promised Land was the only solution for the Hebrew people. After 2,000 years – years of persecution in a hundred lands, years of achievement against all odds – the escapees from the Pogroms in Russia, reinforced by the remnant of European Jewry after the

Holocaust, rejoined their Jewish brethren who had remained in Jerusalem during two millennia of foreign rule, to reestablish the State of Israel.

They were soon joined by Sephardim from Morocco, Yemenite Jews, Cochin Jews and members of the Bene Israel, as well as Manas people from India, Falashas from Ethiopia, Jews from the United States, Canada, South Africa, Australia and many other countries. They drained the swamps and rid the land of malaria. They turned a desert into a fruitful garden. The dream had become a reality.

I traveled with my wife and children to the Holy Land. We felt the warmth of its sunny fields. We saw the beauty of its hills and valleys. The refreshing air of its shores vitalized us. We climbed the mountain to Jerusalem and gazed in awe at the wall of the Temple. We visited the Azubels and Azbels and Ausubels; we spent long hours exchanging stories, and learned how the branches of the tree had fared.

Then one day, on a quiet hillside in the Galilee, I saw a blue-flowered plant clinging stubbornly to the soil, resisting the force of the wind and the desiccating heat of a July sun. I knelt down and scented its menthaceous fragrance, and the words of the psalmist came back to me: "Purge me with hyssop and I shall be clean."

I touched the tiny twigs; some of the flower stuck to my fingers. Lifting the tiny petals above my head, I let them shower me with their cleansing aroma. The flower of God had returned to its native soil; the children *have* come home.